UNDERSTANDING POLICE AND POLICE WORK

UNDERSTANDING POLICE AND POLICE WORK

Psychosocial Issues

A. Daniel Yarmey

NEW YORK UNIVERSITY PRESS
New York and London

Library of Congress Cataloging-in-Publication Data
Yarmey, A. Daniel.
Understanding police and police work : psychosocial issues / A.
Daniel Yarmey.
p.   cm.
Includes bibliographical references.
ISBN 0-8147-9670-2
1. Police.   2. Police—United States.   3. Police psychology.
4. Criminal psychology.   I. Title.
HV7921.Y37   1989
362.2'01'9—dc20   89-12940
CIP

New York University Press books are printed on acid-free paper,
and their binding materials are chosen for strength and durability.

c 10 9 8 7 6 5 4 3 2

Book design by Ken Venezio

To my wife, Judy,
my children, Craig, Linda, and Meagan,
and to the memory of my friend Peter D. Duda

Contents

Illustrations

ix

Tables

Preface

Several years ago, I was contacted by Bill Plomp, now an inspector with the Lethbridge, Alberta, police force, to assist him and a prosecutor in a trial involving eyewitness evidence, including both voice and facial identification evidence. My involvement in this trial introduced me for the first time to the normal working day of police officers and also to their social world and family life. I attended a party at a local hotel with the police and their girlfriends and wives, drank a lot of beer, laughed at the efforts of the hotel security officer's attempts to quiet our party, and generally saw a side of life that up until then was determined mainly by stereotypes. It occurred to me that it was highly likely that many of my fellow researchers in eyewitness testimony, who routinely give advice to police and the courts, also knew very little about police officers and policing. Thus, I thought, why not write a book? I know a little about social psychology and cognitive psychology that may be useful to legal professionals. At the same time, I could learn about criminology, sociology, and the psychology of police-civilian behavior and could pass on my findings to fellow social scientists.

Applied social psychology and cognitive psychology have a solid foundation in science guided by a concern for rigorous empirical methods and theoretical insights. Applied social psychology is also concerned with improving human conditions. Police officers in many respects have to be applied psychologists.

The central concern of this book is the psychological basis of police officers' interactions with society. Applied social psychology and cognitive psychology try to explain such behaviors as stress, prejudice, and discrimination, as well as violence, in terms of the situational context and the thoughts and feelings of the individuals involved. In discussing these and other topics, my goals have been to demonstrate the significance of empirical research and theory and to show the real-life applications of these processes to legal issues.

Acknowledgments

I am grateful to Don Reid of the University of Lethbridge, Peter Leppmann, Fred Eidlin and Eva Matthys of the University of Guelph, Charles Bahn of John Jay College of Criminal Justice, New York, and Bill Barker of the Calgary Police Department, for their perceptive comments. Completion of this book would have been impossible without the excellent typing services and proofreading assistance of Eva Matthys. I am particularly indebted to my late colleague, Peter Duda, for his assistance in working and reworking the first half of this manuscript.

Thanks are also due to Kitty Moore, Senior Editor of New York University Press, for her support and direction in the book's development.

All of my research for this book was financially supported by the Social Sciences and Humanities Research Council of Canada. I thank the Council and the University of Guelph for their continued support.

This book benefited from the encouragement of many friends and colleagues, but my greatest supporter, as always, is my wife, Judy.

I would also like to thank the following:

Stoddart Publishing Co., Ltd., for permission to quote from I. Gadd, *Our Cops: Their Stories,* copyright © 1986 Stoddart Publishing Co., Ltd.

Toronto Star Syndicate for permission to reprint, Kevin Scanlon, "Cop Critics No Experts Chief Says," *Toronto Star*, October 27, 1979.

The *New York Times* for permission to reprint Sam Howe Verhovek, "Man Dies from a Gunshot in Traffic-Accident Dispute," *New York Times*, November 14, 1988, copyright © 1988 by The New York Times Company.

Plenum Publishing Corp. for permission to reprint A. Daniel Yarmey and Judy Kent, "And Justice for You Too," *Law and Human Behavior* 4, no. 4 (1980): 368–70.

Prentice-Hall, Inc., for permission to quote from I. G. Sarason and B. R. Sarason, *Abnormal Psychology: The Problem of Maladaptive Behavior*, 5th ed., copyright © 1987 Prentice-Hall, Inc.

The Canadian Press for permission to reprint "Sketches Led Police to Robbery Suspect," *Guelph Mercury*, January 5, 1989, p. 2.

The International Association of Chiefs of Police for permission to quote from J. W. Osterburg, "The Scientific Method and Criminal Investigation," *Journal of Police Science and Administration* 9, no. 2 (1981): 135–42.

UNDERSTANDING POLICE AND POLICE WORK

1

Introduction

A working knowledge of psychological concepts, theories, and research findings, coupled with practical, on-the-job experience, can make a positive contribution to the training and education of police officers. Although the utilization of principles of psychology in such areas of policing as crisis intervention and dealing with mentally disturbed persons is acknowledged by many officials, some police departments still question the "real" value of psychology in law enforcement (Sobelman and Glorioso 1980). This resistance challenges the social scientist to show the value of psychology to police officers who must deal with the "real world." This book attempts to show how some of the scientific knowledge of psychology and other social sciences can contribute to the understanding of police behavior and the behavior of citizens and other professionals with whom the police are involved.

The police do not need specialists from outside law enforcement to tell them about the technical and vocational aspects of policing. Yet, it is possible that even skeptics may find greater knowledge and effective utilization of psychology in law enforcement to be useful. Chief Neil Atkins of the Santa Barbara, California, police department has stated: "I want an officer with the ability to understand normal human behavior, what it is that causes people to do certain things, and to understand

1

himself" (cited in Langone 1981, 57). Similar views have been expressed by Kroes (1976), a psychologist who considers the police to be "society's victim":

> The officer needs a fuller understanding of his own personal reactions to various stimuli and of what the roles [sic] personality, motivation, cognition, emotion, fears, needs, etc. have in affecting human behavior. Why do we do what we do? Why does the other person behave the way he does? What effect does it have when one behaves a certain way to another individual? Since the police officer's job to a large extent is interacting with people he needs to know the answers to these questions. It would be unreasonable to expect a policeman to become a fully trained behavioral scientist, on the other hand there is a body of practical psychology that the officer needs to know and should be trained in. . . . As one senior police officer stated, "If we can 'arm' our officers with a basic knowledge of human behavior it can be as great a weapon as a firearm." (P.109)

The relationship between psychology and law enforcement is not one-sided, restricted only to police officers. Psychologists and other professionals, such as social workers and lawyers, who work with police or teach courses and do research on police behavior, must have at least a fundamental understanding of law enforcement. Stratton (1980), the Director of Psychological Services for the Los Angeles County Sheriff's Department, has described the naivety of some psychologists wishing employment in a police agency:

> Too often psychologists have misconceptions or stereotypes about police and are unwilling to look at the realities of police activities. The author is reminded of an incident where he was requested to sit in on a presentation by a psychologist for a cadet training program in a law enforcement agency. The presentation was to be made to the top administrators of the department. The psychologist appeared in sandals, blue jeans, T-shirt, and carried a purse. The bulk of his presentation dealt with his plan to teach young officers working in the field issues related to new concepts in art therapy and dance therapy, his rationale being that these disciplines would facilitate the officer's work with the people on the street. Obviously this particular psychologist had very little knowledge of the realities of police work; and even if dance therapy were of some aid to the officer, it is certainly of low priority. (P. 33)

FIELDS OF PSYCHOLOGY

In order to explore the relationships between psychology and law enforcement, I will begin with a brief overview of the many subfields and specialties within psychology. It is not uncommon to hear the layperson say that he or she is a good psychologist. This suggests that many people feel they know more or less what psychology is all about. In contrast, most psychologists have a difficult time defining the term *psychology* beyond saying that it is the scientific study of behavior and experience. Furthermore, psychologists argue among themselves on such matters as the proper or most appropriate research methods to use, the primary subject areas of the discipline, and the theoretical objectives and practical applications of the science of psychology.

The major subfields within psychology and the different settings in which American psychologists work are shown in Table 1.1. Approximately 40 percent of all psychologists work in universities, colleges, and medical schools. Within each subfield psychologists perform several different functions including teaching, research, and the application of psychological theories, principles, and methods of analyses to the solution of individual and social problems.

Table 1.2 summarizes the primary activities of several psychological specialties. Psychologists may specialize in one of several different areas of interest, and it is impossible for one person to be an expert in all aspects of psychology. In fact, it is unlikely that an individual can fully master even one specialty (see Woods 1976). As a consequence, the psychologist typically concentrates on one or two topics within a specialty. Examination of Tables 1.1 and 1.2 should dispel the common belief held by many individuals that psychology is a special branch of medicine (see Posluns 1981; Yarmey and Popiel 1988). Although some psychologists work in mental health settings and diagnose and treat people with psychological problems, clinical psychologists should not be confused with psychiatrists and psychoanalysts. Clinical psychologists do many of the same jobs as psychiatrists, but the first major difference between these specialists is their educational training. Clinical psychologists usually hold a doctorate of philosophy (Ph.D.) degree in psychology. A four-year program of graduate education emphasizes

Table 1.1   Major Subfields of Psychology and Their Work Settings and the Percentage of Psychologists Employed in Each Subfield

Subfield	Percent
Clinical-counseling	56.0
Education	9.8
Experimental	7.7
Industrial	6.3
Social-personality	6.4
Developmental	4.0
Quantitative	1.4
Physiological	1.5
Other	6.9
Total	100.0

Setting	Percent
Colleges and medical schools	43.1
Private practice	14.7
Clinics, counseling centers	14.3
Industry and government	13.0
Hospitals	9.6
School districts	4.6
Others	0.7
Total	100.0

Source: Based on data from Boneau and Cuca 1974, © 1974 by the American Psychological Association by permission of the publisher and author.

course work on the study of normal and abnormal behavior, diagnosis and treatment, supervised field experiences, and research techniques. Part of this training involves a one-year internship in a mental health setting. Once the student has completed these formal university requirements, he or she has to do a further period of supervised practical training and pass a set of certifying examinations.

Psychiatrists, in contrast, first study medicine to earn a doctor of medicine (M.D.) degree. To specialize in psychiatry, postgraduate medical students typically take a three-year residency in a mental health setting where they learn to detect and treat emotional problems. This training involves the use of medical procedures, including drugs and surgery, and psychological techniques. Finally, psychoanalysts are usu-

Table 1.2 Primary Activities of Major Specialists in Psychology

Specialist	Primary Activities
Clinical psychologist	Assesses and treats people with psychological problems; conducts research on normal and abnormal behavior, diagnosis, and treatment.
Counseling psychologist	Counsels people with mild adjustment problems and promotes achievement in educational and work settings; combines research, consultation, and treatment.
Experimental psychologist	Designs and conducts research in a specific area, such as learning, sensation, motivation, language, or the physiological bases of behavior.
School psychologist	Increases the intellectual, social, and emotional development of children in schools by establishing programs, consulting, doing research, training teachers, and treating youngsters with problems.
Educational psychologist	Develops, designs, and evaluates materials and procedures for educational programs.
Industrial and organizational psychologist	Combines research, consultation, and program development to enhance efficiency, satisfaction, and morale on the job.
Social psychologist	Studies how people influence one another.
Developmental psychologist	Studies changes in behavior with age.
Personality psychologist	Studies how and why people differ from one another and how those differences may be assessed.
Community psychologist	Treats people with psychological problems within the community; initiates community action and develops community programs to enhance mental health.
Psychometric (quantitative) psychologist	Develops and evaluates tests; designs research to measure behavioral and mental functions.
Engineering psychologist	Designs and evaluates environments, machinery, training devices, programs, and systems to improve the relationship between people and their environment.

Source: Boneau and Cuca 1974, © 1974 by the American Psychological Association by permission of the publisher and author.

ally physicians or psychiatrists who study and practice the philosophy and teachings of Freud and his followers. This work focuses on particular theories of personality and therapy (referred to as psychoanalysis).

PSYCHOLOGY IN THE CRIMINAL JUSTICE SYSTEM

The modern relationship between psychology and the law goes back to the beginning of this century (see Loh 1981; Sporer 1982). One of the oldest areas of applied psychology is the study of the reliability of eyewitness identification. Psychologists on both sides of the Atlantic were concerned with demonstrating the fallibility of the eyewitness to the judicial system.

As early as 1838, Henke, writing in a handbook of criminal law and criminal politics, called attention to the psychological problems inherent in gathering identification evidence:

> Above all, the identification procedure has to be preceded by a comprehensive interrogation of the witness, wherein he is to describe the characteristic features which could facilitate recognition of the persons or objects to which his testimony or statements refer. Thereafter, in the identification procedure itself, he is, whenever possible, to be confronted with several persons or objects resembling the one to be identified. He should be urged to point out, for example, the identified object, without hesitation, and also to give the reasons why he had identified this one as the real one instead of any of the others. . . . On the one hand, the investigator has to take care, to the best of his ability, to remove any changes that may have occurred in the object to be recognized and that may thus impair recognition: therefore, for example, he must not present the accused in his prison clothes, or with a distorting beard, etc. On the other hand, the investigator must beware of drawing the witness's attention to the correct object through facial expressions, gestures, or external signs that differentiate the object in question from others. (Henke 1838, 705–6, translations by Sporer 1982)

Between 1900 and 1966 only six books in psychology and law were published in English, but since the start of the 1970s there has been an explosion of interest in this relationship (Loh 1981). Contemporary work in applied psychology is recognized as contributing substantially to a wide range of criminal justice concerns, such as law enforcement and courtroom proceedings, assistance to victims, and correctional systems (Brodsky 1976; Megargee 1982a; Tapp 1982).

In the criminal justice system, one highly visible branch of psychology is *forensic psychology*. This subarea may be defined as "the application of psychological principles to the problems and administration of the legal-judicial system—both its criminal justice and civil justice components" (Fenster et al. 1976, 123). Forensic psychologists are primarily involved in the collection, examination, and presentation of evidence for judicial purposes (Haward 1981). This involvement includes three phrases of the judicial process: "(1) *pretrial*—the determination of competency to stand trial; (2) *trial*—the assessment of claims of insanity; and (3) *sentencing*—the preparation of presentence reports to assist judicial decision-making on prison sentences, suspended sentences, probation, or hospitalization. Forensic psychologists are primarily trained in clinical psychology. The nonclinical counterparts of the forensic psychologist are social psychologists and cognitive psychologists who investigate such processes as juror selection, jury decision-making, accuracy and credibility of eyewitness identification, and so on.

Table 1.3 summarizes some of the diverse activities of different psychology specialties involved in the legal system. Police departments, for instance, employ psychologists to administer psychological tests for selection purposes and to diagnose and make prognostic predictions of police officers with emotional problems. Officers in need of counseling often see psychologists either in private practice or, if available, through a psychological services branch of the police agency. Many police academies employ psychologists to teach courses on personality theory, stress, decision-making, interview and interrogation techniques, and the like.

Within prisons, psychologists function as diagnosticians, therapists, researchers, teachers, and consultants to parole boards. Outside of the courts, prisons, and police agencies, psychologists may be found working with victims of crime such as robbery, sexual assault and rape, child abuse, wife battery, and so forth. Nevertheless, psychological contributions to the criminal justice system are far from complete. Judge David Bazelon (1973), asking correctional psychologists whether or not they or the offender benefited from psychological work, has commented:

Table 1.3   Relationships Between Psychology and Law

Specialist	Examples of Activities
Clinical psychologist	Psychopathology of crime; mentally abnormal offender; victims; sex offender; therapy; amnesia; hypnosis; research.
Counseling psychologist	Police officer's stress; family and marital counseling; vocational counseling; research.
Experimental psychologist	Psychology of eyewitness testimony; polygraph; police problem-solving and decision-making; voice prints; research.
Educational psychologist	Courses in preventive law; criminology; legal and police training; research.
Industrial and organizational psychologist	Police administration and management techniques; police morale and job satisfaction; leadership training; selection of recruits; communication; police productivity; research.
Social psychologist	Social psychology of arrests; nature of violence; confessions and interrogation; police-community relations; police roles; judicial attitudes to sentencing; processes of jury selection; jury deliberation; research.
Developmental psychologist	Nature of juvenile delinquency; moral development and socialization of attitudes toward the law; sense of justice; the elderly criminal and the elderly victim; research.
Personality psychologist	Police personality; the antisocial personality; prediction of dangerousness; research.
Community psychologist	Police crisis intervention; hostages; human relations training; research.
Psychometric (quantitative) psychologist	Development of tests to evaluate police performance; research.
Engineering psychologist	Police use of computer technology; driving skills; information (human-machine) processing; research.

Regretfully, I must tell you that the papers prepared for this conference on the role of psychology in corrections do nothing to allay my increasing doubts and uncertainties about what it is that psychologists or any other behavioralists can offer. . . . I certainly hope you will not draw the impression that I consider psychology a worthless discipline that ought to be abandoned. The issue is not whether psychology is good, but what it is good at. . . . On the whole, it seems to me that the institution of correctional psychology has had far too little outside evaluation or scrutiny. Psychologists have not produced any remarkable successes in the corrections field. (P. 150)

Although Bazelon's opinions are open to retort (see Megargee 1982a), his criticisms can be generalized to other specialists working in the justice area. Psychologists have to remember that their field "still awaits full acceptance and recognition within the law" (Tapp 1982, 83). Research is the most important contribution psychologists have to offer the criminal justice system since research is the foundation of all of the services provided in assessment, treatment, training, and education. In the next section, I will look at the various methods used by social scientists to gather information and test hypotheses.

METHODS OF PSYCHOLOGICAL RESEARCH

All research begins with basic questions we want answered. For example, suppose we are interested in the following questions: What makes a police chief an effective leader? What is a good police officer? How do policewomen and policemen react under crisis situations? In order to answer these sorts of questions, psychologists design experiments to test hypotheses or conduct studies that reveal different types of behavior. Most psychological research is conducted either in a laboratory or in field situations. Two major methods of scientific inquiry are used in these settings: *experimental research* (manipulating one or more factors to see its effect on another) and *correlational research* (determining the relationship between two or more factors).

Experimental Research

Suppose we want to know whether policemen differ from policewomen in performance under stress. One strategy is to conduct experiments. A researcher would typically begin by randomly selecting two groups of officers, one male and the other female, who are similar in relevant respects such as age, educational background, experience as police officers, and so on. After choosing some performance measure, say reaction time in making specific decisions, subjects would be exposed to a stress-related situation. If the two groups differ in their speed of reaction (the dependent variable), we might infer that sex differences (the independent variable) were responsible. To follow up, the researcher might want to repeat the experiment but investigate sex differences with different types of performance measures such as strength, endurance, creativity, and so on, as a function of stress versus nonstress. Selection of specific dependent and independent variables should always be guided by theory.

As this example shows, experimental research involves the manipulation of one or more variables (for example, sex of subjects, level of stress, and the like) and the measurement of responses (such as reaction time, attitudes, and so forth) to determine if one or more factors causally influence behavior. Experiments are usually conducted in a laboratory, thus allowing the investigator to control conditions and make precise measurements. Experiments can also be done in the "real world." Field experiments, as they are called, permit the investigator to introduce his or her manipulations in natural settings (albeit with less control) to determine their effects upon behavior. (See Farrington [1983] for a thorough discussion of the use, advantages, and problems of the experimental approach to the study of crime and justice.)

The major value of laboratory research over other research methods is the control that the investigator has over extraneous factors in the environment and the conditions to be manipulated. Changes in behavior can be observed under specific, precise conditions and can be compared against a control baseline condition. Unlike correlational data, which will be described shortly, experimental research allows the investigator to make statements about the effect of changes in one variable on changes in another. In other words, cause-and-effect relationships may be determined with a degree of certainty not matched by any other technique.

Experimental research does, however, have its shortcomings. The main limitation is that in order to achieve good control conditions over extraneous events, the researcher may have to construct situations that are so simple that they are artificial and thus fail to represent real life. Experimental procedures can never be exact analogues to real-life situations. Because of ethical considerations, laboratory and field experiments cannot introduce the same intensity of fear and stress that would occur, for example, in a real-life situation such as in witnessing an armed robbery or homicide. Experimental psychology, in general, has been criticized for its study of aritificial situations, the predominant use of college students as subjects rather than selections from a wide sample of the general population, and the kind of simplified tasks that subjects are asked to perform. Nevertheless, experimental research does provide basic information that may be of value to the scientist and relevant to the needs of the public and that cannot be provided by any other scientifically valid procedure.

Ethical Issues in Psychological Research.   Consider the following situation: You agree to be a paid participant in a psychological study of the effects of punishment on learning. On arrival at the laboratory, you find another subject (unknown to you, a confederate of the experimenter) present. The confederate is supposed to be the "learner" who has to memorize a list of word pairs. You are requested to be the "teacher" who will punish the learner if he makes any mistakes. The confederate is taken to an adjoining room, strapped into a chair, and hooked up to an electrical shock generator. You are shown the shock generator and are told that it will deliver the punishment to the learner. You are not told that the machine is a fake and that no actual punishment will be delivered to the learner. The generator has a control panel of thirty switches to monitor the (apparent) strengths of the electrical current ranging from "slight shock" (15 volts) to "danger: severe shock" (450 volts). When the learner makes a mistake, you are told to administer 15 volts of shock and, with each subsequent mistake, to flip switches with successively higher voltages.

You find that the learner makes a few mistakes at first and does not seem to mind the mild shocks, but after a while, mistakes are more frequent and the shock becomes increasingly severe. Eventually the confederate starts to violently protest the punishment, complain about his bad heart, and plead to be released. Then he stops protesting and responding entirely. You indicate to the experimenter that you are worried about the learner, but you are told to continue no matter how dangerously high the shock might get.

The primary research question asked in this study is whether or not you would obey the wishes of the experimenter: Would you refuse, or would you continue to punish someone at the most severe levels of shock intensity simply because an authority figure told you to carry on?

This study was conducted by Milgram in 1963 and has been repeated in different countries around the world with similar results. Milgram found that 65 percent of subjects continued to obey his orders right up to the highest shock intensity. Most subjects were upset, showed signs of extreme stress and concern for the victim, repeatedly asked permission to stop, but were obedient to the authority figure.

It is unlikely that this research would be conducted today because of the ethical and moral issues now recognized to be involved in such studies. Critics of this particular study feel that it was not ethical to expose people without warning to a situation that would probably cause them high stress and may have lasting negative personal effects. Milgram (1974) argued that the great social importance of this research justified the treatments used. Furthermore, he claimed that extensive explanation and debriefing of subjects was given at the end of the experiment and that participants were given proof that the learner was not harmed.

Whether or not Milgram was justified in his use of deception and invasion of privacy is debatable. Guidelines for ethical standards in psychological research formulated by the American Psychological Association (1979) are now available to assist researchers in insuring that the welfare and dignity of research subjects are not jeopardized.

Guidelines have also been developed to examine the ethical dilemmas faced by psychologists working with the police, court, correctional, and juvenile justice agencies (Report of the Task Force on the Role of Psychology in the Criminal Justice System 1978). The question "Who is the client?" poses the fundamental ethical issue in the field of criminal justice (Monahan 1980; Zelig 1988). In contrast to lawyers, who work within an adversary system and whose responsibility is to defend their clients to the best of their ability, psychologists face a more complex ethical situation. For example, should the clinical psychologist who is hired by the police department to counsel and treat police officers experiencing emotional problems be primarily responsible to the administration who pays his or her salary or to society as a whole or to the police officer who is the patient? These types of issues need clarification (see Norton 1981).

Correlational Research

Whenever an investigator is interested in examining the relationship between factors, such as amount of crime and amount of education, correlational studies are conducted. These studies may be done in controlled laboratory settings, but more typically they are conducted in real-life situations or by surveys.

Naturalistic Observation.   In this procedure, researchers attempt to observe and record behavior in real-life settings. The investigator is a participant-observer who is watching, listening, and interacting with the people being studied. For example, Vincent (1979) used the partici-pant-observer method to study the cultural, institutional, communal, occupational, and personal factors of the policeman's environment that influence his actions and thoughts. Vincent observed the police by riding along in patrol cars, joining them in their leisure activities, and attending police-sponsored gatherings. In addition, he conducted inter-views of officers to sort out hypotheses that were generated from the observations made in the field.

This type of research often leads to "rich" understandings and in-sights not found in experimental work. However, this approach also has disadvantages from an objective, scientific point of view. The data that is gathered may be contaminated by personal biases of the investigator or by the observer's influencing the behavior of the persons being watched. The data is also difficult to replicate, interpret, and evaluate. Although this procedure may lead to the discovery of relationships between two or more phenomena that have been observed, the relation-ships, or correlations, do not imply causation.

Thus, imagine that a participant-observation study indicates that male police officers are more anxious (talk louder, perspire more, show more hurried movements, and so forth) than female officers in violent situations. This result does not necessarily mean that violence causes more "anxiety" in policemen than in policewomen. It is possible that the male officers, but not the female officers, knew that they were being evaluated by an observer and that therefore, the testing, not the violent situation, "caused" the anxiety. It is also possible that other variables the observer was not aware of may have been responsible for the anxious reactions.

Survey Observations.   Often researchers cannot make direct observations because of limitations of time and money, type of information
needed, or the number of investigators required to observe large numbers of people. Nevertheless, information is wanted on such matters as
the extent of criminal activities within a population or attitudes toward
police departments. To gather these data, psychologists turn to various
quantitative methods of assessment: questionnaires, interviews, and
tests. Survey data can be gathered by interviewers asking respondents
questions from a prepared questionnaire, or by mailing the questionnaire to respondents and asking them to complete it and return it by
mail. This procedure allows data to be gathered quickly and relatively
inexpensively on a large sample of people. But this procedure also has
its limitations. The results of questionnaire studies are not always easy
to interpret. Respondents may lie, may not care about the topic being
investigated and respond without thinking, or may not understand the
questions.

The case study is a special form of the survey method in which
information about one individual is gathered in detail. Extensive knowledge about a person's history permits the researcher to make educated
guesses about the causes of current behavior. Preparation of case reports on other individuals, each showing similar behaviors, allows the
researcher to make hypotheses about a common cause. Although this
approach leads to rich and detailed knowledge, there is the danger that
a purely striking coincidence of events may be seen as a true causal
relationship.

Methodological Concepts and Statistics

Once the data from experiments, naturalistic observations, surveys, or
interviews are gathered, researchers use statistical procedures to organize, describe, and interpret the findings. Although statistical analyses
are an important research tool, a description of these tests is beyond the
scope of this book. Instead, a brief discussion of some of the concepts
involved in understanding research findings is presented.

A useful way to understand the nature of the results is to picture
them in graphic form. Figure 1.1 is an example of a graph describing
some hypothetical findings regarding police investigations of weapons
involved in violent deaths. The figure indicates that 50 percent of

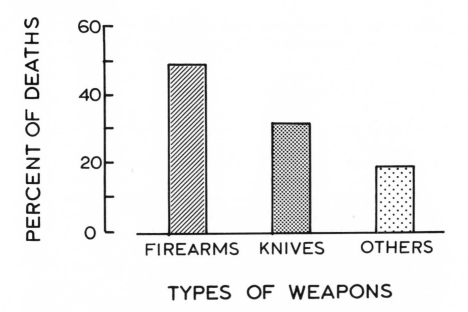

Figure 1.1 Hypothetical Summary of Percentage of Deaths in Every Town as a Function of Firearms, Knives, and Other Types of Weapons.

violent deaths investigated by the Everytown police department involved the use of firearms, while 30 percent of the deaths resulted from knives, and other types of weapons accounted for 20 percent.

Quite often investigators state that their findings showed a significant difference (also called a reliable difference) between the experimental group (the one that received the experimental factor) and the control group. The terms *significant* and *reliable* do not refer to importance or social significance; instead, they are statistical concepts that indicate that the difference in the average score of the experimental group and the average score of the control group is probably real. In other words, if the difference in scores is greater than that which would be expected on the basis of chance, conclusions can be drawn that the experimental treatment caused the difference. If the results shown in Figure 1.1 were of a real study, you might want to know if the differences in percentage of deaths resulting from firearms, knives, and other weapons were reliable or a function of chance. Statistical tests would be applied to these data, and if the tests showed a significant difference, the investigator would conclude that he or she was 95 percent (p <.05) or 99 percent (p <.01) confident that the difference between the groups was real and not a function of chance.

Correlations

A *correlation* is the degree of relationship or association between two or more variables. For example, people who are taller are usually heavier; height and weight are positively correlated with each other. Correlations are called *positive* when a high magnitude of one variable (such as height) is associated with a high magnitude of the other variable (such as weight). A *negative correlation* exists when increases of one variable are accompanied by decreases in the other. For example, there is usually a negative correlation between a police officer's intelligence and how satisfied he or she will be doing a boring, repetitive task. A *zero correlation* occurs when there is no relationship between the variables. The degree of relationship or correlation between two variables may be expressed in quantitative terms by a number called a *correlation coefficient*. Correlation coefficients can range from −1.00 (perfect negative correlation) to +1.00 (perfect positive correlation). A correlation is symbolized by the letter r. Correlations of $r = .00$ indicate no relationship between the variables. Correlations of $r = 1.00$ or $r = −1.00$ are very rare in psychology.

Correlations are useful since they allow predictions to be made. If two variables are strongly related, knowledge of the score of one variable allows us to predict the score on the other variable, within certain limits. For example, applicants for police work are often given a battery of intelligence and aptitude tests involving factors that are known to be correlated with work performance. Knowledge of the applicant's score on these psychological tests allows the examiner to predict his or her probable work performance. However, as stated earlier, correlations do not indicate cause and effect. Suppose a positive correlation was found between a city's crime rate and the city's number of pool rooms—that is, the more billiard halls, the higher the crime rate. Does this mean that pool rooms cause crime or that crime leads people to billiard halls? Not necessarily. Another possibility is that some third variable, such as high unemployment, causes both the increase in crime rate and the greater number of people frequenting pool rooms. We simply do not know which of these or other possible causal relationships may account for the correlation between two factors. The important principle to remember is that correlations indicate that there is a relationship between variables, not that one variable necessarily causes the other.

SCIENTIFIC REASONING: APPLICATIONS IN LAW ENFORCEMENT

Scientific reasoning and police investigations depend upon logic, deductive and inferential reasoning, and the use of theory. A detailed examination of these concepts is presented in Chapter 10, but at this point I want to give a brief introduction by presenting the following police case study, "Investigation of a Murder" (Osterburg 1981).

A detective was called to the scene where a young woman had been murdered in her apartment. He found the table exquisitely set for two with melted-down candles and wine, music playing softly, with the beef stroganoff still warm on the serving tray, and no evidence of forced entry or struggle. The detective hypothesized that she had admitted the killer, probably as her dinner guest. In questioning the woman's family, friends, and business associates, one name, that of her former lover, was constantly mentioned. Indeed, several persons indicated that his behavior during an earlier quarrel had been forgiven and that this was to be a dinner of reconciliation. The hypothesis that the killer was an invited guest is somewhat verified by these facts obtained through interviews; further information, however, is needed. The investigator is now obliged to consider, Can the friend be located at his place of business, home, other usual haunt, or is flight indicated? If the latter, is any clothing or other item, such as his razor, missing from his home, did he cash a large check or withdraw money from his bank account on the morning following the homicide?

If affirmative answers are obtained, and applied inductively, the hypothesis has even greater evidence of support. The former lover may now be considered as the prime suspect. The detective must remember, however, that an inductive result is not necessarily a certainty. Flight may be evidence of guilt, but is not proof.

The suspect may, through coincidence have left for a vacation at what would now seem to be an inopportune time. Obviously, the homicide investigator must next discover the whereabouts of the suspect, assuming that information from his friends and associates has failed to trace him. Deductive thinking, based on the lover as the prime suspect (generalization), leads to other questions (the answers to which are particulars): Where would he be likely to flee? Possible locations are suggested by such considerations as: Where was the suspect born? Had he lived for a long time in some area? Has he a favorite vacation spot? Other facts or details may result from investigative activities which seek answers (particulars) to other questions such as: What else might he do to earn a living? To whom might he write or telephone? Will he make an attempt to obtain his last paycheck by mail, or otherwise? Will he continue to pay union dues? Will he renew a driver's license that he may hold? When sufficient facts (particulars) are acquired, they should allow the investigator, again through inductive reasoning, to determine the whereabouts (location as a generalization) of the suspect and to seek to apprehend him (through deduction) somewhere in the vicinity of the new area in which he was relocated. In summary, the cyclical process of scientific reasoning, from induction to deduction, and vice versa, is obviously applicable to criminal investigation as a means of reconstructing past events. (P. 137)

Several principles mentioned in this case study are common in both scientific investigations and police investigations. (I will leave the discussion of potential errors and fallacies involved in this reasoning process to Chapter 10.)

1. *Deduction* is a process of reasoning that starts from a given premise or generalization to reach through careful, systematic thinking to a particular conclusion. For example, the detective considered the lover the prime suspect *(premise)*. He then deduced where the suspect would flee *(conclusion)*.

2. *Induction* is a process of reasoning from particular facts *(observations)* to a general conclusion. For example, the detective, having ascertained particular facts, used inductive reasoning to determine the most probable location of the suspect. Induction leads to probabilities

and not certainties, and forms the basis of what is referred to as "common sense."

3. *Hypotheses* are tentative explanations or educated guesses of a relationship between two or more events. A hypothesis can be tested by experiment or by a comparison of its predictions with already known facts. Results can support or reject the hypothesis but cannot conclusively prove it. In the case study, the detective made a hypothesis regarding the likely perpetrator and then looked for evidence to support or substantiate his speculation.

4. *Theory* provides the investigator with a foundation for understanding. Good theories have a number of functions in both science and police investigations. They integrate observations and relationships among facts into a single broad explanatory structure. This explanatory framework allows new hypotheses to be derived and tested, which may lead to new facts being discovered. Investigators attempt to use all the factual evidence available and integrate it into a plausible theory. If the theory is valuable, it will generate testable hypotheses. When hypotheses and theories lead to systematically ordered knowledge, which accurately describes regular predictable relationships among events, they are ultimately recognized as scientific laws.

Police investigations and psychological research are similar in many respects, but there are differences between the two disciplines in the amount of control and the certainty that can be achieved. A comparison of these similarities and differences in types of evidence, and proof required, is shown in Table 1.4.

Whereas science strives to develop scientific laws, courts and criminal investigations rarely approach such levels of certainty. What Table 1.4 fails to convey about science is its two research traditions, basic research and applied research. Scientists involved in basic research are primarily interested in discovering knowledge for knowledge's sake. Applied research attempts to provide information that is immediately useful for decision-making (Chavis, Stucky, and Wandersman 1983). Many people can appreciate the value of applied research since it focuses on solving a practical problem. Scientists, however, usually find the division between basic and applied research disturbing because the distinction is artificial and overlaps are common. The objectives of science—that is, "precision, clarity, explanatory value, breadth, parsimony, empirical confirmation, quantification, elegance of theorizing"

Table 1.4 Evidence and Proof: In Science, Law, and Criminal Investigations

Column	I	II	III	IV	V	VI	VII
DEGREES OF PROOF[a]	Intuitive	Speculative	Probable cause	Preponderance of the evidence	Clear and convincing	Beyond a reasonable doubt[b]	Scientific certainty[b]
EVIDENCE Type	Guess; hunch; gut feeling	Impression; surmise	Facts that appeal to a reasonable, prudent person	Additional facts, increasingly supportive, obtained through eyewitness testimony, or the examination of documents, physical things—fingerprint, toolmark, bullet, tape recording, and so on. A forensic scientist may be required to interpret and evaluate the significance of some of this evidence for legal use.[c]			Instrumental data
Quantum	Virtually none	Inconclusive	*Prima facie:* Presumptive but rebuttable	Over 50 percent of the facts in support	Sufficient for moral certainty	Sufficient to preclude every reasonable hypothesis except that which it tends to support	Overwhelming but still probabilistic
Ambiguity or doubt	Considerable	Apparent	Not apparent but quite possible	Some is still permitted	A little may remain	Almost none	Essentially none

USAGE	Discovery	Hypothesis	Somewhere between a hypothesis and a theory	Theory	Scientific law
Science	Not applicable	Basis upon which a civil case is decided	A U.S. president may be impeached. A mentally ill person may be committed involuntarily.	Basis upon which a criminal case is decided	Seldom achieved
Law		Satisfies requirement for an arrest or issuance of a warrant for search and seizure of evidence.	Not applicable		Seldom achieved
Criminal investigation	Useful during the first stages of investigation. The concept of investigative mind-set applies in this range.	Satisfies requirement for an arrest or issuance of a warrant for search and seizure of evidence.		Basis upon which a criminal case is decided	Seldom achieved

Source: Osterburg 1981. Reproduced from the *Journal of Police Science and Administration* 9, no. 2 (1981): 135–42, with permission of the International Association of Chiefs of Police.

[a] Although depicted as seven categories for didactic reasons, such a division may also be viewed as a continuum.

[b] "Beyond a shadow of a doubt" is a colloquial term that falls between category VI and category VII.

[c] Circumstantial evidence falls in categories IV–VI. It is evidence not bearing directly on the fact in dispute, but on various attendant circumstances from which a judge or jury may logically infer the occurrence of the fact in dispute. It is indirect evidence by which a principal fact may be arrived at inductively.

—are shared by both basic and applied psychologists (Hilgard 1971, 2). The only difference between basic and applied research is the greater concern of applied researchers for the immediate utility of their endeavors, not in the quality of their work.

SKEPTICISM OF THE CRIMINAL JUSTICE SYSTEM TOWARD PSYCHOLOGY

The perceived reluctance of psychologists to come to definite conclusions, combined with the perceived lack of immediate relevance of basic research, tends to make some people (police, lawyers, trial judges) skeptical of what psychology has to offer. Psychologists' slow and patient approach to discovery often differs greatly from that of police work, where officers have to act decisively in real-life situations without time to ponder all sides of a problem. Some of the resistance directed toward psychological analysis is based on a belief that human behavior is derived from metaphysical forces that are beyond the grasp of scientific analysis. This argument, which is theologically based, may or may not be true, but it is not relevant to the scientific goals of psychology, which are to describe, explain, and understand human behavior. Descriptions and scientific understandings about human behavior revealed by psychological analysis will often be different from that revealed by other specialists. That is not to say that psychological analyses are necessarily the only correct explanations, but rather that they are statements based upon objective, replicable study using scientific methodology and thus differ from the type of contribution offered by theologians and other specialists.

Another prevalent objection is that psychology is nothing more than "common sense." This criticism was leveled at me by a trial judge when I was called to give expert testimony on eyewitness identification. To paraphrase the judge, "Jurors have been deliberating about questions regarding perception and memory for over 200 years and there is nothing new a psychologist can tell us about these processes" (Yarmey and Jones 1983, 13).

In order to explore the idea that common sense can be used to explain much of human behavior, some of the results from Vincent's (1979) study of police are presented below. As you read each statement, decide whether or not you agree with the explanation.

1. "Police officers differ widely among themselves for the need for capital punishment."

Explanation: It is clear that police officers are not all alike. Some see the need for capital punishment as a deterrent for murder, whereas others do not believe deterrence works. The latter group believes that less drastic measures are more appropriate than condemnation to death.

2. "Police generally recognize social workers and parole officers as respected professionals."

Explanation: With better selection of officers and educational opportunities, police are becoming more professional and better trained in their own work. They see social workers and parole officers as people who have to do a job that is different from but complementary to their own.

3. "Most policemen are not antagonistic to having women on the force."

Explanation: Women are needed in police work because times and attitudes toward women have changed. They can in fact do the things that men can do, and they are especially valuable in dealing with children and domestic disputes.

Your interpretations may resemble the above explanations for each of the three results, but there is one catch: These findings are exactly the opposite of what Vincent actually found. Furthermore, the explanations, although reasonable, are faulty. Vincent discovered that police display a high degree of agreement in the need for capital punishment; that social workers and parole officers are held in low esteem; and that most policemen are opposed to female police.

The purpose of this deception is to illustrate how easily "after-the-fact" explanations can be found to account for particular findings. Common sense explanations are a loose way of thinking that can provide *post hoc* understanding but are not predictive. There is no such thing as *the* common sense. Rather, common sense conclusions are often unclear, ambiguous, inconsistent, contradictory, and vary among cultures and individuals. It is almost impossible to get accurate insights from common sense thinking (Sjoberg 1982). Take, for example, the following folk wisdoms: "One who hesitates is lost," but "Look before you leap"; "Out of sight, out of mind," but "Absence makes the heart grow fonder"; "Never too old to learn," but "You can't teach an old dog new tricks"; "Clothes make the man," but "You can't make a silk purse out of a sow's ear." The major weakness of each of these common sense propositions is that, while both statements are logical, there is no possible way to determine their worth or their differences (Furnham 1983).

Unlike science, common sense does not attempt to distinguish between facts and values (Black 1979). Unlike common sense, psychology is not judgmental. (Unfortunately, some psychologists are judgmental to a fault). That is, what psychology attempts to do in an ideal sense, and what common sense does not do, is to separate facts and values such that descriptions are not confused with evaluations and explanations are not mistaken for justifications. This is not to say that common sense has little or no value. On the contrary, laypersons often have a good knowledge and understanding of psychological concepts developed from common sense (Furnham 1983). Conversely, psychological hypotheses and theories are not totally unrelated to common sense. Psychology draws upon the rich experiences of common knowledge to develop hypotheses, but it further attempts to clarify and test common sense ideas and beliefs. Common sense and intuition are valuable ways of organizing knowledge, but they are not the same as objective knowledge.

Skeptics may accept the argument that common sense notions are not effective substitutes for psychological analyses, but they persist in pointing out that much of psychology is concerned with trivial, irrelevant issues. This criticism is often justified since much of the research, especially applied research on the law, has been focused on irrelevant questions (Elwork, Sales, and Suggs 1981). Applied psychologists never lose the responsibility to learn more about the realities of those parts of the legal process in which they intend to apply their theories and make policy recommendations.

DIFFERENCES BETWEEN
SCIENTISTS AND LEGAL PROFESSIONALS

One of the major role differences between the scientist and the legal professional (police officer, lawyer) is in their approaches to the discovery of truth (Anderten, Staulcup, and Grisso 1980). The law searches for truth in the courtroom from the arguments presented by advocates representing opposite sides. If the charges withstand criticism and the trier of fact is convinced beyond all reasonable doubt, then the court requires a decision of guilt. This approach does not prove that "truth" exists; instead, the logic of jurisprudence assumes that truth has been discovered within the rules of the system. In contrast to the legal system, "The rules of science are predicated on the assumption that truth may be discovered by a single person dispassionately employing the scientific method to make all relevant observations and to test all possible conclusions" (Anderten, Staulcup, and Grisso 1980, 765). Scientific data are distinguished as clearly as possible from inference and belief. The purpose of the scientific canon of objectivity is to minimize the influence of personal beliefs and inference, which are considered to be more fallible than data, and to trust the discrete observations of the scientist rather than his or her authoritative point of view based on credentials (Butterfield 1979).

The two systems differ in their tolerance for indecision. The law needs a decision about truth at a given point in time, based upon the best understanding of the evidence. Science is not pressed to make a definite, immediate conclusion; ambiguous findings are tolerated with the hope that future research will resolve any uncertainties. The purpose of science is to further our knowledge and increase our understanding of how this knowledge may best be used. Law, in contrast, aims to resolve disputes, provide justice, and exercise social control. These differences in purpose and objectives force judges and lawyers to demand answers from scientists as expert witnesses, even though no reliable data are available, or, if there are answers available, the data may be considered as yet incomplete, and the scientific theory it supports tentative. As a result, both the legal system and the scientific establishment are often disturbed with the expectations and products of the other. Scientists typically try to qualify their assertions and take pride in showing where scientific theories are inconsistent because this shows how and where progress is to be made. The court, however, has the responsibility of reaching a decision. It does not want to make decisions that rest solely on currently popular, but transient "scientific" insights. Lawyers who hire expert witnesses do not want their witnesses to qualify their assertions, because this creates the opportunity for the testimony to be discredited on cross-examination. The scientist is put in a position of conflict, trying to be honest about the accepted facts with regard to a particular issue in his or her field, but at the same time, the scientist does not want to appear unsure on the witness stand. The expert's concern for credibility is further complicated by the fact that both sides may call their own experts, and these experts are likely to disagree on some issue. The rules of the court do not provide the opportunity for the two experts to engage in dialogue to determine the bases of their disagreement and come to some resolution. The court has its own mechanisms for resolving disagreement—that is, it is the responsibility of the jury or the trial judge to consider all the permitted evidence and decide upon its worth before reaching a conclusion.

Given that police officers and attorneys are frequently suspicious and dubious of psychologists who enter "their" field, the following chapters have been written in the belief that an understanding of both the strengths and the weaknesses of contemporary psychosocial theory and research can assist those persons interested in the psychology of law enforcement. As Judge Learned Hand stated in 1911:

> How long we shall continue to blunder along without the aid of unpartisan and authoritative scientific assistance in the administration of justice, no one knows; but all fair persons not conventionalized by provincial legal habits of mind ought, I should think, unite to effect some such advance. (*Parke-Davis & Co. v. H. K. Mulford Co.* 1911)

Perhaps this call is being answered now, in current cooperative interactions between the social sciences and the legal system. This book aims to further such cooperation.

In Chapter 2 the focus of interest is the "police personality." This concept is controversial since some individuals feel that such categorization is implicitly negative and critical. I hope that the reader understands that psychological research is not an attack on individuals, groups, or institutions. Instead, such research as investigations of police personality is an attempt to understand normal human behavior and the motivation, interests, and capacities of the police officer.

SUMMARY

This introductory chapter has presented a basic overview of those fields of psychology that are highly relevant to the criminal justice system.

Forensic psychologists are primarily involved in the collection, examination, and presentation of evidence for judicial purposes. However, research is the most important contribution psychologists can make to police and policing since it is the foundation of all of the services provided in assessment, treatment, training, and education. Several methods used by psychologists to acquire data such as the experimental method, survey method, interviews, and case study have been outlined. Ethical principles govern both the research and services that psychologists provide. The question of Who is the client? is the fundamental ethical issue in the field of criminal justice.

Similarities and differences in scientific reasoning and police investigations have been discussed. Much of the skepticism of the criminal justice system toward psychology is attributed to the differences in purposes between legal professionals and social scientists.

2

Personality

John is 25, single, 6′2″, weighs 230 lbs., is intelligent, enjoys the theater and films, and plays professional football. Robert, his brother, is 24, single, 6′2″, 240 lbs., intelligent, enjoys the theater and films, and is a police officer. Although we know quite a bit about John and Robert, we do not know anything about their personalities—what they are really like. It is only when we learn that John is quiet, introspective, ambitious, and sad and that Robert is loud, happy, carefree, sociable, and conventional that we begin to have an insight into them as individuals and how they differ from each other. These characteristics represent what psychologists usually mean when they describe personality because they characterize how people behave and feel. The physical characteristics John and Robert share are very similar. One has chosen to be a professional athlete while the other has selected law enforcement as a career. John and Robert probably shared many of the same family advantages growing up in the same house, attending the same schools, church, clubs, and so on. What is it, however, about John and Robert that accounts for their different career choices? Is it possible, for example, that Robert is an officer because of certain personality characteristics that differentiate him from his brother while at the same time making him more like fellow police officers? Are police officers as a group any different in their personality make-up from other groups who also serve the public, such as firefighters or prison guards? Is there a typical police personality? What personality traits, attitudes, and values does a typical officer have? Does the nature of the police occupation produce a certain working personality? Answers to these questions and other issues related to the personality of police are the primary focus of this chapter.

STEREOTYPES OF POLICE OFFICERS

Television, movies, and magazines have portrayed opposing views of the police (Culver 1978). Some programs picture the police as intelligent, sophisticated super-sleuths, while others suggest they are bumbling, childish idiots. Police have been portrayed as guardians and enforcers of the accepted values and norms and as corrupt, brutal individuals who accept bribes, bully women, and shoot thieves and murderers. As with all stereotypes, some of the police characteristics are positive and others negative, some are true and others false. It is, however, a mistake to stereotype police officers. There are wide differences in personalities, roles, and functions of officers both within and among police agencies, not to mention regional, national, and cultural differences in policing.

THE "IDEAL" POLICE OFFICER

Any description of the "ideal" police officer has to be made in terms of police roles. Policing is characterized as protecting, serving, and keeping the peace. This representation, however, prompts questions as to who is protected and what is served, what laws are enforced and when they are enforced, and at whose expense is the peace kept (Fogelson 1977)? Police departments never publish job descriptions that answer the above questions, but they do have an implicit concept of what is desired in police officers and by extension in police recruits. In general terms, the officer "must have common sense, good judgment, be able to take charge in crisis situations, and, of course, display courage and bravery when the occasion demands" (Vincent 1979, 36). Other writers claim that the "ideal patrolofficer" is the person who takes command or assumes leadership without being directed by higher authority. Such an officer is described as having a superior ability to understand people and keep a cool head under stress, danger, and provocation (Stang 1969). In addition, the ideal officer has been described as being mature, emotionally stable, reliable, and self-reliant, and able to take initiative and responsibility; as having personal integrity and being free of disruptive prejudice; as having qualities of courage, alertness, and an air of authority; as displaying professional traits of knowledge, dedication, and commitment to law enforcement; and as demonstrating miscellaneous traits such as honesty and good health that contribute to effective interaction (Badalamente et al. 1973). Although these characteristics are all relevant to some extent, what is left unsaid is that recruits are selected and socialized toward the "ideal" if they can fit into both the formal police organization and the police subculture (Gray 1975). The legal system has need for people who at times will resort to violence, violate the privacy of citizens, use deception and deceit, and denigrate an individual's character. This behavior is legal when restricted to the enforcement of laws, as in making arrests, using search warrants, and conducting investigations. When laws are not being enforced, these behaviors are illegal. As a consequence of the legal authority under which the police operate, a police subculture exists in which members identify with masculinity, perceive the world as hostile and potentially violent, are suspicious, prejudiced, cynical, and secretive, as well as politically conservative and isolated from both friends and the public (see Rokeach, Miller, and Snyder 1971).

While the above descriptions of the police may be unsavory to many observers, some writers emphasize that it is the role demands of police work and not personality defects that account for such negative characteristics (see, for example, Bayley and Mendelsohn 1969; Dodd 1967; Murphy 1965; Niederhoffer 1967). Since certain traits are necessary for effective police work, the "ideal" police officer must be competent in formal police work and highly supportive of a subculture that values controlled use of violence, group loyalty, and conservativism. Thus, addressing the issues of stereotypes, MacInnes (1962) remarks:

> The true copper's dominant characteristic, if the truth be known, is neither those daring nor vicious qualities that are sometimes attributed to him by friend or enemy, but an ingrained conservatism, an almost desperate love of the conventional. It is untidiness, disorder, the un-

usual, that a copper disapproves of most of all: far more, even, than of crime which is merely a professional matter. Hence his profound dislike of people loitering in streets, dressing extravagantly, speaking with exotic accents, being strange, weak, eccentric, or simply any rare minority— of their doing, in fact, anything that cannot be safely predicted. (P. 74)

Nevertheless, accurately characterizing the ideal police officer and predicting his or her behavior is extremely difficult. Furthermore, the ideal police officer in large urban centers may differ in psychological characteristics from the ideal police officer in rural areas (Bartol 1982). Before examining the literature on police personality, I will look briefly at what psychologists mean by this concept and how they go about assessing it.

TRAITS AND SITUATIONAL DETERMINANTS OF PERSONALITY

Personality is not an easy concept to define. Simply put, personality is an integration of our thoughts, feelings, and acts. It is this combination of characteristics that distinguishes one person from another. Every human being possesses the quality of individuality, each of us having developed genetically and environmentally under different sets of conditions. Such development determines our physical growth and our learning and thinking as well as our social behavior. To understand why people behave the way they do, the field of personality studies is concerned with how various attributes have developed and how they are related to each other.

Individual Differences

For the layperson a sufficient explanation for someone's behavior involves a list of character traits, such as honesty, intelligence, reservation, coldness, and so forth. Thus, it is believed that if somebody behaves in a certain way, it is because she has one or more of these traits determining her actions. The layperson, of course, is not trained in explaining how these traits cause behavior, nor, in most cases, does he or she care. The important question, however, is not so much whether a person is honest or cold, but why that person is perceived as honest or cold.

At one time it was hypothesized that traits were persistent psychic or neurological structures that were either learned or inherited and caused behavior (Cattell 1946). An individual's actions were thought to be relatively constant across widely varied situations because they were prewired in the form of fixed traits. The classical viewpoint is not much different from that held by laypersons. However, according to contemporary trait theorists, traits are what we observe of people; they are not the cause of behavior. When we observe someone over time, we see certain social dispositions or stylistic consistencies. Awareness of these dispositions allows us to infer something about that person's thoughts, feelings, attitudes, and values (Hogan, DeSoto, and Solano 1977).

Situational Forces

Directly opposed to the trait concept is the hypothesis that personality should be understood in terms of situational forces and constraints (Mischel 1968). Many psychologists believe that personality and social behavior are shaped and guided by the situations in which people find themselves. This is not to say that existing situational forces are the only determinants of behavior. Previous experiences in similar situations also serve to predispose people to respond in certain ways.

The differences between the trait approach and situational view for understanding personality may be seen, for instance, in the understanding of the concept of honesty. In the classical trait approach, honesty is perceived to be fixed, permanent, and unmodifiable. In contrast, situationists perceive honesty as a relative behavior that can change depending upon the circumstances faced by the individual. Thus, people will tell the truth in some contexts but will lie in others (Yarmey 1986a). According to this view, we learn more about "honesty" if we focus on the situations that characteristically evoke truth-telling or those that evoke lies, rather than if we try to identify characteristic traits of honest people. Hence, analysis of social forces such as role behavior and normative expectations is the preferred strategy in the situational approach. It is possible, of course, that both individual characteristics and situational circumstances determine behavior (Bowers 1973).

PSYCHOLOGICAL ASSESSMENTS

Men and women wishing entry into police work typically face a number of different assessments in the selection process, including interviews, written examinations, medical examinations, background investigations, physical agility tests, and a battery of psychological tests, such as intelligence, personality, and job simulation exercises.

Intelligence Tests

There is some question as to the usefulness of intelligence scores as predictors of a recruit's on-the-job success. Such scores are valuable predictors of college performance, but there is no reliable evidence that they predict job performance (Spielberger 1979). Early investigators of police officers' levels of intelligence concluded that police officers had below average intelligence (Terman 1917; Thurstone 1922). Contemporary studies indicate, however, that police officers score within the average range on intelligence tests (Matarazzo et al. 1964).

Personality Assessment

Since personality must be inferred from the ways that people behave, think, and interact, assessment must start with an examination of overt behavior and cover several segments of personality. Personality measurement may be subjective, objective, or both.

The most subjective personality measures are scores from projective tests. Projective techniques involve having individuals respond to ambiguous stimuli, such as a complex of photographs or pictures, with the assumption that they will respond by projecting their feelings and unconscious thoughts onto the stimuli. One test of this sort is the Thematic Apperception Test (TAT), in which respondents are shown a number of pictures, each depicting a different scenario, and are then asked to make up a story for each one. It is assumed that the story tells the tester something about the respondent's unique perceptions of the world, what he or she finds important, and reveals his or her emotional needs and desires. Projective tests do not have right or wrong answers, and it is up to the examiner to interpret their meanings. Because of the need to be accountable for test interpretations, it is suggested that these tests are inappropriate for preemployment screening programs for police (Inwald 1984).

Objective tests, on the other hand, do have correct answers or at least have answers that can be compared to some norm or expected responses. One well-known objective personality test is the Minnesota Multiphasic Personality Inventory (MMPI), the most frequently used psychological test for police assessment in the United States (Crosby 1979). This test consists of 550 statements that are to be answered as "true," "false," or "cannot say." The test probes twenty-six areas of interest, including such factors as social activities, family life, religion, marriage problems, and sex-life. Respondents' responses are analyzed and compared to established norms for level of adjustment and neuroticism in an attempt to yield a general picture of personality. These scores are purportedly useful both for selecting the most suitable candidates and for screening out people who are potentially unsuitable for police work because of mental abberations, personality disorders, and the like.

How useful are these assessments for police selection purposes? Clearly, personality tests have their weaknesses as well as their strengths. All tests including personality tests have to be judged for their reliability and validity. A reliable test is one that gives a stable, consistent, and dependable measure. Thus, if an individual is tested once and then tested a second time, say a month later, and the two scores are similar to each other, the test can be considered reliable. A valid test involves procedures that determine whether a test measures what it is supposed to measure. For example, if a test supposedly measures aggression but in fact measures some other unknown characteristic, it would not be considered valid, and we would put little value in its findings.

Most personality tests, such as the MMPI, have been standardized with respect to white American adults with middle-class attitudes and values. Such tests usually produce lower scores for most minority group members, not because they are more maladjusted or more neurotic, but because the test itself is culturally biased in favor of white middle-class Americans. The MMPI is considered to be a poor diagnostic test for behavioral and emotional disorders. However, it does evoke a number of self-reported behaviors that are difficult to fake or deceive without detection, which probably makes it an attractive selection test for police agencies.

Most of the research evidence on the usefulness of personality assessments for police selection is inconclusive or negative (Burbeck and Furnham 1985). For example, MMPI test scores have not been useful in distinguishing between acceptable and unacceptable officers as rated by supervising officers (Schoenfeld, Kobos, and Phinney 1980). Burbeck and Furnham (1985) conclude that "no test has been found that discriminates consistently and clearly between people who will make good police officers and those who will not. . . . The data should be used simply to give indications which a selection board can take into account with other information" (p. 64).

If, as suggested, psychological testing of law enforcement officers is inconclusive, what should administrators do regarding police selection and promotions? One danger, of course, is that all psychological testing will be considered irrelevant and police administrators will throw out the baby with the bath water. A better strategy is to examine more carefully what is expected from psychological testing. In this approach, theoretical perspectives, research, and application of results are integrated with some criterion in mind. Police administrators must be responsible for establishing detailed job analyses in order to determine what skills are considered most important for the different tasks police officers are expected to perform. Psychological testing may then be designed to select candidates most suitable for specific roles.

A valuable analysis of how and where psychological screening could be made more useful for police administrators has been provided by Inwald (1985). A summary of her recommendations is shown in Table 2.1.

Job Simulation Exercises

Situational tests are designed to predict behavior and effectiveness in a variety of job-related settings. This type of assessment has not received wide attention from police administrators perhaps because of the high costs involved in testing large numbers of job candidates. Nevertheless, these types of tests can be useful in assessing characteristics such as reaction time and decision-making under stress and in the observation

Table 2.1 Psychological Screening: Legal, Ethical, and Administrative
Questions

While the standards calling for fully validated tests, complete job analyses, and defensible performance evaluations in law enforcement officer selection may be impossible to meet at this time, meeting the spirit in which these guidelines were intended is a more accessible goal. Thus, the following suggestions are made for the development of psychological testing in law enforcement agencies, which may be of assistance in reaching this goal:

1. Use psychological screening only as one component of the overall selection process. Avoid rejecting a candidate with psychological results as the sole reason; where applicable, find evidence in the candidate's background that supports a negative psychological recommendation.
2. Build in a validation project where psychological test results and ratings can be evaluated in-house to determine their usefulness to the agency. Include an interdisciplinary staff team to evaluate any research design for its appropriateness and ease of implementation in the department.
3. Select as many tests, evaluations, and procedures as possible so that different measures can verify significant findings. Use tests where there is at least some research suggesting they may be valid for the purpose of screening law enforcement officers.
4. Steer clear of accepting arbitrary cut-off scores on psychological tests or scales unless there is clear evidence that such cut-off scores are valid and have been cross-validated in documented research studies in the agency where they will be used.
5. Document all procedures and selection practices by providing written progress reports on testing and research as it develops. Conduct frequent (several times per year) debriefing sessions with administrators and psychologists to outline research results and any changes in design.
6. Conduct an in-house education program with all staff members so that they will understand the limits of psychological testing procedures and the specific goals of the planned program. Allow for feedback from staff members to those conducting the testing program and research so that academic goals will merge with more practical ones.
7. If at all possible, provide for interviews of all candidates who are given written psychological tests. If time and/or monies prohibit this practice, make sure to provide structured interviews to any candidates whose negative written test results suggest they may have significant adjustment difficulties. Any decisions either to accept or reject candidates based solely on written test results may be successfully challenged.
8. Be flexible in the design of any research project or the selection of specific instruments for psychological evaluation. Conduct pilot studies with individual tests to produce local normative data and to determine their overall usefulness for the purpose of screening law enforcement applicants.

Table 2.1 (continued)

9. Use well-defined behavioral measures in both psychological testing and performance evaluations. Avoid subjective psychological instruments and nonspecific performance ratings.
10. Contact other state and local agencies as well as professional organizations to create a network for communication of information and solutions regarding these issues. It is only through combined efforts on the part of law enforcement administrators and mental health practitioners that psychological screening can reach its full potential as a significant component in employee selection procedures.

Source: Inwald 1985. Reprinted with permission from *Journal of Criminal Justice* 13, Robin E. Inwald, "Administrative, Legal, and Ethical Practices in the Psychological Testing of Law Enforcement Officers," © 1985, Pergamon Press Plc.

of certain personality characteristics and social skills that seldom appear in normal activities.

Attempts are made in situational tests to make the tasks and contents of the test as closely related as possible to significant aspects of actual job performance. An example of a job simulation exercise used with police recruit classes is Pugh's script (1985), which is designed to measure ability to relate to a stranger requesting help. An actor asks the recruits, "Excuse me, I'm from out of town, and I want to get to city hall. Can you give me directions?" Recruits' behaviors are recorded on videotape and later assessed by judges in the following areas: (1) approach to the situation, (2) clarity of verbal request or response, (3) consideration given to other's comments, (4) effectiveness of solution to problem, (5) confidence shown in handling situation, and (6) interpersonal skills. An overall rating based on "level of development" is used to predict future performance as a police officer. Pugh (1985) found that job simulation tests based upon verbal fluency and verbal expression are effective predictors of a recruit's job performance after two years on the job.

PERSONALITY PROFILES OF POLICE OFFICERS

Authoritarianism

Of all the stereotypes about the police, the most common is that they are authoritarian. This view appears reasonable, at least at a preliminary level of analysis. When one examines the cluster of traits that are frequently used to describe the police—conventional, aggressive, domineering, power-oriented, and so forth—one finds that these traits also define the authoritarian personality. Authoritarian personalities usually come from homes where discipline is harsh and unloving, fathers are distant and austere, and mothers are morally restrained (Adorno et al. 1950). Children from these homes are expected to be submissive to authority, their parents intolerant of challenges or signs of hostility. Adorno et al. (1950) reasoned that children growing up in such environments are forced to repress and deny their anger toward their parents. Instead, they direct it toward less threatening targets, such as minority group members.

As a consequence of their upbringing, authoritarians adhere rigidly to conventional values of morality and law and order. Obedience and respect for authority become their most cherished values. Authoritarians believe that when people deviate from traditional values, they must be disciplined and punished. Thus, according to this view, a group of individuals, such as homosexuals, for example, deserve to be punished because they deviate from conventional moral standards of decency.

Authoritarians have an orientation toward power in their social relations. They devalue and try to dominate those perceived as weaker, whereas they themselves are submissive toward those they perceive as stronger. Unfortunately, they do not recognize these traits in themselves. They lack insight into their own personality and that of others (see Sanford 1973a, 1973b). Authoritarianism is not demonstrated in every social situation; instead, it is regarded as a behavioral predisposition to be acted upon only if circumstances permit.

As recently as 1972, Balch stated that the typical police officer is almost a classic example of the authoritarian personality. An examination of more recent literature, however, suggests that this stereotype is outdated, if not false (Adlam 1982; Atwater, Bernhart, and Thompson, 1980). To the surprise of critics and perhaps even of police supporters, psychometric tests typically show that police officers score at the low end of authoritarian scales. Furthermore, they are often less authoritarian than civilian groups, including college students, teachers, and lower middle-class and working-class men (see Fenster, Wiedemann, and Locke 1977; Smith, Locke, and Fenster 1970).

Even if police did show higher scores than civilians on authoritarian scales, this would not mean that police necessarily act in an authoritarian fashion, for authoritarian attitudes are not necessarily correlated with behavior (Ray and Lovejoy 1983). Recent findings from Britain indicate that police recruits are not overly intolerant, conservative, aggressive, or, in a word, authoritarian (Brown and Willis 1985). This study also found that levels of authoritarianism decrease as a function of initial recruit training. However, on-the-beat experience leads to a substantial increase in authoritarianism in traditional police areas with high crime rates, but not in low crime areas, where police stress community service. These results suggest that occupational socialization is a determinant of authoritarian characteristics in police (Colman and Gorman 1982).

Prejudice and Bigotry

Police officers are often accused of being bigots and racists. If bigotry is a central trait in the police personality (assuming that there is *a* police personality), police officers should show more prejudice toward racial minorities than that shown by civilians with similar socio-economic backgrounds and social circumstances. Empirical evidence, however, does not support this proposition. Police are no more or no less prejudiced than the community they represent as a whole (Bayley and Mendelsohn 1969; Rafky 1977). This is not to suggest that the police never show prejudicial behavior, such as using insults and pejorative nicknames—they do. But as Skolnick (1966) points out, name-calling is a common form of expression in both the policeman's culture and the masculine working class. Police discrimination toward minority groups can and does occur. But discrimination may be the consequence of police knowledge of higher crime rates in ghettos and more frequent contact with deviant members of minority groups, rather than being a consequence of intrinsic prejudice toward minorities (Lefkowitz 1975).

Need for Control

The need for control is recognized as a powerful personality factor that determines both perception and behavior. Some people, defined as *internals* by test scores, feel that what happens to them is a result of their own actions, that they control their own fates rather than being subject to luck or outside forces. Other people, defined as *externals*, believe the opposite, feeling that their lives are tied to external forces rather than being determined by themselves (Rotter 1966).

A number of behavioral differences distinguish internals from externals. For example, high achievers are more likely to be internals (Rotter 1966). Externals are more likely to be influenced and persuaded to change their attitudes when they receive information from high-prestige sources than from low-prestige sources (Ritchie and Phares 1969). Externals also appear to be more defenseless and more helpless when threatened. They tend to remember more negative than positive information about others and tend to blame the situation or their circumstances for their failures more so than do internals (Phares 1971; Phares, Ritchie, and Davis 1968; Phares, Wilson, and Klymer 1971). Police officers identified as internals believe that they are in control of their actions, can influence outcomes, and are more satisfied with police work than officers identified as externals (Lester and Genz 1978). In addition, experienced officers are more likely to be internals whereas young, inexperienced officers are more likely to be externals (Lester and Genz 1978).

As Gadd (1986) reported:

> No one teaches answers. The good cops have somethin' about their own personality that they'll adapt to the way they work on the street. When I was out in the street in uniform, alot of times you'd walk into a bar, you'd get the kinda response, "I hate you!" or "I hate your guts! You're a real s.o.b.!"
>
> And my response usually to that was, "No, you don't. You may not like my uniform, you may not like my job, you may not like the class of people—the cops—but you don't even know me. I'm a nice guy. And if you knew me, you would like me."
>
> And invariably they would laugh. Some would say, "Well no, I wouldn't."
>
> I'd say, "Oh yeah, you would."
>
> Well, by the time it's all over, the animosity's gone, because now you're kidding back and forth. And it worked all the time. (P. 55)

Cynicism

Some observers feel that police work requires police officers to be suspicious, defensive, isolated, and secretive. Niederhoffer (1967) has labeled this the "cynicism" syndrome—that is, behavior characterized as "loss of faith in people, of enthusiasm for the higher ideals of police work and of pride and integrity" (p. 96). The ever-present possibility of danger in their work environment makes the police wary and suspicious. Officers have been found to be overly controled and somewhat unfeeling (Gudjonsson and Adlam 1983). One way of coping with a hostile environment is to band together with other police officers who share similar viewpoints, life-styles, and feelings. Isolation and secrecy become respected values that distinguish and characterize police officers as a restricted and special group. The more that police officers socialize only with other officers, the greater their tolerance of illegal misbehavior by fellow police officers and willingness to cover up such behavior (Lester and Brink 1985). Socio-occupational isolation, however, has liabilities such as stress and tension. Police officers and their families may feel different from others and become segregated from their nonpolice friends and neighbors. Furthermore, when police promote isolation and secrecy as a police value, they also promote negative attitudes in the public who misunderstand them. Balch (1972) also makes the point that "policemen are also *trained* to be suspicious" (p. 113). Their job requires that they notice the unusual events in normal everyday routines.

Although police are trained to be suspicious and have a job that promotes cynicism, it is not clear whether or not police develop these characteristics as a "working personality." According to one theorist, "The policeman's 'working personality' is most highly developed in his constabulary role of the man on the beat. . . . The policeman's role contains two principal variables, danger and authority. . . . The element of danger seems to make the policeman especially attentive to signs indicating a potential for violence and law-breaking. As a result, the policeman is usually a "suspicious" person" (Skolnick 1966, 44). It is possible that any personality characteristics found to be typical of police may be fostered entirely by the organizational-socialization system of policing (Bayley and Mendelsohn 1969; Niederhoffer 1967; Westley 1970). Both the popular press and the police themselves tend to support this view.

Other data, however, challenges these sociopolitical beliefs. In their review of the psychological research literature, Rokeach, Miller, and Snyder (1971) concluded that "the police [are] generally homogeneous in their attitudes and beliefs . . . [and] that policemen have attitudes and personality characteristics that are distinctly different from other occupational groups" (p. 156). Their research supports the hypothesis that "personality factors and social backgrounds are more important that occupational socialization" (p. 155).

The answer to the question "Is there a typical police personality?" depends, among other things, upon the specificity of response required. If a simple answer pointing to a single dominant personality type is wanted, the research literature is nonsupportive (Balch 1972). There is no evidence for such a thing as a typical police personality showing a cluster of traits that is constant across time and space (Check and Klein 1977). The most representative description of the personality of police officers will be determined by some or all of the following factors: (1) the structures and demands of the police role; (2) occupational socialization; (3) selective attrition of incompatible personality types; (4) organizational selection; (5) recruitment from the working or lower-middle class; (6) self-selection from the working-class men and women who have an interest in police work; and (7) self-selection of men and women with predisposed personality characteristics (Lefkowitz 1975).

SELF-CONCEPT AND SELF-IDENTITY OF POLICE OFFICERS

Socialization of a Police Identity

Learning to be a police officer is a continuous process. It begins at the selection stage, is shaped both formally and informally at the police college, and continues to be influenced at the agency level by police partners, the police subculture, and the larger outside community. Van Maanen (1973) refers to this process as a continuance or metamorphosis. The police socialization process is structured so as to dismantle the personality and self-concept of the recruit and to rebuild it along lines that are occupationally acceptable.

The reconstruction of a recruit's identity into a police identity starts at the police academy (Fielding 1986; Harris 1973). The formal process of training focuses mainly on reconstructing attitudes and values. For example, harassment about a recruit's physical appearance is more than an expression of discipline. The central issue for the recruit to understand is the symbolic meaning of being a police officer. Recruits learn that their physical image is associated with a moral image of respectability, convention, piety, virtue, and honor. Police are instructed to behave courteously for both defensive and pragmatic reasons. Intellectual competence is not a primary concern of police training; instead, recruits learn that they are men and women of action. This image promotes the ethic of masculinity, and the male recruit learns that he must prove his masculinity among his peers. (A discussion of policewomen and their problems in proving their worth is presented later in this chapter.) As a consequence, the self-image of virility, physical strength, power, and loyalty to fellow officers is reinforced. Harris (1973) theorizes that the acting-out of the ethic of masculinity may be responsible for the high defensiveness shown by policemen when their authority is challenged. He suggests that the police may not be as secure with their self-image as they might have us believe. Furthermore, it is those police officers who are least secure in their self-image of masculinity who are most likely to react with violence and aggression to perceived threats to their self-esteem (Toch 1976).

Police recruits have to cope with role expectations that "amplify, rather than reduce, identity problems" (Rubin 1974). Rubin argues that the recruit is defenseless against "a work identity characterized by immaturity, lack of discipline, rigidity, and paranoia". Rubin may be overstating his case, but it is true that the recruit has to cope with a paramilitary bureaucracy and a suspicious, if not hostile, community and that few people are prepared for such conditions.

Gadd (1986) illustrates the predicament of the recruit:

> My first day on the street, you stood roll call. And there's maybe fifty, sixty guys at one roll call for one shift. You walk into the police station, nervous and apprehensive. There's a big area, and you see all these big, tall, older, father-figure type policemen with their guns. They're all standing around with their hands in their pockets, cigarettes and everything. You don't know what to do or how to do it. They try to prepare you, but it's useless. Then the captain walks in with his sergeant and lieutenant behind him. It's a little military thing. (I'm thinkin'), "What did I get myself into! What's goin on here!"
>
> They yelled, "Roll call!" and everybody starts moseyin' over to form a couple of ranks so that they can be inspected. And here I am, all shiny

and new; everything on me was twenty minutes old. They yell, "Attention!" Then the captain calls up everyone's name and gives them an
assignment. He finally gets to me, and, "Did you bring it?"

I said, "Bring what, sir?"

"The note from your mother sayin' you're gonna be out this late!"

My first day, in front of all these guys! I shrunk down to about this
big. So they don't make you feel welcome. (Pp. 5–6)

Self-Concept

Although the police prefer to regard themselves as warriors or crime-
fighters (Wambaugh 1975), this stereotypical image tends to obscure
another very important self-concept: Police officers also perceive themselves as helping persons. This should not be surprising since society
asks the police to "serve and protect" (Chwast 1965). However, the
relationship between warrior and helper does seem incongruous. Thus,
the different self-concepts and values that officers hold merit some
examination.

The term *self* refers to the attitudes and concepts we use to define
ourselves (Gergen 1971). In answer to the question "Who am I?" most
people think first in terms of objective facts such as sex, occupation,
and ethnic group and second in terms of personal traits and goals
(Gordon 1968). One view of the self suggests that we are a product of
our interactions with others (Blumstein 1975). When people mix with
others they also influence and shape each other. Our identity develops
in part from the judgments and evaluations of others who are of significance to us.

The self may be thought of as a set of interconnected hypotheses
comprising multiple selves rather than a single, organized, unitary
dimension. One of these selves is commonly referred to as the *material
self* (James 1950). This self is based on the physical awareness of
sensations from our muscles, joints, stomach, and so on, which are the
"bodily me" (Allport 1955). The second self is the *social self*. This is
the identity that is public and open to evaluations from others. Our
feelings of self-worth or self-esteem are partially dependent on how
people respond to us. Because individuals who are important to us and
whose opinions we value perceive, evaluate, and treat us differently,

each of us has many social selves. The third self is the *spiritual self*, or inner core, the "I" of our identity. The inner experience of self is something that all of us are phenomenologically aware of, although we must infer its existence since we cannot directly examine it.

Over time and with maturity, most people learn to accept themselves —both their good qualities and bad. Psychologically healthy people are described as individuals who have a firm self-identity that forms the basis of self-esteem (Erikson 1959, 1963). In contrast, people who lack a clear understanding of who and what they are have what Erikson calls an *identity crisis*. He suggests that men and women pass through a series of eight psychosocial stages of personality development during their lifetime. How successful individuals are in solving each crisis posed by each stage determines whether or not they build a stable self-concept or identity. Successful solutions result in the person's thinking well of him- or herself, others, and the environment. Unsuccessful solutions, on the other hand, result in lack of self-trust, lack of trust in others or the world, shame, doubt, guilt, inferiority, role confusion, isolation, self-absorption, and despair.

The conflict and adaptations that confront police officers as they progress through their careers have been described by Fagan and Ayers (1982). Twenty-three male police officers between 27 and 55 years of age from a medium-sized city in Kentucky were interviewed. Nineteen of the men came from working-class backgrounds and had been policemen from two to thirty years, with an average of 14.7 years of police experience. This research revealed that police officers do in fact pass through a series of psychosocial stages and that the stress inherent in police work is a significant part of this process. In the early adult transition years (19–22), 78 percent of the sample entered the military. Only two subjects reported having what Erikson would label an *acute identity crisis*. The majority married during this period, led stable lives, and reported little evidence of planning or long-term decision-making in their early adult years. Three of the men became police officers during this period. Between the ages 22 to 28 (entering the adult world period), eleven men left blue-collar work, primarily because of dissatisfaction with their jobs, and found police work, 91 percent having felt attracted to law enforcement because of perceived job security. Most of the officers led settled lives through this period. All of the men who joined the police force at this time initially enjoyed their work, although some could not handle the freedom, excitement and power. The temptation to drink heavily and to be promiscuous was strong.

One police officer stated:

> At that time . . . there were women everywhere. Women would actually chase you. This was a new life. Getting off from work and hitting the bars . . . pulling pranks, drinking on duty. . . . Locking people up; that's a big thing, especially on midnights. You really got the power, whether you want it or not, and at that point, I really don't think any 23, 25, 27 year-old knows how to handle it. (Fagan and Ayers 1982, 278)

Most of the subjects during this period were concerned with doing an adequate job, having a good time, and living a day-by-day existence. Unlike business executives, factory workers, writers, and biologists, who have mentors or leader-models to follow (Levinson 1978), police officers do not have such role-models. Furthermore, as Erikson (1963) characterizes it, young adulthood is a period of intimacy versus isolation. Many of the police officers had difficulty in maintaining close emotional relationships, with 36 percent divorced while in their twenties and many being totally absorbed in their work and heavy drinkers and experiencing high amounts of stress.

According to Levinson (1978), the *age 30 transition period* (28–33) is a stressful, questioning time when commitments made in the early twenties are reconsidered. Fagan and Ayers found that this period was stressful for 78 percent of their subjects. At about age 30, job-related crises centering on conflicts with departmental administration, denial of promotion, disillusionment with the operations of police work, and with life in general were common.

Between 33 and 40 years of age *(settling-down period)*, most subjects recaptured some of their earlier enthusiasm for police work but tempered it with experience. Promotion, further education, and additional responsibility facilitated positive changes. Not all men, however, were successful, and marriage disintegration and excessive drinking did occur for some.

The *midlife transition period* (40–45) was not adequately studied in this investigation because only eight of the police officers were 43 or older. Results that are available, however, suggest that this period is not a transitional one for police. Unlike other professionals, police officers did not dwell on questions such as "What do I really want in life?" "Who am I?" "Where am I going?" Identity searching, death awareness, and other concerns of middle age are not salient issues. In contrast, officers who received promotions were positive in attitude and looked forward to further professional advancement. Those who were not promoted looked forward to retirement and generally complained about their work and their supervisors.

Why Choose a Police Career?

Why does someone want to be a police officer? A cynical answer, and one that is not generally true of those men and women who are accepted as recruits, is that they wish to legitimatize personality weaknesses such as criminal impulses, sadomasochism, inferiority complexes, and the like. A more accurate answer is that the police recruit has a sense of social responsibility and service combined with a desire to be a person of action or adventure. Police work has the potential to satisfy all these needs. This view, of course, is not true of all men and women who join the force. Clinical interviews of male police applicants conducted by Matarazzo et al. (1964) revealed that men chose this work because they wanted to help juveniles and to work with people in trouble. This goal may be contrasted with responses of applicants to fire departments who chose firefighting as a career because of the attractive work schedule (twenty-four hours on, forty-eight hours off), which allows firefighters the opportunity to hold another job or to pursue recreational interests.

The desire for adventure and action is a powerful motivating factor for becoming a police officer (Van Maanen 1973). In spite of the routine services and administrative requirements that comprise most of an officer's daily activities, the fact that danger and excitement can occur at any time provides self-esteem and stimulation. The ever-present possibility of making a "good arrest" motivates the officer and gives meaning to his or her self-image as society's protector.

Other reasons for choosing police work have been summarized by Lefkowitz (1973, 1974, 1975, 1977), according to whom "the predominant psychological motivation to become a policeman appears to be the need for security" (1977, 347). Police officers are well paid relative to many other occupations that attract most of their employees from the working class. Lefkowitz also suggests that the desire for job security is emphasized more by whites than by blacks and Puerto Ricans. In contrast to whites, minority group members choose police work primarily because they wish to maintain law and order and help people (see Hunt 1971; Kelly and West 1973; Reiss 1967).

Police Values

So far I have spoken of the values of police in terms of a personality profile of the "ideal" officer. On a more fundamental level, values can be shown to be central to the self-concept and working identity of the police officer.

Personal values are developed from early childhood experiences, from interaction with parents, brothers and sisters, teachers, church, and other social and cultural institutions. The social origin of most recruits is the working class (Bayley and Mendelsohn 1969), but the police force is a middle-class institution with middle-class values and expectations. Working-class values and attitudes can come into conflict with standards expected by middle-class status. Most successful police officers adopt or believe in middle-class goals such as ambition, the assumption of responsibility, the ability to work for the future, the postponement of immediate gratification, and the respect for personal as well as others' property. These values may conflict in police work with lower-class community values, which reflect such standards as restricted aspirations, a live-for-today orientation, lack of concern for order, neatness and punctuality, and a view that physical aggression is an acceptable solution to interpersonal problems.

The self-concept of officers is shaped by the police role toward conventional middle-class values. Hair is cut and styled in a conservative manner (Preiss and Ehrlich 1966), and speech, mannerisms, and choice of civilian dress is orthodox. The conservative orientation is also internalized and includes a preference for conservative politics and a commitment and conformity to rules, regulations, and the status quo (Butler and Cochrane 1977; Niederhoffer 1967).

Police show an increase in their self-respect or self-esteem when they have a sense of accomplishment. They value a self-image that stresses feelings and thoughts of order, logic, rationality, control, and obedience. However, police put a lower value on independence in work habits, preferring instead a rigid, formal, authoritative structure that sets limits, procedures, and expectations. The preference for organizational control may create conflicts for police officers since formal power is dissonant with a valued self-image of assertiveness, ability to take initiative, and need to be independent in decision-making (Butler and Cochrane 1977; Lefkowitz 1973, 1977).

Perhaps the most troubling aspect of police officers' self-concept and identity is the belief that citizens do not respect them and give them little status or prestige. Since recognition of self-worth, pride, and satisfaction in life are tied closely to an individual's work, this belief may lead to defensiveness and a feeling that they are misunderstood by the public.

PERSONALITY ISSUES AND POLICEWOMEN

Although women have been active in policing in the United States since 1845, the duties, obligations, and roles of women have changed only slightly since their initial entry into the occupation as matrons (Higgins 1951). Utilization of women in policing is tempered by traditional stereotypes of sex roles such that women are perceived as physically weak and unable to handle the emotional, psychological, or physical demands of the profession (Charles 1982; Lord 1986). There has been concern among policemen and administrators whether women can perform customary police roles such as patrol duty, intervening in street fights, pulling victims from wrecked vehicles, and other functions involving danger and strength. Arguments that most of an officer's time is spent in service or noncriminal activities (Cumming, Cumming, and Edell 1965) are not convincing to policemen who are highly aware of the potential for danger and the need for strength on occasion while on patrol. In spite of overwhelming empirical evidence showing that women are as effective as men in police work, policemen generally judge policewomen negatively (Balkin 1988).

Furthermore, there have also been some accusations that the attractiveness of a policewoman is disruptive to the effectiveness of the job performed. In one case in London, a policewoman won a sex-discrimination battle against London police officials who had ruled she was too attractive to share a patrol car with a married policeman. As the *Globe and Mail* reported, "Her family said 25-year-old Wendy de Launay will return to work with police traffic teams. Her partnership with a male police officer on mobile traffic duties was broken up by their supervisor who said she was 'too pretty and attractive' for the job" (April 14, 1984).

Popular beliefs held by front-line male officers and administrators are that policewomen, in contrast to policemen, are indecisive, weak, ineffective, inconsistent, emotionally unstable, passive, nonobservant, lacking in confidence, and less adaptable. However, they are perceived as more understanding, compassionate, and intelligent (Linden 1983; Marshall 1973; Wexler and Logan 1983). Over the years, the set of personality attributes deemed suitable for policewomen has been more or less consistent and stands in marked contrast to the more paramilitaristic image considered appropriate for policemen. In 1933, policewomen were expected to have a pleasant personality, an agreeable attitude toward work with behavioral problems of young women, tolerance, common sense, sympathy, and emotional stability (Bell 1982). By 1945, policewomen were told not to be overly feminine, aggressive, mannish, sentimental, or callous. And in 1953, dignity, sensibility, tact, sympathy, neatness, attractiveness, alertness, interest in others rather than self, and good adjustment were required attributes of policewomen (Tenny 1953).

Very few empirical investigations of the personality characteristics of policewomen have been conducted. Furthermore, the emphasis has been more descriptive than theoretical and has centered mainly on describing differences between female and male police or differences between female police and women in other professions. The descriptive, comparative approach is useful for establishing a preliminary knowledge base, but it has the disadvantage of ignoring all of the individual differences in personality that manifest themselves *within* the female police officer group.

Body Structure and Personality

An old but still popular theory is that a person's personality is directly related to his or her physique. Sheldon's constitutional psychology (1942) contends that body build is inherited and is the foundation of behavior. Sheldon identified three major body types and related a personality to each one: *Endomorphs* are characterized by large stomachs and soft, plump bodies, this body type being related to a temperament of sociability, relaxation, and love of comfort; *mesomorphs* are persons with muscular, hard bodies who love risk-taking, competition, action, and adventure; *ectomorphs* are characterized by tall, thin, and fragile body builds and temperamentally need introspection, isolation, and solitude and have a high level of self-consciousness. Although this theory is not taken seriously by contemporary personality theorists, the stereotypes of body build and personality temperaments are believed by the public and must be reckoned with. Anecdotal observations of male police officers suggest that they tend toward being mesomorphs and men of action. Traditionally, it has been assumed that taller men make better police officers. Shorter officers (less than 5'9.5") show a greater potential for aggression as measured by the Spielberger Trait Anger Scale (Spielberger, Gorsuch, and Lushere 1970) than their taller counterparts (greater than 6'0.5"). However, there is no evidence that shorter officers are more aggressive in their job performance (Willoughby and Blount 1985).

Thirty years ago, Astrand (1956) found that males are 20 to 40 percent stronger than females depending on the muscle group studied. More recently, Charles (1982) deduced that with improved physical training methods and the incorporation of maintenance fitness programs, women and unfit men could attain a degree of strength and conditioning well within the physical demands of policing. While physically fit women will not reach the same high plateau of fitness that well-trained men can reach, this does not mean that the physical level of ability that women may attain is below the physical job requirements of policing. Tests conducted on female athletes show that selected women can surpass the most rigorous demands for strength and fitness needed by any police officer. Through weight training, women's strength can be increased by 70 percent (Wilmore 1973).

One final note. Contrary to the stereotype of policing, physical strength has not been shown to be related to police roles and duties (Sherman 1973). While acknowledging that physical strength is important to the safety and security of both police and the community, "It is even more important that they [police officers] have the ability to plan their actions and utilize their skills with maximum efficiency" (Charles 1982, 203).

Table 2.2 An Overview of Some Differences in Personality Between
(1) Female Police Officers and Female Citizens and (2) Female and Male Police Officers

Reference Group	Compared To	Personality Profile	Reference
Female police officers	Female nurses	—are more changeable, daring, fickle, impulsive, masculine, outspoken, pleasure-seeking, reckless, and spontaneous.	Kennedy and Homant (1981)
Older female police officers	Younger female police officers	—are more conservative, more masculine in attitude. —are less favorable toward expanded women's role and feminist rights.	Kennedy and Homant (1981)
Female state police recruits	Female college students	—are more cheerful, athletic, assertive, happier, forceful, reliable, truthful; are risk-takers, decision-makers; are self-sufficient, masculine, friendlier, aggressive, competitive; show leadership. —are less moody, less analytic, less soft-spoken.	Lester, Gronau, and Wondrack (1982)

Female state police recruits	Male state police recruits	—are similar in high needs to achieve, for exhibition, dominance, and heterosexuality; and similar in low need for affiliation and abasement. —are lower in need for deference, order, abasement, and endurance. —are higher in need for exhibition, autonomy, dominance, change, and heterosexuality.	Lester, Gronau, and Wondrack (1982)
Female police	Male police	—are motivated to be police officers by a desire to help people rather than a desire for security.	Perlstein (1972)
Female police executives	Male police executives	—differed on five leadership traits: women displayed greater flexibility, more concern with personal appearance, greater emotional independence, more self-assertiveness, and greater initiative. —are less persistent, more submissive, less authoritarian, less prejudiced, and more creative. —men are less submissive, sadistic, and hostile to people of different backgrounds.	Price (1974)

Personality Differences Between Policewomen and Other Groups

Table 2.2 presents a summary of the major research findings of personality differences and similarities among female police officers and other groups. An overview of these findings suggests that policewomen are more like policemen in characteristics of personality than they are like college female students of similar age and female nurses. However, just because policewomen score more highly in masculine interests and aggressive tendencies than do other female groups, they are not less feminine as a consequence. Traditional female characteristics such as gentleness, modesty, considerateness, and so on are not absent in policewomen. Also, young policewomen are not prepared to accept stereotypical female-male role prescriptions and are not willing to give up feminine rights. If the traditional masculine stereotype of policing continues into the future, it will exist for political, organizational, and prejudicial reasons, not because females in general are unsuitable for police work as a result of personality deficiencies or weaknesses in physical strength (see Berg and Budnick 1986).

Socialization of Policewomen

Earlier in this chapter, I discussed the self-concept and self-identity of police officers. More accurately, this discussion should have been labeled *policemen*. Gross (1984) rightly indicates that "the experience of becoming a police officer is not the same for men and women, nor should it be" (p. 32). The major conflict facing women focuses on the image the woman has of herself in policing. Female officers typically find that acceptance from their male peers is often at the expense of foregoing many positive feminine qualities. Gross discovered that female recruits entering police training were generally self-confident and idealistic about their work and interactions with fellow male officers. After eight weeks of training, their feelings about peer relations dropped dramatically (80 percent decline) and did not improve significantly after that. Loss of self-esteem, disillusionment, and sex-role conflict were particularly great for traditional "feminine" women.

Women recruits learn that policing is a male occupation and that the image of the "ideal" police officer is usually a strong male figure.

Women also learn from the media that females are predominantly weak, ineffective, manipulative, or flirtatious. These images do little for policewomen in fostering positive mental health or effective policing.

Policewomen often face barriers not experienced by their male counterparts. These include the qualities expected to be a girlfriend, wife, mother, and lover conflicting with the qualities necessary for survival in the academy or the street; denial of feminine qualities of nurturing, empathy, and cartaking; threatening egos of their male police peers or male companions; sexual harassment from training officers and others; fears from administrators and some police wives of sexual involvement with other police officers; and the catch-22 situation of being too competent and therefore threatening, even though competency is extremely valued, as opposed to being less competent and consequently rejected as partners (see Balkin 1988).

Society has changed its attitudes toward women entering into traditional male-dominated organizations, such as medicine and law, and women will be entering law enforcement careers in ever-increasing numbers. The entry and socialization of women into policing will have to be facilitated by police administrators and through the departmental support of "nonthreatened" male patrol officers. Unless experienced policewomen are given encouragement to rise in police organizations and actually attain supervisory or leadership positions, many policewomen will choose to leave the organization (Poole and Pogrebin 1988). Gross (1984) recommends the promotion and maintenance of female support networks among recruits and those experienced policewomen who have retained a sense of femininity in their job. Support networks will provide the opportunity for women to learn to behave responsibly and effectively as women. Female police officers need each other and can best function as each other's teacher, confidants, and approval-givers as they strive for excellence. Gross' recommendations are worthy of support.

SUMMARY

Personality is generally defined as the unique organization of relatively enduring mental states or traits of a person. There is no evidence to show that police officers as a group think and behave in similar ways that reflect a single personality type.

Popular stereotypes of police officers, such as authoritarianism and suspiciousness, have been discussed in this chapter. The self-concept and identity of police officers is seen to be a continuous process that begins to be shaped at the police academy. The role demands of police work, rather than predispositions deriving from personality attributes, probably account for many police characteristics. Policewomen and policemen share many of the same personality characteristics, but policewomen are not less feminine as a consequence.

3

Roles, Role Conflict, and Leadership

Police officers are expected to have good judgment, the ability to make rapid and intelligent decisions, and an understanding of a wide variety of human behavior. They are also supposed to maintain a sense of perspective, to remain calm in emergencies, to communicate clearly and precisely, and to possess leadership skills. With society expecting a great deal from its police, the list of desired attributes is endless. Since police officers are not born to be "cops," they must learn their multidimensional roles.

Critics of law enforcement practices such as Bennis and Cleveland (1980) suggest that the education and training of police officers is misdirected. They argue that 90 percent of classroom time for police recruits is spent on the technical and vocational skills of marksmanship, use of tear gas, and strong-arm tactics, yet investigations of homicides, robberies, and other criminal activities that make use of these technical skills constitute only approximately 10 percent of a police officer's activities. In contrast, the primary functions of order maintenance and community service receive only minimal formal attention.

ROLES AND FUNCTIONS OF THE POLICE

When a patrol officer drives his cruiser down a street in his city, he observes and classifies people into various social categories: shopper, tourist, businessperson, alcoholic, drifter, trouble-maker and so on. These classifications are role categories or positions, which can be defined as follows:

> The term *role* is usually defined as the set of behaviors or functions associated with a particular position within a particular social context. (Wrightsman and Deaux 1981, 14)

> Most behavioral scientists today prefer to define a role as the behavior generally expected of an individual in a given social position. (Berkowitz 1980, 422)

These definitions indicate that roles specify when to act and where. Roles further introduce obligations or demands such that certain actions are prescribed and others are forbidden. Roles involve normative expectations by which we legitimately anticipate that others will behave in certain ways, and these expectations may be shared by most members of society or by as few as two individuals. Societies' subgroups, such as racial minorities, the poor, and adolescents, often have distinctive expectations about the role category police. Thus young adults, for example, characteristically expect more harassment toward themselves from the police than do older persons or primary school children (Bogomolny 1976; Glaser 1978).

Roles are reciprocal in nature, each role being linked to at least one other role. For instance, citizens expect that traffic officers, according to their obligation, will direct pedestrians and drivers with minimal inconvenience to citizens; conversely, traffic officers expect that citizens, according to their obligations, will start and stop on command. Roles do not exist in isolation. Police cannot be guardians of the law and providers of service without countless other role partners, such as lawbreakers and lost children, each of whom makes his or her own unique demands upon the police officer. The reciprocal nature of these roles is most evident in the relationship between the community and the police. That is, the community shapes the behavior of the police and, over time, ultimately produces a force in its own image (Banton 1964; Lopez-Rey 1968). Any attempt to describe the work of police officers must begin with the recognition that police departments are not all the same. Each has a distinct local and national character, and even within the same department police officers differ as a function of their different roles.

Police agencies follow one of three styles of policing: the *watchman style*, the *legalistic style*, and the *service style* (Wilson 1968). The watchman style of policing emphasizes the maintenance of public order. Characteristically, the agency lacks professionalism, and underenforces the law, and the individual officer is permitted a wide latitude of discretion based primarily upon his or her private sense of justice. In contrast, the legalistic style is much more professional. Different police services perform specialized functions, and officers attempt to control by adhering to the letter of the law. The service style is less formal than the legalistic but more controlled than the watch style. Police officers intervene and make contact with a public that expects personal attention to private needs and demands. Police adhere to legal regulations, but, as public servants, police are also expected to be helpful and compassionate. In addition, one part of a control style police administration may emphasize the legalistic style and another part of the same administration may emphasize individuality, with both policies being in conflict with community service values (Toch 1978).

The traditional roles of the police are commonly understood to be law enforcement and the maintenance of public order. If the average citizen is asked to define the primary duties of the police, he or she would probably answer, "Prevention of crime and capture of criminals." Although some police may approve of this "crime-fighter" or "warrior" image and evaluate their work in terms of crime control, these stereotypes are unrealistic and have little resemblance to daily routine (McEvoy 1974).

Table 3.1 presents a summary of the most typical activities of American frontline officers (Badalamente et al. 1973). Police officers work in situations that require them to be problem-solvers, decision-makers, and to use discretion. They perform a wide variety of functions that involve social contacts between themselves and individuals or groups. Specifying a subset of factors of Table 3.1, Table 3.2 presents a sampling of activities in an officer's "social role." The activities listed

Table 3.1 A Patrol Officer's Duties

—Assigned beat or post

—Makes arrest and searches

—Responds to and handles emergency calls

—Collects and safeguards evidence

—Regulates and controls traffic

—Makes necessary reports and records

—Cooperates with other police agencies and allied units

—Interrogates and interviews victims, witnesses, and suspects

—Testifies in court

—Safeguards property

—Advises, directs, and gives information to the public

—Enforces state laws and city and county ordinances

—Performs miscellaneous duties and provides services

—Maintains a professional attitude

—Operates and maintains related equipment

—Investigates citizens' complaints and makes preliminary investigations of major crimes

Source: Badalamente et al. 1973. Reprinted by permission of the *Journal of Police Science and Administration*, copyright 1973 by Northwestern University School of Law, Vol. 1, No. 4, pp. 440–453.

Table 3.2 A Police Officer's Social Role

—Provides assistance in disasters

—Intervenes in attempted suicides

—Intervenes in family crises and/or domestic fights

—Restores order in situations involving student unrest

—Resolves conflicts involving minority factions

—Participates in community-service projects and programs

—Restores order in disturbances involving the mentally ill, alcoholics, and drug addicts and, when appropriate, directs such to rehabilitative services

—Administers first aid

—Locates lost or missing persons

—Restores order in situations involving juveniles

—Participates in human-relations programs

—Mediates disputes between tenants and landlords and, when appropriate, directs complaints to legal services

—Fosters good police-community relations

—Provides comfort and guidance to individuals and families involved in personal tragedies

Source: Badalamente et al. 1973. Reprinted by permission of the *Journal of Police Science and Administration*, copyright 1973 by Northwestern University School of Law, Vol. 1, No. 4, pp. 440–453.

in this table confirm the difficulty in trying to provide a simple definition of police roles and functions. Indeed, some observers believe it is an impossible task (Ward 1970).

POLICE ROLE STRAIN AND ROLE CONFLICT

All individuals typically play many roles in their everyday behavior such as husband, father, wife, mother, neighbor, friend. Some of these roles evoke competing expectations that cannot be fulfilled. Furthermore, even a single role, such as that of police officer, has within it conflicting and varied expectations. Consequently, officers may experience role strain when expectations from one of their roles are incompatible with the demands arising from another. The strain from role conflicts produce feelings of dissatisfaction, inadequacy, tension, anxiety, and frustration. These reactions make it difficult for officers to relate with their partners, which further weakens the interpersonal relationships and the trust, confidence, and respect so necessary for police work. Persistent conflict between citizens and police and between police and fellow officers can be reflected in communication failures, social isolation, and increased hostility.

Role strain and conflict result from three major sources. First, if the expectations that make up the role are ill-defined, correct role performance is difficult. Second, contradictory role expectations, resulting from incompatibilities in the role itself, produce strain. Finally, if there are ambiguities or disagreements among participants over goals and values, relationships among role partners can be strained.

Five types of role strain and conflict in police work are described below.

Quasi-Military Organizations Versus Social Work

In quasi-military organizations, "real" police work is defined in terms of crime control. Police tend to believe that if crime is to be solved, more money has to be spent on policing and officer strength and technology and laws have to be strictly enforced (Manning 1978). These beliefs result in the police judging their own performance against the traditional criteria of numbers of citations, arrests, and summonses. The police reward themselves according to these criteria as do the mass media. Officers who are assigned to other activities find that their work is undervalued or even ridiculed because they are not doing "real" police work.

It is increasingly apparent to social scientists that the use of traditional quasi-military criteria to assess police performance is inappropriate when applied to sensitive interpersonal conflict situations (Badalemente et al. 1973). In fact, the paramilitary police model as an objective for all police is inappropriate (Fry and Berkes 1983). It is worth emphasizing that most calls for police assistance are requests for help from people in distress. These calls require tact and assistance, not force and muscle (Sherman 1973; Webster 1970).

Although the police are not social workers and dislike being labeled as such, their roles are similar in some respects. Toch (1976) states:

> We "know" police are not social workers . . . self-respecting patrolmen would resign in a body if they were rechristened "social workers." But these same officers can generate family crisis units, conflict management units, landlord tenant units, and consumer protection programs. Having generated such programs, they can cheerfully implement them, run them, and man them. Individually, officers act superbly in "social work" encounters. They prevent suicides, reduce fear, settle disputes, make referrals; they comfort the sick or dying; they humor alcoholics, children, psychotics. They do what they do unselfconsciously, waiting for "real police work" to come along. And there is no reward for their work. It draws no headlines, medals, locker room acclaim. Catching burglars does. . . . The situation is different where police departments highlight service functions. While burglars are elusive, community needs are not. (P. 120)

Unlike social workers, who are concerned with assisting individuals and small groups, the police have to interact with the whole community. It is to the police officer that individuals look for help because the officer is always available and dependable. The police mandate is concern for the welfare of the total society (Danish and Ferguson 1973). Most police and citizen interactions reflect a concern for social welfare since most encounters are civil, whereas only 8 percent of interactions are antagonistic (Reiss 1971). By the same token, when citizens have complaints about police, the majority of grievances focus on police attitudes and their lack of social skills (Jones 1986; Marin 1978; Russell 1978). The public does not evaluate police officers primarily in terms of their effectiveness as crime fighters. Instead, citizens are more impressed by police who demonstrate genuine concern for their distress. When officers show empathy, understanding, and interest and take the time to explain their work to civilians, citizens hold the police in high regard.

Clearly, a separation of roles between police work and social work is fundamentally important. In family crisis situations, the police are needed because of their authority to control and to stop a dangerous or violent episode. Once that is completed, a professional social worker's job begins. The social worker assists the family to find and use nonviolent solutions to their problems, whereas the police officer's duty is to communicate to the family that violence is unacceptable. Unfortunately, because of traditional suspicions and cynicism, police officers are often reluctant to develop police–social work interactions (Holdaway 1986; Holmes 1982).

Police officers may have a perception that police work is masculine and social work is feminine (Parkinson 1980). Such sex-role stereotyping may be a defense mechanism to maintain a protective distance between themselves and the public. But the tendency of police officers to ignore and devalue the social worker's role interferes with the kinds of service that police can provide. Partnerships and cooperation between police and social workers have proved to be successful where they have been introduced on a trial basis (see Holmes 1982; Treger 1972). The following two examples of cooperation between police and social workers illustrate the type of professional collaboration possible:

Tom, age 17, was stopped by the police on suspicion of shoplifting, and when searched was found to possess a marijuana cigarette. It was clear to the officer that the boy was troubled, as he appeared depressed and somewhat withdrawn. The social worker was contacted by the police officer and asked to assess the boy's condition. When seen with his family, the stressful home environment became evident. The mother had attempted suicide a few weeks earlier, and the father was using work as a means of escaping family problems. After assessing the family situation, the social worker recommended that the family receive ongoing [social] services. (Treger 1972, 57)

A police officer called the [family trouble] clinic to say that he had a woman in the office who was very upset and needed to talk. Mrs. E. was unsure about whether to press charges of assault against her husband, but had gone to the station from the hospital where she had been taken by the police the previous evening. She agreed to come immediately to the clinic. . . . Various options were explored with Mrs. E., as well as the positive and negative aspects of her marital relationship. (Holmes 1982, 222)

In these examples, a separation of roles between police work and social work is maintained. The skill of the police in defusing a crisis situation or in anticipating the making of a tragic social problem and their contacting other professionals can promote the utilization of an effective interdisciplinary criminal justice team.

Deference to Versus Disrespect for Police

If respect for their occupation is not forthcoming, officers "put heavy emphasis on not taking any crap" (Richardson 1974). Officers are faced with a conflict between trying to do their duty and finding the public uncertain about their value or, at worst, hostile to them. The lack of respect and criticism often shown by the press also leads to tension and insecurity. Society does not know what it wants from police and often acts inconsistently toward its law enforcement officers. The consequence is further police uncertainty, discouragement, and resentment (Blum 1981). For the officer highly involved in his or her job, police work is more than just a way to earn a living. It is also a commitment of self, and feelings of self-worth and self-esteem, to an occupation that dominates his or her life (Westley 1970). Police officers treated with disrespect suffer the stress of personal attacks as well as an assault on their profession.

Competing Expectations

Police are expected to be: (1) the "guardians of society," which gives them the legitimate right to use coercion to prevent crime; (2) the "peacekeepers of society," meaning that they are supposed to maintain public order, arbitrate disputes, and settle conflicts; and (3) "public servants," that is, responsible to community needs (Johnson 1970). Society tends to rely on the police to solve a wide variety of problems that other agencies cannot or are unwilling to manage, such as looking for runaway teenagers or evacuating towns in emergency situations (Johnson 1970; McNamara 1967; Regoli and Poole 1980). However, as mentioned earlier, police administrators have failed to provide clear and consistent guidelines of what is expected of a "good police officer." Police officers often discover that their perceptions of their job are not consistent with their supervisors' perceptions of their roles (Preiss and Ehrlich 1966).

Although police agencies claim that recruits are taught in police training academies how to handle emergency situations, police learn that they have a great amount of discretion in and responsibility for making their own decisions. (Van Maanen 1973). Thus, police officers face crisis situations which they must resolve on their own. These decisions are particularly difficult when the situation is dangerous and emotions run high. Unlike other citizens, police officers can be placed in situations where they must choose between being brave and at risk and being safe and embarrassed for not doing their duty (Blum 1981). Police officers must also learn to deal with pain, misery, cruelty, and death and learn to deny themselves public display of emotion and anger. The tendency to become insensitive to injury is a defensive reaction to the requirements of the job, but it is made at the cost of the distortion of personal needs and emotions.

Conflicting Values

Police generally subscribe to a value system that reflects the institution's authoritarian, quasimilitary structure. Consistent with this view, several social scientists (see LaFave 1965; Reiss 1971) have noted that the police consider themselves morally superior. They feel that they themselves are best suited to judge right from wrong or good guys from bad guys, and they are committed to defending this moral position.

When their authority is challenged, officers are placed in a conflict. They can attack the offender, swallow their pride and forget the incident, or compromise their morality and manufacture a false excuse to arrest the individual (Cain 1973). When the police believe that they are in the best position to judge the culpability of an offender, especially for an offence that violates their moral sensibilities, "street justice," such as harassment or physical force, may be handed out quickly and self-righteously (Reiss 1971; Skolnick 1966). These moral actions, however, violate the basic civil rights of all citizens.

Police officers greatly respect loyalty to their fellow officers. In a profession that involves the likelihood of danger and risk, it is important that an officer knows that his or her partner will assist should danger arise. Loyalty to fellow officers, however, may put police in conflict with administrative directives or with the law itself. Likewise, loyalty to legal and moral principles may put police in conflict with their fellow officers, as in the following incident described by Blum (1981):

> One lieutenant I knew decided that he would always act on the idealistic principle of honesty before loyalty. Consequently, during a grand jury investigation, he testified against several fellow supervisors whom [sic] he know were either inefficient or dishonest. He was commended by the grand jury and the District Attorney, but it was five years before any of his fellow officers would speak to him. (P. 121)

Blum suggests that the solution to conflicts between loyalties can only come about if both individual police officers and the entire departments are committed to the ethical principle of honesty and a code of operating ethics of the highest professional standards.

A more difficult problem is the hypothesized differences in values and beliefs that are said to exist between the police and the community. The study of police values can never be separated from the cultural background in which the investigation was conducted. However, investigations done in the United States (Griffeth and Cafferty 1977; Rokeach, Miller, and Snyder 1971) and in England (Cochrane and Butler 1980) confirm the assumption that the value systems of police officers and civilians differ in some respects. For example, Rokeach and his colleagues found that a sample of 150 American police officers considered peace, beauty, equality, and national security to be less important than did a sample of 560 citizens, whereas police evaluated an exciting life and mature love to be more important.

Likewise, Cochrane and Butler, comparing the values of fifty experienced policemen, twenty-five new recruits, and fifty civilians, found that citizens placed more emphasis on a "world of peace" than did experienced officers and were less concerned than these officers with a "comfortable life," "mature love," and "self-respect." Recruits differed from civilians on only one value: Recruits were not overly concerned with "a world of peace." Recruits also differed from experienced officers in one important way: Recruits attached less importance to self-respect.

The results of these two studies from two distinct cultures cannot be explained by inferring that police officers have a more conservative value system than do civilians. In contrast to civilians, experienced police officers give greater emphasis to personal as opposed to social values. One implication of these findings is that role conflict and role strain will not be reduced by focusing solely on the education of new recruits. As experienced officers become more self-oriented and more socially isolated, differences in values and beliefs will increase and further exacerbate role conflicts.

"Real" Role-Playing: Undercover Police

One of the best examples of role conflict can be found in the work of undercover agents (Girodo 1983). Undercover police officers working in drug enforcement have to learn to physically, intellectually, and emotionally play the role of criminals. This type of activity is exciting and brings tangible rewards of accomplishment and achievement that boost feelings of self-esteem. High emotional and intellectual investment in this work, however, often accounts for an agent's high vulnerability to conflict and emotional distress both during and after an operation. Sometimes losing perspective, undercover police can fail to "turn off" their roles outside of the operational situation when, for example, interacting with the cover team, peers, and family. Operators may begin to lead the life of the role and cover story. High attachment and loyalty to their "new friends" and the life-style provided by this role may result. When undercover work finally concludes, some officers have difficulty in making the transition to more mundane police work.

RESOLVING ROLE STRAIN

Individuals in any role category cannot be all things to all people. Some interests have to be set aside or relegated to a secondary level of importance, whereas other expectations must be given priority. One way for individuals to resolve role strain is to reestablish or rearrange priorities. If individuals cannot do so, institutions may impose a hierarchy of role expectations.

Although police roles are very complex, Radelet (1980) claims that very few police agencies have organizational goals. Furthermore, policies that reflect the values and needs of the community and represent the civil rights of all citizens have not been defined and developed. It is possible that radical decisions such as changing traditional assumptions, goals, and values of the police agency may have to be introduced in order to change conduct and effectiveness of police personnel (Skolnick 1966).

At the personal level police officers themselves have to adapt to role conflict. Some adaptations, such as those that involve hostility, brutality, withdrawal of services, repudiation of police role obligations, or playing off one group against the other, are inappropriate and indefensible.

One proposed solution to resolving role conflicts is professionalization of the police occupation (Niederhoffer 1967). *Professionalization*, according to Filley, House, and Kerr (1976), entails specialized training in a body of abstract knowledge; a code of ethics concerning an obligation to render services to the public; the exercise of autonomy or self-control over work decisions, methods, and activities; collegial maintenance of standards to best assure quality of service, a deep sense of commitment to occupation or calling; and close identification with the chosen profession and use of fellow professionals and professional organizations as important referents. While policing as an occupation has not yet become professionalized and individual police officers cannot claim to be professional (Fogelson 1977; Terry 1985), this is not to say that police officers do not share or are not striving toward these attributes already. A commitment to professionalization is known to reduce role conflict among police (Regoli and Poole 1980).

But police professionalism has different meanings for and impacts on different sized forces. For small rural departments, role conflict is reduced when colleagues, as opposed to "outsiders" who have no specialized knowledge of policing, regulate their work. In larger urban departments, police officers' belief in self-regulation and autonomy and their dedication to their work act to reduce role conflict. Whereas belief in public services reduces conflict among rural police, it does not appear to do so with urban police. Police from large city departments have more occasions to be involved in crime-fighting than do rural police, who broaden their orientation to serve the public and are more receptive to performing public service functions.

LEADERSHIP AND POLICE ORGANIZATIONS

At times a police officer must be dominant and assertive and at other times compassionate and trusting, if he or she is to have influence. Leadership is often thought of primarily in terms of individual characteristics, but, in fact, it depends as well upon the nature and structure of the group, the types of tasks facing the group, and situational determinants. Leadership is perceived as the behavior of individuals who exert more influence than other members of the group toward common goals or purposes.

In the context of conflicts arising from police role ambiguity, leadership becomes a particularly difficult issue. Police officers are primarily peace officers rather than law enforcement officers since most of their time involves the performance of public and social welfare services. Law enforcement officers may find coercive tactics necessary, but peace officers, who handle the mentally deranged, attempted suicides, domestic disputes, and the like, must act as instrumental negotiators (Cumming, Cumming, and Edell 1965). Leadership in these situations involves finding provisional solutions to disruptions and conflicts, and much of the success in these circumstances depends upon officers who must operate without solid guidelines. The public vacillates between wanting police officers to enforce the law and apprehend criminals and wanting them to settle disputes in adversarial situations, such as husband-wife conflicts, without necessarily arresting one or the other party. Since police officers want to do "real" police work, which means law enforcement rather than service, the problem of role ambiguity is a challenge to police authorities. In their role as leaders, police administrators must persuade frontline officers that peace-keeping is a critical aspect of the police role.

Leadership classifications in large police departments are similar to most other public organizations in consisting of four categories: firstline supervisors, middle managers, top managers, and chief executives (Bopp 1974). In police agencies, firstline supervisors are generally uniformed sergeants or investigative squad leaders. Similar to plant foremen in industrial settings, supervisors oversee the department's day-to-day operations — they give out assignments to patrol officers, set work schedules, maintain records, interact with their managers and other supervisors, and so on. Middle managers in police departments are the lieutenants and captains. They are mainly in charge of general policy, maintenance of operational control, and the like. Top managers are usually commanders (deputy chiefs), who operate next in line of authority to the chief. Their responsibility includes many such tasks as determination and interpretation of policy and coordination of administrative processes. Finally, like all chief executives, chiefs of police must be capable of performing managerial and administrative functions rather than technical or specialized tasks (Bopp 1974); they are generalists who have mastered enough technical skills to coordinate the work of specialists. Chiefs of police, as Bopp remarks, "are a unique breed of administrators who must exhibit qualities above and beyond those expected of subordinate commanders. . . . Their job is to enunciate goals, plan programs, develop organizations and staff them for program execution; carry out programming and budgetary responsibilities; evolve essential interrelationships, communication channels, work habits, and organizational doctrine which will convert the available manpower into a team; institute the organization's control and coordination mechanisms; steer the agency's operations; and maintain external contacts" (p. 235).

A large part of the job of being a top manager in police work involves mediating relations between the department and the public. That is, institutional leaders must justify the programs and activities of the police to citizens, the press, public administrators, elected officials, and legislators. Institutional goals are supposedly based on society's values, and it is these values that provide guidance to the administrative process, even though individuals at all levels come and go.

Police leaders are also responsible for minimizing role ambiguity in the minds of the public. Instructing society and public officials regarding the capabilities of the police in terms of both their roles and appropriate public expectations is a leadership responsibility. More importantly, police leaders must educate the public and fellow officers regarding the limitations of the police. The police are not the moral guardians of society, although the public typically sees them as having this function, as do the police themselves (Manning 1978). The police cannot solve society's problems of crime and criminality. Crime control, prevention, deterrence, rehabilitation, and punishment are the responsibility of the whole criminal justice system.

Characteristics of Leadership

Within police organizations, leaders are appointed by formally recognized superiors. Chiefs of police usually follow a traditional bureaucratic "up through the ranks" career path of executive development (Enter 1986). They are not usually "charismatic" people possessing some mystical or magnetic personal power that attracts followers. Nor are they "emergent" leaders struggling from unorganized, informal groups to assert themselves at the top. Instead, technical competence, familiarity with and attention to details, willingness to accept responsibility, organizational skills, ability to discriminate, generalize, and abstract principles, communication skills, and commitment to public service and the ideals of police professionalism determine movement toward higher police leadership categories. Not least important are the personal attributes of sensitivity, responsiveness, and consideration.

But as Gadd (1986) describes promotions to positions of leadership within police departments:

> Most of the good policemen I've known don't fit in. Some of them are rank, some of them aren't. But primarily, you are shunted aside if you don't fit in. The problem that we have is the system itself being controlled by the de facto establishment of the Board of Captains. They usually manipulate promotional examinations to see that their own crazies and buddies make it. (P. 205)

She adds:

> The few who are favored with promotions come to a realization . . . — this job isn't anything like the one they forfeited, because the higher ranking positions all have one thing in common: they deal with daily, nightmarish amounts of paper work instead of people. (P. 203)

Early research on leadership starting in the 1920s followed an approach referred to as the *Great Man Theory of Leadership*. But contem-

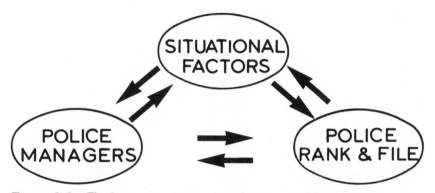

Figure 3.1   The Interaction Approach to the Process of Leadership.

porary research on leadership has abandoned this approach. After years of investigation, the only trait that has consistently been shown to be related to leadership is intelligence, and this factor accounts for only approximately 7 to 9 percent of the variability in task success (Campbell et al. 1970). Research on police demonstrates that there are no universal personality traits that consistently differentiate police leaders from their subordinates (Henderson 1981a). Current leadership research focuses on an interaction approach, illustrated in Figure 3.1.

The interaction approach assumes that there is an exchange of influence in the process of leadership such that the leader (the police chief), the subordinates (top managers, middle managers, supervisors, patrol officers), and the situation have a reciprocal impact upon each other. In order to predict those persons who will assume leadership in a particular group, one must take into account the impact of the situation upon both the leader and the subordinates. A number of situational factors, including the characteristics of the group members, the structure of the group, the nature of the group's tasks, the degree of pressure or stress present, and the clarity of existing role expectations, are correlated with the leader-subordinate exchange of influence.

In formal organizations such as the police, leadership patterns are imposed upon the members by external authority. Police agencies are usually large and are organized in authoritative, hierarchial systems of command. Police appear to prefer this rigid, traditional, authoritarian structure with its highly directive leadership style (Bordua and Reiss

1966). Paradoxically, police report that ideal officers are those who provide leadership without being directed by superiors.

Varieties of Leadership Behavior

When all of the factors thought to be important for leadership are analyzed, two variables emerge as critical. The first is *consideration*—that is, the extent to which the leader is seen as warm, friendly, and trustworthy in personal relationships with subordinates and willing to explain actions and allow participation in decision-making. The second is *initiating structure*—that is, the extent to which the leader organizes tasks and determines standards of performance for the group, follows routines, and defines the limits of the leader-subordinate relationship (Fiedler 1967).

The degree of pressure or stress present in the group also influences what a leader does and what is most readily accepted by subordinates. Stress can arise from external sources, such as threat or danger to the group, and/or from internal sources, such as intragroup conflict, task complexity, short decision time, or performance incompetence. Supervisors under conditions of stress tend to use authoritarian styles of leadership. While group performance in stressful situations has been found to improve with authoritarian methods of control, under low stress conditions a democratic style of leadership enhances group performance (Hamblin 1958).

Leadership behavior varies from situation to situation and what works well in one situation may not necessarily work well in another. Leadership behaviors extend over a wide range of different activities including such functions as command and modeling, emotional support, maintenance of the status quo, tactical work, diplomacy, and so on.

Leadership Styles and Effectiveness

Regardless of whether we are talking about business, politics, or police groups, in order for leaders to stay as leaders they have to be effective in influencing others to do what is required to accomplish group tasks. Leadership effectiveness has been studied by several different theoretical approaches (see Blake and Mouton 1964: Fiedler 1981). One theoretical issue that is particularly relevant to policing concerns the question of whether the democratic style or the authoritarian style of leadership is more effective. This issue was first examined in the classic study conducted by Lewin, Lippitt, and White (1939). Adult leaders were randomly assigned to groups of 10-year-old boys who were engaged in various hobbies. Each adult was instructed to behave in either an authoritarian, democratic, or a laissez-faire manner toward his group. The autocratic leader dictated policy and controled activities, was aloof from the group, and was subjective in his praise of the children's accomplishments. In contrast, the democratic leader encouraged the boys to discuss policy and activities. He allowed them to choose their workmates and select their own tasks and evaluated their work fairly and objectively. Under the laissez-faire leader, the group was essentially leaderless. The boys were given freedom to do as they wished, and little, if any, comments were made about their work.

As can be expected, leadership styles definitely had an effect on the group. The laissez-faire condition was worst in terms of both quantity and quality of work. The autocratic groups produced the most work, but the boys were more aggressive toward one another and more dissatisfied than members of the democratic groups. The quality of the work in the democratic condition was judged superior to that of the other groups. Other investigators have confirmed these early findings about members' preferences for democratic leaders, but evidence about group productivity either fails to show differences or indicates that the authoritarian leadership condition is more productive (Yukl 1981).

Although many aspects of police operations must be authoritarian, there is at least one police program that operates along more democratic lines; team policing. Team policing refers to law enforcement practices and organizations in which the officers are treated more democratically; status and rank differences are deemphasized; power is greatly decentralized; effective job performance is emphasized and is goal-oriented rather than focused on rights, obligations, and methods of performance; priority is given to commitment to organizations-wide goals and progress. And officers have flexible assignments as to time, place, and method of operation. In such a context, emphasis is given to stable and close ties with neighborhood residents, and participative planning is encouraged within broad departmental guidelines (Kuykendall and Roberg 1982). When properly carried out, neighborhood police teams can have positive results over conventional programs in terms of improved crime and clearance rates (see Davis 1973; O'Malley 1973; and Rand 1970). Team policing also has a positive influence on police attitudes and community perceptions of law enforcement (Bloch and Ulberg 1972).

SUMMARY

Police officers and citizens alike have a set of role expectations that operate to define their role relationships with each other. These roles evoke competing expectations, role strain and role conflict. Five contexts in which police role strain occurs are the quasimilitary organizations of police versus their social-service functions; deference to versus disrespect for authority; competing expectations regarding the roles of guardians of society, peacekeepers of society, and public servants; police values; and undercover work.

Role strain and role conflict can be resolved through rearrangements of individual and organizational priorities and a commitment to professionalization. Police leadership must solve the dilemma of being an authoritarian agency in a democratic society where conflicting role expectations are held by both the police themselves and the public they serve and protect.

The stresses inherent in this work are of concern to both police officers and psychologists. The next chapter will look specifically at police stress and the ways in which stress may be managed.

4

Stress

Observers of police behavior are consistent in their opinion that police work involves high levels of stress. According to Fennel (1981), "The peace officer's principle enemy is not the burglar or armed robber. Rather, the major source of suffering and death for peace officers and their families is the inability to cope with psychological stress" (p. 170). The assistant for psychological services in the Dade County, Florida, Public Safety Department, William Garrison, is even more outspoken in his claims of damage from stress. Garrison states that "police work is probably the most psychologically damaging field in the world. The mental health of policemen is really being tested, and every one of them is going to run into serious problems sometime in his career" (cited in Langone 1981, 84). Garrison's sentiments, although frequently expressed in police circles, are a mixture of myth and fact, which, if accepted at face value, could be damaging to police officers because of their negative, pessimistic overtones (see Malloy and Mays 1984; Terry 1981, 1985). Lester (1979), for example, found no evidence for higher rates of divorce, alcoholism, or mental illness in police officers than in nonpolice. In fact, police on the whole do not experience an extreme amount of general job stress (Lawrence 1984). This finding is significant since it challenges many of the conclusions drawn from nonempirical studies of police stress. All life events involve some stress, and moderate stress is not dangerous. Instead, it is the constant or excessive stress that has to be coped with or controled. Recognition of individual differences in the ability to tolerate stress and the use of methods available either to prevent stress or to assist in its control are a more positive way to deal with stress. Some officers, because of their intelligence, personality, constitutional strengths, attitudes toward illness, adaptability, and social support, will not be debilitated by stress. Other officers will have to become involved in programs of self-management training, control techniques, and systematic support groups to alleviate stress.

WHAT IS STRESS?

Stress is a normal, universal experience of life. Both unpleasant and pleasant experiences can have stressful results—winning a lottery, getting a promotion, being fired, having a death in the family are all examples of stressful events. The common element among these experiences is the intensity of the demands placed upon the person that require some kind of adaptation or coping. When stress become excessive, the person may experience disruptions of emotional well-being and physiological functioning and loss of cognitive control, reflected in fragmentary thinking, poor concentration, and inadequate memory. Chronic stress is associated with a large number of physical illnesses including coronary heart disease and high blood pressure. It is important, however, to emphasize that not all stress is bad. A certain amount of stress can enrich human experiences and make life more interesting.

Several years ago, Holmes and Rahe (1967) developed a list of stressful life events that was used to measure a person's total amount of recent life stress. Death of a spouse was ranked as the most stressful life event and "minor violations of the law" was ranked as the least stressful of the forty-three events tested. Holmes and Rahe's rating scale makes an important contribution to an understanding of life stresses by drawing attention to such events as retirement or a change to a different line of work as costly psychological events since people often take them for granted. Knowledge of the events that most people find stressful can assist in the identification, preparation, and ability to cope before the magnitude and consequences of stress escalate. Following

Table 4.1   Law Enforcement Critical Life Events Scale

Event	*Value*
1. Violent death of a partner in the line of duty	88
2. Dismissal	85
3. Taking a life in the line of duty	85
4. Shooting someone in the line of duty	81
5. Suicide of an officer who is a close friend	80
6. Violent death of another officer in the line of duty	79
7. Murder committed by a police officer	78
8. Duty-related violent injury (shooting)	76
9. Violent job-related injury to another officer	75
10. Suspension	72
11. Passed over for promotion	71
12. Pursuit of an armed suspect	71
13. Answering a call to a scene involving violent nonaccidental death of a child	70
14. Assignment away from family for a long period of time	70
15. Personal involvement in a shooting incident	70
16. Reduction in pay	70
17. Observing an act of police corruption	69
18. Accepting a bribe	69
19. Participating in an act of police corruption	68
20. Hostage situation resulting from aborted criminal action	68
21. Response to a scene involving the accidental death of a child	68
22. Promotion of inexperienced/incompetent officer over you	68
23. Internal affairs investigation against self	66
24. Barricaded suspect	66
25. Hostage situation resulting from a domestic disturbance	65
26. Response to "officer needs assistance" call	65
27. Duty under a poor supervisor	64
28. Duty-related violent injury (nonshooting)	63
29. Observing an act of police brutality	62
30. Response to "person with a gun" call	62
31. Unsatisfactory personnel evaluation	62
32. Police-related civil suit	61
33. Riot/crowd control situation	61
34. Failure on a promotional examination	60
35. Suicide of an officer	60
36. Criminal indictment of a fellow officer	60
37. Improperly conducted corruption investigation of another officer	60
38. Shooting incident involving another officer	59
39. Failing grade in police training program	59
40. Response to a "felony-in-progress" call	58

Table 4.1 (continued)

Event	Value
41. Answering a call to a sexual battery/abuse scene involving a child victim	58
42. Oral promotional review	57
43. Conflict with a supervisor	57
44. Change in departments	56
45. Personal criticism by the press	56
46. Investigation of a political/highly publicized case	56
47. Taking severe disciplinary action against another officer	56
48. Assignment to conduct an internal affairs investigation on another officer	56
49. Interference in a case by political officials	55
50. Written promotional examination	55
51. Departmental misconduct hearing	55
52. Wrecking a department vehicle	55
53. Personal use of illicit drugs	54
54. Use of drugs by another officer	54
55. Participating in a police strike	53
56. Undercover assignment	53
57. Physical assault of an officer	52
58. Disciplinary action against partner	52
59. Death notification	51
60. Press criticism of an officer's actions	51
61. Polygraph examination	51
62. Sexual advancement toward you by another officer	51
63. Duty-related accidental injury	50
64. Changing work shifts	50
65. Written reprimand by a supervisor	50
66. Inability to solve a major crime	48
67. Emergency run to "unknown trouble"	48
68. Personal use of alcohol while on duty	48
69. Inquiry into another officer's misconduct	47
70. Participation in a narcotics raid	47
71. Verbal reprimand by a supervisor	47
72. Handling of a mentally/emotionally disturbed person	47
73. Citizen complaint against an officer	47
74. Press criticism of departmental actions/practices	47
75. Ansering a call to a sexual battery/abuse scene involving an adult victim	46
76. Reassignment/transfer	46
77. Unfair administrative policy	46
78. Preparation for retirement in the near future	46

Table 4.1 (continued)

Event	Value
79. Pursuit of a traffic violator	46
80. Severe disciplinary action to another officer	46
81. Promotion with assignment to another unit	45
82. Personal abuse of prescription drugs	45
83. Offer of a bribe	45
84. Personally striking a prisoner or suspect	45
85. Physical arrest of a suspect	45
86. Promotion within existing assignment	44
87. Handling a domestic disturbance	44
88. Answering a call to a scene involving the violent, nonaccidental death of an adult	44
89. Change in supervisors	44
90. Abuse of alcohol by another officer	44
91. Response to a silent alarm	44
92. Change in the chief administrators of the department	43
93. Answering a call to a scene involving the accidental death of an adult	43
94. Move to a new duty station	43
95. Fugitive arrest	43
96. Reduction in job responsibilities	43
97. Release of an offender by the prosecutor	41
98. Job-related illness	41
99. Transfer of partner	40
100. Assignment to night shift duty	40
101. Recall to duty on day off	39
102. Labor negotiations	39
103. Verbal abuse from a traffic violator	39
104. Change in administrative policy/procedure	38
105. Sexual advancement toward you by a citizen	37
106. Unfair plea bargain by a prosecutor	37
107. Assignment to a specialized training course	37
108. Assignment to stake-out duty	37
109. Release of an offender on appeal	37
110. Harassment by an attorney in court	37
111. Administrative recognition (award/commendation)	36
112. Court appearance (felony)	36
113. Annual evaluation	35
114. Assignment to decoy duty	35
115. Assignment as partner with officer of the opposite sex	35
116. Assignment to evening shift	35
117. Assignment of new partner	34
118. Successful clearance of a case	34

Table 4.1   (continued)

Event	Value
119. Interrogation session with a suspect	33
120. Departmental budget cut	33
121. Release of an offender by a jury	33
122. Overtime duty	29
123. Letter of recognition from the public	29
124. Delay in a trial	28
125. Response to a "sick or injured person" call	28
126. Award from a citizens' group	27
127. Assignment to day shift	26
128. Work on a holiday	26
129. Making a routine arrest	26
130. Assignment to a two-person car	26
131. Call involving juveniles	25
132. Routine patrol stop	25
133. Assignment to a single-person car	25
134. Call involving the arrest of a female	24
135. Court appearance (misdemeanor)	24
136. Working a traffic accident	23
137. Dealing with a drunk	23
138. Pay raise	23
139. Overtime pay	22
140. Making a routine traffic stop	22
141. Vacation	20
142. Issuing a traffic citation	20
143. Court appearance (traffic)	19
144. Completion of a routine report	13

Source: Sewell 1983. Reproduced from the *Journal of Police Science and Administration* 11, no. 1 (1983): 109–16, with permission of the International Association of Chiefs of Police.

Holmes and Rahe's procedures, Sewell (1983) developed a scale of critical life events for police officers. Table 4.1 shows in rank order the 144 events perceived by police to be their most critical professional life events.

MODELS OF STRESS

Stress is defined as the "perceptual phenomenon arising from a comparison between the demand on the person and his ability to cope "(Cox 1978). Researchers typically analyze stress in terms of three models. The first approach known as the response-based model, considers stress in terms of behaviorial responses—that is, what a person does in response to negative environments. The second model, the stimulus-based model, views stress in terms of the situations that cause the stressful reactions. The third approach, known as the interactional model, sees stress in terms of an imbalance between the demands of the environment and the person's ability to cope.

Response-Based Model

This approach attempts to identify and understand the syndrome of physiological responses and psychological reactions that occur in disturbing environments. The late Hans Selye (1976), an endocrinologist, pioneered much of the research on stress. Selye proposed a model of stress referred to as the *general adaptation syndrome*. When an animal or human encounters an emergency situation, response called an *alarm reaction* occurs in resistance to the stressor. The sympathetic nervous system and the adrenal glands are activated, producing the energy needed to maximize the body's defenses, and the body prepares for "fight or flight." Individuals in an alarm reaction may experience a dry mouth, perspiration, shortness of breath, and a faster heartbeat. If the stress continues, a second stage called *resistance* begins. The sympathetic nervous system and the adrenal system reach their optimal level and remain highly mobilized, but because of the prolonged emergency state, other bodily systems become weakened. As a consequence, defensive reactions to new stresses are debilitated, and the body's ability to fight off infection is lessened. If the body continues in this weakened state, a third stage called *exhaustion* begins. This is the final stage; collapse or even death can occur because of the sustained inability to cope. An individual in the exhaustion stage may show such physical disabilities as headaches, high blood pressure, ulcers, heart attacks, and psychological distress, including depression and psychotic behavior.

Although Selye's contributions to stress research have been invaluable, a major weakness of his model is its primary concentration on the physiological reactions to stressor agents, while ignoring the role of psychological processes, such as emotional tension, social and behavioral adaptations, and the cognitive interpretations that evoke the alarm reaction. Furthermore, in order to predict whether a certain environmental event will produce a stress syndrome, a great deal more information must be known about the characteristics of stressors.

Stimulus-Based Model

Many different characteristics of environments are recognized as stressful. Each of the following situations can make harsh demands on a person: noxious environmental stimuli, isolation and confinement, demands for quick thinking and decisions, frustration, group pressure, and disturbed physiological processes (such as the results of disease, drugs, sleep loss). Physical stressors such as noise and extremes of temperature can also be combined with psychosocial stressors to threaten a person's well-being. Attacks on self-esteem, fear of failure, and interaction with rude, hostile, or violent people also act to create stressful environments.

Environmental stressors typically share three characteristics: stimulus overload, conflict, and uncontrolability. Stimulus overload involves situations that are so intense—cold, heat, noise, pressure of work, and so on—that the individual can no longer adapt. Conflict occurs when a person must choose between incompatible, contradictory, or mutually exclusive goals or courses of action. The uncontrolability of events, especially when these events are unpleasant, is highly stressful. If unpleasant situations that are known to cause pain can be controled in terms of their onset and their duration, the actual pain and stress experienced is lessened (Weiss 1972). Furthermore, the mere belief that control is possible is sufficient to reduce the stress of a negative situation (Glass and Singer 1972).

Four basis types of situational conflicts have been identified:

1. *Approach-approach conflict.* In this situation, people are faced with two equally attractive goals, but selection of one necessarily means giving up the other. Stress occurs because of the necessity to choose and manage any feelings of doubt that the selection made was the best course of action.

2. *Approach-avoidance conflict.* In this type of conflict, people are presented with a single goal or activity that has both positive and negative consequences. For example, the stress experienced by a police officer who wants to be friendly with local residents but is afraid that they may be hostile and abusive results from such a conflict.

3. *Avoidance-avoidance conflict.* Here an individual is faced with two equally unattractive goals. Choosing one leads to a negative consequence, as does avoiding choosing. Either course of action is stressful. If the individual decides to avoid making any choice at all or to escape by leaving the field, he or she often feels that things have gotten out of control or that things are being forced on to him or her, and this pressure adds to the sense of stress.

4. *Double approach-avoidance conflict.* In this type of conflict, a person faces two courses of action, and both courses have a positive and a negative feature. For example, a potential police recruit would like to join a small, rural police force because of the relaxed lifestyle but with low pay. If he joins a large, urban police force, he will make more money but will have to live a hectic life.

All of these conflict situations are stressful because the individual cannot determine from the stimuli themselves what response or course of action is appropriate. The major limitation to an understanding of stress solely in terms of environmental stimuli is the difficulty in specifying what it is about a particular stressor that is stressful. Also, not all people find the same events equally stressful.

Interactional-Based Model

This approach emphasizes two factors, (1) perceptions of threat to important personal motives and needs and (2) the coping methods used to master stressful situations. Stress is both a perceptual process and a result of a person's relationship with his or her environment. Individuals experience stress when they perceive that the situation they are in poses a threat to their well-being or personal needs. The interactional model holds that stress occurs when the person is unable to cope with the perceived stressor. If there is an imbalance between the perceived demands of the situation and coping skills, stress will be high. When coping skills match stressor demands, stress will be low (Lazarus 1968). Successful coping reduces the potency of physical and psychosocial sources of stress; unsuccessful coping may lead to exhaustion, ulcers, heart attacks, or psychological difficulties.

HEALTH, PERSONALITY, AND STRESS

For some people, the pressures of everyday living may be as dangerous to health as major life changes are for others. Correlational research suggests that poor people have more health-related problems than do wealthier people. One of the reasons for poorer health may be the strain associated with poverty. Certain occupational groups—such as physicians and surgeons, but not carpenters and medical technicians—have a disproportionately greater incidence of coronary heart disease (House 1974). Persons having a high risk of heart attack often hold jobs that entail comparatively high work overloads, high responsibility for the work of others, and role conflicts (Jenkins 1971a, 1971b). Low job satisfaction and low self-esteem may also predispose people to heart disease (House 1974). However, it is not clear that certain jobs necessarily increase a person's chances of having a heart attack; it is possible that the risk of heart attack is present in heart-attack prone people because of other factors (Hinkle et al. 1968). For example, certain precursor conditions such as hypertension, heavy smoking, high cholesterol levels, and a family history of cardiovascular disease tend to predispose individuals to heart conditions.

Heart attacks are also related to a particular personality pattern called *Type A* (Friedman and Rosenman 1974). The heart-attack prone Type A person is described as hard-driving, aggressive, ambitious for achievement and power, competitive, impatient, compulsive, and preoccupied with an enhanced sense of time urgency. Type A individuals report an inability to relax and feelings of guilt if away from work for even a short period. *Type B* persons, on the other hand, are characterized by a relative absence of these coronary-inducing traits and situational pressures. Type B individuals are not driven to assert their control over situational demands and stressors (Glass 1977). Type A persons tend to experience greater feelings of helplessness than others in uncontrollable stress situations. They show a constant state of being "on guard," as demonstrated in their inability to depend upon others and their fear of new experiences, such as going on vacations, attending the ballet, playing with children, and the like. The Type A man is preoccupied with proving his masculinity and hates any sign of femininity in himself. Frequently, there is fear of tender emotions and personal intimacy, these emotions being typically ignored or avoided as unimportant psychological needs. However, the combination of a Type A personality pattern with some critical life event such as the death of a spouse may create what is perceived as an uncontrolable stress, which is a precursor of a heart attack (Glass 1977). The Type A pattern is seen more frequently in men than women. However, when found in women it increases coronary risk about as much as in men (Haynes, Feinleib, and Eaker 1983).

POLICE STRESSORS AND REACTIONS

The complexity and seemingly boundless number of job-related stressors and the immediate and long-term responses to stress found in police work (see Table 4.2) have been summarized by Kroes (1976) and others (see, for example, Eisenberg 1975; Kroes and Hurrell 1975; Territo and Vetter 1981).

Job-Related Stressors

One of the most complete studies to investigate stressors within police work was conducted by Kroes, Margolis, and Hurrell (1974). One hundred officers within the Cincinnati, Ohio, Police Department were interviewed, and results indicated that several aspects of police work are sources of stress: (1) the court system, which was perceived as soft on criminals and insensitive to scheduling police testimony; (2) department administration that lacked specific policy and poor internal communication; (3) equipment either in disrepair or unavailable; (4) negative and hostile community relations; (5) shift work causing physical strain and poor family and social relationships; (6) heavy responsibilities and crisis situations; and (7) social isolation.

A major source of job-related stress for police officers is threat to self-esteem. Young officers first joining the police force see themselves as trained professionals dedicated to public service. They expect to be recognized and appreciated by the public for their efforts to correct social problems. Some officers find, however, that over the course of their career, their ability to reach these goals are constrained, recognition is fleeting, promotions may be based more on political considera-

Table 4.2 Short-Term/Chronic Stress Reaction

Immediate Response to Stress

Job-Related Stressors	Personality	Health	Job performance	Home life
Administration	Temporary increases in:	Temporary increases in:	Job tension	"Spats with spouse"
Job conflict	Anxiety	Smoking rate	"Flying off the handle"	Periodic withdrawal
Second job	Tension	Headaches	Erratic work habit	Anger displaced to spouse and children
Inactivity	Irritability	Heart rate	Temporary work decrement etc.	Increased extramarital activity etc.
Shift work	Feeling "uptight"	Blood pressure		
Inadequate resources	Drinking rate etc.	Cholesterol level etc.		
Inequities in pay and job status				
Organizational territoriality				

Long-Term Response to Stress

	Personality	Health	Job performance	Home life
Job overload	Psychosis	Chronic disease states:	Decreased productivity	Divorce
Responsibility for people	Chronic depression	Ulcers	Increased error rate	Poor relations with others
Courts	Alienation	High blood pressure	Job dissatisfaction	Social isolation
Negative public image	Alcoholism	Coronary heart disease	Accidents	Loss of friends etc.
Conflict values	General malaise	Asthmatic attacks	Withdrawal	
Racial situations	Low self-esteem	Diabetes etc.	Serious error in judgment	
Line-of-duty/crisis situations	Low self-actualization		Slower reaction time etc.	
Job ambiguity etc.	Suicide etc.			

Source: Adapted from Kroes 1976, with the permission of the Psychological Services Unit, Dallas Police Department and Charles C. Thomas, Publisher, Springfield, Ill., from W. H. Kroes, *Society's Victim—The Policeman*, 1976.

tions than on job performance, and the work is more boring than first anticipated. The conflict between a person's expectations about being a police officer and the realities of the job are difficult to cope with, especially when they are unexpected. Failure to meet career expectations or ideals held by oneself or by others may lead to self-doubts and self-disparagement. The disintegration of an officer's positive self-image has the consequence of adding further stress as well as creating an individual who is more susceptible to the influence of other stressors (Cooper 1982; Hylton 1980).

Posttraumatic Stress

Not all police work is stressful, but one exception worth emphasizing is the stress involved in police-citizen shootings in the line of duty. A police officer involved in a shooting situation either as the victim or as having killed another person in the line of duty may not show immediate signs of stress, instead experiencing reaction days, weeks, months, or years later. This is referred to as *posttraumatic stress disorder*. Similar reactions may be observed among rape victims and hostages of terrorists.

The typical scenario involving shootings between police officers and citizens leading to delayed stress reactions include the following conditions. First, the officer's very survival is threatened. The situation also occurs without warning, and events are essentially uncontrolable. Following the shooting and death of a citizen, the officer may be treated as a homicide suspect, stripped of his or her weapon and authority, suspended from duty, and isolated from peers. Many departments seem to appear to be insensitive to the stress and mental health needs of officers in this trauma (Nielsen and Eskridge 1982).

Immediately following a shooting, most officers deny the death and emotionally insulate themselves. The officer will continue to use these defense mechanisms for an indefinite period, but once the defenses are relaxed, he or she will begin to experience symptoms of stress—sleep-pattern disturbances, flashbacks, depression, fears, anxiety, helplessness, self-doubt, guilt, alienation, and cynicism (Carson 1982).

Most of our knowledge on postshooting stress is drawn from anecdotal evidence rather than from findings of empirical or clinical studies. Two exceptions, however, are the investigations by Nielsen (1982) and Loo

(1986). Nielsen systematically interviewed a sample of sixty-three police officers from Utah, Mississippi, and Colorado who had shot a suspect within the last eight years. Results were analyzed in three categories: officer characteristics; incident characteristics; and stress-response reactions.

1. *Officer characteristics.* Seventy percent of shootings involved officers 30 years of age or younger working as patrol officers on patrol assignments. Fifty-one percent of these officers had been employed in policing three years or less.

2. *Incident characteristics.* Eighty percent of shootings occurred between eight P.M. and five A.M. Domestic disputes and stake-outs each accounted for 19 percent of shootings and burglary accounted for 16 percent of shootings. Thirty-five percent of all shootings occurred within 39 seconds of the officer's arrival on the scene, 52 percent within 60 seconds, and 100 percent within 8 minutes. Officers generally fired between three and five rounds during the incident, whereas suspects fired far fewer rounds—25 percent fired once, and 40 did not fire a round.

3. *Stress-response reactions.* Identifiable cognitive distortions occurred in most officers at the point of firing. Sixty-four percent of officers reported a perceptual distortion of slow motion, 43 percent reported experiencing tunnel vision (a perceptual distortion in which the experience of space is narrowly confined and misrepresented), and 25 percent reported auditory blocking.

The most frequently reported physical reactions experienced during the week following the shooting incident were nausa/upset stomachs (92 percent), headaches (25 percent), and general fatigue (14 percent). Thought intrusions (59 percent), depression (52 percent), anxiety (33 percent), sleeping disturbance (27 percent), fatigue (25 percent) and an inability to concentrate (22 percent) were the most frequently reported emotional symptoms occurring in the week following the shooting. The most frequent attitude changes in the three months following the shooting were increased cautiousness (51 percent) and apathy (24 percent). Twenty-five percent of the officers were embittered and expressed less enthusiasm for police work.

Loo (1986) surveyed fifty-six Royal Canadian Mounted Police Officers involved in shootings between 1970 and 1982. Many of Nielsen's (1982) findings were confirmed. Officers were found to experience most stress reactions within three days of the shooting incident. For the month following the shooting, officers reported being preoccupied with the incident, experiencing sleep disturbances, anger, and flashbacks, and reexamining personal values. Contrary to anecdotal evidence, police officers did not express undue remorse or guilt over having shot someone. The average time taken for normalization of working, social, and family life affairs was twenty weeks.

The empirical work of Nielsen and Loo are important contributions to the understanding of police stress. Although both studies depended upon self-report measures, which are susceptible to various types of response biases and memory failures, the data are significant first steps in understanding police officers' reactions to involvement in shooting incidents.

Management Versus Frontline Officers

Many of the job-related stressors listed in the first column of Table 4.2 are discussed throughout this book, but one stressor I wish to emphasize here is police management. Policing is not unique in its bureaucratization, but the split between frontline police officers and supervisors has become more compartmentalized and structured over the years (Kroes 1983). According to Kroes, management is not seen as an ally of line officers but, instead perceived as adversaries in an "us against them" division. This split has occurred because of perceived differences in purpose. Line officers see their concerns to be justice issues, whereas they consider management to be public-relations representatives rather than police officers. For management, image can be more important than solid policing. These differences result in lying, distortion of facts, and pressure on line officers to maintain a false front. The appearance of officers and their off-duty behavior is more closely monitored and punished than poor policing performance. Frontline officers feel that they are merely objects of concern rather than individuals of value and worth and believe that management will not support them when trouble occurs. Kroes (1983) states that many police departments totally dismiss job-related stressors as inconsequential to their staff. The results of such perceptions of management are frustration, poor morale, disinterest, and "stress" for the line officer.

Management, however, may have a different view of stress, as Gadd (1986) relates from her interviews of police officers:

I heard a statement that just about knocked my socks off. They were interviewing the administrator and talked to him about stress. They said, "How do you spot an officers under stress?"

That man, as knowledgeable as he was, said, "We don't have stress in this department. We hire people that aren't under stress, so we eliminate stress through hiring. . . ."

The things that are gonna bother you most [in the force] are the infighting rather than the fighting on the street. You can handle the fighting in the streets; you expect it. But the infighting—the backstabbing, the cliques, the unfairness of administration, and the inability of some administrators to be fair because of the restrictions placed on 'em —is tremendous in alot of places.

What keeps most cops in this business is that somewhere along the line they know that the next corner they go around is gonna be the most exciting time they've ever had in their lives. Their adrenalin is going to pump; it's gonna be life and death. They're gonna make it, they're gonna live through it, it's gonna come out right, and it's gonna be the biggest thrill they've ever had. I think that's what keeps an awful lot of people in it." (P. 246)

Death Notification

Job-related stressors for patrol car officers amount to a very small proportion of frontline duties (6 percent of calls [Cruse 1972]), but those that do occur are often extreme. Police officers, having to confront acutely suicidal persons and view mutilated accident and homicide victims, quickly adapt to the realities of death, but one of the toughest jobs of all is telling people about the death of a loved one. Police generally receive very little training in handling such crises (Hall 1982). When an officer has to break the news that someone in the family has been murdered, killed in an accident, committed suicide, the officer must often handle this complex situation according to common sense.

Learning of the unexpected death of a loved one evokes an immediate reaction of shock, immobilization, and withdrawal (see Kubler-Ross 1969; Parkes 1975). Close relatives of homicide victims, for example, face a two-phased pattern of reactions: an immediate period of acute grief and a long-term reorganization phase. Immediate post-homicide reactions appear to be more powerful and more difficult to control for family survivors than those that occur in response to other kinds of death. A profound sense of violation and loss, compounded by the violent nature of the death and mixed with obsessional thoughts and vengeful desires to hurt the killer, are common reactions.

Gadd's (1986) description of informing victims' families captures the tremendous difficulty of this task.

> We had a head-on collision involving the driver of one car and six teenagers in another. The end product was seven dead people. These young people were badly, badly torn up; it was a tremendous impact. There were portions of bodies lying in the road. There would be an arm and part of a shoulder, or one leg and half of the torso, And heads, just heads! You didn't know whose head went with whose body. It was just gruesome!
>
> Then comes the solemn task of going from house to house, knocking on each door, saying, "I can't tell you how sorry I am to have to inform you that your daughter was killed in an automobile accident tonight."
>
> The response was everything from fainting to actually screaming and hitting you in the face and chest, saying, "You lying sonofabitch! You lying bastard!" They just instantly go hysterical.
>
> Any one incident of that is bad enough, but to have to go in one night to seven different families . . . (P. 48)

How are the police to handle such communications? There is no specific formula on how to do this since each incident is different. Police must handle each case with tact and compassion. Although this may seem obvious, concern for the emotional well-being of survivors must be coordinated with the officer's need for professional detachment in order to carry out certain basic police tasks. Police must determine the cause of death, involve the family in assisting in the identification of the victim, protect the deceased person's property, and arrange for family disposition of the body (Hall 1982).

Death notification is not an enactment of a planned script. Both the police and the family bring to this interaction their characteristic backgrounds and past experiences as well as their personal attitudes, beliefs, and values. Police officers must learn what nonverbal behaviors are consistent with compassion in order to ensure the communication of tact and respect. A sensitivity to the normal feelings of pain, loss, and grief and to reactions of denial, the verbal and nonverbal facility to communicate this understanding is needed. How an officers gives bad news is nearly as important as the news itself.

STRESS REACTIONS

The right-hand side of Table 4.2 shows four immediate and long-term responses to stress, each of which is examined below.

Personality

The most common reactions to stress are *anxiety* and *depression*. The anxious person feels tense, nervous, fearful, restless, and apprehensive. Anxiety usually occurs in anticipation of a stressful encounter. Depression, on the other hand, usually occurs after the occurrence of serious stressful experiences and involves feelings of loneliness, worthlessness, fatigue, blame, and pessimism. Recognition and identification of emotional signals are the first steps in the coping process; otherwise, long-term personality reactions to stress such as alcoholism, suicide, psychosis, chronic depression, and similar problems become a possibility (see Table 4.3). According to one estimation, 25 percent of police officers in American police departments have serious alcohol abuse problems (Hurrell and Kroes 1975). Alcohol abuse is probably much greater than reported since many officers will not officially report their dependence for fear of departmental discipline (Violanti, Marshall, and Howe 1985). Suicide is not common among young officers, but when it does occur, it is typically associated with family problems or divorce (Territo and Vetter 1981). Suicide among older officers is usually related to alcoholism, physical illness, or impending retirement.

Relatively little empirical research has been conducted on the relationship between personality variables and police stress. One factor, however, that may predict the likelihood of police stress is the concept of locus of control, which was introduced in Chapter 2 (Rotter 1966). Individuals who believe that events in their lives are primarily controled by their own actions (internals) are distinguished from individuals who attribute the cause of events in their lives to chance or fate (externals). In contrast to internals, externals perceive more stress in their lives, although they do not experience a greater number of stressful life events

Table 4.3 Fifteen Most Prevalent Warning Signs of Stress in Police Officers

Warning Signs	Examples
1. Sudden changes in behavior, usually directly opposite to usual behavior	From cheerful and optimistic to gloomy and pessimistic
2. More gradual change in behavior but in a way that points to deterioration of the individual	Gradually becoming slow and lethargic, possibly with increasing depression and sullen behavior
3. Erratic work habits	Coming to work late, leaving early, abusing compensation time
4. Increased sick time due to minor problems	Headaches, colds, stomach aches, etc.
5. Inability to maintain a train of thought	Rambling conversation, difficulty in sticking to a specific subject
6. Excessive worrying	Worrying about one issue to the exclusion of any others
7. Grandiose behavior	Preoccupation with religion, politics, etc.
8. Excessive use of alcohol and/or drugs	Obvious hangover, disinterest in appearance, talk about drinking prowess
9. Fatigue	Lethargy, sleeping on job
10. Peer complaints	Others refuse to work with him or her
11. Excessive complaints (negative citizen contact)	Caustic and abusive in relating to citizens
12. Consistency in complaint pattern	Picks on specific groups of people (youth, blacks, etc.)
13. Sexual promiscuity	Going after everything all of the time—on or off duty
14. Excessive accidents and/or injuries	Not being attentive to driving, handling prisoners, etc.
15. Manipulation of fellow officers and citizens	Using others to achieve ends without caring for their welfare

Reprinted by permission of the Psychological Services Unit, Dallas Police Department. Cited in Territo and Vetter 1981.

(Tyson 1981). Lester, Leitner, and Posner (1985) found that police officers categorized as externals experienced high subjective stress and that stress was reliably related to low self-confidence and Type A behavior. In contrast, officers who held high belief in internal control failed to show subjective perceptions of stress.

Control over the environment, however, is not simply a personality factor. Police officers learn that their working environment is potentially dangerous. Although the fear of being injured or killed by an assailant is generally assumed to be a major factor in police stress, it is not as significant as suspected (Lawrence 1984). This is because police are generally aware of potential danger, and danger is part of the job for which they are well trained and technically well equipped. The courts and the state give the police the right to use reasonable force to protect themselves. Police experience greater stress in situations in which they have little or no personal control, such as inconsistent judicial decisions, randomly scheduled court appearances, insensitive administrative procedures, and a hostile community.

Health Disorders

Extreme police stress has been found to be associated with thirty-five physiological effects including every ailment from headaches and sinus attacks to shrinking thalamuses, spastic colons, and grinding teeth (Terry 1981). Excessive stress can stimulate adrenal production of desoxycorticosterone (DCA), which inhibits the nervous system. Consequences of DCA production are depression, apathy, fatigue, and feelings of weakness (Henderson 1981b). Constant tension can affect the gastrointestinal system and produce vomiting, nausea, diarrhea, and so on, and can also affect the cardiovascular, respiratory, and circulatory systems. Fell, Richard, and Wallace (1980) found that 60 percent of all stress-related causes of death in police resulted from diseases of the circulatory system.

Job-Performance Disorders

Martin Symonds, a former police officer and presently the psychiatrist in charge of New York City's psychological police services section, underscores the heavy responsibility of police officers: "You take an ordinary guy, a high school graduate, and ask him to make instantaneous judgment of the sort that Supreme Court Justices have time to deliberate" (quoted in Langone 1981, 84).

Stress on the job can impair the officer's abilities to perceive, remember, and think. Under nonstressful conditions, a person is able to selectively attend to and remember various events relatively accurately and make decisions and communicate with few difficulties. Extreme stress can severely disrupt these cognitive processes. For example, in life and death situations, officers do not have time to organize their thoughts in a logical, coherent manner. Under prolonged stress, officers who are prone to anxiety may worry about failure, which, in turn, interferes with concentration and problem-solving. Fear of failure and negative evaluation has been found to increase with police experience and seniority (Gudjonsson 1984). The common denominator of per-ceived stress in police officers is performance anxiety—that is, fears of doing something wrong, of being criticized, investigated, tried, sus-pended, fired, seen as inadequate, or of being the defendant in a civil suit (Jacobi 1975).

Home Life

Although Terry (1981) suggests that police divorce rates in the United States are lower than the national average, several researchers have commented on the correlation between marital problems of police offi-cers and job performance (see Blackmore 1978; Hageman 1978; Sten-mark et al. 1982; Stratton, Tracy-Stratton, and Alldredge 1982). Earlier the point was made that a law enforcement career is more than just a job for the officer; it is also an identity and an orientation toward life that affect not only the officer but also his or her family and spouse. The role conflicts an officer experiences between family obligations and official police responsibilities can create a split between the officer and family members. The emotional pressures of police work can influence the quality of the officer's marriage and family life. Conversely, the strains of marital discord, separation, and divorce can influence the nature of the officer's interactions with the public and fellow officers.

Specific job-related problems that affect family and marital life of policemen include the following stressors and reactions (Territo and Vetter 1981). (Stress affecting policewomen is treated separately be-low.)

1. *Erratic work schedules.* Because of shift work and overtime re-quirements, not enough time can be given to sharing the responsibilities of home life with a spouse. Social events with friends and family on weekends and holidays cannot be easily arranged.

2. *Emotional exhaustion. Burn-out* is conceptualized as a syndrome composed of distinct and independent reactions to one's job, emotional exhaustion, depersonalization, and feelings of low personal accomplishment (Jackson 1983). Police officers are susceptible to burn-out from a number of job stressors. Police officers' feelings of emotional and physical exhaustion result from the persistent periods of extreme involvement in their work. High emotional strain is produced by feelings of personal responsibility for the well being of others.

These feelings are extremely intense when the officer must share the emotions of the moment with people who are experiencing traumatic injury or grief. Over time, negative attitudes and cynicism may develop toward the job and the people being served. When this occurs, officers may depersonalize or dehumanize even crime victims, treating them more like objects and less like individuals. Finally, burned out police may feel a sense of hopelessness. They begin to feel that their involvement in their job is not accomplishing anything of value. Feelings of ineffectiveness, failure to meet personal objectives, and even self-blame cloud their views of the job and personal well-being.

3. *Negative public image.* Most police are proud of their work, but they are also very sensitive to public criticism and opinion. Public disrespect of police officers, such as calling them "pigs," affects both the officer and family members and can lead to social isolation of police families from their communities.

4. *Overprotection.* The suspiciousness needed in police work may transfer to personal relationships. Overprotection, lack of trust and confidence, and authoritarian control, all for the sake of family welfare, can lead to frustration in children and spouses. In particular, teenagers may reject the authority represented by their father's occupation.

5. *Hardening of emotions.* One of the defense mechanisms officers use to deal with the misery encountered on the job is suppressing their own feelings of anger, disgust, or grief. To protect the family from the grim realities of policing, the officer often maintains a stoic image at home. Distortions of work-related emotions result in distorted personal emotions and further lack of communication and sharing of life experiences.

6. *Sexual problems.* According to Territo and Vetter (1981), "Sexual problems between the officer and his spouse may be either a symptom or a cause of emotional conflict and estrangement, and often are both"

(p. 204). Male officers are often away at night and may be attractive "prizes" in the eyes of many women. The frustrations of police life may also lead to a lack of intimacy, and either or both partners may resort to sexual promiscuity as a solution to their problems. Infidelity is thus a common source of marital conflict.

7. *Identity problems.* Male police officers typically believe in a traditional, conservative image of family life where the wife stays at home and is the mother and spouse of the wage-earner. Problems may result when wives of policemen want an independent identity, the opportunity for personal growth, status, and prestige as separate persons. Interpersonal difficulties may occur if an officer believes that his wife has outgrown him and her social status as a police officer's wife.

Wives of overly stressed policemen have considerable difficulties themselves. As one police officer's wife remarks,

> I can't understand how seemingly normal husbands turn into such machos. Arguments end in "Because I said so." Our children feel as though they really can't discuss problems with their father because he relates in terms of the law and logic, and not the emotions involved. Sometimes I feel that if I don't do what he wants, I'll be arrested. (Quoted in Maslach and Jackson 1979, 59)

POLICEWOMEN

In addition to having many of the same stressors experienced by males, female police officers have their own separate sources of stress. Wexler and Logan (1983) suggest that stress for policewomen is often related to the following factors:

1. *Negative attitudes of policemen.* Questions about their sexual orientation, blatant antiwomen comments, and refusal to talk to women are frequent experiences of policewomen.

2. *Training.* Training officers often verbally abuse, punish, and attempt to intimidate female recruits into resigning. The types of physical training skills given to women disregards physical size and muscular differences between females and males. Although some policewomen need training in assertiveness and decision-making, little consideration is given by male supervisors for these so-called "natural" "male" behaviors.

3. *Rumors.* Policewomen feel particular stress when policemen spread rumors about their sexuality, trustworthiness, or capability. Not willing to be part of the gossip mill, policewomen often feel isolated and lonely. They fail to develop the occupational comradery usually found among their male counterparts.

4. *Group blame.* Policewomen frequently experience the stress of minority group status. When a policewoman fouls up, her fellow female officers believe that policemen take this as proof that all policewomen are inadequate, as, indeed, they sometimes do.

STRESS AND COMMON DEFENSE MECHANISMS

All people use a number of psychological techniques to defend themselves against stressors that threaten their well-being or integrity. These mechanisms are not consciously chosen but instead involve some self-deception to reduce stress. Five of the most common defense mechanisms are discussed here.

1. *Repression.* The unconscious mechanism of keeping anxiety-provoking ideas out of awareness is the self-protection technique of *repression.* For example, some police officers may experience panic on their first occasion to use deadly force in the line of duty. They may find the panic so frightening that the memory of this experience is unconscious. This unconscious distortion of reality is dangerous since it leaves the officers feeling guilty or resentful, without allowing the officer to understand why he or she feels this way. Furthermore, the officer does not know how to deal with these feelings alone. Repression is distinguished from *suppression,* which is the active control of removing something that is bothering us from our thoughts by thinking of something else. Officers who discover themselves thinking of some embarrassment they have suffered in the past, such as failing initial examinations before being accepted into the force, and then consciously removing it by thinking of more positive actions are suppressing feelings of inadequacy.

2. *Denial. Denial* is the refusal to perceive danger or threat. It is seen in police officers who refuse, for example, to recognize that they are victims if they are shot, or refuse to accept responsibility for an injury to their partners, pretending that the unfortunate event was bad luck, or even refuse to see that there is a problem.

3. *Rationalization.* This is a technique in which logical explanations, justification, and excuses are given for certain behaviors and feelings. Police officers who pocket stolen goods may rationalize their dishonesty by saying the store is covered by insurance and won't miss the camera, film, and so forth, anyway.

4. *Intellectualization.* In this defensive technique, emotions that normally accompany stress are blocked from conscious thought. Thus, a police officer who investigates the abduction, sexual assault, and murder of a young child may remain calm and detached in dealing with the parents and emotionally insulated and logical in dealing with the problem. By attending only to the intellectual aspects of the crime, officers protect themselves against the anxieties deriving from discovering the murdered child, but they also distort their feelings and perceptions of the world.

While excessive use of defense mechanisms is the beginning of serious psychological disturbance, defense mechanisms are useful coping strategies in emotionally intense situations. As the intensity of the loss recedes with time, the healthy individual can slowly adjust by adopting other coping strategies that are superior and less damaging.

STRESS PREVENTION

Several strategies to counteract the effects of stress are now available (Alkus and Padesky 1980). I will examine some of these programs in this section. Table 4.4 outlines specific treatment programs and activities for the prevention and treatment of stress in police officers.

Cognitive Reappraisal

One of the conditions precipitating tension is the perception of stressors that threaten important needs or motives. The realization that stress is in many respects a cognitive phenomena suggests that an individual can reduce stress by modifying her or his perceptions of the environment. Through a process referred to as *cognitive reappraisal* a person is trained to reexamine his or her initial perception of a situational stressor, evaluate alternatives, and consciously convert a negative appraisal into a positive one (Lazarus 1976; Sarason 1975). Since most situations are

Table 4.4   Promoting and Maintaining Mental Health in Law Enforcement

PREVENTION

—Recruitment selection criteria and procedures	—Develop job-related psychological standards and tests
—Participation in training and development courses	—Present mental health topics to existing recruit and in-service courses
—Periodic medical/health examinations	—Ensure that periodic examinations are performed to provide early identification of problems and at-risk officers
—Special-purpose psychological assessments/follow-ups	—Assess members prior to and following extremely stressful duties (e.g., undercover work)
—Seminars and workshops for supervisors	—Present short sessions (up to one week) to help train supervisors in health issues and interpersonal skills
—Assistance program	—Use the employee assistance program (EAP) model to develop an assistance program tailored to law enforcement organizations
—Occupational health and safety	—Ensure that the organization is sensitive to hazards such as the handling of dangerous materials in forensic labs and lead levels on firing ranges
—Life-style and health promotion	—Provide education and encouragement, especially in nutrition and exercise, to promote healthy life-styles
—Stress management	—Provide stress inoculation and stress management training tailored to law enforcement needs
—Peer support	—Develop peer support networks to provide officers with emotional support and referral services for situations such as posting and relocation
—Preventive counseling services	—Provide counseling services in such areas as aptitude/vocational career counseling or life enrichment
—Spouse programs	—Provide information and skill training in stress management, for example, for spouses of law enforcement officers
—Management consulting	—Provide advice and consulting services on current or anticipated mental health issues

Table 4.4 (continued)

PREVENTION

—Health research projects   —Conduct program evaluation and re-
                                          search projects in support of policy
                                          and program development

—Preretirement/career transition   —Provide information sessions and
                                          counseling relating to retirement and
                                          career changes

TREATMENT

—Counseling services   —Provide professional counseling ser-
                                          vices for individual, work group, and
                                          marital problems

—Treatment   —Provide medical and other health
                                          treatment services (e.g., marital
                                          counseling) as required

—Therapy   —Provide brief therapy or other psy-
                                          chological/psychiatric therapies as
                                          required

—Self-help   —Develop and advise self-help groups
                                          for a variety of problems (e.g., drug
                                          abuse, weight control)

—Peer counseling   —Develop and manage networks of peer
                                          counselors (law enforcement officers)
                                          to complement the work of health
                                          professionals

Source: Loo 1987, 21–22. Reproduced with permission of the Minister of Supply and Services Canada from Robert Loo, "Policies and Programs for Mental Health in Law Enforcement Organizations," *Canada's Mental Health* 5, no. 3 (Sept. 1987).

not all positive or all negative, people can reduce stress by trying to focus on positive factors of potential stressors. People are thus given a sense of responsibility for controling a stressful situation by actively blocking negative thoughts and emotions from awareness. Training in cognitive reappraisal on mock situations known to evoke high anxiety can enhance the performance of officers (Sarason et al. 1979). Anxiety may be aroused, for example, in such routine activities as traffic-stop field interrogations, arguments between customers and shopkeepers, and building searches. The development of perceptual sensitivity and appraisal of stressors can be accomplished through role-playing, modeling, and self-monitoring of responses during stressful situations. In stressful situations, officers can learn to perceive emotional cues that serve as signals to begin coping responses. Of special interest, however, is the observation of Saranson et al. that in spite of the fact that stress-management programs are successful, some police officers fail to see their value, are suspicious of their intent, and feel that training in appropriate police procedures is sufficient to deal with the stress of policing. For some officers, special training in stress management was considered unnecessary and even perceived as a sign of weakness.

Anticipatory Socialization

Police officers often experience a sense of *learned helplessness* (Seligman 1975) as a result of failing to accomplish certain objectives through the job. Unrealistic expectations usually end with failure, which, if experienced frequently, leads to stress reactions such as burnout. Learned helplessness is commonly defined as passive behavior that is produced when an individual has been unable to avoid repeated aversive events.

One prevention program that can help decrease the severity of this failure-stress relationship is *anticipatory socialization* (Jackson 1983). Systematic training on the differences between idealized police work and the realities of police work can be given. Once these difference are exposed and examined, police officers can be taught how to cope effectively with anticipated frustrations. Forewarning can lead to preparation.

Any method that directly and intentionally inhibits stress-related emotional reactions and their symptoms, such as the use of sedative drugs, participation in physical exercise, and relaxation training, may be used to reduce tension. The use of alcohol, barbiturates, and benzodiazepines will promote sleep and lessen stress-induced physiological arousal. Although sedatives work to control stress in the short term, their use as a permanent coping strategy is not recommended because of the potential for their abuse, and the fact that they do not facilitate learning of stress reduction techniques for long-term control.

Physical exercise is an effective technique for controling stress. Exercise facilitates both the bodily and emotional well-being of the individual. Excessive body fat is related to a number of serious health problems, especially coronary heart disease. Strokes, kidney failure, and heart attacks are linked to high blood pressure. Failure to engage in regular vigorous exercise creates a serious health hazard (Wood et al.

1982). Physical exercise reduces stress because it gives the individual a sense of mastery and self-control over stress reactions as well as producing a postexercise relaxation state in which stress-related thoughts are inhibited.

Officers can also use relaxation training techniques to gain rational control over the many "automatic" physiological reactions evoked by stressful situations (Farmer and Monahan 1980). These techniques involve systematic relaxation, hypnosis, and meditation (see Barber and Ham 1974; Goleman and Schwartz 1976).

Social Support Systems

Many police departments now have in-house psychological service units that focus on high-risk police personnel (Alkus and Padesky 1980). Individual officers coping with stress do not have to go it alone; instead, they can seek out the company of other officers as well as the support of their spouse and family. The celebrated "choir practice" of officers joining with other police over beers and drinks in local taverns is an example of the "informal" social support group (Wambaugh 1975). Although this network is useful, the need for a systematic approach to peer group support is recommended (Farmer and Monahan 1980). A systematic approach can avoid the difficulties inherent in informal groups—alcohol abuse, for example—and replace these with effective officer-to-officer counseling. Such programs do not propose to train selected "paraprofessionals" as counselors for stress management. Rather, they focus on the necessity of training all police personnel in interpersonal communication techniques so that the individual can become better able "(1) to listen effectively, (2) to verbalize feelings in appropriate and nonthreatening ways, (3) to problem solve, and (4) to view himself as a potentially helpful person to colleagues, not as an "expert" but, rather, as a colleague" (Farmer and Monahan 1980, 59).

In general, social support provides three major benefits (Caplan 1981). First, the individual can get information and problem-solving guidance to deal with his or her problems. Second, social support provides the affection, care, and nurturance that allows the stressed individual to build and enhance self-esteem and confidence. Finally, social support encourages and reassures individuals that they are in control and are able to master their stress (Gottlieb 1981).

Families have the potential to provide critical support for officers. By its very nature the family provides an intimacy where self-disclosure can be made in a context of total acceptance, without the need for a "macho" image (Farmer and Monahan 1980). Some police agencies now provide orientation programs for wives and husbands to make them more aware of the many responsibilities involved in policing. Ride-along programs, familiarization with firearms, and training in interpersonal communications skills are also provided for spouses of officers (Territo and Vetter 1981).

Organizational Reform

Patrol officers experience stress when there is poor internal communication, a lack of specific policy (Kroes, Margolis, and Hurrell 1974), and inconsistent departmental goals (Toch 1978). Since employees given the ability to influence events in their workplace are more highly motivated and intrinsically rewarded by their jobs (Deci 1980), greater use of participatory management in police administration, can clarify role expectations (Jackson 1983) and lessen officer frustration (Stotland 1975). Participatory management might involve representatives of front-line officers on committees responsible for departmental policy, rules, and procedures. Topics open for discussion could be limited to specific stress-related issues that have the greatest impact on the daily routine of officers. For the system to work, employees must be part of the decision-making process, and management must act on the advice given by employees. When supervisor-employee discussions are perceived as open and honest, an atmosphere of support that works to prevent stress is created (Stratton 1978).

SUMMARY

Stress is a normal, universal experience of life. Stress becomes excessive when the perceived threat to physical or psychological well-being is combined with an individual's feeling that he or she cannot cope with the threat. Stress can also affect health; there is a strong relationship among health, personality, and stress, particularly coronary heart disease.

Police officers are susceptible to many job-related stressors that have both immediate and long-term physiological and psychological consequences. In addition to having many of the same stressors experienced by policemen, policewomen have their own separate sources of stress. Police can defend themselves against stressors by using different psychological techniques that allow for control over stress-inducing events or seeking social support from family, friends, colleagues, or professional counselors.

5

Attitudes and Prejudice

The first modern police force was formally established in 1829 by Sir Robert Peel in London. The objectives of the police were to make the streets and the community safe by patroling and to develop and maintain public good will and support. Police officers cannot serve, protect, and maintain order in a free society unless they have the cooperation and the support of the public. Since the police do not control the causes of crime and are not present when individuals or groups make decisions to commit crimes, they are dependent upon the public for information useful in making arrests. The need for public support in the enforcement of law was made explicit in the United States by the President's Commission on Law Enforcement and Administration of Justice (1967):

Police-community relationships have a direct bearing on the character of life in our cities, and on the community's ability to maintain stability and solve its problems. At the same time the police department's capacity to deal with crime depends to a large extent upon its relationship with the citizenry. (P. 144)

The attitudes of citizens and police that both determine and result from police-community interactions are the primary focus of this chapter. I will consider the many individual and social variables that lead to attitudinal and behavioral difficulties in relations between the police and the community. Racial and cultural factors involved in prejudice and discrimination as well as national differences in attitudes toward police, specifically in the United States and Canada, will be reviewed. Finally, I will look at the role of the mass media and its influence on creating and maintaining certain beliefs about the police.

The police are a regulatory agency with legitimate authority to control those actions of the public that violate the law. This authority is often a source of conflict when attempts by the police to maintain social order are perceived by citizens as a threat to individual freedom. Police effectiveness depends upon the quality of the relationship between the police and the public, and the quality of this relationship depends, of course, upon the services provided. Negative reactions toward police are found, for example, among some crime victims who are dissatisfied at the police response to their victimization or their inability to prevent crime (Poister and McDavid 1978).

Attitudes toward the police are related to the psychological make-up of the individual, his or her social group membership, and the structure of society. How does the community at large perceive the police? An answer to this question is not as obvious as it may seem. Three distinct and contradictory images of police-community relations exist (White and Menke 1982). The first is a positive image in which the majority of the public, regardless of their racial differences, respect and support the police (President's Commission on Law Enforcement and Administration of Justice 1967). The second image is a negative one. This is most clearly seen in young, lower-class, black males, living in ghetto neighborhoods and is related to the minority group's perceptions that its members are more frequently stopped and searched, unnecessarily frisked, and treated in a more harsh, unfriendly, abusive, and degrading manner than are whites (Erez 1984). The third perception involves ambivalent attitudes, with the public skeptical and even distrustful of police power at the same time that the public recognizes the legitimacy of the police and accept their necessity and functions (Reiss 1967). The lower the social standing of citizens, the greater the hostility shown toward the police.

Ambivalence, however, can be more complex. People are not always rational or logical in their evaluations of others or of institutions. Individuals can hold one attitude at a general level, such as belief in the general honesty of the police, and another attitude at a more specific level, such as the belief that some police are dishonest and take bribes (White and Menke 1982). Thus, there may be general and diffuse support and acceptance for the police, but there may also be specific instances of disrespect because of negative experiences with one or more officers.

In order to introduce the extensive research literature on police-community attitudes, the next section reviews a general understanding of what is meant by the term *attitude* and its theoretical relation to behavior.

ATTITUDES

Definitions

Attitudes are defined as positive or negative evaluations of people, objects, ideas, or events (Bem 1970). When we question a citizen's attitudes toward the police, we are asking about his or her feelings of liking or disliking *(affects)*, whether he or she is inclined to offer support or opposition *(behavior)*, and what he or she believes to be true or not about them *(cognitions)*. Generally, we assume that there are consistent relationships among these components. For example, a woman who believes that police are lazy may feel negative toward police officers and, as a consequence, may act in a hostile manner when stopped by the police. However, the various components do not always have a logical relationship. For instance, a man who believes that police are helpful and courteous may feel positive toward law enforcement, but he may avoid helping an officer who is in difficulty.

Part of the misunderstanding regarding the concept of *attitude* is due to the lack of specificity attached to the term. Clearly, some attitudes are more general than others. People can have an attitude toward police, toward a specific police department, toward a particular officer, and so on. Usually people have a vague, general attitude toward the idea of police, but they may have specific attitudes about their local police force and about certain individuals who are police officers. The more general an attitude, the more likely that it is stable and important. But general attitudes do not lead to good predictions about behavior. Knowing a person's general attitudes toward police does not allow for accurate predictions of how he or she will behave in the presence of a police officer.

Attitude-Behavior Relationships

At one time, it was generally accepted that thoughts and feelings determined behavior. Similarly, it was believed that people acted in accordance with their attitudes. If one wanted to change someone's behavior, it was thought that one had to change that person's attitude. This view, however, is no longer accepted as the primary method for changing behavior. Knowledge of attitudes does not effectively predict behavior (Wicker 1969). People do not necessarily behave in ways that are consistent with their verbal statements. They may say, for instance, that they object to cheating, but this attitude need not necessarily be related to the likelihood of their cheating. Since people do not always act the way they profess to feel or think, it is not surprising that attempts to change behavior by attacking attitudes usually fail. Dangerous behaviors, such as drinking and driving for example, are seldom affected by appeals for attitude change. Other measures that directly control behavior, such as vigorous enforcement of laws and relative certainty of punishment, have proven to be more influential (Ross 1983).

Attitude-behavior relationships are thus not related in simple, unilateral cause and effect terms. Behavior is controled by many factors. Some of these are internal, such as attitudes and personality traits, while others are external, such as the situation or social context a person is in. Our behavior is often tailored to fit what we think others want to hear and see. For example, people often think one way privately, but behave in the opposite way publicly because they want to please their audience. General attitudes predict behavior only in terms of average behaviors over periods of time (Fishbein and Ajzen 1974). Thus, general attitudes toward police will not predict whether people will assist an officer in trouble on any particular occasion. Public assistance for an officer is dependant on a number factors in addition to attitudes, such as physical strength, courage, time constraints, the weather, the presence of other people, and so on. However, when attitudes correspond closely to concrete situations, attitudes can be accurate predictors of behaviors.

The results of a study by White and Menke (1982) show how the public's attitudes toward police can differ as a function of the specificity of questions given. Of 809 people asked to respond to the *general* statement "For the most part, police are just," 77 percent indicated positive attitudes and 14.5 percent were unsure of their perceptions. When the statement was made more *specific*, as in "Cops often carry a grudge against people who get in trouble with the law and treat them cruelly," only 46.6 percent of the public indicated a positive attitude toward police, while 26.3 percent were unsure of their perceptions. The level of public satisfaction with the police depends upon the specificity of inquiry; highly specific questions evoke a greater rate of dissatisfaction than more general question.

The attitude-behavior relationship also depends upon how automatic the behavior in question is. When we are forced to act automatically, without time for our feelings to be aroused, attitudes are nonfunctional —that is, they do not affect our behavior. Thus, a police officer suddenly encountering a "police-hater" on the street may find the civilian courteous in a reflexive response to the officer's friendly greeting. Attitudes are potent, however, when they are acquired first-hand and become solidified in experience. Someone who has had a specific and emotionally unpleasant experience with a police officer, such as being abused following a minor traffic offense, is likely to have negative attitudes toward police. These attitudes will persist and can predict the quality of his or her subsequent interactions with the police. Because police play a regulatory role, people may express some degree of dissatisfaction with police regardless of their type of contact, but this does not mean that they generally disapprove of police (Maxfield 1988).

Does Behavior Determine Attitudes?

In the previous section I noted that specific attitudes can predict specific behaviors whereas general attitudes only predict general reactions. If we turn the issue around, we can ask: Do people infer their attitudes from their behavior? Under what circumstances do people begin to believe what they say?

Consider the following experiment by Zimbardo and his associates (Zimbardo, Haney, and Banks 1973; Haney, Banks, and Zimbardo 1973). In order to investigate the consequences of being a prisoner or a prison guard, twenty-one adult male student volunteers were selected as participants in a simulated prison experiment. All of the students were given intensive psychological tests and clinical interviews and were chosen for their stability and maturity. Half of the students were assigned at random to play the role of "guards," and the remainder served as "inmates." All were instructed to assume and play their roles as realistically as possible.

To enhance the realism of the experiment, the "prisoners" were arrested by city police at their homes, charged with a felony, read their rights, spread-eagled against a squad car, body-searched, handcuffed, and driven to the station for finger printing and history-taking. Prisoners were then taken to a mock prison where they were stripped, skin-searched, sprayed for lice, given prison clothes, blankets, soap and towel, and put in a cell with two other inmates. "Guards" simulated the normal eight-hour shifts of real correctional officers. They wore khaki uniforms and carried whistles, handcuffs, and billy clubs as symbols of authority. Although instructed not to use physical force, they were given wide discretionary power to maintain "law and order" in their cell block.

The experiment lasted six days. During this time, a symbiotic relationship emerged. The more aggressive the guards became and the greater their sense of control and mastery, the more passive, depressed, and hopeless the prisoners became.

As one guard commented later:

> "I was surprised at myself. . . . I made them call each other names and clean the toilets out with their bare hands. I practically considered the prisoners cattle, and I kept thinking: I have to watch out for them in case they try something." (Zimbardo, Haney, and Banks 1973, 42)

This study showed that normal, healthy men who stepped into a role they knew to be artificial began not only to believe the role but to adopt behaviors usually associated with that role. The prisoners became resigned to their fate and behaved in ways that helped to justify their victimization. The guards' aggressive behavior and the prisoners' passivity were attributable to situational factors in the mock prison environment rather than to any character defects and personality maladjustments. The prisoner role and the guard role demanded new behaviors appropriate to the situational context. The new roles and new behaviors resulted in the development of new but temporary attitudes. Similar types of learning most probably occur in police officers. In Chapter 2, I suggested that the occupational role of policing socializes the police recruit and the experienced police officer to internalize certain values that are necessary for the job. The attitudes and values of policing are developed, in part, at least, from acting out the role requirements of being a police officer.

Other research has shown that when people publicly behave in a particular fashion and believe that they freely chose to act this way and are not coerced, attitudes developed from these actions are extremely powerful and long lasting (DeJong 1979). People also begin to believe what they say to others, provided they believe that their statements were not coerced but freely expressed (Klaas 1978). In other words, the folknotion that "saying is believing" is a scientifically respectable belief (Higgins and Rholes 1978).

Thus, while the popular opinion is that attitudes control or determine behavior, there is substantial evidence that under certain circumstances public behavior can influence and change attitudes.

Theories of Attitude Change

One of the purposes of this book is to present evidence and discussion on the need for attitude changes in both the police and the general community if there is to be a working relationship between the two. Several theories of attitude change have been formulated by social psychologists, but I will restrict our review to just three of these approaches: *cognitive-dissonance* (Festinger 1957), *self-perception* (Bem 1972), and *role-playing* (Elms 1969).

1. *Cognitive-dissonance theory.* Sometimes, what people publicly say or do is discrepant with their private beliefs or attitudes on the matter. The dissonance that is aroused by this inconsistency is disturbing, and people are motivated to restore a balance between behavior and beliefs. They can change their attitudes to make them consistent with their behavior, or they can rationalize their behavior, or they can seek out new information to justify the apparent discrepancy between their public actions and private beliefs. Thus, a police officer who dislikes blacks but is asked to give public lectures on good race relations, may feel pressured to change his or her beliefs about blacks so that private attitudes become consistent with what he or she has publicly declared.

On the other hand, the officer may not feel any cognitive dissonance or necessity to change private attitudes on the grounds that he or she was coerced into giving the lectures, a rationalization that in turn justifies self-deception.

2. *Self-perception theory.* According to self-perception theory, the same processes we use to attribute cause and effect in the behavior of others can also be used in our perceptions of self. If we stand back and observe our own behavior, we can infer attitudes and intent from the actions we took. People want to have a harmony or balanced state between their emotions and beliefs, and both of these psychological states have to be consistent with their actions. In order to have this balance, two attribution principles function in self-perception. The first is called *insufficient justification.* People are often unaware of the many subtle pressures inherent in a situation that act to determine their behavior. When we try to understand why we did something and there is insufficient justification to attribute the cause to some external forces, we may infer that our personality or some internal state caused our reactions. The second principle is called the *overjustification effect.* People may initially feel that their actions are the result of internal motivations, desires, and attitudes. However, when they become increasingly aware of the potency and control that situational factors exert over behavior, they may disregard their own internal disposition to behave and attribute their actions solely to situational forces. Such reasoning can act to produce attitude change. For example, if white police officers and inner-city blacks help each other, they may gradually see themselves as people who cooperate with each other. Cooperation may lead them to the inference that they are genuinely helpful and friendly and certainly not prejudiced people.

3. *Role-playing theory.* The techniques of role-playing have been used to produce changes in people's attitudes and opinions in such diverse settings as mental health centers, educational institutions, and police academies. In this approach to attitude change, individuals are asked to play roles they would normally not perform. It is assumed that this technique allows people to gain insights into how others see the world and how they might behave if they were in other positions. Individuals may also learn something about themselves by acting according to the way they think they really would respond if they were in particular situations. These new insights may produce attitude change.

For example, having a police officer play the role of a battered wife or an abusive husband under different situational conditions may provide further understanding of domestic relationships.

NEGATIVE ATTITUDES

Prejudice

Prejudice is an attitude, and, like any attitude, it is learned from and maintained by the social environment. *Prejudice* can be defined as an unjustifiable aversion and hostility toward members of a particular group solely on the basis of membership in the group. Prejudice involves negative feelings, mental images, and predispositions to act but does not necessarily determine actual behavior. When prejudice is displayed in overt negative behavior, we use the term *discrimination*. Thus, prejudice may or may not result in discrimination. Furthermore, discrimination has more than one cause; it does not always emerge from prejudice. Discrimination may result from institutional practices that arbitrarily deny power, privilege, and status even though there is no obvious prejudicial intent. For example, elderly persons are denied the right to serve as jurors in many jurisdictions once they reach the age of 70 regardless of their health, interest, or other considerations. Many elderly people consider this restriction discriminatory, especially when trial judges are allowed to sit on the bench until the age of 75 (see Yarmey, Jones, and Rashid 1984).

Prejudices more often that not have their bases in dominant group–minority group relations. A *minority group* is a social, not a numerical concept. Thus, in some American cities and in the Union of South Africa where blacks are a larger racial group than whites, blacks are nevertheless the minority group. A minority group can be either a highly visible racial group distinguished on the basis of genetic physical traits, such as Orientals, and blacks, or a less visible ethnic group, such as Jews, East Europeans, and the Irish. Members of ethnic groups are characterized more on the basis of socially acquired habits and lifestyles than on the basis of hereditary features. The common characteristics that all minority groups share are disadvantages in power, privilege, and status relative to that of the dominant group. Minority group members are often oppressed and victimized both physically and psychologically.

The *dominant group* creates and maintains the social order. It defines what is worthy and valued. Members of dominant groups are characterized as having: (1) feelings of superiority; (2) the perception that minorities are inherently different and alien; (3) perceptions of exclusive right to power, privilege, and status; and (4) a fear that the minority intends to seek the power, privilege, and status of the dominant group (Blumer 1961). As a consequence, minorities become self-conscious social units. Individuals who identify with the minority develop strong feelings of solidarity for others like themselves.

Prejudices against the poor, the young, the old, women, and racial minorities are so fully accepted and ingrained in society that they are often perceived as normal. Since dominant groups of society shape the laws and policies that govern it, attitudes become institutionalized. In turn, attitudes of individuals are influenced by the social institutions that have legitimized dominant cultural beliefs. Institutionalized prejudice involves the decision-making and control of events, resources, job opportunities, privileges, beliefs, and values.

Sexism

Sexism involves the discriminatory practices against one sex (usually women), particularly in employment and other social roles, and the institutionalized practice of systematically making decisions simply on the basis of anatomical traits that result in oppression, ridicule, or embarrassment. How men define women in the course of socialization, education, employment, recreation, and so on, has a profound effect on how women come to define themselves. Even when women reject these definitions, the social message being communicated has an impact in terms of psychological costs of feelings of rejection, hopelessness, frustration, and anger.

Sexism is clearly demonstrated in some policemen's attitudes toward policewomen. To quote one observer, "Possibly nowhere has prejudice been more obvious than in perpetuating an unrepresentative police force by deliberately excluding minorities and women" (Caiden 1977, 129). Compared to other institutions, police forces throughout the world are male dominated.

Caiden (1977) states that policemen fear that police work will be devalued as an occupation if women are patrol officers. Furthermore, police leaders believe that their community is threatened by evil forces and that the "weaker sex" should not fight these barbarians or be publicly exposed to them. The attitude that women's place is in more civilized settings, such as in the home (barefoot, pregnant, and in the kitchen) persists. Policing is viewed as man's work, dangerous, violent, brutal, and heroic. Many policemen believe that society itself would be in disrepute if women were allowed to do combat, not because women could not perform the task, but because it would be an indictment of what men perceive as worthy in society. Women find it difficult to fight this type of sexism because it is based on historical beliefs of chivalry, ignorance, and fear. It is a value-related issue having to do with women's "proper" place in society rather than with women's competence as police officers.

Objections by policemen that women would be unable to perform the dangerous functions of patrol work and that the public would not accept them have been refuted by empirical research (Bell 1982; Linden 1983). An evaluation study comparing the performance of eighty-six male and eighty-six female patrol officers in Washington, D.C., revealed that policewomen were equally effective in managing angry and upset citizens (Sherman 1975). Patrolwomen made fewer arrests and tended to be less aggressive than men, but there were no critical incidents where women were reported as being unable to perform their duties satisfactorily. Citizens did not report feelings of insecurity when policewomen answered their calls for assistance; in fact, citizens reported greater satisfaction in dealing with policewomen in handling service calls and domestic quarrels. Policewomen seem to add a social dimension to policing that many men so far either lack or are unable to express. Patrolwomen appear to have more capacity for sympathetic listening, compassionate understanding, and human responsiveness. These observations are significant when it is remembered that most police work is service-oriented and nonviolent.

Not all studies, however, have reported positive attitudes toward female police officers. These studies show that there are elements of sexism in the public's perceptions of policewomen. Many citizens are disturbed by the idea of women carrying firearms since they believe women are less capable in shooting and are more likely to wound innocent bystanders (Anderson 1973). On the mistaken assumption that brawn is necessary to manage dangerous situations, the public generally believes that women are unable to handle violence. The public and some police do not appreciate the fact that the ability to think clearly and quickly, rather than brute strength, is more likely to save lives (Milton 1972). Spouses of male police officers have been especially negative toward female officers assuming patrol car duties. Some wives believe that female officers put their husbands at physical risk and that women are too emotional for police work. Wives also object to their husbands spending eight hours daily in patrol cars with other women (Bell 1982).

As Bell (1982) remarks, "The main obstacle to overcome for women entering the police profession remains discrimination from within the police organization" (p. 119). But as Bell also adds:

> Policing is a voluntary occupation, and women realize the risks and rewards involved when they enter the profession. When the unsupported myths regarding women's limitations can be cleared away long enough to examine their contributions, then the assets of policewomen outweigh their perceived liabilities; the same as it does for men. (P. 120)

Racism

Racism is the differential treatment and control of individuals on the basis of their membership in a racial group. Racial prejudice begins in childhood—in the home, playground, school, and so on. The development and maintenance of racial bias are supported by the wider social and political institutions of society. Consequently, racism is stronger in some regions of the United States than in others, and it is more prevalent in the working class than in the middle class and in older persons than in younger people (Maykovich 1975; Middleton 1976). My discussion here will be limited to the biases of whites against blacks, but this is not to say that other forms of racism, such as black racism, are unimportant.

It is an error to believe that prejudice is fixed forever and cannot be altered. Research indicates that when whites and blacks share the same goals and interact in a cooperative manner in order to reach common objectives, prejudice is usually lessened. A good example of this cooperation was seen in World War II, when black soldiers and white soldiers had to depend upon each other. The primary factors for the lessening of racial hostility are interdependent contact rather than separate and parallel contact, cooperative rather than competitive behavior, and equal status rather than whites controling and demonstrating their superiority of power. Mere contact between blacks and whites of unequal status and without common goals will not reduce racial tensions (Blanchard, Adelman, and Cook 1975; Blanchard and Cook 1976; Blanchard, Weigel, and Cook 1975).

Antiblack feelings have been reduced in the United States since the end of World War II. Whites have become more accepting of formal equality between the races in terms of supporting black rights to fair housing laws and equal political rights. Old fashioned "red-neck" racism, such as overt acts of discrimination and beliefs in negative stereotypes—blacks are lazy, dumb, shiftless, and so on—is now out of style. However, some observers argue that this kind of racism has merely been replaced by a different form of prejudice called *symbolic racism, "the expression in terms of abstract ideological symbols and symbolic behaviors of the feeling that blacks are violating cherished values and making illegitimate demands for changes in the racial status quo"* (McConahay and Hough 1976, 38). These writers suggest that the relatively affluent, middle-class American white population, particularly northern white suburbanites, perceive blacks as *"too* pushy, *too* demanding, *too* angry, things are moving *too* fast, and blacks are getting *more* than they deserve" (p. 38). McConahay and Hough's research indicates that personal experiences and emotional states have little relationship to this new style of prejudice. Instead, it is related to political and economic conservatism, religious and secular traditionalism, and unacknowledged negative feelings toward blacks. These perceptions are indirectly expressed in such symbolic acts as voting against a well-qualified black by supporting an inexperienced, unpopular white, or by resisting suburban community integration by middle-class blacks, or subverting affirmative action programs (Hamilton and Bishop 1976; Greeley and Sheatsley 1971). In fact, in their extensive review of the literature, Crosby, Bromley, and Saxe (1980) conclude that "antiblack prejudice is still strong among American whites" (p. 560).

The most vivid and well-documented example of police racism in the United States was the opposition to the civil rights movement in the deep South during the 1960s (Caiden 1977). Southern police forces were indistinguishable from the white supremacist culture, which was determined to maintain the status quo. This alignment, however, is not really surprising. The police have traditionally been supporters of the status quo and more concerned with enforcement of the law than with defending the democratic process. Southern police openly sympathized with white racists, and they refused to protect blacks and white civil rights activists from the Ku Klux Klan and to enforce federal laws or Supreme Court decisions regarding civil rights.

> Into the 1970's, southern police used high-pressure hoses, clubs, whips, electric cattle prods, and savage dogs to break up demonstrations. They armed themselves with sawed-off shotguns and machine guns. They resorted to saturation policing (i.e., overwhelmed residents through concentrated force) and massive overkill. They made mass arrests. They physically prevented people from registering to vote. They harassed civil rights supporters. They ignored white racist attacks on school children, and allowed white vigilantism wide latitude. Several deaths resulted from their activities and other killings occurred with their tacit approval. (Caiden 1977, 35)

During this period, police racism was also apparent in urban black ghettos of the Northeast and the West. Local ghetto residents resented the white-dominated power structures of society. Law enforcement officials were perceived as the representatives of society and were held responsible for the lamentable conditions of the ghetto. The police, in turn, did not empathize with or like the ghetto residents (Levy 1968). In contrast to their treatment of whites, they treated ghetto residents more aggressively and more abusively through demeaning acts and taunts, illegal search and seizure, and false arrests and excessive force. The greater the prejudice of white officers toward blacks, the greater the likelihood that black suspects would be arrested (Friedrich 1977).

The ghetto riots of the 1960s were sparked by accusations of police racism, and the police were the first targets of violent attacks (Caiden 1977). By the mid-1970s, the attitudes of police agencies had changed, although some critics still felt that "the picture presented by police-community relations in black and other minority communities today is a dismal one" (Holman 1977, 91).

In order to reduce alleged racism and to control crime, police departments have attempted to form partnerships with the community. The distance between the police and its public has narrowed and is reflected in such police projects as the establishment of store-front and mobile centers, crime prevention programs, and neighborhood advisory committees (Bent and Rossum 1976). Whether or not these endeavors are meaningful and honest attempts to address real problems, rather than mere public relations programs, is debatable, according to some observers. Many black leaders continue to perceive the police as biased toward minorities. Black resentment toward the police is based on many charges: police brutality, police corruption, lack of police service and protection, more frequent use of deadly force on blacks than whites, an absence of effective mechanism for protest, little or no participation in the program development of police-community relations units, and so on. Clearly, some police officers are prejudiced toward the racial minorities. The more white officers dislike blacks, the greater is the expression of negative, coercive behavior (Friedrich 1977).

Although prejudicial behavior by police cannot be condoned in a free society, even those police who are not prejudiced against minorities can be labeled racists because the police role institutionalizes and rewards suspicion and distrust of citizens (Banton 1964). Those citizens who look different, have different moral standards, and whose demeanour challenges authority appear to violate the white officers' identification with the legal and moral order of white middle-class society. Police officers routinely look for a set of cues as evidence of suspicion and criminality. Minority group members, because they are often poor and different from the police officer's perceptions of "good" citizens, are set apart as distinct from the majority and are the recipients of police distrust. Furthermore, police officers working in ghettos may have frequent contact with hostile residents. Police officers, of course, perceive risk to themselves and to others in such contacts. Both prejudiced and unprejudiced officers may produce negative attitudes in minority group citizens because they expect to receive hostility. This misunderstanding can have self-fulfilling consequences:

> Police expect a hostile citizen reception and hence take a more authoritarian attitude in order to assure that actions will be seen as legitimate and authority will not be questioned. . . . The public, expecting the worst from the police, may alter their perceptions so that criticisms of police behavior are more likely. This shared misunderstanding produces

more conflict between citizens and police. Instances of police brutality are covered by the media, and the cycle continues. (Smith and Hawkins 1973, 135)

CITIZEN ATTITUDES TOWARD POLICE

Explanations for variations in attitudes toward police can be examined in terms of two categories; individual factors and contextual variables. Individual factors include consideration of such variables as personality, age, sex, race, and socio-economic status. Contextual variables focus on culture and social structure and include issues such as neighborhood composition, community beliefs, experience with police, and the likelihood of victimization.

Individual Variables

Personality.   Most personality theories state that temperament and adult prejudices are developed and shaped in childhood. The prejudices of adults most closely associated with a "law and order" mentality is the authoritarian personality (Adorno et al. 1950). Authoritarians are described as fascistic, ethnocentric, conservative in values, and rigid in beliefs. They dislike and blame minority groups for their own misfortunes, are intolerant of weakness in others or themselves, are preoccupied with power and status, and are respectful and submissive toward authority figures. In U.S. society, one very conspicuous authority figure is the police officer. As expected, authoritarians hold positive attitudes toward the police. This hypothesis was confirmed by Larson (1968), who interpreted this attitude as an expression of a need for authoritarians to find security in a threatening world through their identification with the police. The police are not necessarily liked by authoritarians; rather, they are perceived as allies who will keep minority group members, criminals, or anyone unconventional away from them. The stronger the beliefs in conservatism in a community the more positive the attitudes toward performances of the local police, toward the police in general, and toward the powers given to the police (Zamble and Annesley 1987).

Age.   Young people and the elderly tend to have unique relationships with the law and the rest of the criminal justice system. Police resent juveniles, whether they are offenders or not, when they fail to respect and defer to their authority (Piliavin and Briar 1964). Studies conducted in the 1950s indicated that deviant juveniles are most negative toward police (see, for example, Chapman 1953). However, more recent work showed that adolescents without prior police contact were more disrespectful toward police than arrested youths, who were less negative and shared many attitudes and beliefs with the police (Rafky 1973, 1977). Furthermore, youths with greater contact with the juvenile justice system were found to be more positive toward the police, the courts, trial judges, and probation officers than their less experienced counterparts (Giordano 1976). These results challenge the theory that deviant juveniles necessarily hold a sense of injustice or hostility toward law enforcement agencies. It is possible that these juveniles feel they "deserve" the treatment they receive (Erez 1984). Being a juvenile delinquent has certain costs that are understood and accepted by these offenders as part of an equitable relationship with the police and the courts.

As Derbyshire (1968) found, young children (third grade) from economically depressed areas have more negative attitudes toward police than their counterparts from higher socio-economic areas. Several investigators have found that adolescents do not understand the role of the police, although the vast majority of nondelinquent adolescents have favorable attitudes toward the police (see Amoroso and Ware 1981; Moretz 1980; Winfree and Griffiths 1977). Amoroso and Ware (1981) suggest that adolescents may not like the police per se, but they respect the power and authority that society grants to law enforcement agencies.

In contrast to juveniles and most other groups, elderly citizens are very positive in their evaluations of police. Citizens over 65 evaluate police more favorably than trial judges, prosecutors, and defense lawyers (Yarmey 1984). The elderly are especially vulnerable to crime (Goldsmith and Goldsmith 1976). Physical and mental trauma resulting from criminal victimization have a greater immediate effect and relatively more serious economic after effects for the older person. Elderly people also express substantially higher levels of fear of victimization, although some observers argue that this fear is created by the media and is unwarranted (Cook and Cook 1976). Nevertheless, the problems confronting the elderly are real and not contrived; nor are they transitory. Thus, as expected, older citizens are highly positive toward the police and society's legal institutions (Pope and Feyerherm 1976; Yarmey 1984).

But just as it is a mistake to categorize all juveniles as hostile to police, it is equally erroneous to believe that all elderly are supporters of police. Although older people are susceptible to victimization, some elderly people also are criminal offenders (see Wilbanks and Kim 1984). Shoplifting accounts for most (75 percent) of the crime committed by the elderly. People over the age of 65 have significantly lower arrest rates than people under 65, but the elderly are much more likely to be arrested for violent crimes, particularly assault and homicide. An analysis of Uniform Crime Report statistics between the years 1964 and 1983 revealed that the pattern of property crimes for which elderly people are arrested is becoming increasingly similar to that of the nonelderly population (Covey and Menard 1987). One-quarter of all arrests of older persons is for driving under the influence of alcohol, and there are proportionately more elderly drunk drivers than in any other age category. Surprisingly, the profile of the elderly offender is not of a destitute, lonely, grief-stricken or absent-minded individual. Instead, many are in good health and economically secure. Elderly women commit more thefts and take more valuable items than do their male counterparts. Most senior citizens convicted of an offense and imprisoned (0.5 percent of inmates in the United States) are first offenders *(Liaison* 1983a).

It is generally believed that police officers do not treat most crimes committed by older citizens seriously, perhaps because of the perception of the elderly as nondangerous and not totally responsible (Wilbanks 1988). However, Wilbanks' analysis of data gathered in 1980 in California found little evidence that the elderly are treated less harshly than younger persons by the criminal justice system. We can only guess about the attitudes of the elderly offender toward the police since this research still needs to be conducted. They may be positive toward the police since they do not perceive themselves as deviants and are not treated as dangerous offenders when stopped by the police. On the other hand, most elderly offenders know right from wrong and can appreciate what side of the law the officer is on.

Sex.   Although differences between males and females in attitudes toward police have been found, some researchers feel that sex differences are not an important predictive factor (Bayley and Mendelsohn 1969; Smith and Hawkins 1973). Females are generally more positive toward the police than are males (Thornton 1975). This result is logical since the majority of police contacts are with males, males are arrested at much greater frequency, and female suspects receive more polite treatment from the police (Friedrich 1977). Male-female differences are also found in the quality or types of complaints made about police. The greatest complaint from men is physical abuse, and their least likely complaint is verbal abuse. In contrast, the principal complaint about police from females is officers' verbal abuse (Wagner 1980).

Race. American-based studies have consistently shown that overall whites are more positive toward the police than are blacks or other racial minorities (LEAA 1977). My discussion here will be restricted to the experiences of black Americans with the police.

The perceptions of blacks toward police are based on both historical and contemporary factors. As mentioned earlier, in contrast to whites, blacks have been more harshly treated by the police and by the courts for the same types of crime (Johnson 1985). Black ghetto residents are more likely than poor whites to have contact with police because they are more frequent victims of crime, and the more serious their victimization, the more likely it is that they will give negative evaluations of police. In addition, blacks perceive inadequate police services as a racial factor. Hostility toward the police has a ripple effect: Few blacks will report crimes to police, and this in turn influences the quality of police services that can be provided (Hahn 1971); when blacks are complainants, the police are less likely to write crime reports, and this confirms blacks' view of police indifference (Friedrich 1977). The perceived inequity in the provision of police services, regardless of its cause, is a fundamental reason for black's dissatisfaction with the justice system.

Equity and Police-Black Relationships. *Equity theory* is useful in understanding the relationship between blacks and the police (see Walster, Walster, and Berscheid 1978). Simply put, this theory suggests that people and groups compare their rewards or the outcomes of events with their investments in those events. People also look around and see what others are receiving for exactly the same amount of personal effort, and they expect to be rewarded to the same degree as others in comparable circumstances. Equity occurs when people perceive that the relative rewards and costs of contributions and investments to social relationships are equal for all. Feelings of injustice occur when people get less than they perceive as fair relative to their contribution and relative to what others receive. Inequity results in distress, frustration, anger, and hostility toward those who caused the injustice or benefit from it. Demanding more rewards is the most obvious way for victims to reestablish equity. A second method is to make the other party uncomfortable or suffer through retaliation.

One of the traditional beliefs of American society is that "All people are created equal" and that each citizen is entitled to a fair share of educational, social, and economic opportunities. It is difficult to disagree with the observation that most blacks have not benefited economically or in many other ways for their treatment at the hands of whites since the end of slavery. In fact, blacks suffer from a disproportionately high victimization rate (President's Commission on Law Enforcement and Administration of Justice 1967). The response of black militants in recent years has been to retaliate by rioting, sniping at firemen and police, breaking, entering, and looting, burning, and destroying. Twenty-five years ago, James Baldwin (1963), a civil rights leader writing about blacks' attempts to obtain minority rights in the United States, concluded: "Neither civilized reason nor Christian love would cause any of those people to treat you as they presumably wanted to be treated; only fear of your power to retaliate would cause them to do that, or seem to do it, which was (and is) good enough" (p. 35). Contemporary black militants, however, are not content with minority rights; they want full citizenship and believe that black violence is necessary for this end. Walster, Walster, and Berscheid (1978), however, make the point that "retaliation will be beneficial *only* if the recipient of the violence feels that he is responsible for black's suffering. Retaliation against those who feel themselves to be innocent observers of injustice would seem to be a disastrous strategy" (p. 46).

To the extent that blacks have a negative attitude toward the police, this attitude may occur from one or more of the following reasons: (1) police are seen as the representatives of an oppressive white system; (2) police have been observed in instances of wrong-doing or abuse; (3) police have violated constitutional rights of minorities; or (4) blacks expect more protection, sympathy, understanding, and courtesy from the police than is received (Erez 1984).

Few police officers, especially black police officers, feel they are personally responsible for blacks' suffering. Furthermore, recent investigations have failed to find support for the hypothesis that police harass, question, chase, or warn blacks more than other races. Erez (1984) found that police give greater attention and harassment to persons known to be currently criminally active, regardless of their race.

Unfortunately, the police perceive many citizens as holding more hostile antipolice sentiments than is in fact the case (Bayley and Mendelsohn 1969). This belief has self-fulfilling consequences that perpetuate police-citizen misunderstandings. According to a 1977 U.S. Department of Justice study (LEAA), "Even among the most critical (young/black/other) respondents, only about one-quarter said that their local police are doing a poor job" (p. 13).

Socio-Economic Status. Police officers are said to differentiate the public along a general continuum that can be divided into five groups (Westley 1970) corresponding to the amount of respect and quality of treatment given to each group by the officer. Children receive the most positive concern, followed by the "better class of people," the slum dwellers, blacks, and criminals in that order. These perceptions are based on the group's supposed attitude toward the police, their values, their political power, and their respect for police goals.

Police believe that children are innocent and that children respect or at worst fear the law. Even juvenile delinquents are initially given the benefit of doubt, with officers inclined to perceive these offenders as still children. The "better class of people" is defined as those individuals who live in better residential neighborhoods and include people engaged in skilled trades, professionals, and the rich. Westley (1970) claims that the police deliberately try to develop the friendship of this class through politeness. Police feel that this class perceives them as servants and consider themselves superior to the police. The political power of this group forces the police to accept this relationship as long as members of the group are within the law. Slum dwellers are those people who live in the run-down areas of town and include migrants, and immigrants. This group are perceived by the police as morally weak, potentially criminal, and ignorant of the law. Members of this group supposedly respond more to fear than to persuasion and show respect for the law only when the law is enforced. Their lack of political power allows harsh treatment. The police believe that this group does not respect them, and they expect open hostility from them. According to Westley, police believe that blacks respect only force and power. Police perceive blacks as little better than slum dwellers, not labeled criminals only because they have yet to be caught. The criminals are the enemy. They understand force and are treated accordingly.

Westley drew his impressions of police-public attitudes from non-systematic observations and casual conversations with police officers rather than from scientific research. Notwithstanding this shortcoming, Westley's comments are useful for understanding the stereotyped relationships between individuals' socio-economic status and their attitudes toward police. What little empirical research has been done in this area is equivocal (see Decker 1981). Persons with the lowest incomes, especially the urban poor, show the greatest dissatisfaction with police (Albrecht and Green 1977). However, socio-economic status is also related to neighborhood culture. Thus, the poor in some neighborhoods may be more satisfied with the police than the poor in other neighborhoods (Jacob 1971). These attitudes may be determined in part from the harsher treatment the lower class receives from the police (Black 1979; Friedrich 1977). When negative attitudes are found among the middle class, they are often based on the belief that police spend too much time on "less serious offenses," while major crimes go unsolved (Keller and Vedder 1965).

Contextual Variables

Personal Experiences with Police.   It has been estimated that approximately 90 percent of police-citizen interactions are civil and the remainder antagonistic (Reiss 1971). The vast majority of police contacts are service-oriented, in response to people in distress or in response to calls for help from witnesses or victims of crime. Rather than proactive and involuntary, most contacts between citizens and police are voluntary, with police reacting to and being supportive of citizens in need of help. It would be expected then, that reactive encounters would be more positively received than proactive contacts.

This hypothesis has been supported. Citizens are more negative toward police in proactive encounters (Reiss 1971), and, as a corollary, the police are more antagonistic in proactive encounters, but only toward suspects (Friedrich 1977). However, all proactive encounters do not lead to negative attitudes. For example, the receipt of a traffic ticket in itself has no reliable effect upon attitudes toward the police (Klein, Webb, and DiSanto 1978; Smith and Hawkins 1973).

The general public is much more supportive of the police than the police themselves believe. In particular, officers who appear to be personally concerned about citizens' welfare and show warmth, friendliness, and tact are highly respected (Carlson and Sutton 1979; Jones 1986). However, mere contact between the police and citizens, including casual and friendly greetings, does not influence attitudes toward the police (Smith and Hawkins 1973). Superficial positive experiences do little to improve attitudes toward the police, but negative experiences act to substantially lower citizen evaluations (Jacob 1971).

Citizen-Police Contact: Consensus Model and Conflict Model.

Two criminology theories that discuss citizen-police contact may be helpful in explaining attitudes toward police. The first model is called the *consensus model* (Klein, Webb, and DiSanto 1978). According to this model, society is a complex system that is unified at a general level by shared cultural values. Criminal laws are one of the many codifications of society's values that are legitimized through high social consensus of reasonableness. Police are seen as representatives of the people and have the responsibility to insure that society's values are respected. Attitudes toward the police in this model are primarily the result of specific citizen-officer encounters rather than a function of group membership. Membership in social groupings affects attitudes toward the police only insofar as individuals in some contexts have more contact with police in conflict situations. The major predictors of attitudes toward the police in this model are the quality and the consequences of contact-specific encounters with the police.

The second model is based on Marxian philosophy (Marx 1963) and is called the *conflict model*. Society is viewed as a disunited system of groups struggling against each other in order to uphold and promote their own values, goals, and world-views. Criminal laws are a part of a political process that is supported by the state, which wealthy groups use as a legitimate means to maintain their power, status, and domination over the weak and the poor. According to Chambliss (1974) "The criminal law is . . . first and foremost a reflection of the interests and ideologies of the governing class" (p. 37). Crime is a product of the economic conflict between the oppressed and the oppressors. The function of the police in this model is to coerce acquiescence on the part of the powerless. Since minorities have more contact with the police and are coerced into obeying laws that are in conflict with their own goals and world-views, a minority individual's negative attitudes toward police is a direct result of categorically different treatment by the police.

Neighborhood and Community Beliefs.   The role played by neighborhood culture in determining attitudes toward police has been emphasized by a number of writers (see Jacob 1971; Schuman and Gruenberg 1972). The more contact that minority group members have with others holding similar perceptions within a given geographical area, the more negative will be the effect on their attitudes toward the police. Furthermore, as the proportion of a neighborhood's minority population increases, there is a corresponding increase in contact between members of that minority who have negative attitudes toward police and a strengthening of community beliefs and ideology about police (Apple and O'Brien 1983). Residents of small cities and towns are more likely to have positive attitudes toward police than residents of large cities, perhaps because smaller areas are more conservative in orientation (Zamble and Annesley 1987).

Likelihood of Victimization.   A reasonable prediction is that those citizens who have been victims of crime or live in high crime-rate neighborhoods or perceive continual victimization of others and themselves have little confidence in the ability of police to control crime. Consequently, they have more negative attitudes toward police than citizens in less crime-prone areas (Decker 1981). American blacks as a group, for example, are disproportionately more victimized by crime than are whites, Puerto Ricans, and West Indian blacks (Kleinman and David 1973). Recent victims of criminal acts hold similar attitudes toward police as do nonvictims. However, recent victims who are *not* satisfied with police performance hold more negative attitudes toward police than individuals who are satisfied with police action (Smith and Hawkins 1973). Citizens who experience more serious victimizations also hold more negative attitudes toward the police (LEAA 1977).

CULTURES, ATTITUDES, AND THE POLICE

The customs, social relationships, thought processes, and values of cultural groups have to be understood and appreciated if the criminal justice system is to be truly responsive to all of its communities. In this section I will look at the Hispanic and Native American cultures, which were arbitrarily chosen for review, not because they are distinctly different from other ethnic or cultural groups in their interactions with the law.

Hispanics

A lack of appreciation for cultural differences probably accounts for much of the hostility and mutual distrust between these groups and the police and courts. According to Carter (1983), the values and norms of Anglo-American culture have been applied to Hispanics without recognizing their cultural differences. Hispanic Americans are persons of Spanish ancestry from Cuba, Mexico, and other Latin American countries. While there are wide variations in traits, norms, dialects, and other characteristics within this group, there are some general similarities. The Hispanic family is maternally oriented, although the father is the ultimate figure of authority. The family plays a central role in social relationships, and loyalty is a cherished value. The oldest male in the household is the leader, and more respect is given to older persons than to the young and to males than to females. An arrest of the oldest male in the family may be perceived as an attack on the whole family, and this attack must be opposed in order for familial relationships to be maintained. Loyalty, respect, and obligations are extended to friends and distant relations. Loyalty and obligations, however, are identified with personal self-images. If the police attempt to disrupt or share existing loyalties and obligations, this is perceived as an attack on an individual's honor. The individual (usually male) is duty-bound then to defend his honor and his individuality.

Machismo is a real male attribute. Males are supposed to be strong, reliable, and protective. An insult or damage to the family or to an individual cannot be forgotten, and revenge is usually handled personally rather than through outside authorities such as the police. Carter

(1983) found that only about 25 percent of his sample of 312 Hispanic subjects evaluated the local police as good. This rating was significantly lower than evaluations of the police by the general American white population.

Native Americans

To be a Native Indian American means a higher likelihood of being poor, unemployed, uneducated, badly housed, and prone to alcoholism and having worse health and a shorter life-span relative to the white population (Solicitor General of Canada 1975). Native Americans living in Canada have much greater contact with all branches of the law than the white population: more arrests, more convictions, more imprisonment, and greater numbers of rearrest proportionately (Hylton 1981a, 1982; La Prairie 1984).

A number of cultural factors have been seen to contribute to the difficulties between Native Americans and the police (James 1979).

1. Inadequate verbal skills may suggest to the officer that the Native American is hostile or uncooperative. Native American nonverbal communication habits such as shrugs, downcast eyes, and shuffling feet often are seen as signs of disrespect by whites.

2. Native Americans believe in living in harmony with nature. They believe in their right to take from the environment that which is required in order to live. Consequently, fishing laws, trapping, and hunting regulations often bring them into conflict with the law. The demands of the larger society, including the justice system, undermine Native Americans' ability to live in harmony with nature.

3. Native American culture places great value on sharing resources and necessities of life. The white person's concept of theft is not always meaningful in the native society in which goods are shared without permission of the original owner.

4. Many Native Americans are indifferent to concerns of time, which may result in the failure of a defendant to appear in court at a precise hour on a specific day or failure to pay a fine by a due date, or failure to keep an appointment with a parole officer. Justice officials may interpret any of these time-related indiscretions as breaches of the law and contempt for the courts.

5. Many Native Americans support a cultural ethic of noninterference

from others in the resolution of conflicts. They see conflicts among themselves private matters, rather than as community matters that would involve the police. If police do intervene, witnesses and victims typically do not press charges, offer statements, or testify.

Police departments have the responsibility to serve and protect all ethnic and cultural members of their community. In order to understand these groups, police will have to know a great deal about their history and values. They will have to take the time to be participant-observers of their customs and traditions. Police officers will also have to analyze their own feelings toward these cultures and not let their own prejudices interfere with their job as peace officers (Ryan 1981).

DIFFERENCES IN PUBLIC ATTITUDES TOWARD POLICE IN CANADA AND THE UNITED STATES

Although the spirit of police community extends across the border dividing Canada and the United States, policing in these two countries has some dissimilarities. Not all social and political problems that are important in the United States are shared by Canadians. For example, instances of police brutality associated with civil rights and race riots in the United States during the 1960s and 1970s, the after-effects of the Vietnam War, and the hippie movement had relatively little impact in Canada (see Alcock 1978).

The historical differences between the United States and Canada probably account for some of the differences in attitudes toward police. From the earliest days of frontier settlement, Americans and Canadians have differed in their respect for public authority. Canadians are much more likely to defer to legal authority than are Americans. In American popular culture, the hero is the rugged individualist, the cowboy, the frontiersman, and even the vigilante. In Canada, the hero is the uniformed, disciplined Mounted Police Officer who represents traditional authority (Lipset 1972). Surveys indicate that the Canadian public holds the police in high regard (Klein, Webb, and DiSanto 1978; Koenig 1975; Moore 1983; Thornton 1975; Yarmey and Rashid 1983). In contrast to American research findings, Klein and his colleagues found that Canadians with the lowest income levels were most favorable in their attitudes toward police.

The American West was opened up by pioneers and settlers who depended upon guns for their survival. Many Americans still believe that it is their basic right to own a weapon, including a handgun, and this right is guaranteed in the Second Amendment of the Constitution. In contrast, the Canadian West was not opened by pioneers but was secured by the Northwest Mounted Police moving into the frontier settlements before and along with the settlers. Canadians' emotional ties to guns have been much less strong than their neighbors' to the South. Furthermore, Canadian federal gun laws restrict legal ownership and use of handguns to only those persons holding a permit authorized by the police.

At least two other historical and perhaps enduring differences between the United States and Canada probably contribute to national differences in perceptions of police. First, Americans believe in and will defend their right for life, liberty, and the pursuit of happiness as stated in the American Constitution. In contrast, Canadians have traditionally been more concerned with peace, order, and good government (Kalin and Gardner 1981). Second, the United States has intentionally tried to assimilate all of its people into one American culture, while Canada has formally decided to pursue the concept of multiculturalism within a national structure.

Much criminal law and the basic principles of criminal trials, such as the presumption of innocence and the right of an individual to lawfully refuse to answer questions to the police or to the courts, are similar in the United States and Canada. Both countries use an adversarial system of justice and trial by jury, and have similar rules of arrest, rules of lawful search, and exclusionary rules for hearsay evidence. However, the Supreme Court of the United States has been much more diligent than its counterpart in Canada in protecting individual civil rights (Brannigan 1984). Judicial concern for procedural safeguards (due process) of civil rights is more evident in the United States than in Canada. For example, since the Miranda case in 1966, American police officers prior to any questioning must warn accused persons of their right of silence and assure a continuous opportunity to exercise it. In contrast, police in Canada must advise an arrested person of the right to counsel but they are not required to warn arrested persons of their right to remain silent.

In the United States any evidence against a person that is illegally gathered may not be admitted for trial in court (absolute exclusionary rule) whereas in Canada:

> The illegality of the manner in which evidence is gathered has no bearing on the guilt or innocence of the accused established by such evidence. These matters are viewed as quite independent. The reasoning is this: because a policeman broke a law does not mean that the suspect is then absolved from the illegal behaviour discovered by that policeman. By contrast, the American judiciary has linked these by providing for the exclusion of illegally gathered evidence. The American court has reasoned that, without such controls, there would be no curbing the illegal acts of the police. For example, in the *Rochin v. California* case (1952), drug enforcement officers illegally entered the premises of Rochin's home, saw Rochin swallow two pills, and tried to forcibly open his mouth to retrieve them. When this failed, they took him to the hospital to have the contents of his stomach forcibly pumped out. He was later convicted of possession of morphine. In a judgment quashing the conviction, the judge noted: "This is conduct that shocks the conscience, illegally breaking into the privacy of the petitioner, the struggle to open his mouth and remove what was there, the forcible extraction of his stomach's contents —this course of proceeding by agents of government to obtain evidence is bound to offend even hardened sensibilities. These are methods too close to the rack and screw." In Canada, Rochin would have been convicted and invited to sue the officers for trespassing and assault; in view of the conviction, the damages would be trifling. (Quoted in Brannigan 1984, 77–78)

All of the above differences in police and judicial practices between these two countries are the result of different national values and attitudes. According to Brannigan (1984) "In the US, the police and the laws are constituted for the people and by the people and hence the police must be exemplary in their behaviour, otherwise their evidence will be excluded. In Canada, citizens tolerate a more autocratic and secretive government and bureaucracy that is responsible only indirectly to the citizenry, as well as to the Queen, through Parliament" (p. 72).

THE MASS MEDIA AND ATTITUDES TOWARD POLICE

Television, radio, and news publications, reaching millions of people daily, disseminate selective information about crime and criminal justice system. Information about police and their practices and the public's reactions to these disclosures, are popular and often controversial topics. The police, like all social institutions, are dependent on the media for "fair" presentations and evaluations of their services. Crime news and police dramatizations on television have several effects on the public, such as the promotion of exaggerated fears of crime seriousness and rising crime rates (Gebotys, Roberts, and DasGupta 1988; Payne and Payne 1970), impressions that violent street crimes are prevalent, and trivialization of the significance of white-collar crime (Graber, 1978; Hindelang 1974). The media, however, are not solely responsible for cultivating apprehensions of crime victimization. Individuals who are highly fearful of crime spend a greater proportion of their time watching television, and some people willingly choose to selectively expose themselves to programs about crime. However, television itself is not the direct cause of people's fear of victimization. This fear is related to knowledge of the crime rate in local neighborhoods (Doob and MacDonald 1979).

Television Images of Crime and Police

According to Haney and Manzolati (1981), television teaches us what crimes to fear, what types of people commit crimes and for what reasons, what the police respond to, and how they react to law breakers.

Much of television drama likewise misrepresents the realities of police-citizen interactions and how the courts operate. Contrary to the stories presented to the viewing public, crime in the real world often is understandable and justifiable. Thus, criminals can be both villains and victims, and crimes can result from situational causes or pathological social conditions rather than from personal defects of individuals. Television dramas rarely go beyond depicting criminals as "crazies" or pathological liars consumed with greed.

The realities of police work are similarly distorted. Apart from the "red-neck," bumbling TV police chief, police are typically presented as larger-than-life heroes. Most shows focus on police investigations, not on routine police work. In them, the police seldom make mistakes, and innocent people are not harassed, arrested, or sent to jail. The high uncertainties manifest in most police work are seldom depicted. Instead, the viewer sees decisive, detached, problem-solvers, who are certain that their decisions lead to the correct course of action. Television dramas show police breaking laws and violating constitutional rights, but these actions are never labeled *crimes*. Police are not punished for their violations; instead, their actions are presented as necessary and essential for the good of society. The viewing public either does not know or is not able to discriminate between legal police behavior and felonies and may believe that police in real life can also do whatever they please.

The distortions of police dramas have real consequences. Legislators, prosecution and defense attorneys, judges, and jurors are susceptible to forming stereotypes and expectations regarding both criminals and the police. The moral certainty and legal infallibility of police practices depicted on television can predispose all but the most cautious viewer to believe that an arrested person is a guilty person. Real-world decisions and attributions of responsibility and punishment can be influenced in part by the subtle and pervasive conditioning effects of television dramas.

Police News Coverage

A year-long content analysis of six Illinois daily newspapers, three national early evening television newscasts, and two local Chicago television newscasts revealed several different types of coverage about police and crime (Graber 1978). News about the police and about individual crimes is handled mainly by newspapers and local television stations. Consequently, individuals who learn the news from national newscasts receive little information about police activities. Significantly, more emphasis is given in all news sources to criminal acts and to suspects than to police activities. This emphasis contrasts directly with television police dramas, which focus mostly on crime fighters and crime-fighting.

Stories containing information about the police role in capturing suspects, aiding victims, or protecting the community from further harm

seldom give explicit evaluations of police performance. Evaluation stories are usually given as part of a general feature about police work,
but, according to the study, only 43 percent of these stories appeared in
the first section of the paper. In contrast, 61 percent of all crime stories
appeared in the first section. Police were positively evaluated in 60
percent of these stories; negative or mixed evaluations accounted for the
remaining 40 percent.

Even when police stories are featured in news stories there is insufficient data for a truly objective evaluation of the police (Cohen 1975).
The police themselves are responsible in part for this failure since they
do not provide data on such matters as police turnover and morale and
success and failure rates in various types of crime prevention programs.
The media, on the other hand, are not in the business to educate the
public on how police departments work on a daily basis. Instead, the
media are interested in communicating unusual events of public significance, such as "crime waves" (see Fishman 1978, 1981). Furthermore,
the public wants primarily to be entertained by the media rather than
educated and would probably ignore much of the information supplied
for proper evaluation.

News personnel play the role of gatekeepers in screening, rejecting,
and selecting which police stories pass from the source to the public.
News choices are not simply a reflection of the amount of newsworthy
happenings, but rather are designed to attract large audiences within
fixed time and space constraints. As Gadd (1986) remarks:

> The public's feelings towards its police force is influenced alot by the
> media, and the officer is fully aware of that as alot of his movements are
> carefully observed. While the press provides the citizens with a valuable
> service, it more often than not becomes a pain in the backside for the
> officer who feels, "They're very inaccurate. I've seen articles written up
> on things where I have been there personally, and thirty per cent of the
> things in the article were inaccurate. . . . We had an accident where the
> t.v. cameras showed a police officer striking this fellow. What they didn't
> show was the fellow had bitten onto the officer's hand. To get him to let
> go, that officer began striking him, but the cameras only showed part of
> what was happening, so people got a very bad impression of the police.
> . . . We had a siege here where a fellow came out of a public area with
> two shotguns. Two policemen started walking towards him, and he pulled

the shotguns out, ready to shoot them. As a result, a police sniper just shot him dead. They way that was edited by the t.v. cameras and used that night, the police had just shot him for no reason. You never saw the guys walking down the street; you never saw him lifting the guns up in a threatening attitude. You just saw a man walk out in front of the store, then dead. They had cut it all just to make a sensation." (P. 198)

However, it is also important to recognize the role of police as gatekeepers when they produce crime reports that become the raw data journalists use to write the news. According to Fishman (1978), "News organizations may choose what crimes to report, but the pool of occurrences from which they draw is preselected and performed within police departments. . . . The police crime-reporting apparatus systematically exposes the media to incidents which perpetuate prevailing law-and-order themes in crime news" (p. 372). Providing information to the news media allows the police to have control over social disorder and management of their public image, which is defined in terms of "law and order," not in terms of social services.

Police-Media Relations

In its simplest form, the relationship between the press and the police is a pure exchange of information—a simple question by a reporter and a straightforward reply by a police spokesperson. But sometimes, the interaction may be adversarial and mutually distrustful (Kiernan 1979).

Police chiefs are often responsible for establishing the tone of police-media relations. Reese (1983) surveyed the opinions of 104 chiefs of police in California cities with populations between 10,000 to 50,000. Ninety-nine percent of the chiefs reported fair to excellent relations with the news media, but disagreed as to what constituted good or poor relationships. Conflicts often centered on the public's "right to know" and the accused's right to a fair trial. Good or excellent media relationships (84 percent) were attributed to the existence of a written police-media policy. Several characteristics such as openness, candor, and fairness on both sides were perceived as necessary for positive police-media relations. Major problems perceived by chiefs of police were media sensationalism, inaccuracy, editorializing, and limitations on time and space.

If individual reporters embarrass the chief or the department or betray the trust extended to him or her, the tenor of all media-police exchanges in that department are hardened and communication exchange stops. Reese (1983) found that 21 percent of the chiefs perceived the media as "open," 21 percent called them "trustworthy," and 48 percent saw them as "fair." Police chiefs perceive newspapers, in contrast to television, as substantially more objective, more complete, and more accurate.

The views of new police recruits, however, are more negative toward the media than those of police chiefs. In a study of sixty-nine police cadets, Lazin (1980) found that the majority of cadets believed that the press was hostile to the police. Only seven cadets felt the press acted in a professional, objective manner in its coverage of police-related incidents. Similar results were found by Berg, True, and Gertz (1984). Following the 1979 race riot in Miami, Florida, a clear majority of officers in this city believed the news media gave biased accounts against police. Furthermore, young officers (under age 30) were more negative and cynical toward the community and toward police work than officers over 30.

Positive relationships between the police and the media are necessary if the police are to have the general support of the public. A bad press can have a good chief removed from office, and a good press can maintain a bad chief in power (Kiernan 1979). At the same time, the adversarial role is of prime importance in police-media relations in a free society:

> As appealing as the idea of total cooperation between police and media may seem, keep in mind that this degree of "cooperation" is far more typical of repressed nations—where the public is told only what the ruling party wants it to hear—than of democracies. Our judicial system is predicated on the adversarial concept of justice. Fairness and proper representation by competent and legal procedure is inherent in the adversary system. A case can be made for the need for gatekeepers, watchdogs, and monitors, and this tends to suggest that an adversarial relationship between police, the media and the public is more appropriate to a free society. (Reese 1983, 38)

SUMMARY

Neither citizens nor police are neutral toward people, groups, institutions, objects, or issues around them. Their beliefs, feelings, and behavioral tendencies toward others are grouped together as attitudes and are relatively long lasting. Prejudice is a negative attitude toward the members of a social group.

This chapter has presented a review of police-civilian attitudinal and discriminatory practices involving women, racism, personality factors, age differences, personal experiences with police, neighborhood situations, and community beliefs. Cultural differences among communities and their respective attitudes about crime have been reviewed, with a focus on blacks, Hispanics, and Native Americans. Attitudes toward police in Canada and the United States have been compared, and historical differences in the settlement and growth of the two countries have been shown to probably account for national differences in policing and attitudes toward the law.

Much of our attitudes toward police and toward crime is determined by the mass media, although the media are not solely responsible for cultivating apprehensions of crime victimization.

6

Social Influence, Control, and Deterrence

Much of the social influence and power that people have over others often is self-evident; however, subtle and indirect pressures that influence and control behavior are not so readily recognized. In this chapter, I will consider some of the strategies and techniques used by assailants, police, and the courts to influence and control victims, suspects, citizens, and others. All people are mutually influenced by promises, threats, rewards, and punishments (French and Raven 1959). Police officers use legitimate threats as well as physical force to control people. Even a simple "good morning" may be interpreted as a stimulus control over the behavior of citizens on the street. To the extent that people fear the loss of what they value—be it money and personal safety or less tangible values such as approval, esteem, or respect—they are influenced by other parties.

According to one view of police control:

A policeman's principal concern is to physically control the people he is policing. While he sometimes wants to hurt or humiliate them, that is not nearly so often his purpose as it is the consequence of his efforts to control them. When he intervenes in a person's life, his attitude is basically instrumental. He mainly wants to place himself as quickly as possible in a position that will allow him to control the person, if that is required, or hopefully to discourage any inclinations to resist him or his order. (Rubenstein 1972, 302)

Police power has several distinguishing characteristics. First, it is *legitimate power* given by the state, and citizens generally accept this power because of social structures and cultural values (Elliott and States 1980). In addition to legitimate power, police officers utilize *coercive power* to control antisocial behavior and *expert power* to control crime and perform general service functions. The limits of individual officers' influence over citizens are set by institutional and organizational forces. Law enforcement agencies emphasize the paramilitary nature of policing. Police officials are very sensitive to "orders from above" (Bordua and Reiss 1966), such as inquiries from the mayor's office or the police commission. Police organizations are characterized by a strict hierarchical system of chain of command, strict subordination, accountability, and trust between the ranks because of their highly decentralized operations. A police officer's commitment to obedience in this quasimilitary organization is rewarded by acceptance and is in itself a sign of membership.

AUTHORITY AND POWER OF POLICE

Each time a police officer interacts with a citizen, the nature of their reciprocal roles is influenced by the differences between them in authority and power (Elliott and States 1980). Police authority is legitimately ascribed by the state. Regardless of the particular individual who is wearing the "blue" uniform and/or carrying the badge, he or she has the legitimate power to impose sanctions (French and Raven 1959).

Power is the ability to influence the actions and behavior of people to do something they would not ordinarily do (Kipnis 1976). Police officers have the duty to demand certain behavior from others even when the exercise of power is personally disagreeable. On the other hand, power can have its rewards insofar as it is enjoyable (Christie and Geis 1970) or satisfies personal needs such as dominance and avoidance of feelings of weakness (Veroff and Veroff 1972).

Police have the power to arrest and if necessary to use violence in making arrests, privileges that usually are beyond the authority of civilians. Power, however, is exercised at the cost of rejection or dislike from those over whom power is held. Because society accepts the legitimacy of police orders, individuals usually comply, but they may not enjoy doing so. If people refuse to comply, officers are put in the position of deciding how important the order is, what alternatives exist, and whether or not to persist with the original order, which may now necessitate the use of threats or force.

Unfortunately, most people, including police, understand the term *power* to mean "force." At times, police have to use force, but on most occasions "influence" is the appropriate control mechanism. Henderson (1981b), drawing on the writings of Rollo May (1972), cites five basic kinds of police power with which police officers must cope: exploitive, manipulative, competitive, nutrient, and integrative.

Exploitive power is seen in the worst types of police abuse and corruption (see the *Knapp Commission Report on Police Corruption* 1973). It is associated with raw force, it presupposes violence or the threat of violence, and it disregards the most minimal recognition of human rights of its victims, particularly drunks, drug addicts, low-income persons, homosexuals, prostitutes, and ethnic minorities.

Manipulative power is defined as power *over* another person. The views of B. F. Skinner (1953) are relevant here. All behavior, according to Skinner, is subject to the effects of reinforcement and punishment, controled by the presence or absence of environmental reinforcement. In short, humans could be said to be the victims of forces that shape their behavior. The police and courts use manipulative power to shape behavior through such reinforcing stimuli as praise and citations and such punishments as fines and jail sentences.

Competitive power is power *against* another person. Competition typically denotes the process of trying hard to win. Competitive power can be positive and facilitate high performance by members of the police force. In many instances, both competition and cooperation occur almost simultaneously, as, for example, when a police officer attempts to capture (win over) a gang of terrorists while cooperating with fellow police officers in an assault on the gang. Competition can, of course, be negative as well. It can be self-defeating, stressful, and motivated by relatively unhealthy aggressions against community residents or fellow police officers. Police who compete with fellow officers for arrest records, for example, may achieve success while alienating both community residents and other police officers.

Nutrient power is power *for* the other person. It derives from a humanistic concern for the welfare of others for whom one is responsible. Police supervisors should understand that both junior officers under their control and community residents are more amenable to influence when concern for their well-being, as opposed to the use of power or forcible intervention, is used to direct their actions.

Integrative power is power *with* another person. When police develop a sense of trust and cooperation between themselves and the community, both parties benefit. In this type of relationship, police are not perceived as an enemy or threat, but instead seen as respected allies who have the power to influence crime and violence.

In a society based on democratic principles, the police are able to influence others only if people accept their authority as legitimate. The ability to control should not rest solely on the use of threat or physical force. Instead, expert power acquired through education, training, and experience allows the police to serve and protect with maximum efficiency and rewards for both the police and the community. The words of George Bernard Shaw are relevant here: "Power does not corrupt men; fools, however, if they get into a position of power, corrupt power" (quoted in Henderson 1981b, 83).

COMPLIANCE

Conformity

Police tactics that quietly persuade and influence citizens in nonthreatening ways did not grow out of formal psychological training, but these procedures have received extensive empirical investigation over the years. The pressure to conform is apparently at a maximum with groups of five persons. Groups larger than five or six persons do not extract more conformity; rather, if at least one person acts as an ally with a dissenter, conformity is significantly decreased. Even one ally breaks the group's unanimity and lessens the pressure on the dissenting individual (Allen and Levine 1971; Stang 1972, 1976). These research findings have practical significance for the courts and their decision in some jurisdictions to use six-person juries rather than the traditional twelve (see Strasser, Kerr, and Bray 1982). It is much more likely for a dissenter in a twelve-person jury to find a single supporter and thereby reduce the pressure to end the discussion and reach a decision of guilt or innocence. Group pressure and conformity to authority, as we will see later in this chapter, also can be used by the police to induce confessions from suspects.

Several factors influence conformity. People conform and obey in order to avoid feelings of embarrassment and guilt. The need for information, the need to be correct, and the need to be accepted by others are also powerful motives. (Deutsch and Gerard 1955). Individuals tend to conform when the task is difficult or ambiguous (Asch 1956), or when they feel inferior or less competent than other group members (Ettinger et al. 1971). Middle-status members of groups tend to conform more than leaders or low-status members, presumably because they have the most to lose or gain (Dittes and Kelley 1956).

The classic studies by Solomon Asch (1956) provide a good example of how people are pressured to conform to the judgments of others. Subjects were given the relatively easy task of judging the similarity of lengths of lines. Small groups of people were shown a standard line and three comparison lines (A, B, and C). Each person in the group publicly stated which of the three lines was the same length as the standard line. Although the task was easy and everyone in the group agreed on their answers—at least for the first few trials—the task suddenly became difficult for one person. Unknown to the last person in the group to give his answer, all other group members were confederates of the experimenter. They were instructed to give some obviously wrong judgments after the first few trials. The true subject was now placed in the conflict between trusting his own perceptions or reporting the same but obviously wrong answers as all other group members. Asch found that approximately one-third of his subjects yielded to group pressure on one-third of all trials by conforming with the erroneous group consensus. Postexperimental interviews with conforming subjects indicated that they felt embarrassed by or guilty over being different. Asch demonstrated that groups as small as three or four can produce as much conformity as groups as large as sixteen, providing that the erroneous majority is unanimous in its judgments.

Contrary to popular opinion, little evidence is available to show reliable personality differences in conformity. Although some people appear to always "go along" with the group, only about 20 percent of the subjects in one study showed consistency in conforming in four different conformity situations (Vaughan 1964). Conformists typically have low self-esteem (Stang 1972), greater feelings of inferiority, more rigidity, more authoritarian attitudes, and excessive self-control (Crutchfield 1955). However, personality differences are not good predictors in explaining conformity because people who conform in one situation may not conform in others.

Obedience to Authority

Whether or not an individual complies with a direct command or request to behave in specific ways depends upon his or her fear of punishment, rejection, or embarrassment. Thus, compliance is primarily a function of normative social influence. Public compliance, however, should not be confused with private acceptance. This latter concept refers to changes in attitudes and beliefs resulting from group pressure. An individual may comply with an order from an authority but may not change his or her attitudes. Private beliefs and attitudes will change along with public compliance only if the individual feels that the group's wishes are congruent with his or her interests.

In Chapter 1, a description of Milgram's (1963) obedience to authority study was given. To recapitulate briefly, in this study, adult men of all ages, occupations, and social positions in the New Haven, Connecticut, region obeyed the instructions of an authority figure to give (supposedly) massive amounts of shock to another person. Most subjects complied simply because the authority said, "You must go on. The experiment requires it." When this study was conducted, few people predicted that most subjects would administer near maximum (extremely dangerous to life) levels of shock. In fact, psychiatrists predicted just the opposite results—that is, that less than 0.1 percent of the subjects would comply completely (Milgram 1974).

Several possible explanations account for this high rate of obedience. One of the best uses the idea of *diffusion of responsibility*. To the extent that subjects believed that the experimenter would be responsible for any harm to the victim, they could rationalize their actions by saying, "I was just following orders" and "I am not responsible." Another valuable explanation involves the concept of *normative support*. People may believe they obey orders because that is the right thing to do and other people would agree that it is proper. Some people justify their compliance by arguing that their behavior has beneficial effects—that is, "shocking people in an experiment contributes to the advancement of science." This view is expressed when people believe that the ends or goals always justify the means, especially if the goals are grand and historically significant and the means are perceived as merely ordinary concerns. Some people follow orders because they have complete trust in the legitimacy of authorities. Others obey because of the coercive power of the authority to punish noncompliance. Often compliance results from situational forces the individual feels unable to resist because of such factors as a desire to uphold a commitment, the awkwardness of withdrawal, politeness, and cognitive reevaluation of the situation that produces deindividuation.

Deindividuation is a process in which people begin to regard their victims more as objects or concepts and less as humans. When this happens to soldiers in battle, for example, they begin to believe that they are not killing fellow humans but rather merely eliminating the "enemy." The enemy is not perceived as having human fears or anger; instead, he or she is understood in terms of the simple, black-and-white category of "evil" and the like. Similarly, suicide jumpers standing on building ledges are often seen not as people in need of help, but as "crazies" who are there to provide entertainment for onlookers. Once the deindividuation process starts, the individual begins to see himself or herself less and less as a separate, socially responsible person. The deindividuated person becomes a face in the crowd. Normal inhibitions and personal controls over behavior are relaxed, and hostility and overt expressions of aggression are more vigorously expressed. The greater the opportunity for obscuring of identity, combined with a lack of self-monitoring and concern for individual responsibility, the greater the deindividuation (Cannavale, Scarr, and Pepitone 1970).

Some people claim that on really important issues, they wouldn't comply, but that on trivial matters they give in rather than waste energy arguing with the authority. One can ask, however, how "trivial" was the delivery of near-lethal shocks to the "victim" in the Milgram experiment? Perhaps people obey orders because of the material rewards offered. In the Milgram study the payoff for punishing another human

being to the highest level of shock permissible was only $4.50—hardly
a large amount of money even for the 1960s.

Although it is conceivable that only people with certain kinds of
personality traits are predisposed to obey or conform, this explanation
lacks empirical support. So-called weak personalities are used as explanations or excuses for behaviors that are difficult to comprehend or
justify. For example, the "inhuman" behavior shown in the Nazi Holo-
caust of World War II has been explained by pointing to "crazy"
leaders, "weak" followers, and so on, with the implicit suggestion that
if you or I were in Germany at the time, we could say "I wouldn't have
done that" or "It couldn't happen here." Subjects in Milgram's obedience study were carefully screened, however, before they participated;
no one was a sadistic, cruel, or neurotic person, yet most obeyed the
instructions to the fullest. Clearly, the demands of a situation can be so
powerful that normal, healthy individuals feel compelled to comply even
though the induced behavior is discrepant with their personal values
and beliefs.

Most people misunderstand the obedience situation. They underesti-
mate the extent to which a person usually obeys an authority figure, and
they wrongly assume that individuals can always resist this type of
pressure "if they truly wanted to." People persist in believing that a
person's character, rather than the situation, is the more important
determinant of behavior (Ross 1977).

Although during basic training the U.S. Army now provides instruction pertaining to moral responsibility and illegal actions in combat,
research by Cockerham and Cohen (1980) suggests that another My Lai
incident remains quite possible. Bureaucratic organizations such as the
military depend upon the premise that members must obey orders if
efficiency is to be achieved. Obedience to orders is a normative expectation of everyone. Cockerham and Cohen found that 51 percent of 736
paratroopers were either undecided or disagreed with the statement that
"A soldier should have the right to disobey an immoral order, even in
combat," and 38 percent of the sample were either undecided or disagreed with the statement that "A soldier who intentionally kills innocent
civilians should be treated as a criminal." It was also found that those
soldiers who were most committed to the military system—that is,
highest ranking, career-oriented, and most satisfied with military life—

were most likely to comply with legal orders in combat even if the orders were immoral. However, they indicated that they would not comply with definite illegal orders, such as an order to commit a war crime.

Cockerham and Cohen argue that the likelihood is high that these self-reported attitudes would predict obedient-type behavior in paratroopers, an elite unit with high primary group solidarity and discipline. Such factors operate on the individual to force him or her to follow group standards. Group norms are supported and rewarded by significant others and act to strengthen preexisting attitudes held by the individual. Since the police subculture values group loyalty, secretiveness, and isolation from the public (Rokeach, Miller, and Snyder 1971), and "real" police are defined in terms of quasi-military criteria (Manning 1978), it is likely that similar expectations to orders operate in police organizations as well.

The Power of a Uniform

I vividly remember an incident from my college days that personalizes the meaning of the social power of the uniform. Driving home one weekend from my summer job as a park ranger, I left my working clothes on—a jacket, shirt, tie, and hat that closely resembled the uniform of the highway police. The feeling of power to be able to slow down and control traffic as I drove my "unmarked cruiser" was a "high" that has been matched only by my present role as a youth football coach (I get to wear a baseball cap, blow a whistle, and carry a clipboard). Uniforms serve to identify the wearer and give status, group membership, and legitimacy. People follow orders of someone in a police uniform because they assume the officer has the legitimate right to give orders. Uniforms suggest coercive, informational, and expert power. They also elicit normative support and trust in most people (Joseph and Alex 1972; Mauro 1984). However, traditional uniformed police officers also elicit greater anxiety than nonuniformed officers (Colbert 1980). Depending upon the situation, uniformed police officers are positively evaluated when police intervention is required, but negatively perceived in nonintervention situations (Muchmore 1975). "Clothing in the criminal justice system seems both to express and to be the cause of attitudes, actions, and reactions" (Shaw 1973). Traditional police uniforms have a history of stereotyping associated with them that may affect the credibility of the wearer and his or her need for instant recognition (Gundersen 1987).

In one experiment on the social power of a uniform, pedestrians in Brooklyn, New York, were stopped in the street by an experimenter dressed in civilian street clothes or as a milkman or as a guard. They were told to "Pick up this bag for me" or "Give a dime to a stranger for a parking meter" or "Move away from the bus stop." Compliance with the orders from the civilian and milkman was low, but 82 percent obeyed the guard's order to pick up the bag, 89 percent followed his order to give a dime to a stranger, and 56 percent complied with the request to move on. It was concluded that the guard, unlike the civilian and milkman, was obeyed because he gave a legitimate order (Bickman 1974).

COERCION

Compliance Through Threat

Everyone uses *threat* in one manner or other to influence and control others. However, threats are a two-party transaction that is dependent upon the nature of the demands made by the source and the perceptions of the receiver. The receiver and the source of the threat may not be attending to and thinking about the same things. The receiver, for example, may focus on the dangers associated with the threat and what will happen if he or she does not comply with demands. The source, on the other hand, may focus on what he or she expects to accomplish by threatening the victim.

Threats have a number of distinguishing characteristics. They are most effective when situational cues evoke guilt or anxiety. For example, the glimpse of a highway police cruiser in your car's rear-view mirror as you are just about to race for work is an effective control. Threats are a form of coercive power used to influence or deter others from committing a crime or misdemeanour. Providing that threats are credible, compliance with demands may follow, but if the source is not believed, his or her threats will have little effect on behavior. However, a less credible threat may force the source to prove that he or she is serious, which may increase the chance of violence. This section will consider how compliance is generated with the use of threats in rape situations. Although males can be raped, I will restrict my attention to exploring the social forces established by the offender to control the female victim. (A detailed examination of sexual assault and rape victimization is presented in Chapter 9.)

Coercion Tactics in Rape.   Definitions of *rape* extend over a continuum anchored at one broad end by the radical feminists' view that all coerced sex is rape, whether the coercion is physical or psychological or economic, to a narrow restrictive end, which states that rape is a myth, that there is no such thing as rape (see Burt 1980; Holmstrom and Burgess 1978). Whether or not the victim resists the assault is a key determinant for many people's decision that rape occurred. Did she want to have sex, or was she forced? Was the sexual behavior a product of personal motivation or environmental coercion? The answers to these questions suggest that the issue of consent is fundamental to an understanding of rape.

Rapists attain power over victims through strategies based on physical force, linguistic control, and various situational manipulations. These types of controls place the victim in circumstances requiring quick and sometimes irrevocable decisions. For example, the victim must decide how she should respond to an attack: Should she resist or not, and what are the likely consequences of this decision?

Unlike the advice normally given by bank managers, for instance, that victims should comply with the demands of a robber in order to avoid injury or even death, rape victims have been given conflicting recommendations. Feminists typically advocate physical resistance, claiming that fighting the rapist minimizes the probability that rape will be successful. Furthermore, it is their opinion that physical resistance promotes the chance for psychological recovery if the rape is completed. In contrast, the police usually assert that women should not physically resist since aggression may trigger further violence and result in greater chances for injury or even death (Curtis 1976).

A study by Griffin and Griffin (1981) using nation-wide survey data of a subsample of 242 women from 72,000 households showed that a full range of threatening behaviors is used in rapes: gestures, verbal commands, physical force, and brandishing of weapons. Fifty-one percent of rapists used nonphysical threats, 42 percent physically attacked the victim, and 7 percent threatened victims with weapons.

Linguistic Control Strategies.   In addition to physical force, rapists gain power and control over victims either before, during, or after rape through linguistic strategies (Holmstrom and Burgess 1978, 1979). In-depth interviews of 115 adult, adolescent, and child rape victims revealed that rapists' talk is a prominent characteristic of sexual assaults. Ten major themes were found:

1. and 2. *Threats and orders.* The victim is told to cooperate or be hurt or even killed: "If you resist, you're dead woman"; "Do what I say or your kids will get it."

3. *The confidence line.* If the victim is known to the rapist, he builds on their existing familiarity. If the victim is a stranger, his conversation is directed towards establishing trust and normalcy. In both instances, victims are manipulated into situations where the rapist is in control. "Can I give you a ride home?" "Want to come over to my place and hear my new stereo?" Confidence lines also are given with the assistance of female accomplices: "We know of a good party—why not join us?"

4. *Personal inquiries of the victim.* The more personal information the rapist learns about the victim following the assault, the greater her vulnerability. Even if the victim refuses to answer questions such as "Where do you live?" "Do you live alone?" and "What's your telephone number?" the mere fact that the rapist asked these types of questions reinforces her fears that she could be raped again. Rapists also inquire about personal habits and preferences with regard to sex, money, and drugs in order to gain information that may be used later to discredit the victim.

5. *Personal revelations by the rapist.* Regardless of whether or not the information is true, a rapist often tells the victim how tough, how dangerous, or how lonely and deserving of sympathy he is in order to gain and maintain control. These revelations usually are made at later stages in the rape with the intention that the victim will more readily adapt to her plight and be influenced against trying to have the police arrest the rapist.

6. *Obscene names, dirty sex, and racial epithets.* Rape can be understood in terms of its social and psychological meanings of power, anger, hatred, contempt, and conquest. Humiliation of the victim by insults ("slut") and obscene names with sexual and cultural ambivalence ("black bitch," and "white whore") serve to support the rapist's need for power.

7. *Inquiries about the victim's sexual "enjoyment."* Some rapists have fantasies about themselves as being great lovers. They need the victims's confirmation of how much pleasure she has received, combined with the illusion that she wants him again as her lover. "He kept wanting to know if it felt good, and I had to say yes to keep him happy. . . . He also wanted to know if he could come and do it again." Rapists may ask whether the woman is enjoying her rape in order to taunt and ridicule her. Holmstrom and Burgess (1979) discovered that if victims reply, they answer in the affirmative as a defensive measure.

8. *Soft-sell departures.* On completion of the act, rapists often depart by showing concern for the victim, giving sympathy, and apologizing. These measures are taken in an attempt to pretend that the situation is normal and that nothing really out of the ordinary has happened. For example, one victim reported: "I got up and put my clothes on. He asked if I was hungry, if I wanted to eat. He kept apologizing. . . . He said he was sorry I was so upset" (Holmstrom and Burgess 1979).

9. *Sexual put-downs.* Victims are often humiliated and devalued by the rapist's suggestion that they (rather than the rapist) are sexually inadequate. For example, one victim reported, "He said I wasn't worth it, that he didn't get any pleasure from it" (Holmstrom and Burgess 1979).

10. *Possession of women.* For some rapists, the need for power and control over the victim extends not just for the short term but indefinitely into the future. A rapist may talk of keeping the victim as his lover, wife, or whore.

Situational Control Strategies.   Analyses of rape cases reveal that situational forces separate from the control strategies used by the assailant should also be considered in order to understand the causal processes that operate in rape. The likelihood of an individual becoming involved in a rape incident depends upon one or more of the following situational factors (Gibson, Linden, and Johnson 1980):

1. *Facilitating times.* Over 80 percent of 281 rape cases analyzed occurred between 8:00 P.M. and 7:59 A.M. In particular, those rapes that take place outdoors or in motor vehicles usually occur in this time period.

2. *Facilitating places.* Rapes are most likely to occur in the privacy of unobtrusive locations such as empty homes, automobiles, vacant

streets, lots, parks, and the like. The residence of the victim or the offender or some other residence is the most frequent place for rapes (44 percent). Rapes between acquaintances or friends are twice as likely to occur in one or the other's residence (56 percent) compared to when the rapist is a stranger to the victim (28 percent). Women living alone account for 51 percent of rapes in residences. A relatively high proportion of rapes (24 percent) take place in motor vehicles following hitchhiking or acceptance of a ride from a passing driver, and of these victims, 80 percent are strangers to the motorist.

3. *Facilitating hardware.* Gibson, Linden, and Johnson (1980) found that a weapon was used in 22 percent of the rapes in order to secure victim compliance and cooperation. Knifes were most frequently employed, but some victims were threatened with guns, beer bottles, chains, clubs, or even an axe.

4. *Facilitating others.* Twenty percent of the rapes involved more than one offender. The confederates' major role during gang rape was to keep the victim subdued and compliant.

5. *Facilitating circumstances.* Alcohol was present in the victim, in the offender, or in both parties in 69 percent of the rape situations.

THOUGHT CONTROL, INTERROGATION, AND CONFESSIONS

In this section, I will look at thought control techniques, such as brainwashing, and review several different psychological procedures used by the police to induce confessions. A detailed examination of the legal restrictions placed by the courts on the investigating officer when interrogating a suspect is beyond the scope of interest of this book and will not be reviewed (see Kaci [1982] regarding the admissibility of confessions in the United States under Miranda). Similarly, the legal implications of obtaining confessions from juveniles will not be treated here.

Brainwashing

Why did many of the followers of Reverend Jim Jones follow him to Jonestown, Guyana, and commit mass suicide by drinking Kool-Aid

laced with cyanide? Why did the newspaper heiress Patty Hearst participate in a bank robbery with her kidnappers, the Symbionese Liberation
Army, and then blast a Los Angeles store with a submachine gun in
another SLA holdup? Complete and convincing answers to these questions may never be known. Defense lawyers for Patty Hearst argued that
Hearst embraced her captors, renounced her family as "fascist pigs,"
assumed a new identity as "Tania", and become a guerrilla in the SLA
as a result of two months of brainwashing. The courts, however, have
not accepted brainwashing as a basis for a defense of "duress or necessity." (See Alldridge [1984] for a discussion of the legal issues involved
in using brainwashing as a defence to criminal liability.)

Deliberate coercive persuasion or *brainwashing* was first recognized
by the Western world following the thought-control techniques used by
the North Koreans and the Chinese on American prisoners during the
Korean War (Schein 1956). The purpose of brainwashing was to control
and to coerce the POWs to renounce their values and beliefs and to
adopt those of their captors. Although this thought-control program was
not overly successful (only twenty-one POWS chose to stay in Korea
following the war), the concept of brainwashing continues to arouse
interest, fear, and confusion.

Several elements used in brainwashing techniques are now well
recognized (Back 1977) and used in one form or other by terrorists
groups and some religious groups seeking converts to their way of life.

1. *Rigid environment.* Individuals are taken away from familiar surroundings to an isolated environment that is totally controled by others.
Maximum environmental pressure can now be exerted on the individual.

2. *Loss of identity.* An individual is often given a new name, coupled
with attacks on his or her self-concept, personal values, and beliefs.
Under persistent pressure, the self begins to crack and to be recreated
in the image of the manipulator.

3. *Extreme emotional arousal.* The individual is overly stimulated,
excited, and fatigued. Praise and friendship are offered in a situation
fraught with exhaustion, uncertainty, despair, and fear of the unknown.

4. *Guilt.* The individual is made to feel inadequate and guilty for past
beliefs and behaviors. The person is told that he or she can be cleansed
by joining and trusting new friends. Confessions of sins are encouraged
even if the confessions must be fictionalized. Once the individual begins

to confess, old values and beliefs are more easily discarded and replaced by new beliefs.

5. *Positive reinforcement.* Each time the individual complies with seemingly trivial responses, he or she is praised and rewarded with favors. Eventually, the individual is shaped by his or her captors to comply with more important requests, especially requests involving confessions, self-criticism, and information.

Police Interrogation Techniques and Confessions

Although police brutality and the "third degree" is not unheard of today, it is safe to say that modern practices of in-custody interrogation are psychologically based and similar in some respects to brainwashing techniques. Police manuals and texts document the most effective psychological strategies to employ for successful interrogation (see Inbau and Reid 1962; O'Hara 1970; Wicks 1974). The following categories and discussion summarize most of the interrogation techniques used by the police (see Driver 1970; Zimbardo 1967; Zimbardo, Ebbeson, and Maslach 1977).

Demand Characteristics of the Interrogation Environment. Interrogation is usually conducted as soon as possible after the criminal act, but for some suspects interrogation is deliberately timed for after-midnight arrest or a weekend arrest in order to increase uncertainty and suggestibility. The interrogation area is manipulated to give the suspect the expectation that the forces of the law are invincible. The suspect may be "softened up" by being put into isolated and unfamiliar surroundings and deprived of sleep and/or food. The interrogation room is designed to be plain but comfortable and free of distracting materials such as pictures or a telephone. Close attention is given to ecological details such as lighting and furniture arrangement. Lighting must be bright enough to enable interrogators to observe nonverbal behaviors but not too bright to suggest the "third degree" to the suspect. Furniture is arranged to emphasize the relative differences in status and to allow the investigator easy access to and manipulation of the suspect's personal space. For example, the interrogator may sit on the edge of a desk looking down at the suspect who is seated close by.

Environmental manipulations of this sort act to increase suggestibility as a result of perceptual or sensory deprivation (Kubzansky 1961) and to confirm the interrogator's authority, power, competency, and ability to control events (Inman 1981). Because the suspect is deprived of familiar surroundings and supportive friends, he or she is dependent on the investigating officer.

Perceptual and Judgmental Distortion.   Attempts may be made to distort the suspect's understanding of the crime and his or her decision-making. Although the police have only selective knowledge about any crime, they present an image of confidence and total certainty of the suspect's guilt. Questions are put to the suspect in the context of confirming what is supposedly already known and inquiring why the suspect committed the crime, rather than asking if he or she did the act (Wicks 1974). Interrogators encourage self-doubts in suspects by stressing the futility of alibis or denials of guilt.

A suspect's understanding of his or her situation is limited by police deception and lies. For example, in *Miranda v. Arizona* (1966), the court cited a trick recommended by O'Hara (1970): "The accused is placed in a line-up, but this time he is identified by several fictitious witnesses or victims who associated him with different offenses. It is expected that the subject will become desperate and confess to the offense under investigation in order to escape from the false accusations" (pp. 105–6).

Lies made during interrogation to encourage confessions, such as "your buddy has confessed" or "your fingerprints were found at the scene," are not uncommon. The courts grant legitimacy to this type of questioning with one limitation: Police lies may not be of such a nature that an innocent person would be induced to commit a crime or falsely confess to having committed one (Klockars 1984).

Deliberate distortions of suspects' decision-making occur through the making of threats and promises. It is the responsibility of the court, of course, to interpret the legal meaning of "threats" and "promises" since confessions must be free and voluntary and "not . . . extracted by any sort of threats or violence, nor obtained by any direct or implied promises, however slight" *(Bram v. United States* 1897). Be that as it may, several recent example of police threats and promises may be cited.

> In one case, *State v. Jackson* (1983), a detective stated falsely to a murder suspect, with the intent of inducing a confession, that bloodstains had been found on the suspect's pants, that the suspect's shoes matched footprints found at the scene of the crime, that the murder weapon had been found with the suspect's fingerprints on it, and that a witness had seen the suspect running from the murder scene. The detective also attempted to coerce a confession through various forms of intimidation, such as reminding the suspect that death was the maximum penalty for murder and threatening to testify falsely that the suspect, a black man, had raped and killed a white woman. . . . In a second case, *McGee v. State* (1969), interrogators falsely asserted that bloodstains, fingerprints, and lie detector results conclusively proved a suspect's guilt. The suspect, a 19-year-old male who had been treated previously for emotional problems, including two psychiatric hospitalizations, and who had only a third-grade education, subsequently confessed. (Sasaki 1988, 1593)

What drives a person to confess? Since it is difficult for lawyers to prove illegal or unconstitutional police manipulations of suspects, judges and/or jurors may have difficulty in appreciating why a supposedly uncoerced person gives a confession unless it is true. Hilgendorf and Irving (1981) suggest that confessions, especially false confessions, are best understood in terms of perceiving the suspect as a decision-maker. According to the *optimizing decision strategy*, it is probable that suspects subjectively weigh the perceived consequences of a confession, seeking to minimize their own suffering through a probable reduction in severity of sentencing in contrast to the likelihood of conviction and harsher sentences. Even "innocent" individuals may decide to confess and accept a plea bargain if the consequences are likely to minimize the punishment (Bordens 1984). This model assumes, of course, that people are rational and capable of optimizing their decisions. The courts insist that confessions be made voluntarily; however, most individuals are unable to optimize their judgments in circumstances that debilitate decision-making—that is, conditions of threat, physical confinement, social isolation, compliance to perceived authority of the police, and so forth. Vennard (1984) found that the three most frequent reasons for suspects' making alleged false confessions were: (1) a promise made by police to grant early release from custody if a confession is made; (2) prolonged detention in a police cell; and (3) actual or perceived threats of violence by police.

Kassin and Wrightsman (1985) suggest three psychological types of false confessions: (1) The *voluntary confession* is given by people who voluntarily go to the police to confess to crimes they have not committed. The motives for these confessions are "a morbid desire for publicity or notoriety"; "a desire to aid or protect the real criminal"; "the guilt-ridden individual who believes that confessing to the crime will relieve him or her of guilt about some real or imagined previous transgression"; and "the mentally disordered person who cannot adequately distinguish between reality and fantasy" (Gudjonsson and MacKeith 1988). (2) The *coerced-compliant confession* is given to obtain some immediate reward, such as being allowed some favor, or to escape from an intolerable situation. (3) The *coerced-internalized confession* is given because the individual lacks confidence in his or her own memory to reconstruct the event and a willingness to accept the suggestions offered by the police (Gudjonsson and MacKeith 1982).

Distortion of the Social-Psychological Situation.   Modern interrogations are conducted in a supportive atmosphere in which the interrogator projects friendship, patience, respect, dedication to professionalism, and fairness (Wicks 1974). The suspect is encouraged to trust the officer who wants to be seen more as a friend or counselor concerned with the suspect's welfare than as an officer attempting to obtain incriminating information (White 1979). In *State v. Reilly* (1974), the court learned that the interrogator manipulated the relationship between himself and the 18-year-old suspect so that he was viewed almost as a father figure. Since the young man wanted to please his "father," a confession was relatively easily induced. Similarly, in *State v. Biron* (1963), an officer presented himself as a fellow Catholic and assumed the role of religious counselor by extoling the benefits of confession.

Perhaps the most celebrated deceptive manipulation used by the police is the so-called "good cop–bad cop" routine. One of two police officers working together begins the interrogation as a friendly, sympathetic questioner who ingratiates himself to the suspect. After a period of time, "bad cop" announces that he knows the suspect is guilty and begins to berate and vividly show his hostility toward the suspect.

"Good cop" steps in once again and resumes a friendly approach. He indicates that he disapproves of his partner's behavior, and when "bad cop" leaves the room, "good cop" indicates that he can get his partner to leave the suspect alone providing the suspect cooperates and makes an immediate confession. The "good cop–bad cop" routine can also be played by a single officer who alternates between being friendly at first, then angry and demeaning, and once again concerned, helpful, and sympathetic. The friendly-ally approach followed by the assaultive-opponent act is intended to manipulate the suspect's feelings of self-worth, trust, fear, decency, dignity, honor, and guilt.

When two or more interrogators display repeated assurances and certainty of the suspect's guilt—"We know what you've done—we know where you went, who you talked to, and who was with you—so why not admit it?"—the suspect is faced with the situation of being the only person disagreeing with the unanimous opinion of the group. The tendency of single individuals to yield to unanimous judgments of others may act to induce a confession of guilt even from an innocent person (see Asch 1956).

Utilization of Personality and Clinical Psychology Phenomena. In this technique, the suspect's personal motives, needs, and interests are questioned and analyzed in the context of a therapeutic relationship with the interrogator. Wicks (1974) recommends an indirect approach to interrogation that attempts to mollify the suspect to confess to the crime because he or she is told: (1) It wasn't really a serious crime; (2) the victim was more at fault or blameworthy than the suspect; (3) the suspect will feel better and less guilty for confessing; (4) the suspect will have the respect of the interrogator; and (5) the crime was probably more accidental than intentional, and the suspect wasn't completely at fault. These pseudolegal excuses and psychological ploys of sympathy and illusions of empathy serve to convince the suspect that he or she is honorable and worthy—providing confession is made. If the suspect adopts the role of being an honorable, trustworthy person, his or her confession will be compatible with this self-image (Biderman 1960). Furthermore, the more that the suspect confesses, the more he or she begins to believe in the correctness of admission, especially if the confession is given without any overt threats (Bem 1966). Another danger of these manipulations is the likelihood that individuals who have pathological tendencies toward self-accusation or who suffer from guilt anxiety or who have an acute need for love and attention may confess to crimes they did not commit.

Verbal Distortion and Harassment.   Repeated use of such phrases as "you're to blame," "you're guilty," "tell the truth" increases the suspect's uncertainty and confusion. Suggestive metaphors such as the following act to influence the suspect's judgment:

> Right up to your ears you're implicated. That hole is getting bigger, you're digging it deeper. You're the fellow who's going to determine how long you're going to be buried. . . . You're the one guy who's got the shovel; you're the one fellow who's digging the hole. You just figure out how deep you want to dig that hole, how far down you want to bury yourself; and you just keep right on digging. Of course, if you would start telling the truth, we could throw a little of that dirt back in, and make it a little shallower. (Quoted in *State v. Biron* 1963, 177)

Verbal distortions and harassment may constitute implicit threats or promises that lead a suspect to believe that his fate will worsen if he fails to confess, or that it will improve in some way if he does confess.

Police Responses to Charges of Coercion

To counteract the charge that a confession was not made voluntarily and intentionally, police forces have begun to videotape interrogation sessions. The apparent objectivity of this procedure, however, can be illusory. Bias can be created by the focus of attention given by the videotape technician in recording the session. Lassiter and Irvine (1986) experimentally demonstrated that the point of view from which a confession is taped influences whether viewers judge the confession to be voluntary or coerced. When the camera was focused primarily on the suspect (view of the front of the suspect from the waist up and showing part of the head and one shoulder of the detective), observers judged the confession to be voluntary. When the camera focused primarily on the interrogator, the confession was judged to be the result of a high amount of coercion. When side views of both the detective and the suspect were shown, the confession was judged to be the result of a moderate degree of coercion. In order to minimize bias in judgments of coercion, Lassiter and Irvine recommend that interrogation sessions be videotaped from the perspective of the suspect. This would permit observers to judge whether or not coercive influences were at work during the taping session.

Justification for Confessions

Some legal scholars (see McConville and Baldwin 1982; White 1979) argue that police interrogations are unjustified since confessions are obtained largely in cases where the evidence against the accused is already convincing. Furthermore, these authors emphasize that considerable research evidence shows that the laws designed to protect the rights of citizens during interrogation are ignored and violated by the police. If these critics are correct, why do police continue such practices?

Justification for the continued use of interrogation to induce confessions cannot be attributed to evil intent or naïveté of police. Instead, the police continue to use a variety of interrogation techniques for a number of legal and psychological reasons (McConville and Baldwin 1982). (1) In addition to suspect confessions, interrogation of suspects may produce evidence about accomplices, recovery of stolen property, and clearance of other unsolved cases. (2) Confessions usually lead to guilty pleas. (3) A confession convinces the police that the accused is the correct person. (4) The police see themselves as professionals whose duty is to present the strongest possible case to the courts. The prosecution must prove the case beyond reasonable doubt. Regardless of other available evidence, confessions allow the police to present to the court a clear and coherent picture that can confirm the guilt of the defendant. Confessions permit the police to understand the motive for the crime and provides evidence of intentional behavior. (5) Police interrogations and suspect confessions are part of the ritual of being a police officer. Interrogations are intrinsically interesting and exciting, and they provide an opportunity for the confirmation of police norms and values of control, authority, power, formality, identity, tradition, honesty, fairness, and so on. Interrogations and any resulting confessions legitimize police behavior and confirm society's expectations of law enforcement. Furthermore, suspect confessions legitimize fellow officers' perceptions of police and the wider occupational culture of policing. (6) Interrogations and confessions are considered a vital part of policing because they set the suspect apart from law-abiding citizens and the police apart from the suspect. This is most clearly seen when the accused apologizes or shows remorse. Suspect apologies and remorse confirm officers' belief in their own moral worth and value in spite of the fact that confessions may have been induced by trickery and deceit. Any moral dilemmas of this sort can be resolved by reationalizations such as "we're just doing our job" or "we know the guy is guilty."

Such rationalizations, however, do not satisfy critics, even if the trickery or police lies are legal in the opinion of the courts. For example, White (1979) states:

> The use by law enforcement officers of any tactic that challenges a suspect's honour or dignity raises a fundamental question for our system of criminal justice . . . a basic postulate of the fifth amendment is a concern for protecting the dignity of the individual. Interrogation tactics that are calculated to make the suspect feel that he is not a decent or honorable person unless he confesses constitute direct assaults upon that dignity. (Pp. 627–28)

Where does this leave the conscientious police officer who wants to do the best possible job of policing yet stay within the law? White (1979) argues that whenever an interrogation strategy puts a citizen's constitutional rights at real risk, the practice should be absolutely prohibited. Coherent guidelines must govern police interrogation practices, and the judicial system must vigorously scrutinize such practices. Otherwise, the criminal justice system does not and will not operate within constitutional confines.

INFLUENCE AND CONTROL IN THE DETERRENCE MODEL OF CRIME PREVENTION

Legislators and officers of the court have believed for approximately two hundred years that lengthy prison sentences and the death penalty are effective means of making citizens law-abiding (Beccaria 1953). Severe penalties given by trial judges to convicted defendants supposedly have a general deterrent effect on other potential offenders because of fear of punishment. *Deterrence* is commonly understood in terms of *general deterrence* or *prevention*—that is, the impact of a punishment threat on those who have not been punished—and *specific deterrence*—that is, the impact of punishment on the punished (Gibbs 1975). These two concepts are logically independent and may not have the same effects. General deterrence is assumed to work because people have a nonspecific fear of punishment and may also have respect for society's formal criminal laws. In contrast, a person who has been arrested, convicted, and punished may develop a greater respect for the law by having personally experienced each of these processes. On the other hand, specific deterrence may not work since people may learn that the law is a paper tiger and that legal punishments are less aversive than once believed.

Justification for the use of punishment in criminal law is found in the writings of philosophers, early criminal justice writers, and other social scientists. Immanuel Kant, for example, believed that offenders should be punished for their crimes simply to support the absolute principle of "justice," regardless of any possible deterrent effects (see Van den Haag 1975). In the eighteenth century, Jeremy Bentham (1962), a foremost English representative of the classical school of criminal justice, based his theory of criminal law on a general deterrence model. According to Bentham, humans are rational beings with free will who choose to maximize pleasure and minimize pain. When someone considers breaking the law, he or she calculates a rough ratio between the potential pleasure to be received and the risk of being detected and punished. For criminal law to be effective, potential lawbreakers must know that the legal penalty for the offense is greater than the pleasure derived from the crime. Furthermore, the certainty of the punishment was considered by classical theorists to be more important than the severity of the punishment (Andenaes 1983).

Toward the end of the nineteenth century and into the first half of the twentieth, many theorists and practitioners adopted the belief that punishment was an unjust retributive act of revenge that had little purpose. Treatment and rehabilitation became the rallying cry of criminologists, psychologists, and penologists. Punishment was redefined to meet the needs of the individual offender. With the introduction of indeterminate sentences, prisoners were detained as long or as short as necessary for a "cure." However, by the 1960s, another change in criminological thought emerged. Penologists and others lost confidence in the belief that treatment and rehabilitation can function as the bases for a system of legal sanctions. Interest once again centered on deterrence and other forms of punishment, such as fixed sentences in proportion to the seriousness of the offense, as favored means of social control.

Effectiveness of the Deterrence Model

Common sense suggests that people will not commit crimes if the legal consequences of detection and conviction are severe. However, extreme penalties, such as the Middle-Eastern practice of cutting off the hands of thieves, are morally unacceptable in Western society even though they may be effective deterrents. Penalties must be perceived as reasonable, humane, and just if the deterrence model is to have a valid moral basis for legislators, judges, law enforcement officials, and the general public. Before specifying some of the factors needed for deterrence, it must be acknowledged that certain crimes involving children, the mentally deficient, psychopathological states, extreme passion, and politics will not be deterred regardless of the certainty and severity of punishment. Even crimes involving the death penalty for "statutory rape" would not deter a man from having sex with a young girl if he believed her consent freed him from charges (Gibb 1975).

General deterrence depends upon a number of factors:

1. *Public knowledge and severity of the punishment.* Obviously, if people are not aware of the law and the differences in penalties for criminal activities, their illegal behavior will not be deterred. While the public understands the significance of more serious crimes, they are not well informed about differences in penalties in relation to the seriousness of the crime. Survey research of Arizona residents, for instance, indicated that most citizens were ignorant of the differences in severity of punishments between first-degree burglary and second degree (Gibbs and Erickson 1979).

2. *Credibility of the threat.* Awareness of the law and the penalty imposed on lawbreakers has little effect on behavior if people do not believe they will be apprehended and, if detected, do not believe they will be prosecuted. Certainty of punishment as opposed to severity is considered by most authorities to be the more important characteristic for deterrence (Andenaes 1983).

Credibility of a deterrence threat also depends on how the courts and the police administer the law. When penalties are perceived as unjust because of undue harshness (as in sentences of ten years or more for simple possession of marijuana), the public may fail to report crimes to the police, the police may decide not to press charges, prosecutors may recommend that charges be dropped, and judges and/or juries may not convict. Without credible punishments, decision-making at different levels of the justice system may be affected and tends to reduce the deterrence effect of the law.

3. *Types of offenses and rational decisions.* The concept of deterrence depends to a great extent on the type of crime being committed and its related penalties. Thus, motorists may be deterred from drunk driving if they know that imprisonment is certain, but they may not be overly concerned with a fine for speeding. Drunk driving is affected by the introduction of tough legislation, providing the threat of punishment is swift, certain, and severe. In addition, the law must be well publicized so that the public is fully aware that intoxicated drivers will be punished (Ross 1983).

Certain types of offenses referred to as *instrumental acts* are more likely to be deterred by criminal sanctions than other more *expressive acts* (Chambliss 1969). Instrumental acts, such as shoplifting, are crimes committed as a means to an end. In contrast, expressive acts, such as drug use, are committed because the act in itself is pleasurable. According to Chambliss, a deterrent will be most effective for instrumental acts, whereas expressive acts are resistant to penalties. Although this model is logical, other researchers doubt its analytical value (see Andenaes 1983). Finally, the deterrence model assumes that people are rational and decide to commit crimes by weighing the risks of being caught relative to the rewards to be gained. Critics of this model argue that most crimes, especially those involving passion, drugs, or alcohol, are not the result of rational thinking, but the consequence of impulse and spontaneous reactions.

4. *Labeling theory.* It is argued that people often behave consistent with the labels others attach to them. Thus, if an individual is punished for breaking the law and is labeled a dangerous criminal, he or she may be motivated thereafter to live up to that social definition.

Is Capital Punishment a Deterrent to Homicide?

The death penalty has generated legal, moral, and political controversies for the past two centuries. Abolition groups throughout the world have attempted to eliminate or restrict capital punishment with varying amounts of success. They believe that the death penalty is unjustified on the grounds that it is cruel, inhuman, and degrading of the right to life. Following World War II, the death penalty was abolished or at least greatly restricted in several countries. More recently, interest has developed in the reintroduction of capital punishment where it has been repealed, and strong demands are being made for its broader application. Whenever there is a noticeable increase in despicable crimes, a large portion of society enthusiastically demands the reinstatement or use of the death penalty. Many supporters of capital punishment argue that the protection of the public requires the execution of murderers, traitors, kidnappers, and rapists. Furthermore, they believe that the death penalty does deter such crimes (Thomas 1977).

Public opinion polls in recent years show that over 65 percent of North Americans favor capital punishment for murder (Rankin 1979; Vidmar and Dittenhoffer 1981). However, in the United States Supreme Court decision of *Furman v. Georgia* (1972), Justice Thurgood Marshall postulated that (1) people are generally uninformed about capital punishment, and (2) if they were aware about the facts of deterrence (capital punishment does not deter crime) and about the facts of actual application of the death penalty (it is cruel and applied unfairly and capriciously), they would be opposed to it. Marshall's hypothesis has been supported by research done in both the United States (Sarat and Vidmar 1976) and Canada (Vidmar and Dittenhoffer 1981). The greater the public's knowledge of issues involved in the death penalty, the greater the number of people who oppose it. For example, the general public is generally not aware of the high relationship between race and capital punishment in rape cases. A study of 1,265 cases in eleven Southern and U.S. border states from 1945 to 1965 showed that blacks were sentenced to death seven times more frequently than whites. The probability that these differences could have happened by chance were one in thousand. This study also indicated a cross-racial effect. Blacks convicted of raping whites received the death penalty in 36 percent of the cases. In contrast, only 2 percent of the blacks who raped blacks or whites who raped whites received the death penalty (Wolfgang and Riedel 1976). The conclusion can be drawn that racial discrimination is a primary factor in the execution of rapists.

Although the research literature examining the deterrent effect of the death penalty is controversial, most social scientists have concluded that capital punishment is not an effective deterrent to murder. Prior to 1975, the general consensus among most social scientists was that capital punishment did not deter homicide rates. This conclusion was based on studies that (1) compared the homicide rate between contiguous states with and without the death penalty (Sellin 1959); (2) compared longitudinal changes in the murder rates associated with the abolition or reinstatement of the death penalty (Samuelson 1969); and (3) compared homicide rates of states having relatively high rates of execution with states having relatively low rates of execution (Schuessler 1952). In 1975, Isaac Ehrlich published the results of an econometric study of homicide rates and use of capital punishment in the United States for the period of 1933 to 1969. Ehrlich reported that the use of capital punishment reliably lowered the homicide rate and concluded that executions significantly deter homicide. Furthermore, he estimated that each execution deterred seven to eight potential murders. Other researchers, however, have not been able to replicate these findings, and Ehrlich's econometric model and research results have been discredited (see Lempert 1983).

The Death Penalty and the Police

Most police officers support the use of capital punishment (Crawford and Crawford 1983, Fagan 1986). One officer put his feelings this way:

> Why should we keep them for years in the slammer? They only come back to haunt you when they get out. I figure my life is worth his. All those bleeding hearts say that capital punishment isn't a deterrent as far as murder is concerned. It sure puts a stopper on the guy who has murdered. He won't murder anybody anymore. It is scary out there if you allow yourself to think too much. Here are all these murderers coming out on the street after a long stretch. Do you think they are rehabilitated? Hell, put them in a position where they are going to get caught and sent back, and they are going to kill, for sure, and it's us that they are going

to kill. Those politicians and judges aren't the ones that have to face these guys; it's us, and the fewer of them the better! (Quoted in Vincent 1979, 93)

Although the police may reluctantly accept the conclusion that the death penalty in general does not deter homicides, the police probably feel more protected in carrying out their duties knowing that the death penalty is in effect. The death penalty in their view is an added measure of protection against lethal assaults. This belief has recently been put to an empirical test. Bailey (1982) found that the rate of police killings from 1961 to 1971 did not differ between abolitionist states and retentionist states. Furthermore, the actual use of the death penalty was not an effective deterrent to police killings. Bailey concluded that capital punishment is not the solution to resolving the danger to life of police officers.

> The greatest burden of responsibility for preventing assaults on police must fall upon the police themselves. . . . Paramount in solving the assault of police problem is the great need for special training of police officers . . . to anticipate and handle potential assaults . . . in the long run, only the police can effectively take measures to prevent assaults. (Creamer and Robin 1970, 494)

SUMMARY

Police power is the legitimate capacity ascribed by the state to alter the actions of others. Five types of police power have been distinguished: exploitive power, manipulative power, competitive power, nutrient power, and integrative power. Conformity and compliance occur when citizens change their behavior or their beliefs as a result of social pressure. In general, people find it difficult to resist the demands of authority.

Examples of coercion tactics used by rapists to control their victims and coercive persuasion techniques used by police to induce confessions have been presented in this chapter. The effectiveness of punishment as a deterrent to crime and the question of whether capital punishment is a deterrent to homicide have been discussed.

7

Psychological Theories of Criminal Behavior

In the nineteenth century, "slum poverty" was the generally accepted explanation for the cause of crime and the development of delinquency. In the early part of the twentieth century, experts spoke about the "absence of love" in childhood as the primary cause of crime. Criminologists, sociologists, and psychologists no longer attempt to understand the cause of crime in a single isolated dimension; instead, recognize several complex factors each of which may interact with other factors. Many of the theoretical explanations for the causes of crime, be they sociological, economical, or political, are beyond the scope of this book and will not be included in this review. However, I will look at the major psychological and psychobiological theories of delinquency. For these purposes, *crime* is defined as "a kind of human behavior that is *deviant* by certain established standards of authority in society" (Radelet 1980, 483). Researchers, however, fail to use common and consistent behavioral criteria to define the term *delinquency*. Consequently, unless otherwise stated, I will define the term using the legal criteria— that is, an individual is a delinquent when so adjudicated by the courts.

Kurt Lewin's (1951) highly regarded and often cited conclusion is that "there is nothing so practical as a good theory" (p. 169). A good theory both guides new research and practice and integrates existing knowledge to allow better understanding and explanation. Some psychological theories have proven useful in providing tools to ascertain what happens in the mind of a delinquent before, during, and after he or she commits the criminal act. Other psychological theories focus more on understanding the reasons for delinquent behavior and how it is acquired, what situational and personal forces maintain the behavior, and what is needed to change the behavior. The fact that a delinquent's behavior may be better understood from theoretical insights, however, does not mean that legal conventions are to be abandoned and legal responsibility absolved. Laypersons, along with many legislators, trial judges, attorneys, and police rely upon "fireside inductions" (common sense, anecdotes, introspection, practical experience, and cultural stereotypes) to construct, explain, or enforce laws (Meehl 1971). Psychologists and other social scientists are generally skeptical about fireside inductions since they believe that generalizations about the causes and control of human behavior should be subjected to scientific investigation whenever possible. Nevertheless, common sense and cultural beliefs about human behavior cannot be ignored since they are not necessarily incorrect and may not be anymore unreasonable and contradictory than academic theories.

Before I review the different theories of what causes one person to be a criminal and someone else to obey the law, the belief that people can be categorized into criminal typologies on the basis of personality types and behavioral tendencies has to be rejected (Sarbin 1979). Psychological typologies, such as introverts and extroverts, are theoretical and empirical constructs that have been put forward for other reasons than to explain crime. Still, social typing of criminals is commonly practiced, even though it is a process that has more to do with beliefs, racial and ethnic prejudice, and observations of public behavior that serve the immediate purpose of the observer than with explanation and understanding.

Classification of people into criminal and noncriminal categories on the basis of social typing distorts the reality of crime and criminality. Crimes of violence or street crimes such as assault and armed robbery typically receive the greatest attention from both the public and legal authorities. These crimes are most often associated with the poor and ghetto cultures. Middle-class delinquents (such as embezzlers and forgers) and white-collar crimes of "successful" society (such as corporate violence [see Monahan, Novaco and Geis 1979]) are probably more damaging to society, but they receive the least attention from the criminal justice system. When police or others classify people into criminal or noncriminal categories, they focus primarily on the poor and rely on stereotyped beliefs that are related to class differences and the belief in the likelihood that these people are dangerous. The social alienation and cynicism towards the law and the criminal justice system from those person who are the most disadvantaged members of society can be readily appreciated.

Descriptions of the frequency of crime and criminality are dependent upon official statistical reports gathered by law enforcement agencies. Most crimes are not solved or are not reported to police. Consequently, our understanding about criminal types is biased, depending as it does primarily upon a complex perceptual and social filtering process of cleared police complaints. Knowledge about criminal types may include only information about the least competent, those who draw police attention, or those who want to be captured, rather than those who are successful enough to remain undetected. Thus, present categorizations of criminal types based upon social typing is incomplete and, worse, mythical (Sarbin 1979).

LAY EXPLANATIONS OF
CRIME AND DELINQUENCY

Lay understanding of delinquency has been assessed by a number of surveys. In one public opinion poll, nearly two thousand respondents were given ten statements representing popular explanations for crime and asked to select those they thought most important. Over 70 percent chose one or more of the following: "Nowadays people feel they can get something for nothing and not have to work for it"; "There is so much emphasis today on getting rich quick that people feel money is the most important thing"; "Parents do not have enough authority over children today"; and "So many people get away with breaking the law that the rest feel it is not so bad to break it." Secondary cause of crime chosen by between 50 percent and two-thirds of the sample were: "People being persuaded to buy things they didn't really want and couldn't really afford"; "School teachers not having enough authority over children"; and "People working in boring jobs and not having enough to do in their spare time." A substantial minority of the sample thought that an important cause of crime was the fact that "People were less religious than they used to be." The two least preferred explanations for crime chosen by this sample were the effects of war and its habituating influence on violence generally and the fear of war and uncertainty about the future (Banks, Maloney, and Willcock 1975).

In a study specifically interested in laypersons' causal explanations of delinquency, Reuterman (1978) found that the public acknowledges that multiple factors are responsible for delinquency, but that women, more than men, tend to favor explanations centering on problems in the home and family. A CBS/*New York Times* poll conducted in 1977 showed that two-thirds of their sample blamed crime and delinquency on "conditions of unemployment" and the "leniency of the law," while 60 percent felt that "a lot of blame" can be attributed to "the way judges apply the law" as well as to "the breakdown of religion and morality in families" (Jensen 1981). Starting with a list of over forty-five explanations for delinquency, Furnham and Henderson (1983) found that laypersons have six primary explanations for delinquent behavior: defective education, mental instability, temptation, excitement, alienation, and lack of proper parental guidance. Thus, lay theories of criminal behavior can be said to encompass sociological factors (education and unemployment), family practices (parents), and psychological and biological explanations (mental instability, inability to resist temptation, and search for excitement). More recently, in a survey that examined offense-specific explanations for delinquency rather than following the more traditional global approach used by other investigators, Hollin and Howells (1987) discovered that the public believes that robbery and burglary are caused through long-term failures of parenting and the education system, whereas sexual assaults are a result of mental instability of the offender.

Obviously, a grain of truth runs through most lay theories of delinquency, but at the same time, there is a mixture of errors, fundamental oversights, and simplistic generalizations in public beliefs. Each of the following theories of criminal behavior focuses on different descriptive levels of knowledge that lead to different causal explanations and different proposed solutions to problems. The worth of these theories depends upon their ability over time to generate and survive the test of scientific empirically-based research and provide explanations that lead to more thorough understanding of the complexity of the problems involved in crime.

PSYCHOBIOLOGICAL THEORIES

Genetic Factors

A popular but false theory commonly referred to as the *bad seed explanation* for criminality is the notion that individuals are destined to be criminals because of their heredity. This idea is nonsensical because criminality is not directly inherited anymore than intelligence or mental illness are directly inherited. Instead, all behavior, including criminality, is influenced by the genetic inheritance of physiological and biochemical potentialities. Genes affect behavior by influencing how the nervous system functions. However, behavior is never solely determined by heredity since all genetic factors also interact with environmental factors. All behavior, including antisocial acts, is the product of an interaction between a person's heredity and his or her environment. If criminality is related to genetics, then inherited predispositions, such as fearlessness and aggressiveness, must interact with a powerful negative environment in order to increase the probability that a person will engage in criminal activities. Similarly, if those genetic potentialities that are said to be important in the development of criminality interact with a powerful positive environment, there will be a high probability that the individual will develop behavioral tendencies compatible with more socially approved occupations that also value these characteristics, such as law enforcement or deep sea diving. People are not predisposed to a life of criminality just because they have a family history of antisocial behavior. Genetics do not determine behavior. They do, however, play a role in behavior, including criminal behavior (Mednick 1986).

The evidence for a relationship between heredity and criminality is based on several American, Danish, and Swedish adoption studies and studies of identical and fraternal twins. Children with criminal biological parents who are adopted in infancy are more likely to develop criminal behaviors than are children with noncriminal biological parents. These results occur even if the adoptees of criminal biological parents are raised by noncriminal adoptive parents (Cadoret et al. 1975; Cloninger et al. 1982; Mednick, Gabrielli, and Hutchings 1984). In a study of 14,427 Danish male adoptees, Mednick and his colleagues discovered that if neither their adoptive or biological parents had been convicted of a crime, 13.5 percent of the adoptees became criminals. If the adoptive parents were criminals and the biological parents were not criminals, 14.7 percent of the adoptees had a criminal record. The proportion of adoptees who became criminals rose to 20 percent if they had at least one biological parent who had been convicted of a property crime. If both their biological and adoptive parents had been convicted of property crimes, 24.5 percent of the adoptees became criminals. These results support the hypothesis that genetic influences play a small but significant role (along with a supportive environment) in the cause of crime. This study also showed that 4.09 percent of the adoptees were chronic offenders (three or more court convictions) and were responsible for 69.4 percent of the court convictions received by all the adoptees studied. These results support the often expressed idea that a small number of offenders is responsible for the majority of known crimes.

Twin studies of adult criminals also implicate the role of genetics in criminality (Cloninger et al. 1978; Fuller and Thompson 1978). Identical twins have an identical genetic make-up, whereas fraternal twins are no more alike genetically than ordinary brothers and sisters. The home environment of any twins, however, is likely to be similar. Evidence indicates that identical male twins are more like one another in criminality than are fraternal male twins. If one identical twin is convicted for criminal behavior, the likelihood that the other would also be convicted is 35 percent, but if the twins are fraternal the probability is only 12 percent (Christiansen 1970). Since the concordance rate of heredity and criminal behavior is far from perfect (100 percent), these results indicate that genes influence the predisposition for the development of criminal behavior in supportive environmental conditions.

The relationship between the so-called supermale XYY chromosomal syndrome and criminality, particularly violent criminality, is also important in behavior genetics. Males typically have 46 chromosomes and two of them are the sex chromosomes X and Y, commonly referred to as the *XY chromosomal configuration*. In 1965, researchers reported that an extra Y-chromosome configuration (XYY) discovered in some men was related to abnormally high levels of aggressive behavior, mental retardation, and tall stature (Jacobs et al. 1965). Investigators at that time discovered that a number of infamous murders (Robert Peter Tait in Australia, Daniel Hugon in France, and John [Sean] Farley in the United States), possessed an extra Y-chromosome. Defense lawyers were quick to use the XYY abnormality as the basis of their defense, arguing that their clients were not responsible for their actions because of this chromosomal syndrome. This early work has been discredited because of the faulty research methods used. More recent studies using valid methodological and statistical research designs have failed to find support for the hypothesis that XYY men are particularly violent or aggressive (Witkin et al. 1976). Also, men with an XYY chromosome pattern are no more likely to commit criminal offenses than are men of similar intelligence with the normal XY chromosome pattern (Theilgaard 1983).

Physiological Processes

Central Nervous System.   While genes influence the growth and structure of all living organisms, one of the causes of behavior is the internal chemistry of the body and the brain. From a strict biological point of view, the *central nervous system* produces behavior by creating muscular, skeletal, and glandular reactions. When individual nerve cells or neurons function properly, electrical energy sweeps across nerve cells and causes complex chemical reactions to occur in the synapses (gaps) between neurons. These chemical reactions act as transmitters or inhibitors carrying messages from one part of the body to another. When neurons are disturbed, damaged, or drugged, the chemical process is upset, and this may result in memory loss, poor judgment, learning failures, and under- or over-reaction to stress. Scientists can monitor the electrical activity of the central nervous system using electroencephalographic (EEG) scalp recordings.

Researchers applying these techniques to the study of incarcerated individuals have found abnormal physiological functioning of the central nervous system (that is, a slowing of the EEG frequency) in a significant number of criminals (approximately 50 percent) compared to 10 percent of individuals in the general population (see Mednick and Volavka

[1980] for a review of the literature). These inmates show slower EEG wave activity than would be expected on the basis of their chronological age—a finding suggesting that they may be maturationally slow in cerebral development and thus retarded their socialization and cognitive awareness (Forssman and Frey 1953).

The finding of abnormal brain activity in criminals may be attributed to a number of factors such as heredity, brain injury, drugs, or even the antisocial behavior itself. Which of these factors is a cause or a consequence of criminal behaviors is an important issue. That is, is the abnormal brain activity found in some criminals a cause of their criminal behavior, or is the excessive amount of slow EEG activity a consequence of involvement in criminal activities? Support for the hypothesis of a causal link between criminal behavior and heredity has been found in neurophysiological studies conducted by Mednick and his colleagues. In a study conducted in Denmark in 1972, EEG recordings of 129 boys ages 11 to 13 were obtained (see Mednick et al. 1981). Six years later, some of these children had been arrested for a variety of offenses (mainly involving property). EEG recordings for boys who had become delinquent showed excessive slow-wave EEG activity as compared to nonoffenders (Mednick et al. 1981). In 1981, a follow-up study was conducted on these same subjects, now about age 21 (Gabrielli and Mednick 1983). Using the same EEG recordings obtained in 1972, an attempt was made to discriminate from police registers the repeat offenders from one-time offenders and nonoffenders. Results showed that the 1972 EEG recordings continued to discriminate between groups and that "chronic" offenders (individuals arrested five or more times) had the greatest increase in relative percentage of slower EEG activity (Gabrielli and Mednick 1983).

Autonomic Nervous System. Similar results have been found in studies focusing on the *autonomic nervous system* (ANS). One of the functions of the ANS is to mediate the physiological processes that are associated with emotion. Some criminals have been found to show significantly different ANS responses to various stimuli compared to noncriminals. In particular, prisoners who suffer from antisocial personality disorders (formerly called *sociopaths* or *psychopaths*) have been found, in contrast to less psychopathic prisoners, to exhibit significantly less ANS responsiveness (change in heart rate, blood pressure, respiration, muscle tension, and so on) and less emotional apprehension in anticipation of noxious stimuli like electric shock (Hare 1965).

The most salient characteristics of antisocial disordered persons are ". . . unreliability; insincerity; pathological lying and deception; egocentricity; poor judgment; impulsivity; a lack of remorse, guilt, or shame; an inability to experience empathy or concern for others, and to maintain warm, affectional attachments; an impersonal and poorly integrated sex life; and an unstable life-plan with no long-term plans or commitments" (Hare 1986, 189). Hare emphasizes that the asocial and antisocial behavior of criminal antisocial personalities is evident in adolescence and continues throughout much of the lifespan. Antisocial persons repeatedly fail to learn from punishment and are unresponsive to aversive feedback from family, friends, or formal agencies when they break moral and legal regulations. This failure to learn from punishment is probably related to their high rate of recidivism. Hare states that although socioeconomic and family dynamics contribute to psychopathology, it is almost certain that constitutional and genetic factors are the primary contributors (Hare 1986).

It may be concluded that the results of central nervous system studies and autonomic nervous system studies support the hypothesis that there are some brain states and genetic conditions that are important predisposing factors in criminal behavior. However, as stated earlier, physiological, biological, and genetic potentialities must interact with a powerful, supportive environment to increase the probability that criminal behavior will be produced.

Sensation-Seeking Behavior.   For some individuals an involvement in criminal activities such as robbery and assault may be engaged in not for material gain, but as an exciting alternative to a life that is usually boring and monotonous. Persons who have an excessive need for thrills may be pushed in this direction because of their physiological make-up (Zuckerman 1978), and such needs may be satisfied through delinquent activities.

The construct of sensation-seeking is derived from a theory that humans are driven or motivated to obtain and maintain an optimal level of emotional arousal. Zuckerman (1979) has found that individuals with high sensation-seeking needs are more extroverted, more thrill-seeking, more impulsive, more anti-social and nonconformist, and less anxious.

Other researchers have shown that adolescents who need higher levels of stimulation and live in recreational and culturally barren communities are likely to engage in delinquent behavior. For these adolescents, sensation-seeking drives may be satisfied through anti-social acts (Farley 1973; Farley and Farley 1972; White, Labouvie, and Bates 1985).

Thus considerable evidence is now available to support the hypothesis that biological factors are related to a propensity to develop criminal behavior under proper environmental conditions. The fact that scientific knowledge of biological factors could be used to diagnose an individual's potential criminality at childhood and adolescence is disturbing to some people. Most people want to believe that criminal behavior can be changed with proper treatment and rehabilitation programs. Some are reluctant to accept any scientific evidence that links crime to biological factors because it suggests to them the deterministic position that nothing can be done about crime and that the offender is untreatable. Resistance to the concept of biological determinants of crime also centers on ethical concerns and civil rights issues. Critics suggest that identifying children from biological diagnostic tests and labeling them as potential adult criminals is unethical since the children and others may develop a fatalistic attitude that they are destined to be criminals. Critics also appear to believe that if biological determinants of criminal behavior are accepted, the only intervention techniques possible would be medical in nature, such as psychotropic drugs and psychosurgery.

What these critics fail to appreciate is that all intervention practices, including any that may arise from a better understanding of biological factors that predispose criminality, are subject to ethical and civil rights concerns. Furthermore, knowledge of genetic predispositions of criminality does not imply that treatments must be medical or biological. Identification of biologically at-risk children would facilitate the isolation of specific environmental interventions, such as the introduction of family counseling and remedial and educational upgrading, and, most importantly, attempts to stabilize the home conditions for the child, particularly in early adolescence. Mednick (1986) found that "if the adolescent period was spent in a stable family, the biological predisposition did not result in delinquency outcomes. It was only in unstable family circumstances during early adolescence that the biological factors seemed to be criminogenic" (p. 209).

Interestingly, the biological model is appealing to some people but for the wrong reasons. School administrators may find attributing delinquency to biological factors useful since it absolves them of any blame for delinquent behavior (Wertlieb 1982).

PSYCHOLOGICAL THEORIES

Psychoanalysis

Although Sigmund Freud did not specifically focus on criminal behavior, his theory of personality development influenced several other analytic theorists.

Briefly, Freud's psychodynamic theory of personality development works as follows:

Freud (1940) proposed that three distinctive personality components, id, ego, and superego, emerge in early childhood. The *id* is the primitive core of personality and contains all of the basic bodily and instinctual drives that press for immediate gratification. The id operates strictly on the "pleasure principle." The *ego* emerges as a part of personality as the young child learns that the id's pleasure-dominated desires often produce pain and may best be satisfied by a logical, rational approach to situations. Thus, the ego operates on the "reality principle." As the child develops, he or she begins to identify with parents and internalize their values and standards of morality. This process results in the *superego* splitting off from the ego into a conscience concerned with moral issues, self-sacrifice, idealism, and heroism. The superego combines with the ego to keep the person on a moral track and serves to check the pleasure-seeking tendencies of the id. When the ego behaves morally, the person's superego is gratified, but when the ego is pressed to do something immoral, the superego creates feelings of shame and guilt. Freud (1940) hypothesized that the ego was constantly forced to work out compromises between its three harsh masters, the id, the superego, and reality. The greater the intensity of the conflicts among these masters, particularly the demands of the id to express primitive drives, the greater the anxiety generated in the individual. In order to cope with these anxieties, the individual normally attempts to manage his or her resources with various types of defense mechanisms, such as denial or repression. Overutilization of defense mechanisms, however, may result in behaviors symptomatic of abnormality. The principle argument of psychoanalysis pertaining to delinquency is that it results from a lack of effective personal controls due to faulty early childhood training. Faulty early training or parental neglect results in the child's having little ability to control his or her impulses (Aichhorn 1935). An antisocial character structure that interferes with the child's ability to adequately handle realistic demands from society and from a changing environment may develop in these circumstances (Friedlander 1947).

According to psychoanalytic perspectives, faulty development in early childhood may produce criminal behavior because of one or more of the following reasons:

> (1) Criminal behavior is a form of neurosis which does not differ in any fundamental way from other forms of neurosis (e.g., while some neurotics work too hard, others set fires. [An examination of the psychoanalytic view of fire-setters is presented below.]); (2) the criminal often suffers from a compulsive need for punishment in order to alleviate guilt feelings and anxiety stemming from unconscious strivings; (3) criminal activity may be a means of obtaining substitute gratification of needs and desires not met inside the family; (4) delinquent behavior is often due to traumatic events whose memory has been repressed; and (5) delinquent behavior may be an expression of displaced hostility. All of these interpretations would suggest that, although an original difficulty arose in the child's early environment, by the time delinquent behavior occurs such causal factors are operating contemporaneously within the offender. (Warren and Hindelang 1979, 172–73)

Fire-Setting.   Sixty percent of nonsanctioned firesetting activity comes from children and adolescents (Mieszala 1981). In 1982, 55 percent of all persons arrested for arson were under 18 years of age (U.S. Federal Bureau of Investigation 1983). The economic, medical, and social consequences of these fires runs into the millions of dollars in damages and hundreds of lives lost or injured in any one year (Kolko 1985).

In diagnostic terms, fire-setting is categorized as a conduct disorder along with such behavioral problems as assault, destructiveness, theft, and lying (American Psychiatric Association 1980). Until very recently, psychoanalytic perspectives have dominated the psychiatric and psychological literature on fire-setting (Harris and Rice 1984). Psychoanalytic theory perceives the firesetter as having severe personality problems that are related to sexual disturbance and urinary malfunction.

Freud (1932) stated, "In order to possess himself of fire, it was necessary for man to renounce the homosexually tinged desire to extinguish it with a stream of urine" (p. 405), adding that "the warmth radiated by fire evokes the same kind of glow as accompanies the state of sexual excitation, and the form and motion of the flame suggest the phallis in action" (p. 407). Contemporary psychoanalysts continue to follow Freud's lead and link fire-setting to sexual excitement. Macdonald (1977) offers the following advice to police and arson investigators: "The compulsive firesetter's obvious pleasure from his fire is shown by his bright eyes, flustered face, saliva at the corner of his mouth, and even wet pants from involuntary urination due to his excitement. The investigator will want to talk to anyone seen masturbating in the area of the fire" (p. 223).

I am not psychoanalytically oriented. However, regardless of my personal biases, psychoanalytic perspectives on fire-setting have some critical limitations. Psychoanalysts have drawn their conclusions from the case-history technique using only a small number of patients. Relatively few cases are cited in the literature, but they are cited by several authors, and only those cases that fit the theoretical orientations of these therapists ever are published. Psychoanalysts would have readers believe that there is much more known about fire-setters than is actually the case (Harris and Rice 1984).

Kolko and Kazdin (1986) have developed an experimental model of fire-setting that emphasizes three principal areas: learning experiences and cues, personal repertoires, and parents and family influences and stressors.

1. *Learning experiences and cues.* Fire-setters often have early exposure to fire and become interested in fires through father who work in fire-related occupations (firefighter, furnace stoker, and the like). Accidental fires caused by young children often result from curiosity in playing with matches. Fire-play in very young boys is almost universal and can become part of a child's behavioral repertoire very early in life. Children whose parents smoke and carelessly leave matches about or adults who play with match sticks or peer pressure to participate in group firesetting are antecedent conditions that encourage fire-play and fire-setting.

2. *Personal repertoire.* Given the opportunity to play with matches, few young children can resist experimenting, but most will be unaware

of the dangers inherent in the activity. For some children, cognitive immaturity is compounded by social and personal ineffectiveness. Juvenile fire-starters are often socially immature, angry, overcontrolled, and unable to solve problems in a socially acceptable manner. This group of children and adolescents frequently displays covert antisocial behaviors such as property destruction, cruelty to animals, lying, running away, and truancy. Fire-setting may be the result of curiosity, thrill-seeking, cognitive retardation, emotional disturbance, stress, and anxiety and pathological need for attention, aggression, revenge, jealousy, spite, power and control.

3. *Parental and family influences and stressors.* Fire-setting is highly related to minimal parental supervision. Fathers are frequently absent over protracted periods, and mothers are often uninvolved with the child. Homes of adolescent and child fire-starters are often pathological — that is, there is a presence of one or more of the following conditions: alcohol abuse, psychoses, mental retardation, physical abuse, maternal overprotection, and a history of suicide and homicide. Fire-setters are often the victims of extreme stress, such as family deaths, divorce, separation, or the addition of a new sibling or stepparent.

In sum, firesetters are driven by complex emotional forces. Some firesetters are crying for help, others are acting out their anger and aggression against authority, and still others, are profoundly emotionally disturbed (see Kolko 1985). Fire-setters are more likely to receive beneficial assistance when interventions are guided by behavioral and social considerations rather than focusing on the psychoanalytic dynamics of anxiety disorders.

General Psychopathological Theory

Most clinical psychologists diagnose and treat delinquency in terms of *general psychopathological theory.* Clinicians using this approach typically test their patients for such characteristics as brain damage, intelligence, personality dynamics, and abnormality. These standardized, objective tests are supplemented by both structured and unstructured clinical interviews. The results of such testing are often presented to trial judges and may lead courts to recommend in-depth psychotherapy by professional therapists and/or counselors. The underlying assumption of this approach is the belief that the psychological make-up of the delinquent is the cause of the delinquency. One problem, however, with psychopathological explanations of delinquency is that they often involve circular reasoning. That is, you cannot say that someone who commits a crime must be mentally ill and then turn around and say that the disorder caused the crime. Theories must explain and predict behavior rather than merely describe or define it. (I will have more to say about circular reasoning and police involvement with mentally disordered persons in Chapters 10 and 11).

Research evidence indicates that 5 percent of the persons sentenced to prison are diagnosed as psychotic. This percentage closely matches the estimates of psychoses in the general population (Sutherland and Cressey 1970). Very few psychotics commit crimes (Erickson 1938). The fact that a person is diagnosed as psychotic, however, does not prove that the psychoses caused the criminal behavior. Psychotic prisoners are much more like nonpsychotic prisoners in their social backgrounds than they are like psychotic persons in the general population (Silverman 1946). These results suggest that social backgrounds are related to crime, while severe mental illness is only slightly related to criminality.

Hare (1986) estimates that between 15 and 25 percent of criminal prisoners can be accurately classified as suffering from antisocial personality disorders (psychopaths). These individuals begin their criminal careers at a much younger age than nonpsychopathic criminals and commit a disproportionate number of all crimes. It is likely that their criminal activities are underrepresented in official crime statistics. However, they are not considered to be mentally ill by psychological standards or insane by legal standards. Thus, the concept of psychopathology is related to, but is not an explanation for, crime.

Researchers have found little evidence for attributing personality traits or any of the diagnostic categories of abnormality to the causes of crime (Waldo and Dinitz 1967). If the courts insist on clinicians examining most offenders for possible deep-seated emotional disturbances, their request is more a statement enforcing social control than one of clinical diagnosis and treatment (Miller 1974). Many delinquents display behaviors that are socially unacceptable and even dangerous and bizarre, but this does not mean that they are mentally ill (Hoffman 1984).

Not all psychologists, however, dismiss the possibility of a causal connection between personality and crime. A highly contentious theory proposed by Yochelson and Samenow (1976) and Samenow (1984) suggest that prisoners' criminality is a function of thinking errors that occur from a unique set of cognitive patterns. After working for a number of years with individuals who had been hospitalized for psychiatric evaluation or treatment related to criminal prosecution, this psychiatrist-psychologist team came to the conclusion that criminals have qualitatively different ways of thinking about themselves and their social environment from the vast majority of law-abiding citizens. Although their thoughts are internally logical and consistent, criminals' judgments and decisions are faulty as judged against commonly accepted notions about responsible thinking. They deny any personal responsibility for their criminal activities and blame others, such as schools and "bad" company, for leading them into crime. Many criminals see themselves as "good" people, although they admit committing a large number of crimes for which they have never been arrested. As far as they are concerned, their actions do not injure others, and if anybody is hurt, it is they themselves because they are serving time.

According to Yochelson and Samenow, criminals are in control of and are responsible for their actions rather than being society's victims. Crimes are rationally planned and cannot be attributed to mental illness or "poor" home life or any other environmental explanation. People become criminals as a result of a series of choices they start making at a very early age (as young as 3). It is these choices, accompanied by criminal thought processes of suggestibility, perfectionism, anger, pride, concrete thinking, lying, and fear, that mold lives of criminals. "Crime is like alcoholism: 'once a criminal, always a criminal' " (quoted in Wrightsman 1987, 350). All of these factors constitute for Yochelson and Samenow the "criminal personality."

Yochelson and Samenow describe criminals as having great self-doubt and feelings of worthlessness that they constantly cover up. They will change to law abiding behavior only when they are aware of their free choice to make socially responsible decisions and then decide to act accordingly.

This theory is controversial and has been criticized for methodological weakness by social scientists (see Hylton 1981b). No control groups were studied, and conclusions were drawn from data obtained from intensive interviews of a relatively small sample of selected criminals

—"hard-core" criminals or people in hospitals for the criminally insane. Furthermore, Yochelson and Samenow fail to explain how the "criminal thinking pattern" is caused and what factors force criminals to make their choices at an early age.

Learning Theory

In contrast to the idea that delinquency is symptomatic of internal forces such as repressed impulses, ego deficits, and weak superego development as suggested by psychoanalysts, *learning theory* assumes that deviance, like any other behavior, is learned from the individual's experiences in his or her environment. Learning theory is a major area of study in psychology with many subareas. I will focus, however, on operant conditioning and social cognitive learning.

Operant Conditioning. One of the most prominent learning theory researchers, B. F. Skinner (1969), and his followers explain behavior entirely in stimulus-response set terms. If inappropriate behavior *(deviance)* is frequently rewarded *(reinforced)*, then the strength or probability of that behavior being shown in similar situational circumstances is increased. Individuals learn delinquent behavior by being reinforced for such behaviors. For example, if a person's peer group reinforces him or her for stealing by praise or encouragement, there is a strong likelihood that stealing may be used to get attention or praise in the future. Even negative reinforcements can strengthen deviant behaviors. For instance, if the police punish juveniles and young adults for loitering, this attention may strengthen the disturbing behavior since it may be seen as an interesting diversion in an otherwise boring evening. Conversely, police can control and change the behavior of potential offenders by withholding reinforcements for inappropriate behaviors and rewarding only acceptable behaviors (Ayllon and Azrin 1968).

Social Cognitive Learning. Much of human behavior is acquired through observational learning. People learn through imitation, identification, and modeling the actions, attitudes, and emotional responses displayed by influential others (Bandura 1977). What the child learns in the early affective relationship with his or her parents provides the foundation for the transference of these learned behaviors to other social contexts as the child matures. The home and family provide the context for early social learning about rules, expectations of behavior, and relationships with authority. Teenagers' problems with the law, such as criminal violence, failure to conform to society's rules, and difficulty in relating to police, often can be understood by investigation of child-rearing practices (Sears, Maccoby, and Levin 1957; White and Straus 1981).

Observational learning occurs through real-life forms and through pictorial presentations such as magazines, movies, and television. Offenders may learn delinquent behaviors from watching cartoons and television crime shows or imitate the behavioral and emotional responses of others who they observe successfully violating school and society regulations. People may learn how to be successful burglars and robbers by watching others steal and sell what they steal. Children and adolescents involved in delinquent behaviors such as use of drugs usually grow up in families who use drugs and learn their families' values related to drug use (Jacquith 1981).

According to this approach, delinquent behavior is learned through association or close, personal acquaintances with other delinquents. The best predictor of the extent of a young person's involvement in delinquent activities is the size of his or her delinquent network (Johnson 1979). Delinquency is a product of differential association, learning, reinforcement, and imitation. However, it is possible that other factors rather than associations cause juveniles to become lawbreakers; having delinquent friends may be a result of delinquent behavior rather than a cause of it (Hirschi 1969).

DELINQUENCY

Learning Disabilities and Delinquency

The possibility of a causal connection between learning disabilities and criminal activities has interested psychologists and other professionals for the past two decades. Such a relationship has been difficult to prove, however, because of a general confusion in defining the term *learning disabilities* and the lack of consensus regarding the multitude of behaviors said to be associated with learning problems. One observer even feels that learning disability is not a scientific category but a political concept designed to direct funding to otherwise unclassified persons (Farnham-Diggory 1978). In an attempt to bring order to the verbal chaos surrounding this issue, researchers are insisting on restrictive definitions of learning disabilities such as the following:

> *Children, youth and adults with learning disabilities are those who manifest a significant discrepancy between their estimated learning potential and actual performance. This discrepancy is related to basic disorders in the learning processes, which may or may not be accompanied by demonstratable central nervous system disfunction and which are not secondary to sensory loss, mental retardation, primary emotional disturbance or environmental disadvantage.* (Brosseau and Lock 1979)

The best estimate of the frequency of learning disabilities in juvenile delinquents in the United States has been provided by the American Office of Juvenile Justice and Delinquency Prevention (Keilitz, Zaremba, and Broder 1979). Comparison of a sample of 397 males, 12 to 15 year old, adjudicated juvenile delinquents with a sample of 984 officially nondelinquent boys of the same age revealed that 32 percent of the delinquent group and 16 percent of the nondelinquent group had learning disabilities. It is clear that there is a substantially greater prevalence of learning disability in juvenile delinquents, but whether or not the learning disability caused the delinquency is uncertain. A subsequent study involving over 1,600 juvenile delinquents and nondelinquent boys confirmed the relationship between learning disability and delinquency, but a significant, negative correlation between learning disability and self-reported delinquency was found (Broder et al. 1980). These researchers rejected the claim that learning-disabled boys are more involved in delinquent behaviors than delinquent boys who are not learning-disabled. Instead, they argued that learning-disabled boys have been labeled and treated differently by the juvenile justice system. They assert that the learning-disabled are incorrectly perceived as more criminalistic than their counterparts because of their inability to appreciate the nature of the criminal justice process and their general inadequacy to defend themselves. The case of *In re Gault* (1967) gave juveniles many of the same rights and privileges as adult defenders, such as the right to be notified of charges against them, to be represented by an attorney, to confront and cross-examine witnesses, and to remain silent. However, learning-disabled juveniles frequently fail to comprehend these rights (Wall and Furlong 1985).

Learning disabilities are a reality, but there is little proof that there is a causal linkage between the disability and delinquency (Cellini and Snowman 1982; Coons 1982). Learning disabilities may be related to school failure and, as a consequence, indirectly related to delinquency. A learning-disabled child who consistently fails may be subject to a labeling process by which he or she is evaluated negatively by teachers, peers, and parents. Eventually the child will accept the negative self-image and probably leave school early. Without marketable skills and with considerable time on his or her hands, the learning-disabled child may find support only from association with delinquency-prone people who can easily lead the child into crime. Furthermore, the child may wish to punish society in order to compensate for his or her negative self-concept. Involvement in delinquent acts may be a form of social defiance. Scientific validation for this "school failure rationale," however, is still needed.

Moral Development

Earlier in my discussion of laypersons' theories of the causes of crime and delinquency, I cited the following reasons: "So many people get away with breaking the law that the rest feel it is not so bad to break it"; "There is a breakdown of religion and morality in families"; "Parents do not have enough authority over children today." What determines people's moral judgments, their beliefs about "right" and "wrong"? Psychologists who take a social learning perspective think of moral development as a continuous and cumulative learning process that grows over time. An individual's behavior, including moral judgments, are seen as variable and dependent on situational contexts. Depending upon the circumstances, a person may have learned that honesty is required, but in another situation, he or she may be dishonest. This conceptualization may be contrasted with the moral development approach of Lawrence Kohlberg (1969).

Drawing primarily on the cognitive developmental work of Piaget (1965), Kohlberg theorizes that children pass through six invariant, universal stages in moral development: *the preconventional level* (stages 1 and 2); *the conventional level* (stages 3 and 4); and *the postconventional level* (stages 5 and 6). Each successive stage is considered to be morally superior to the preceding one, and each level represents the individual's

Table 7.1 Kohlberg's Stages of Moral Reasoning

Stage of Moral Reasoning	Moral Behavior Is That Which:
Preconventional morality	
Level 1	Avoids punishment
Level 2	Gains reward or benefit
Conventional morality	
Level 3	Gains approval of others
Level 4	Is defined by rigid codes of "law and order" and doing one's duty
Postconventional morality	
Level 5	Is defined by a "social contract" generally agreed upon for the public good
Level 6	Is based on abstract ethical principles that determine one's own moral code

Source: Adapted from Kohlberg 1969. Reprinted by permission of David A. Goslin.

particular way of valuing human life and relationship to society's rules (see Table 7.1). This theory argues that children, adolescents, and adults reason differently about moral issues as a function of their level of cognitive and moral development. An individual's developmental level determines his or her capacity to make successively higher and more sophisticated moral judgments.

The relevancy of this approach to delinquency are in the possibilities for understanding differences in the moral thinking between offenders and nonoffenders and the opportunity to make stage-related interventions for changing moral judgment and moral behavior. This research is also relevant to the issue of consent and responsibility—that is, at what age and under what social conditions children can be expected to understand and be competent to give or refuse consent (see Tapp and Levine 1977) Research with adolescents generally shows that delinquents, in contrast to their nondelinquent peers, are less mature in areas of cognitive development, especially in their egocentricity, which is reflected in a poor ability to perceive other's viewpoints (Chandler 1973).

Delinquents are at a lower stage of moral reasoning than nondelinquents of the same age and intelligence (Blasi 1980; Kurtines and Greif 1974). In particular, psychopathic delinquents, as opposed to other types of delinquents, seem to account for most of the relationship between moral development and delinquency (Campagna and Harter 1975; Fodor 1973). Most noncriminal adolescents and young adults (75 percent) are classified at the conventional level of morality, whereas the majority of adolescent offenders are classified at the preconventional level of morality. Their moral judgments are decided by two major determinants; the need to avoid punishment and the desire to gain rewards or benefits (Kohlberg and Freundlich 1973). People at the conventional level of morality behave morally much of the time, which suggests that growth in moral reasoning to the third stage will generally "protect" a person from delinquent behavior (Blasi 1980).

Legal scholars (see Zimring and Hawkins 1971) and social scientists (see Tittle and Logan 1973) now recognize that individuals are much more likely to obey the law if the behavior in question elicits disapproval from others important to the person. The impact of legal sanctions is negligible in controling behavior if these sanctions are not also supported by general social disapproval.

Psychologists have know for over fifty years that there is no relationship between knowing what is right or wrong and behaving lawfully or unlawfully (Arbuthnot, Gordon, and Jurkovic 1987). Teaching moral rules to young people will affect behavior only if this information is integrated into a larger, internally consistent cognitive and moral worldview that will generate behavioral choices (Jurkovic 1980). To illustrate this point, Arbuthnot and Gordon (1988) offer the following example:

> A teenage career thief-in-the-making may well know that stealing is "wrong," that is, disapproved of by the larger society, against the law, and likely to result in negative consequences if he is caught and convicted. However, this knowledge will have little impact on him if he wants the money that he can get by stealing, has no concerns about the effects of the theft on the victim, lacks the capacity to view his actions in terms of ultimate effects on the maintenance of mutual trust and respect among members of an orderly society, doesn't think he will be caught, or if he is that he will escape punishment, and/or even if he is that he will reap the admiration of his peer group . . . for this adolescent, stealing is not a moral question . . . it is simply a matter of pragmatics. . . . Moral behavior, then, is not simply a matter of knowing what is right and what is wrong. (Pp. 382–83)

Delinquency can be prevented or at least minimized if the potential career thief can reach stage 3 moral reasoning. This stage can be acquired through interventions that rely on small dilemma-discussion groups of a Socratic nature. Changes in reasoning to stage 3 will most likely be accompanied by changes in moral behavior (Arbuthnot and Gordon 1988).

Religiosity and Delinquency

It has been argued that religion encourages the development of moral values and that if a person is religious, he or she more willingly accepts society's norms and values (Erikson 1966). The proposition that involvement in formal religious activities counteracts engagement in delinquent activity has been supported by some researchers (for example, Rhodes and Reiss 1970), but others have reported no relation between religiosity and delinquency (see Hirschi and Stark 1969). Religious saliency and a belief in the efficacy of personal prayer and orthodoxy have been found to be more highly related to minimizing delinquent behavior than church attendance, according to Elifson, Petersen, and Hadaway (1983). This study showed that victimless crimes (drug use, alcohol, gambling, and unsanctioned sexual behavior) were more strongly related to religiosity than were delinquent acts involving a victim, a finding that suggests that the churches' strong appeals to their members against illegal use of drugs, gambling, and so on have had a positive influence on some antisocial behaviors. Nevertheless, Elifson and his colleagues emphasize that religion by itself is not a strong predictor of legal behaviors. This is probably due to religion being so closely interconnected with family and other moral influences in society. Religious and nonreligious people operate within the same general legal boundaries. Religion is only one of many potential influences, along with family, friends, and peer group, that encourage young people to be law-abiding citizens.

Family Factors and Delinquency

This chapter has reviewed the major biological and psychological factors related to delinquency and crime. All of these variables are related to each other, and it is meaningless to talk about a linear causality of delinquency. However, of all the major environmental variables influencing behavior, the family certainly has a central position. Negative aspects of family environments related to delinquency (marital conflicts, broken homes, frequent moves, poverty, drug use, alcoholism, child and wife battery, parental absence or indifference, rejection and hostility, discipline, hypocritical morality, mental illness, overindulgence, physical birth trauma, and so on) seem to be countless (see, for example, Coates, Peterson, and Perry 1982; Figley and McCubbin 1983). I will conclude this chapter by looking at some of the family influences that promote healthy growth and development and, in their absence, failure and possibly delinquency. Although police officers are not responsible for family life in society at large, they can at least contribute to the community's promotion and support of the healthy family.

The family is the primary socializing agent for the child, providing him or her with nurturance, training, status, and other developmental elements. At adolescence, other socialization sources come into play, with the most significant being the individual's peer group. Although not all authorities would agree, a healthy family can counteract movement toward delinquency, even in the face of heavy peer pressure to participate in the delinquency.

What is a healthy family? Family health can be viewed in one of the following ways: (1) *asymptomatically*—that is, in terms of the absence of symptoms, which suggests health; (2) *optimally*—that is, in terms of looking for the ideal and the positive with special reference to the offsprings' success; (3) with reference to an *average*, or that which fits most families in terms of statistical measures; and (4) *transitionally*, by focusing on universal processes of maintenance and growth of the family in relation to the social system (Walsh 1982).

It is my assumption that healthy families hold fairly elaborate storehouses of knowledge and strategies, or what psychologists call *schemata*, about themselves and about other people. (A thorough discussion of schemata is given in Chapter 10.) Families draw upon those schemas to guide their selection and evaluation of social behaviors. Thus, a healthy family's *self-schema* might include such separate but related factors as: interpersonal intimacy, closeness, involvement, self-worth, values, standards, direction, clear boundaries, autonomy, flexibility, initiative, love, trust, happiness, recognition, sharing, openness, mutual respect, acceptance, consideration, commitment and support. It might exclude such factors as: guilt, excessive control, emotional blackmail, disharmony, rejection, hostility, immaturity, and sexual ambivalence. The individual's healthy family self-schema involve a set of core convictions, beliefs, and assumptions about the social environment that allows the family to ignore certain aspects of the world, follow certain pathways, make decisions, and accept the consequences of those decisions. The life of the family is organized by this schema of values and affections, which continue to emerge and guide the family toward its goals. This schema provides meaning for members of the family and others and carries the moral values of the person and of society. Family maladjustments occur when the healthy family schema breaks down (see Scott and Scott 1983).

Healthy families have healthy children, and healthy adolescence is incompatible with juvenile delinquency. Healthy teenagers seldom have an identity crisis, their relations with parents are "generally" good, and there is little evidence for a so-called generation gap. Healthy teenagers tend to follow their parents' values and life-style. They have many friends and feel competent and self-assured. Finally, healthy young people can and do deal with distress. They tend to share their painful feelings with others rather than blocking or turning inward their fear, depression, or anger (King 1971).

SUMMARY

Crime is behavior that is deviant by certain established standards of authority in society. Lay understandings of causes of crime and delinquency focus mainly on education, unemployment, family practices, mental health, morality, and need for excitement. Psychobiological factors including genetics, central and autonomic nervous system activity, and sensation-seeking behavior and their causal relationship to crime have been explored in this chapter. Theories of crime from the perspectives of several major psychological theories—psychoanalysis, general psychopathology, learning theory, and moral development—have been described. The family is the principle environmental factor influencing the socialization of the child, with the healthy family fostering well-adjusted, moral children.

8

Aggression and Violence

The relationship of the police officer to violence in society is unique and statistics, laboratory studies and post-event analysis are, in a sense, irrelevant to his function and, to a certain extent, must remain so. . . . Academics, the courts and the media can examine violent events in the cool light of day after an examination of all possible alternatives, precedent and neat legal arguments. . . . But, it is the policeman or policewoman, as an individual and very human being, who must deal with violence, coldly and nakedly, as it happens, not as it was or might have been. . . . The issue is far removed from the unreality of inevitable post mortem discussions, where the closest thing to violence are the verbal barbs used in academic arguments. . . . [Critics] must discard the notion that they can be instant experts in police matters and attempt to empathize for a moment with that very human being, who just happened to be dressed in blue and who had to make a decision in relation to the matter in question. ("Cop Critics No Experts Chief Says," *Toronto Star*, October 27, 1979)

Because of the nature of police work, police officers must expect and be able to cope with violence. Society has given the police the power and responsibility to enforce the law and to use justified force if necessary. Recent research indicates that police officers prefer not to use excessive force and are more conservative than comparable citizens (firefighters) in their violence-prone attitudes (Brodsky and Williamson 1985), although there are situations in which unethical means of enforcing the law, including unjustified violence, are used (Felkenes 1984). Police officers often experience extreme stress reactions in dealing with violence and may have to seek psychological help in order to cope with their distress (Kroes and Hurrell 1975).

Most individuals, be they academics, jurists, or media people, probably appreciate the sentiments expressed by Chief Harold Adamson in the quotation cited above. However, this does not mean that the reality of criminal violence, including police violence, should be accepted without critical examination. Aggression and violence, from street crime to domestic violence, threatens not only the quality of life but also citizens' and police officers' lives.

Three types of violence are generally encountered by police officers: (1) violence against the officer (such as being physically attacked, shot at, or verbally assaulted), (2) violence of citizens against citizens or institutions (such as rape, physical assault, family violence, robbery, murder, terrorism, and hostage-taking), and (3) violence police officers use against citizens (such as crowd control and use of deadly force). In this chapter I will focus on a general overview of the theoretical issues involved in the psychology of aggression and criminal violence. An examination of two specific types of criminal violence, rape and sexual assault as well as spouse abuse, and the different police responses made in crisis intervention in these two types of criminal situations are presented in Chapter 9.

DEFINITIONS OF
AGGRESSIVE AND VIOLENT BEHAVIOR

There is no universally accepted definition for either *aggression* or *violence*. Although both of these concepts are described in terms of physical acts or verbal behaviors that can physically and/or psychologically harm others or oneself, "there is no single kind of behavior which can be called 'aggressive' nor is there any single process which represents 'aggression' " (Johnson 1972). The lack of clear identification and interpretation of what is or is not aggressive behavior has important implications for citizens, police, and the courts. For instance, the improper labeling of a mild insult or threat between a police officer and a citizen or between two citizens, can lead to retaliatory behavior that can escalate into violence. The judgment that an action is aggressive depends upon a complex consideration of factors such as who is the aggressor, who is the victim, what is the purpose, and what are the consequences (Mummendey 1984). The same action, for example, committed by a Hells Angel biker and by a priest against an innocent bystander with serious consequences to the bystander may be considered aggressive when performed by the biker but not by the priest.

Anglo-American law recognizes distinctions between kinds or degrees of violence (Goldstein 1986). Society and the courts consider some types of violent acts socially and legally acceptable, but legal violence has its limits. It is legal, for example, for parents to punish their children, but not to batter; it is legal for teachers in some jurisdictions to use corporeal punishment on students, but not excessive strapping. Legal interpretations of violence often are a matter of degree, and the law is not always precise on the dividing line. Illegal acts of violence depend upon considerations of such factors as aggressor age, means, intentionality, forethought, responsibility, damage to victim, and so on.

Psychological theorists (see Baron 1977; Kaufmann 1970) agree that aggression has at least three common characteristics: (1) overt behavior is directed against a victim; (2) there is intent to harm the victim; and (3) there is a reasonable expectation that the act will injure the victim. Violence is the most extreme form of aggressive behavior and is defined as the "overtly threatened or overtly accomplished application of force which results in the injury or destruction of persons or property or reputation, or the illegal appropriation of property" (Megargee 1982b). The courts ultimately must decide on the meaning of "intent to injure."

One example of how aggression can be differentially categorized into a typology of human behaviors is shown in Table 8.1 (Buss 1971).

This typology shows that aggression includes both direct and indirect physical and verbal acts that can be active or passive in content. Active varieties of aggression involve the intentional delivery of physical or psychological injury to another, whereas passive varieties primarily cause psychological injuries to others. Police officers, like everyone else, face all eight types of aggression both in their work and in their private lives. It is significant that modern policing is cognizant of

Table 8.1 A Typology of Human Aggressive Behaviors

	Active		Passive	
	Direct	*Indirect*	*Direct*	*Indirect*
Physical	Punching the victim	Practical joke; booby trap	Obstructing passage; sit-in	Refusing to perform a necessary task
Verbal	Insulting the victim	Malicious gossip	Refusing to speak	Refusing consent, vocal or written

Source: Buss 1971. Reprinted by permission of the author and Academic Press from A. H. Buss, "Aggression Pays." In J. L. Singer, ed., *The Control of Aggression and Violence* (New York: Academic Press), 8.

psychological injuries and does not dwell solely on the physical varieties of aggression.

Aggression is subdivided into two basic types, *hostile* and *instrumental*, according to the type of primary goals or reinforcers that the aggressor seeks (Baron 1977). In hostile aggression, the primary goal is to inflict pain and injury on the victim. Seeing the victim suffer through the delivery of physical or verbal punishment is reinforcing to the aggressor. This sort of aggression is always accompanied by anger on the part of the aggressor. Bank robbers, for example, who have to bloody customers' heads or humiliate the bank manager in the process of a hold-up, exhibit an extreme form of hostile aggression. Instrumental aggression also involves an intent to injure. However, the primary goal is some external reward such as money, power, or recognition. Instrumental aggression, unlike hostile aggression, is a means to an end rather than an end in itself. The aggressor, who may or may not be angry, is willing to hurt or kill in order to attain his or her goal. Thus, a bank robber may shoot at a police officer in order to avoid arrest but the robber's immediate goal at that point in time is to escape capture rather than to injure or kill. A clear distinction, however, between hostile and instrumental aggression is difficult to differentiate empirically. All aggressive acts are instrumental insofar as they seek some end—as in seeing a victim suffer or stealing his or her possessions or both of these purposes.

Extreme aggression and violent behaviors that are prohibited by federal or state legislation amount to criminal violence. For the purposes of this book, *criminal violence* is defined as "engaging in or threatening behavior that is (1) directly injurious or destructive, or potentially injurious or destructive, to persons or property, and (2) currently prohibited by state and/or federal laws and statues" (Megargee 1982b).

OFFICER-CIVILIAN VIOLENCE

Police officers are normally not aggressive, although in some situations they are expected to be assertive. Police assertiveness involves the use of legitimate physical or verbal force to achieve goals, such as restricting citizens' mobility in crowd control. *Assertiveness* involves communicating directly without intent to harm or injure others. Any physical injury or emotional distress to citizens is incidental to the officer's attempt to take control. Obviously, there can be great differences of opinion over whether or not police behavior is perceived as aggressive or assertive.

When police officers are beaten, shot at, critically wounded, or killed, these acts and consequences have repercussions on all of society. Such incidents typically stimulate the press and senior police officials to seek greater public support. Calls for greater availability and use of bullet-proof vests, permission to obtain and use heavier, more lethal weapons, and the need to hire more police to combat the evils of the street are frequently heard. The image of police officers as warriors against the unlawful masses becomes reinforced, often at the cost of minimizing the valuable police practices of engaging in public support and social services and keeping the peace.

According to Toch (1976):

Violence-inspired responses may not only create new violence for the police and the community, but for individual officers and citizens. Officers may be more likely to kill suspects who make "furtive movements" towards guns that never materialize. If a stimulus is ambiguous, an officer is more likely to infer the possibility of danger if his perceptions are conditioned by fear. Reactions to low probability violence (if it is extreme enough) can increase the chances of violent reactions, which in turn create occasions for fear. Riots illustrate this process, because they often break out when police incidents are viewed by hostile spectators against a backdrop of past police-citizen confrontations. (Pp. 13–14)

Although police are involved in many varieties of criminal violence, a review of all types of violence directed against police, such as robbery-related assaults, ambush attacks, and the like, is beyond the scope of this book (see, for example, Meyer et al. 1982; Meyer et al. 1981).

Most police contact with the public involves traffic cases such as speeding, driving while intoxicated, and reckless driving. The offender may be frightened, resentful, feeling guilty, frustrated, or angry. The interaction between the officer and the offender may be civil at best; at worst, it may be violent and deadly assaultive (Westley 1970). Individual differences exist among officers on the likelihood of being assaulted. In addition to the factors of chance and accidental misfortune, some police officers are particularly prone to assault (Renner and Gierach 1975). Differences in victimization among officers can be attributed to a number of sources, such as the training and skill of the officer, the officer's willingness to take risks in crisis situations, and the officer's psychological composition (Meyer et al. 1982).

Police officers in the United States are assaulted most frequently by unemployed, young, poor, nonwhite males who have been drinking (Chapman 1976). Meyer et al. (1982) suggest that these youths are probably extremely frustrated with their lives and, with the help of alcohol, vent their frustrations in aggressive social acts. Use of alcohol does not directly cause violent behavior, but it does promote "deindividuated" behavior (Zimbardo 1970), in which there is a reduction of self-awareness and self-evaluation and a lack of concern for the evaluation of others. Such a state is a potent antecendent of aggression. Deindividuated persons feel a sense of anonymity and perceive themselves as less accountable for their actions. This loss of personal identity may act to increase impulsiveness and aggression in persons who are normally not violent. Aggression may be more than simply stored up anger.

Police-civilian assaults are typically unplanned and arise from stressful situations that initially involve relatively minor infractions. Officers are most frequently assaulted on the street or highway, in the jail or booking area, or in a private residence. They are least likely to be attacked in open areas, schools, colleges, and hotels (Chapman 1976).

Police-suspect violence often occurs in situations in which the civilian fails to show proper respect for and recognition of the legitimacy of police power and police officers fail to explain the reasons for their actions (Chevigny 1969). Officers and assailants usually have an opportunity to communicate with each other before an assault. The failure of the offender to submit to the officers' authority is a strong stimulus for confrontation (Brent and Sykes 1980).

Many police-citizen interactions may be crisis situations for the citizens but routine, perhaps boring, occurrences for the officers. Because of their familiarity with interrogations and possible bias in questioning certain citizens, officers may use inappropriate strategies of interaction. When police lack social skills, they usually provide the civilian with few alternatives for response other than compliance with what may be perceived as unreasonable demands, resistance or attempts to escape (Toch 1976). If the officer is unable to effectively communicate his or her expectations, the officer may become frustrated and angry and continue to use inappropriate strategies, which can make both parties emotionally upset. Very little is needed in such situations to provoke aggression and violence (Brent and Sykes 1980).

Relatively few officers are violence-prone, but this minority is distinguished by their excessive concern for proper respect and self-esteem (Westley 1970). This subgroup of officers is most responsible for police brutality (Toch 1976). Some civilians, of course, are also violence-prone and overly concerned with self-esteem. A major antecendent of anger in people is insult and humiliation. Deliberate attacks to self-esteem, for example, are far more powerful causes of anger than frustration from failure to attain some material goal (Feshbach 1986). When an officer ridicules and disparages a person's reputation, especially in front of the individual's friends or relatives, the results are often predictable, with one critical difference. Police officers are usually "protected" by their fellow officers both during and following a violent incident, whereas the offender may be protected by his or her friends during an incident, but not after the incident, which makes civilians more vulnerable than the police (Toch 1976).

Predictors of Violence

General police-civilian assaults can be perceived as a sequence of interpersonal actions and reactions that grow in psychological intensity.

Violence may occur when there is a perception of disequilibrium in power, particularly in situations in which civilians fail to recognize the legitimacy of the police, or when civilians perceive unjustifiable restrictions of their civil rights. Violence may be utilized by civilians as the final way to restore balance and reclaim lost powers.

Physical confrontations leading to assaults often have a predictable pattern involving five interrelated phases: a triggering stage, an escalation stage, a crisis stage, a recovery stage, and a postcrisis depression stage (Kaplan and Wheeler 1983). If officers can become aware of their reactions to cues that are associated with the triggering stage of violence, they may be able to prevent a trivial incident from exploding into a violent incident.

Individuals entering an interpersonal conflict have a behavioral and emotional baseline of responsive readiness. The triggering phase is the first emotional and behavioral movement away from this baseline. One or both parties may feel agitated, which could serve as a warning, if heeded, that the assault cycle has been triggered. An officer's giving an order or threat, placing a person under arrest, trying to intervene as a third party in a dispute, handcuffing, and the use of body contact are the most frequent acts to precede an assault. Suspects may trigger the violence cycle by verbal abuse, resisting an officer's command, making a threat, or attempting to flee (Meyer et al. 1982). Specific "dangerous" behaviors of civilians vary, and officers cannot predict accurately that any one person will become assaultive unless they know the history of that individual. However, officers can "listen" to their own bodily cues and judge whether or not they are moving into stage two, the escalation phase of violence.

When the intensity of behavioral and emotional responses escalate, the feasibility of rational and diversionary intervention strategies diminishes. Anderson and Bauer (1987) suggest that officers will sometimes get even with a civilian who has been unusually insulting by using tactics that promote the escalation of violence. "One technique is to use body language, such as intrusive eye contact or moving into the other person's body space, to push the citizen into making a physical attack (e.g., 'I get right up into his face and talk just a little too loud and, most of the time, I can get him to take a swing at me'). This allows the officer to take violent defensive action" (p. 382). Apart from an officer's intent to get even with an obnoxious civilian, the possibility of assaults are increased when officers or civilians move into another person's *buffer zone,* or *critical defense zone.* This is that distance between twenty-four and forty-eight inches surrounding a person socialized in North American culture. The probability of an assault between two violence-prone persons increases geometrically with a decrease in distance. Violence is especially likely to escalate when a civilian invades an officer's critical defense zone if the officer is violence-prone, in a dangerous setting, and perceives the offender to be dangerous (Blau 1984; Hays, Roberts, and Solway 1981). Violence also escalates when officers believe that suspects are attempting to run. Escape behaviors are often a signal that a weapon will be drawn by a suspect, and officers are likely to protect themselves by using deadly force when such signals are salient (Geller 1982).

Once a civilian or officer or both are in the crisis phase, control of aggressive actions is usually beyond rational appeal. At this point, the principle concern is safety and survival. On conclusion of the assaultive incident, participants begin to recover and return to their baseline behavior. However, Kaplan and Wheeler (1983) emphasize that physiological arousal continues to be high during this period and can last as an active agent up to ninety minutes after extreme emotional incidents. Improper intervention tactics during this period can reactivate assaultive behaviors. In the final phase of the assault cycle (the depression phase), participants typically are mentally and physically exhausted. Some people will be very remorseful, ashamed, distraught, or in shock, depending upon the seriousness and consequences of the incident. At this stage, participants usually regress below their normal baseline behavior.

CAUSES AND CORRELATES OF
VIOLENT BEHAVIOR

Students of criminal violence acknowledge that the causes and correlates of aggressive and violent behavior seldom result from a single factor, but are the consequence of complex interactions of biological, psychological, sociological, political, and economic factors. Not all violence is considered to be "bad" or "wrong," however, since violence is widely accepted in American culture as a legitimate means for accomplishing positive social functions such as social control or producing social change in the family, in educational, business, and industrial settings, and in the general community (Coser 1956). The following discussion centers mainly on the psychological and sociopsychological explanations of aggression and violence. Theorists disagree over whether the phenomenon of aggression is determined by innate factors, is a product of frustration, or is learned. Explanations and approaches to understanding the psychology of aggression fall into three major theoretical categories: instinct theory, frustration-aggression theory, and social learning theory.

Instinct Theory

According to *instinct theory*, human aggressive tendencies are innate and inevitable. Freud (1950) argued that human beings have two basic instincts, an energizing life force, *eros*, and a death instinct or destructive force, *thanatos*. People are driven toward their own destruction, and aggression occurs whenever the death instinct is directed toward others. If there were no outlets to express this drive, aggression could be turned inward and result in depression, masochism, or suicide. Freud's psychoanalytic theory of a death instinct has not won large support among psychologists or even among Freud's own supporters, since it is not credible that people are destined to self-destruct.

Another instinctual theory, put forward by ethologist Konrad Lorenz (1966), argues that humans have the same innate aggressive instincts as animals. Consequently, humans are born to defend their territory and fight for survival. This innate fighting instinct is said to be a natural, healthy characteristic. According to Lorenz, the fighting instinct spontaneously builds up aggressive energy until it is released through an aggressive act. The greater the build-up of aggressive energy, the more likely that aggressive behavior will erupt. In order to avoid violent outbursts of aggressive energy, Lorenz advocated its release in less destructive ways, such as participation in competitive sports or by letting off steam by yelling at the televsion while watching others engaged in emotional activities. The supposed cleansing of stored aggressive impulses through such steam-releasing activities is known as catharsis. There is little research support for the catharsis hypothesis. In fact, empirical evidence indicates that watching others participate in highly arousing activities increases rather than decreases hostility (Berkowitz 1970).

Instinct theories of aggression would have us believe that all humans, regardless of their culture, have the same innate instinctual impulses to show aggressive behavior, generate similar levels of aggressive energy, and exhibit similar amounts of aggressive behavior. These assumptions are false (Berkowitz 1969). Furthermore, instinctual arguments drawing upon animal behavior research provide only interesting metaphors for discussing the complexity of factors involved in human violence. Metaphors, by themselves, are not sufficient explanations for aggressive behavior.

Frustration-Aggression Theory

The original and now out-dated formulation of the *frustration-aggression theory* stated that aggression is always a consequence of frustration (Dollard et al. 1939). According to this early theory, aggression presupposes the existence of frustration, and the existence of frustration always leads to some form of aggressive drive, which, in turn, promotes aggressive behavior. For instance, this theory suggests that, when young boys or girls are continually prevented from achieving their main objectives (passing school grades, finding a part-time job, and so on), they become frustrated. In frustration, they will attack the source of the frustration (vandalize the school, for instance). If they cannot overcome the frustration through direct contact with the source of their anger, they will displace their aggression onto a substitute object (such as picking on a smaller child) in order to eliminate their frustration.

The original frustration-aggression theory gradually lost favor among theorists since it became apparent that frustration does not always result in an overt aggressive response (Berkowitz 1969). Frustration may lead to many other types of responses, such as depression, withdrawal, and escape. Not every act of aggression can be traced to some original frustration, and frustration may follow as well as precede aggression.

Berkowitz (1974) revised the original frustration-aggression hypothesis by proposing that learned and innate sources of aggression coexist. According to Berkowitz, frustration arouses anger and creates a "readiness" for aggressive behavior. Behaving aggressively against a person who annoys you may or may not reduce your anger, but, if you are successful in that activity, the experience may encourage you to be aggressive in other situations (see Doob 1970; Geen, Stonner, and Shope 1975; Konecni 1975).

Frustration by itself is not a sufficient cause for aggression. Instead, if a person is highly frustrated, he or she will behave aggressively when provided with situational cues that may provoke or facilitate aggressive behavior. For aggression to actually occur, an individual in this ready state must associate the situational stimuli with aggression. Consider the following factors. When a weapon is available and individuals are emotionally aroused, the presence of the weapon may increase the intensity of the violence. Berkowitz has made the controversial conclusion that "guns not only permit violence, they can stimulate it as well. The finger pulls the trigger, but the trigger may also be pulling the finger" (quoted in Goldstein 1986, 92). A more conservative conclusion has been suggested by Goldstein (1986): "When an individual is bent on aggression in the first place, the presence of a weapon will eventuate in its use, and the consequence of the aggressive act will be much more severe than if no weapon were available" (pp. 142–43). These writers clearly support the role of weapons in aggression; the greater the availability of weapons, the greater the likelihood that they will influence the occurrence, the severity, and the lethality of violent behavior (Zimring 1977).

One report supports this more conservative view.

Canadian Consul General Milton Blackwell was recently robbed at gun point after parking his car in a downtown Detroit garage. Blackwell, as a member of the Canadian foreign service, has served in Singapore, Hong Kong, Mexico City, and Bonn. Yet, in an interview with the *Detroit Free Press*, he said, "Nothing quite like this has ever happened to me."
Blackwell's experience is not surprising. As a Canadian citizen, he resides in a nation where handguns are tightly controlled. And every nation in which he has lived has strict laws to keep handguns from falling into wrong hands — except the United States.
America is the only western nation without strong handgun laws and the consequences are horrifying. In 1980, handguns killed: 8 in Great Britain, 77 in Japan, 24 in Switzerland, 18 in Sweden, 23 in Israel, 8 in Canada, 4 in Australia, and 11,522 in the United States. (Lautman 1984, 2)

And the following report shows how the presence of a weapon helped to escalate a situation into a deadly event.

> An argument after a minor traffic accident on the turnpike here this week-end left a computer analyst from New Jersey dead and a truck driver from North Carolina charged with killing him. . . . Everett Lee Lyons, 46 . . . was charged with firing the shot that killed Mr. Kearney, 49. . . . Sergeant Zukowsky said that after the car's fender and truck's tire brushed just south of the Exit 18-W toll plaza, the two drivers pulled over and Mr. Lyons and Mr. Kearney got out and exchanged harsh words.
>
> After Mr. Kearney punched Mr. Lyons in the mouth, Sergeant Zukowsky said, Mr. Lyons went to the cab of his tractor trailer, pulled out a .25 caliber semiautomatic handgun, and fired the single, fatal shot. Mr. Kearney was the passenger in a Mercedes-Benz driven by his brother-in-law, who was not injured in the incident. Mr. Lyons walked to the toll plaza after the shooting, surrendering his gun to a state trooper there and asking for medical attention for his bloody lip, according to Dominic Sidonio, toll collector who said he watched the incident from his booth.
>
> "I don't think it had really hit him, what he had done," Mr. Sidonio said yesterday. "He was really kind of calm. The trooper said 'O.K., where's your gun?' and he said, 'Oh, it's right here,' and gave it to him." Mr. Sidonio said that Mr. Kearney punched Mr. Lyons and that he was "pretty aggressive," but neither he nor the police said they had any reason to believe that he had threatened Mr. Lyons with anything other than his hands. (*New York Times*, November 14, 1988)

The availability of weapons, however, is only one of many environmental factors that encourage aggressive and criminally violent acts. Other situational factors, such as family, peer, and job environments, the availability of victims, alcohol, and so forth, are all likely facilitators or inhibitors of violent acts (see Monahan and Klassen 1982).

Aggression can also occur in the absence of frustration—out of boredom, for example. However, frustration-aggressive responses can be modified by learning. Individuals can learn not to respond to frustration with aggression, and aggression is unlikely to follow frustration if a nonaggressive response has proven to be more effective. For instance, a frustrated person may lash out and start a fight, but he or she can also learn to avoid or escape this situation by walking away or using appropriate social skills to defuse the situation. There is also a cognitive basis in most instances of frustration and aggression. If frustration is considered "legitimate"—that is, it is not perceived as the fault of the person who caused it—the tendency towards aggression is minimal (Berkowitz 1981).

Social Learning Theory

A brief overview of *social learning* was presented in Chapter 7 in the review of psychological causes of criminal behavior. That discussion is continued here. According to Bandura (1973), the leading proponent of social learning theory, aggression is a learned response. People learn to be aggressive either through direct reinforcement or through observational learning. Supporters of this theoretical view claim that there is no need to propose any innate or continuous drive toward aggression. Aggression should not be understood as inevitable. Instead, it is suggested that individuals behave aggressively only under conditions that stimulate learned responses or support aggressive behaviors. Since aggressive behaviors are learned in response to specific situations and cues, nonaggressive responses to these same stimuli can also be learned. Bandura argues that aggression has a circular effect. One act of aggression leads to further aggression, and this pattern of behavior will continue until the circle is broken by some sort of positive or negative reinforcement. For example, a young boy may model himself after an admired, aggressive father. As long as his father's violent behavior (such as wife-battering) is tolerated by other members of the family or by the police and the community, the boy will continue to have an adult role model of aggressive behavior and will learn aggressive behaviors. If society punishes the father for his violent actions, the cycle may be broken, and the child may learn about the consequences of undesirable behaviors.

Marvin Wolfgang, a professor of sociology and law, has theorized that there is a "subculture of violence" based on social learning. That is, within the larger society, there are socio-economic communities in which violence is expected, tolerated, and even required if one wants to remain a member of the social group (Wolfgang 1959; Wolfgang and Ferracuti 1967). Favorable attitudes to solving problems through violence are transmitted from parent to child in social development. These expectations and values are assumed to be directly responsible for criminal assaults later in adolescence, when peer influence and group pressure to conform are powerful factors determining behavior. Traits of toughness and machismo and quick violent responses to challenges are valued. According to Wolfgang (1959), "Quick resort to physical combat as a measure of daring, courage, of defense of status appears to be a cultural expectation, especially for lower socioeconomic class males" (p. 189). Respect and approval from bystanders are given by hitting an antagonist; however, "The juvenile who fails to live up to the conflict gang's requirements is pushed outside the group. The adult male who does not defend his honor or his female companion will be socially emasculated. The 'coward' is forced to move out of the territory, to find new friends and make new alliances" (Wolfgang and Ferracuti 1967, 160).

Although this theory is influential (see Clinard 1974; Gibbons 1973), it has been criticized for being circular. It explains group differences in violence by positing subculture values, then points to differences in violent behavior as evidence that the groups differ in their values. There is no evidence that people who behave violently have positive attitudes toward violence (Ball-Rokeach 1973). Values of toughness and machismo are not favored, ideal values among the poor or among young males or nonwhites (Erlanger 1974). It is possible that the reason that violent behavior and lower social class appear to be related variables is the greater likelihood that the police will become involved in violent disputes in this community, whereas lawyers and social counselors may be called upon and will keep disputes private when there are similar problems in middle-class communities (Stark and McEvoy 1970). Finally, Berkowitz (1978) has shown that members of low-income groups are likely to be violent because of frequent frustration and threats to their self-esteem. In contrast to the predictions of the subculture violence hypothesis, Berkowitz found that men were much more likely to attack a foe when their pride was wounded. Anger and pleasure in hurting an antagonist were the reasons for violence, rather than seeking the social approval of others. According to Berkowitz, hostile aggression, instrumental aggression, and self-approval are the salient factors in understanding violence in the lower classes.

I will conclude this overview of psychological factors associated with violence with a summary of a general model of aggression (Goldstein

Table 8.2   Factors Associated with Aggression and Nonaggression

Short-Term	*Long-Term*
Aggression	
Characteristics of the actor:	*Characteristics of the actor:*
Immediately prior aggressive acts	Deindividuation
Loss of cognitive control of behavior	Impulsivity
Low identifiability	Low level of moral judgment
Moderate amount of alcohol ingestion	Negative labels for targets
Moderate emotional arousal	Positive labels for aggression
Consequences of actor's behavior:	*Consequences of actor's behavior:*
Cognitive justification for aggression	Rewards for aggression
Devaluation of victim	*Parental characteristics:*
Environmental factors:	Aggressive models, unpunished
Abundant opportunities for	High punitiveness
aggression	*Environmental factors:*
Availability of a weapon	Aggressible situations
Familiar environment	Exposure to aggression in others
Familiar or similar target	
Recent exposure to violence	
Nonaggression	
Characteristics of the actor:	*Characteristics of the actor:*
Aggression-anxiety, guilt	Ability to delay gratification
Arousal of pleasant emotions	Ability to take role of others
Fear of punishment	High level of moral judgment
High identifiability	Inclusive concept of "we"
Immediately prior nonaggressive acts	Individuation
Environmental factors:	Negative labels for aggression
Presence of authority figure	Positive regard for others
(for those low in moral judgment)	*Consequences of actor's behavior:*
Unfamiliar environment	Rewards for nonaggression
	Parental characteristics:
	Affection, control, nurturance
	Nonaggressive models
	Environmental factors
	Nonaggressible situations

Note: The characteristics of the actor listed under short-term factors are temporary or transient states, most often induced by the physical or social environment, rather than enduring traits of the actor.

Source: Goldstein 1986. From *Aggression and Crimes of Violence*, Second Edition, by Jeffrey H. Goldstein. Copyright © 1975, 1986 by Oxford University Press, Inc. Reprinted by permission.

1986). Aggressive behavior depends upon the interchange of several simultaneous factors. First, there must be a stimulus for aggression; then, any inhibitions of aggression must be overcome; and finally, the environmental conditions at the time—in terms of opportunity and capability for aggression as well as an available victim—must be supportive. Short-term and long-term factors involving characteristics of the aggressor, consequences of the aggressors behavior, and situational factors operate either to facilitate or to inhibit the likelihood of aggression. Table 8.2 shows a list of factors that are related to aggression and nonaggression.

I will continue this discussion of aggression and violence in chapter nine with a look at how many of these factors are related to sexual assault and spouse abuse.

SUMMARY

Aggression is behavior intended to hurt others. Aggression may be physical, verbal, even passive. In hostile aggression, the primary goal is to inflict injury; in instrumental aggression, the injury is a means to some other goal. Aggressive behavior has been investigated in terms of instinctual and biological theories, frustration-aggression theory, social leaning theory, and cognitive theory.

Police officers generally encounter three types of violence: (1) violence against officers; (2) violence of citizens against citizens or institutions; and (3) violence police officers use against citizens.

9

Criminal Victimization

The psychological effects of violence on victims of crime are well documented (see, for example, Bard and Sangrey 1979; Greenberg and Ruback 1984; Janoff-Bulman and Frieze 1983; Kilpatrick, Resick, and Veronen 1981). Criminal victimization often has a persistent impact on a person's emotional and cognitive well-being. Individuals may show symptoms of shock, anxiety, depression, sleep disturbances, flashbacks and recollections of the traumatic event, loss of emotional control, guilt, helplessness, memory loss, inability to concentrate, an exaggerated startle response, and obsessive fantasies about the crime and the assailant. Beliefs in self-worth and self-esteem are often shattered. These responses are known collectively as *posttraumatic stress syndrome* (Stekette and Foa 1987).

In order to cope with their victimization, individuals may resort to a number of avoidance behaviors such as changing their residence and phone number, enrolling in self-defense courses, and becoming detached from friends and acquaintances (Skogan and Maxfield 1981). Victims of violent crimes experience a profound threat to their autonomy. They no longer feel free to go where they please, shop where they want, or bank where it is most convenient. They are forced to rethink many of the assumptions and expectations they hold about the world and about themselves. If the world appeared comprehensible, orderly, meaningful, and fair, victims cannot understand how it is that they have experienced such an incident (Lerner 1980). General trust and confidence in others is undermined. Individuals now recognize that serious crimes do not happen only to other people. Any illusion they may have had about their own invulnerability is challenged, if not destroyed (Perloff 1983). A sense of helplessness, apprehension, and intense anxiety about being victimized in the future may preoccupy the victim.

Crimes of violence account for 12 percent of all criminal victimizations in the United States. (Frieze, Hymer, and Greenberg 1987). Although anyone can be a victim of violent crime, the most typical victim is a young person between 12 and 24 years of age, black, single or divorced, unemployed, from a low-income family, and living in an urban area (Zawitz 1983). Crime is more likely to occur in certain geographical regions of urban areas than others. Victimization is correlated with such factors as race, history of family violence, geographical proximity of residences between victims and assailants, and even such characteristics as the physical appearance and walking styles of "easy marks" (Grayson and Stein 1981; Lamborn 1981). I will continue the review of aggression and violence in this chapter by looking specifically at the crimes of sexual assault, spouse abuse, and victimization of the elderly.

SEXUAL ASSAULT AND RAPE

Rape is any form of forcible sexual assault, and rapists are men who have sexually assaulted a nonconsenting woman. Males also get sexually abused (Risin and Koss 1988), but I will focus mainly on female rape victims. Suffice it to say that male rape victims experience many of the traumas experienced by female victims, but males do not usually think themselves vulnerable to being raped.

Many of the physical and psychological symptoms of victims of crime described above are shared by rape victims, but, in addition, victims of rape may display a group of symptoms that are unique to this crime. These symptoms are referred to as rape trauma syndrome (Burgess and Holmstrom 1974, 1979). Two specific phases of reaction to a sexual assault are commonly experienced. Immediately after the attack and for a few days thereafter, victims are in the *acute phase,* which involves a state of shock, disbelief, fear, anger, revenge, humiliation, guilt, and self-blame. Victims may appear either emotionally overcome and semihysterical or silently composed. Following this acute phase, victims go through an *integration and resolution* period in which they attempt to come to terms with the reality of their experience. It is during this period that victims alter their lifestyles. Sleep disturbances, severe emotional distress, disturbed sexual relationships, and difficulties relating to men are common. Conflicts and taboos about sexuality and the mythologies surrounding the responsibility of women as victims of rape compound the normal problems of criminal victimization. Self-blame, shame, anger, and guilt continue to preoccupy the victim.

Less than 10 percent of completed rape cases are reported to the police. Furthermore, only 3 percent of completed rape cases result in arrests (Kidd and Chayet 1984; Kilpatrick et al. 1987). This low report rate may be attributed to a number of factors. It is likely that symptoms of the rape trauma syndrome, specifically feelings of guilt and shame, act to prevent some women from reporting the crime. Women who are sexually assaulted are often perceived as both maligned victims and subtle instigators of the incident. They may suffer physical and emotional distress as victims, but they may also be blamed for enticing the rapist and engaging in vindictiveness and malice (Wood 1973). Some victims will not contact the police if they feel that nothing can be done at that point. If the police are perceived as insensitive to a victim's distress and if the courts are perceived as soft on rapists, victims may fail to cooperate with the criminal justice system (Ashworth and Feldman-Summers 1978). Others are concerned that the rapist or his friends will retaliate if charges are made. Public admission of a sexual assault may be humiliating and may result in rejection from the woman's husband, lover, or father. Countless women choose not to seek assistance from health care or victim services, and over 50 percent of raped women experience posttraumatic stress disorders 15 years after the crime (Kilpatrick et al. 1987).

Rape Myths

A number of cultural myths and stereotypes about rape affect the victim, the victim's family and friends, the relationship of the victim with the investigating officer, the course of the investigation, and ultimately the trial process itself. Many of these myths are deeply rooted in our cultural heritage. They show themselves in rape jokes and risqué remarks, which tell us much about the jokesters' attitudes toward the crime and attitudes toward women (Schrink, Poole, and Regoli 1982). I will discuss these myths in the context of three theoretical models about rape victimization: the victim precipitation model, the social control model, and the situational blame model (Koss 1985).

The Victim Precipitation Model. The idea that rape victims have a causal role in precipitating their victimization was introduced by Amir (1971), who stated:

> Once the victim and the offender are drawn together, a process is set in motion whereby victim behavior and the situation which surrounds the encounter will determine the course of events leading to the crime. If the victim is not solely responsible for what becomes the unfortunate event, at least she is often a complementary partner. . . . Theoretically, victim precipitation of forcible rape means that in a particular situation the behavior of the victim is interpreted by the offender as a direct invitation for sexual relations or as a sign that she will be available for sexual contact if he will persist in demanding it. (P. 493)

If rape victims precipitate their victimization, the following beliefs must be true: A woman cannot be raped unless she wants to be; most women will eventually enjoy it; only attractive and young women are raped; nice girls don't get raped; victims ask for it by the way they dress and walk; victims are promiscuous, seductive, or aggressive.

Blaming the rape victim is a popular theme in films, novels, and "pop psychology" literature. Clinical and social-psychological evidence shows that victim precipitation rape myths are ridiculous, but they are still accepted as probable explanations by many segments of society (Alexander 1980; Feild 1978). Females of all ages are sexually assaulted, including very young children and elderly women. The seductive infant and provocative 80- and 90-year-old woman must invite assaults if we are to believe that victims precipitate rapes (Calhoun et al. 1980). Up to 70 percent of rapes are at least partially planned beforehand by the assailant (Amir 1971). Rape is a crime of violence in which women, regardless of their physical appearance, social class, education, marital status, or race, are victimized. Women are raped in public washrooms, churches, parks, alleyways, cars, private residences, and elsewhere, every hour of the day and in every season. Even if a woman truly was seductive and provocative, a sexual assault is still a crime if a woman changes her mind. There is no law against being provocative, especially in a society that encourages women to be sexually attractive. There is no law against saying no. But there is a law against forced sexual relations (Groth 1979).

One reason that responsibility for being raped is attributed more to the rape victim than to the offender may be that people have a need to believe in a "just world" (Lerner 1980). Many believe that the world is a just place where good things happen to good people and bad things happen to bad people. They believe that people get what they deserve or deserve what they get. Since most people see themselves as good, decent, and intelligent, they are inclined to believe that disasters could not happen to anyone like themselves. Other people, those who are disrespectable, provocative, or careless and lacking foresight in their actions, are viewed as responsible for their fate. If they have been victimized, they must have in some fashion precipitated or deserved this consequence.

Perceptions of a victim's physical appearance, character, and behavior during a sexual assault also contribute to assigned blame. Although people believe that attractive women are more likely to be raped, several studies show that unattractive women are assigned greater blame for their victimization (see Deitz, Littman, and Bentley 1984; Seligman, Brickman, and Koulack 1977). It is reasoned that in order to attract male attention, unattractive women precipitate their victimization by being especially provocative and seductive. The belief that "she led him on" and other rape myths are most widely accepted by older men and women (average age of 58 years) (Yarmey 1985a) and by men and women whose thinking is guided by sex-role stereotypes (Burt 1980), the belief that women should be traditional and submissive, men assertive and dominant. In a sample of 598 adults in Minnesota Burt (1980) found that over 50 percent agreed with the statement that "in the majority of rapes, the victim was promiscuous or had a bad reputation." Young men and older men and women also have been found to attribute less blame to rapists who assault provocative women than to those who assault demure women (Yarmey 1985b).

These results suggest that our society regards women who look and act provocatively as suitable targets for sexual assault. To the extent that rape myths are accepted, women are denied the label of "real victims", their injuries are minimized as self-inflicted, and they are blamed for precipitating their own victimization (Hall, Howard, and Boezio 1986; Weis and Borges 1973).

The Social Control Model.   According to some theorists, women are socialized through their sex-role training to accept beliefs and attitudes that support rape as normal. This training makes women more vulnerable to the likelihood of sexual assault (Koss 1985). For example, it has been suggested that rape is only a minor crime; that the issue of rape tends to be overdramatized, its significance overexaggerated; that women often lie about being raped; that women mean yes when they say no; that rape is merely an impulsive, uncontrollable act of sexual gratification; that rape is an impulsive, biological need of sex-starved or insane men; that it is not possible for a husband to "rape" his wife.

Females in our culture are socialized to be demure and sexually attractive. They are expected to be submissive, passive, tender, fearful, and compliant toward men, whereas males are characterized as powerful, aggressive, opportunistic, dominant, and adventurous (Bem, 1981). According to feminist perspectives, men are socialized to prove their masculinity through force and domination and are expected to be the initiators of sexual activity. Sexual aggression, assault, and rape are the consequences of cultural glorification that measures masculinity in terms of sex, power, and violence (Brownmiller 1975; Weis and Borges 1973).

If a male is the recipient of unwanted sexual advances from another male, it is assumed that he would forcefully defend himself. Males, in general, consider aggression an appropriate response for any victim, including female victims. Women may, in fact, be disparaged by men for not resisting (Krulewitz 1981). Similarly, people with traditional conservative attitudes regarding sex-role norms believe that a respectable woman would vigorously fight to protect her virtue, and if there is no evidence of brutality resulting in serious injuries, it may be assumed that the act was consensual (Clark and Lewis 1977; Krulewitz and Payne 1978). Women face the dilemma of being perceived as less intelligent and more blameworthy for their victimization by other women if they resist a rapist, but if they fail to resist, men consider them dumb and blameworthy (Krulewitz and Nash 1979). If women are raped by an acquaintance, they are less likely to be physically assaulted and more likely to believe they contributed to their own victimization (Oros, Leonard, and Koss 1980).

Women are often perceived as extensions of men's possessions and as legitimate objects of sexual aggression. Furthermore, many women are socialized to believe that it is their responsibility to control the nature of the "romantic" interaction with males. If women do not take control, males may argue that their sexual aggressiveness was consensual (Williams 1984). Sexual assault is so closely associated with attitudes toward women and sex-role socialization that sexually assaultive adolescent males are supported by their male peer group (Ageton 1983). Males who are sexist tend to hold tolerant attitudes toward sexually coercive behavior in other males; sex-role stereotyping is directly related to acceptance of rape myths (Feild 1978).

Rape prevention programs in some rape crisis centers now include teenage and adult males, as well as females. It is argued that rape is primarily an expression of men's power over women, and men do not take rape seriously because they do not usually think of themselves as potential rape victims. Males in these programs are put through a series of exercises in empathy and role-playing in which they must relate to and deal with their feelings about being victimized in a homosexual rape. It is felt that only when men can empathize with the injury, pain, and humiliation women experience from rape, will they recognize males' responsibility for rape prevention.

Men fill most positions of power in the criminal justice system, but very few men have experienced rape or have experience as potential rape victims. It is probable that many men fail to identify with and appreciate the female experience of rape (Krulewitz 1981). The control and prevention of rapes and the detection of offenders are not going to be resolved by revolutionary developments in eyewitness identification techniques or other technical forensic innovations in the near future (one exception may be in the analysis of genetic codes from semen or other body traces). Consequently, police activities have to concentrate upon the victim both as a provider of evidence and as the recipient of a primary police function—that is, protecting the citizen from the consequences of crime (Blair 1985).

No support has been found for the hypotheses that rape is the result of an irresistible impulse or an impulsive biological need of men or that rapists suffer a "disease of the mind" (Glueck 1925). Studies of convicted rapists indicate that less than 5 percent were psychotic at the time of the rape (Abel, Becker, and Skinner 1980). There are no predictable symptoms of psychiatric disorders that are causally associated with rape. Amir (1971) found that 49 percent of convicted rapists had previous arrest records dealing with property crimes, which suggests that for some rapists, sexual assault is but one violent crime committed among others. Clinical research reveals that rapists experience high frustration in attempting to prove their masculinity, and sexual aggression may be the result of compensating for feelings of inadequacy. Rape may be a means by which men try to prove their dominance, mastery, strength, and self-worth. Rape has very little to do with sexual gratification. Instead, it is the use of sex to conquer, control, exploit, dominate, hurt, retaliate, and express anger and rage (Groth, Burgess, and Holstrom 1977).

Convicted rapists, of course, may not be representative of men who have not been arrested for sexual assault. However, the few studies that have been conducted on men who have reported on their sexual aggression indicate that they are not distinguishable in terms of social class, educational level or background, or ethnic or racial group (Alder 1982; Smithyman 1978). Most "official" rapists (71.4 percent) come from unstable, impoverished backgrounds — that is, broken homes, alcoholic fathers, and general neglect. Children raised in these circumstances show high levels of aggression at home with mothers and playmates. Difficulties at school, expulsion, frequent fights, fire-setting, and destruction of property are common in the histories of rapists (Tingle et al. 1986). The lack of love and nurturing in early child development may account for the failure of sexually aggressive men to develop and maintain affectionate and meaningful sexual relationships with their partners.

Recent research indicates that convicted rapists lack a number of social skills that are important for normal relationships between men and women. Such social learning deficits can produce stress, frustration, and anger toward their targets. For example, convicted rapists and sexually aggressive males have been found to misperceive social cues from women. They interpret ambiguous female behaviors as "come-ons," misconstrue women's rejections as positive invitations, and fail to believe that *no* means no (Lipton, McDonel, and McFall 1987; Malamuth and Check 1980a, 1980b). Convicted rapists also have inadequate conversational skills, skills that are at least minimally necessary in normal social interactions with women (Marshall and Barbaree 1984). These social learning deficits are related to the impoverished home environments these men experienced in their formative years, rather than to mental illness or biological impulses.

The Situational Blame Model.   Rape victims are often blamed for the circumstances in which the assault occurred, including their use of defensive strategies to avoid or escape the attack. Women encounter such myths as: Since rape occurs only among strangers, if I avoid strangers I will not be raped; rape occurs only when you are alone at night, out in the street or in parks and dark alleys; rape occurs only in large cities. None of these statements can be empirically supported. Almost 40 percent of all sexual assaults occur in the daytime, and, when a man is determined to sexually assault, he will often be successful regardless of how many precautions a woman may take (Scheppele and Bart 1983). Rapists are most likely to complete their assault with an acquaintance, rather than a stranger, inside a dwelling, and using a weapon (Quinsey and Upfold 1985).

Some observers feel that by offering women training in rape prevention, false beliefs are strengthened, thereby making women even more vulnerable, guilt-ridden, and self-blaming if they should be raped (Kidder, Boell, and Moyer 1983). Several rape prevention strategies have been suggested, but none of them is foolproof. Researchers have concluded that stranger and acquaintance rapes are most likely to be avoided when victims actively resist by screaming, yelling, fighting, or running away. Attempts to reason, flatter, quarrel, cry, or plead with a rapist more frequently lead to completed rapes than avoidance (Bart and O'Brien 1985; Levine-MacCombie and Koss 1986). A woman's decision to physically resist or to reason with the offender normally depends upon her perception of the likelihood of physical injury as compared to her judgment of the effectiveness of reasoning with a particular assailant in that particular situation (Macdonald 1971). If the situation appears to be minimally threatening, little resistance would be expected since women may believe that it would be silly to make a scene. However, women in obvious danger have to decide whether active resistance leading to the chance of escape is worth the risk of extreme brutality or

whether passive resistance, although perhaps not a deterrent to the
crime the crime being completed, will result in no injury. Passive
resistance, however, does not significantly reduce the chances of serious
physical injury (Griffin and Griffin 1981). Active evasive action appears
to be the recommended pattern of resistance.

Police and Victims of Sexual Assault

Police officers who respond to a call are typically the victim's first and
sometimes only contact with the criminal justice system. How the police
deal with victims has both immediate and long-term consequences for
personal adjustment (Frieze, Hymer, and Greenberg 1987) and for
cooperation between the victim and the state (President's Task Force on
Victims of Crime 1983). Victims who are treated callously by the police
are unlikely to assist in the prosecution of the case. Evidence indicates
that police demonstrate less serious attention to men accused of sexual
assault when the incident involves a victim who has a "bad" reputation
and fails to immediately report the incident (Holmstrom and Burgess
1978) and is an acquaintance of the offender and unwilling to prosecute
(Williams 1976).

It is probable that some male police officers still show callous or
indifferent treatment and judgmental attitudes toward rape and toward
rape victims similar to the insensitivity prevalent in the early 1970s
(Brownmiller 1975; Greer 1975; Wood 1973). However, a recent national survey of the attitudes toward rape of 2,170 county and municipal
law enforcement officers found few officers oblivious to the crises of
rape victims, although they accepted some rape myths (LeDoux and
Hazelwood 1985). As a group, the officers rejected the myth that a
raped victim is not a true victim. Police believed that rape is motivated
by men's seeking power over women, but they did not perceive rape as
a means by which rapists seeks proof of their manhood. Officers did not
equate sexual assault with mental illness, but they did not believe
rapists to be "normal" either. Police showed uncertainty whether or not
rape is a sexual crime or a crime of violence. Respondents indicated
they were suspicious of victims who yell "Rape!" if they have had
previous consensual sex with the offender and disbelieved women who
"provoke" rape through their dress or behavior. Finally, there was a
small subset of officers who accept the myths that "nice women do not

get raped" and "most charges of rape are unfounded." LeDoux and Hazelwood conclude that it is the responsibility of supervisors to ensure that prejudicial officers are not assigned to sexual assault cases.

The current practice in larger police agencies of assigning special sexual assault and rape analysis units to deal with all sexual offenses is an indication that police are sensitive to the special needs of rape victims. Male and female officers in these units are (or should be) given special training on all aspects of sexual investigation; evidence gathering, interview techniques, attitudinal training, and psychological training on rape trauma syndrome and other forensic issues (Blair 1985).

Crisis Intervention.   Although the majority of rape victims have positive perceptions of police being helpful and concerned about their feelings (Burgess and Holmstrom 1979), officers have been criticized for responding inappropriately by pressuring victims to minimize the seriousness of the incident and urging them to readjust quickly to the demands of everyday living (Rosenbaum 1987a). During police interviews, victims are in the acute stage of the rape trauma syndrome. They are highly dependent and suggestible. Identification evidence gathered at this point can easily be tainted by leading questions. Victims seek support, protection, reassurance, recognition, information, and advice. They need to regain a sense of order, control, and confidence in the community, especially in the police, who are perceived as the key representatives of social order (Fischer 1984). To the extent that these needs are unfulfilled, dissatisfaction with the police sets in, and the psychological damage of the victimization is compounded by the perceived insensitivity of the system. It is as if the victim experiences a second wound in "the victim's perceived rejection by—and lack of support from—the community, agencies, and society in general" (Symonds 1980).

The ways in which a police officer responds to a victim soon after the incident are the most important factors in the victim's psychological recovery. According to crisis theorists such as Bard and Sangrey (1979), "Minutes of skillful support by any sensitive person immediately after the crime can be worth more than hours of professional counseling later" (pp. 31–32). According to a number of agencies (President's Task Force on Victims of Crime 1983; American Psychological Association 1984):

Police training will be most effective if it prepares officers to (a) be immediately sensitive and responsive to victims' emotional crises; (b) encourage victims to engage in a healthy ventilation and expression of the full range of their emotions; (c) make interventions that result in a reduction in the victims' injured pride, feelings of self-blame, and likelihood of self-destructive reactions; (d) identify victims who may require subsequent assessment and treatment by mental health professionals; (e) empower troubled victims to take remedial actions that will reduce feelings of helplessness and impotent rage; and (f) make well-informed and appropriate referrals to adjunctive service agencies. (Rosenbaum 1987a, 505)

In order for these recommendations to be successfully implemented, police departments will have to be sensitive to social, economic, and cultural differences among victim groups (Skogan and Wycoff 1987) as well as to the cynicism and suspiciousness of experienced officers (Niederhoffer 1967; Skolnick 1966). Officers of both sexes have to be available, if required, contact must be maintained from initial questioning of the victim until trial, and information about the progress of the case must be provided (Blair 1985). Regarding the issue of whether police women should conduct rape investigations, the conclusion of a nationwide survey indicated:

The gender of the officer is not as important as the qualities he or she possesses. Both men and women can be motivated, sensitive and understanding. The majority of rape victims express no preference concerning the sex of the investigating officers. (National Institute of Law Enforcement and Criminal Justice 1975–1978)

SPOUSE ABUSE

One of society's most violent institutions over the course of history has been the family. A person is more likely to be assaulted or killed in the home by another family member than outside the home by other persons (Gelles and Straus 1979). Although family violence includes such phenomena as child abuse and assault of elderly relatives, I will limit this review to a discussion of the battered wife and abusive husband.

Gelles and Straus (1979) have defined *battering* as any "act carried out with the intention of, or perceived as having the intention of, physically hurting another person" (p. 20). This definition includes two categories of battering: (1) *physical battering* and (2) *psychological battering*. The first category is the use of hands, feet, or objects to inflict pain on another and includes sexual abuse. The second category is not so well understood. Psychological battering includes such activities as verbal or nonverbal threats of violence, repeated humiliation and degradation, and creating an environment of terror. It can involve intimidation through such actions as punching walls, throwing objects that just miss hitting their target, and destroying belongings and pets (Edleson, Eisikovits, and Guttmann 1985).

Although females are less aggressive than males in general (Maccoby and Jacklin 1974) and are expected on the basis of traditional sex-role norms to be more "proper" than men in public, research on aggression within families shows very similar assault rates for husbands and wives and for sons and daughters (see Gelles and Straus 1979; Lefkowitz et al. 1977). Society's complex rules of behavioral expectations involving aggression are applied differently inside the family home than outside. However, the dynamics of violence from males are not equivalent to that of females. Women do not hit as hard as men, and it is very rare that a man will experience the continuous, consistent sort of beatings a battered wife encounters. Men usually leave soon after the violence begins. Furthermore, men are much more likely to inflict psychological forms of violence than are women (Fiora-Gormally 1978).

Batterers

Popular views of battering husbands suggest that they are alcoholic, working-class, uneducated men. Men who assault their partners are believed to be crazy, psychopathic, or just plain bullies. In fact, however, spouse abuse occurs at all socio-economic levels (Loving 1980). Most violent husbands are under the age of 40, with the greatest number in their twenties. They are either generally violent, antisocial, and sociopathic men who frequently have fights in bars, at work, at school, and so on (Gondolf 1988), or they are relationship-specific violent men (Brisson 1981). Therapists consider the relationship-specific wife-beater a possible candidate for treatment, but not the generally violent man

(Bascelli 1985). Generally violent men who are also wife-beaters perceive violence as a part of their life-styles. They may stop wife-beating only when prosecuted. Many batterers who are in counseling are unaware of the immediate reasons for their blind rage and seldom connect prior psychological events, such as self-doubts, jealousy, and anxiety, with their aggressive behavior. Furthermore, few of these men connect their use of violent behavior to long-term consequences such as divorce or criminal prosecution (Edleson 1984).

Several studies have confirmed that many wife-beaters come from homes in which they were victims of child abuse or saw their fathers beat their mothers (see Roy 1982). Although early experiences do shape basic personality and aggressive behaviors are likely to be incorporated into an observer's or victim's own behavior patterns, these factors do not justify wife-battering.

The relationships between battering and the use of alcohol has also been misunderstood. Many people, including medical practitioners, police, and trial judges feel that there must be a direct causal connection between excessive drinking and violence (Mitchell 1988). When police arrive at the residence of a disputing couple and one or both are drunk, it is easy for the officers to draw the inference that violence was caused by drinking. Bard and Zacker (1974) found that alcohol led to family disputes requiring police intervention in only 14 percent of cases. Studies show a correlation between battering and presence of alcohol, but only a minority of women report alcohol to be a consistent contributing factor to violence (Roy 1982). Also, analysis of data from wives' reports show that drinking by abusive husbands is not significantly different than that of nonabusive husbands (Rosenbaum and O'Leary 1981). A recent study involving a sample of 5,159 households indicated that alcohol was used immediately prior to domestic abuse in the minority (24 percent) of cases (Kantor and Straus 1987).

The stereotype promoted by television and films that it is "drunken bums" who beat their wives is not supported by empirical evidence. Still, drunkenness is not totally absent as a correlate of wife-beating, but whether it is a cause of violence or an excuse for violence has to be differentiated. Recent reviews reject simple cause-and-effect theories of drug use and increased violence (Myers 1982). Some aggressive people become more aggressive with alcohol use, but they can also become less aggressive. Intoxication promotes an illusion of irresponsibility and encourages lessened impulse control, which may lead to silly or foolish behavior rather than aggressive behavior. Mitchell (1988) remarks, "intoxication encourages people to sing in public not because drunks sing so well but because they become less concerned about singing badly" (p. 85). Similarly, intoxication may encourage a batterer to be aggressive not because he is always violent but because he is threatened or annoyed and is less concerned about the consequences of his actions in that particular situation.

Battered Women

Pervasive conventional wisdom suggests that battered women who stay in the home are masochists and either like to be beaten or want to be beaten. Battered women have been characterized as "aggressive, efficient, masculine, frigid, and thus, legitimate threats to their husbands" (Walter 1982). Myths about battered women include the belief that a woman is free to leave such a relationship if that is what she truly wants, and that she could have informed police and friends if she were really injured.

Why do abused women stay in relationships with abusive men? Many women do leave these types of relationships after an average of six years (Browne 1987), but others stay for a number of reasons, some of which are not widely appreciated. The common characteristics of wife-beating and the distorted perceptions that result from this continuous treatment are together referred to as the "battered woman's syndrome" (Walker 1979). The severity and frequency of violence toward women varies substantially across couples, and any one factor, of course, will not be present in all women.

Many battered women face external constraints on their freedom of movement. They may be economically dependent upon their mate, they may lack employment and educational skills, and they may have no place to go. Family members and friends may blame them for their fate, and social service agencies may not be helpful. Calling the police for help may not be a workable solution since some abused women know that doing so will further enrage their husbands and result in greater beatings once the police leave. If the woman has children, her freedom to leave is further constrained by her concern for their welfare. Some women will stay with an abusive man for the sake of the children as long as he is not violent toward the children. Even if there is access to a shelter for battered women, victims cannot stay there indefinitely. Once women leave the shelter, they may fear retaliation involving further injury or death. A common phrase used by abusive husbands seems to be, "If I can't have you, no one will" (Browne 1983).

Internal constraints also act on the battered woman. Many women who stay in an abusive relationship have a poor self-image or low self-esteem, are emotionally dependent, and believe in traditional ideas about women's "proper place." Many of these women grew up as victims of child abuse and see the violence in their relationship as normal and natural. For these women, violence would have to be extraordinary in order for them to consider leaving (Loseke and Cahill 1984).

Once battering occurs in a relationship, the frequency and severity of abuse escalates over time (Dobash and Dobash 1979). Violence occurs in a three-stage cycle. Beginning with a period of *tension-building* (Walker 1979), friction, anger, name-calling, and minor abusive episodes gradually build and finally explode into an *acute battering incident*, the second stage. At this point, the man loses control and physically beats the woman. Most injuries occur at this time. The battering incident is followed by a period of loving, kind, and remorseful behavior, the *calm stage* the husband promises to make amends and showers his mate with affection. The intermittent repetition of this abusive cycle and the battered woman's psychological responses in each of the three stages—anger, frustration, resistance, pain, powerlessness, depression, relief, hope, love, and attraction—act to establish a traumatic emotional bond between the woman and her partner (Dutton and Painter 1981). The bond between the victim and her batterer is said to be similar to the emotional ties found between abused children and their parents, hostages and their kidnappers, and cult members and their leaders.

Battered women are usually more concerned with survival rather than with planning how to leave, particularly during the acute battering stage. Because she is unable to do or say anything that will stop the beatings and is unable to leave the situation, the woman is described as being in a state of learned helplessness (Seligman 1975). The woman may now view the situation as being out of her control. Passivity, fragmentary thinking, lack of concentration, and distorted perceptions and memory are common characteristics of learned helplessness. Even when given the chance to escape through legal solutions, such women usually do not respond since they believe that nothing will alter their situation. Battered women who kill their mates typically do so during an attempt to escape. In most cases, the murder was not intended and may be argued before the courts as motivated by self-defense. Standards of women's self-defense were set in the Joan Little case in North Carolina *(State v. Little* 1975) and, more particularly, in the Inez Garcia case in California, which involved self-defense for battered women *(State v. Garcia* 1977). Battered women usually do not have a history of violence. Nearly all call the police and the ambulance and are not aware that they have critically wounded their mate until informed later that he is dead (Walker, Thyfault, and Browne 1982).

The above discussion implies that ordinary citizens, police, other professionals, and social institutions share a normative expectation that assaulted women will leave their husbands. Women who stay are perceived as deviant, their behavior requiring explanation (Loseke and Cahill 1984). However, not all battered women who stay need professional help, many perceive themselves as less traditional than "other women" (Rosenbaum and O'Leary 1981; Walker 1983), and many report having higher self-esteem than "other women" (Walker 1983). It is possible that some abused women remain with their abusive husbands because of their personal and long-term commitment and deep attachment bonds to this specific mate. He is seen as an uniquely irreplaceable individual in spite of what outsiders perceive as a poor relationship. These women reject the notion that they are deviant by staying in a situation that has been abusive.

In contrast to the belief that battered wives are passive victims of abuse and trapped by forces beyond their control, some battered wives are successful in getting their husbands to stop the violence (Bowker 1983). These women use three types of activities to get the abuse to stop: (1) personal strategies, such as talking, threatening, promising, passive defense, aggressive defense, hiding, and avoidance; (2) informal help sources, including family members, neighbors, friends, and shelters; and (3) formal help sources, including the police, social service agencies, and lawyers. None of these strategies is superior to another. What is most important, according to Bowker (1983), is that women clearly and unambiguously insist that the violence cease immediately.

Police and Domestic Disputes

Many spouse abuse cases involve repeat calls from the same household. Repeat calls are a source of great frustration to law enforcement officers since police feel their presence has proven ineffective, and they feel poorly trained to handle family conflict calls in general (Loving 1980). The police are also criticized for their responses to domestic violence, accused of underenforcement of the law and crude applications of crisis intervention skills.

Underenforcement of the Law.   Police do not believe that intervention in domestic assaults on women is legitimate police work and do not perceive battered women as legitimate victims (Brown 1984). This view is first communicated during training and in police manuals (Bae 1981). Training in domestic crisis intervention techniques is not a priority for recruits or for veteran officers, even though police routinely experience at least one domestic disturbance daily. The charge that police departments and police officers systematically underenforce the law when investigating family disturbances is based on a number of empirically supported arguments. Underenforcement of the law starts with the responses of desk dispatchers who give low priority to domestic dispute phone calls. Patrol cars may or may not be sent, and, if dispatched, the arrival time is slower than for other calls involving disputes between unrelated parties (Berk et al. 1980; Oppenlander 1982). Patrol officers may not be in a hurry to get to a residence since they view these calls as "social work" rather than "real" police work. However, police responses to domestic disputes take as much time as any other single activity (Breslin 1978).

Police perceive intervention in family violence as an extremely dangerous activity, and they prefer to avoid it for personal and professional reasons. The low priority given by the department results in few occupational rewards or recognition for officers who charge batterers. Officers rationalize that the home is a private sanctuary and that problems within that environment are civil, not criminal matters and are best resolved by the parties themselves (Oppenlander 1982). Because of their minimal training, officers are not formally prepared to appreciate the needs of the battered woman. Officers feel incompetent to deal with her emotional distress, and because the visit is not regarded as criminal in nature, they may overlook the physical evidence of the assault (Jaffe and Burris 1981). Officers may even feel that the woman somehow deserved the beating.

Police officers are reluctant to arrest the abusive mate since they feel that arrests are generally useless in family disputes (Brown 1984). The victim often refuses to cooperate as a witness, may turn on the police, and, if an arrest is made, often wants the charge withdrawn at a later time (Homant and Kennedy 1982). Many police believe that bringing charges against a husband will only make the violence-prone man even more angry at his wife and promote further attacks when the man is released by the courts. The police are also aware that some prosecutors and judges may be sympathetic to abusive husbands and may fail to take family violence seriously. As a result, an assailant may not be vigorously prosecuted and, if found guilty, may receive the most lenient of sentences (Burris and Jaffe 1983).

Crisis Intervention.   Because of changes in policy and in the law, police in most jurisdictions no longer have to witness a family assault before they bring charges, providing they have reasonable and probable grounds to believe that the assault has occurred (Waaland and Keeley 1985). However, the most common police response is to talk to the offender, and arrests are rarely made (Brown 1984).

Police training in the use of domestic crisis intervention skills is long overdue. These skills are necessary if for no other reason than simply to defuse a potentially explosive situation (Dolan, Hendricks, and Meagher 1986). Training programs that emphasize police safety, rapid police assistance, effective crisis intervention skills, referral assessment, and working connections with social agency networks are needed (Levens and Dutton 1980). What battered women most want from police officers is someone who is understanding but firm, shows compassion while remaining impartial, and provides information about services and alternatives available in the community (Kennedy and Homant 1983). In contrast, studies indicate that police rarely refer victims to a social service agency and seldom suggest the use of community agencies, such as temporary shelters, family counseling, alcoholism programs, or mental health clinics, even though most police officers are aware of appropriate referral services (Brown 1984; Jaffe and Burris 1981; Oppenlander 1982).

Table 9.1   Police Crisis Intervention Skills

A. Observing and protecting against threats to your safety
   1. Consider your prior experience on similar calls.
   2. Anticipate that the unexpected may actually happen.
   3. Form a tentative plan of action.
B. Calming the situation
   1. Observe and neutralize threats to your safety.
   2. Create a first impression of nonhostile authority.
   3. Calm the emotional citizen.
C. Gathering relevant information
   1. Explain to the citizen what you want him to discuss with you and why.
   2. Interview the citizen so as to gain details of the crisis as clearly as possible.
   3. Show that you understand the citizen's statements and give answers to his questions.
   4. Revise your plan of action if appropriate.
D. Taking appropriate action
   1. Carefully explain your plan of action to the citizen.
   2. Check that the citizen understands and agrees with your plan of action.
   3. Carry out your plan of action.

Source: Adapted from Goldstein et al. 1977. Reprinted with permission from A. P. Goldstein et al., *Police Crisis Intervention*, © 1977, Pergamon Press Plc.

Effective police crisis intervention consists of four separate skills, which are outlined in Table 9.1.

The use of each of these procedures, combined with an understanding of the dynamics of spouse abuse (or other types of crises), can promote appropriate police responses. Goldstein et al. (1977) suggest five courses of action that an officer might take in a crisis situation, mediation, negotiation, counseling, referral and arbitration, each of which differs in the amount of assistance that police officers give in helping citizens resolve their problems. They also differ in their long-term effectiveness (see Figure 9.1).

1. *Mediation.* Long-term problem-solving in husband-wife disputes is most effective and most lasting when the individuals themselves solve their own problems. An officer's role in mediation is to facilitate citizens' solving their own problems rather to give answers or make suggestions. Help is given by listening to and clarifying separately each participant's suggested solutions, acting as a go-between with proposals,

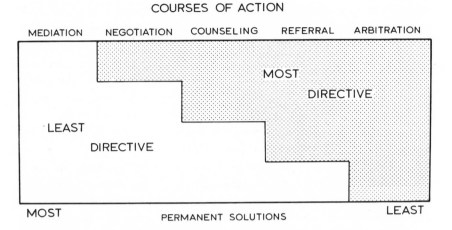

Figure 9.1 Levels of Directiveness and Effectiveness in Five Courses of Police Action in Crisis Situations.

promoting a cooperative, give-and-take atmosphere, and supporting in a nonjudgmental way the final agreed-upon solutions made by the couple.

Certain ground rules must be announced at the beginning of the mediation session. Husband and wife are to remain seated at a distance from each other. While one person is speaking, the other is not to interrupt. Speakers are to try to report specific facts of the incident that brought them to this immediate crisis and separately relate the history of events that led up to the present problem. The person that phoned in the complaint should start by presenting his or her side of the issue. After each person has spoken and has had a chance to respond to the facts the other has raised, the mediator should separate the couple into different rooms and speak to each one privately. The primary purpose of meeting separately and then finally as a group is to convince both parties that there is a problem they must solve. The mediator should let the couple do most of the talking and allow frustrations to be expressed or "vented" in the presence of a sympathetic listener. He or she should interject with questions such as "How do you see this problem?" and, later in the discussion, "How do you think this problem should be resolved?" The police officer has to keep suggestions concrete and realistic. He or she may offer "what if" statements if the couple is stalemated. Tentative solutions may lead to some sort of compromise that both the husband and wife can discuss and resolve on their own.

2. *Negotiation.* If mediation is unsuccessful or is not attempted because the parties were not ready to resolve the crisis on their own, the officer may have to be more directive by suggesting solutions or compromises. The officer should state his or her own view, but avoid taking sides. The officer's role is to show that he or she is objective but also has some control over their immediate future.

Negotiation involves bargaining, a form of social exchange in which individuals engage in a mutual trade of offers, compromises, and perhaps concessions. For some disputes, officers may want to propose extreme initial solutions to the crisis since research indicates that participants seem to lower their expectations considerably after hearing large demands (Yukl 1974). Initial suggestions, however, cannot be so extreme that they anger either party since this may result in the termination of negotiation in disgust. Free and open negotiation between a husband and wife, along with the officer, can enhance the possibility of compromise and agreement if it is perceived as an honest attempt to reach a solution (Kelley and Thibaut 1978). The techniques of mediation and negotiation, however, are useful only in spouse abuse cases that do not involve physical injury as a result of violence or the use of a weapon. When there is physical injury as a result of assault or aggravated assault, criminal procedures leading to possible arrest are more appropriate (Loving 1980).

3. *Counseling.* As counselors, police officers must be directive, open, genuine, and supportive. They must actively offer suggestions and advice and assist the couple to express and understand their feelings, wishes, and expectations. The police officer-as-counselor is not there to resolve all the predisposing problems of the husband and wife, but to try to encourage the parties to acknowledge their differences and seek professional help.

4. *Referral.* If the police officer-as-counselor is effective, the couple will be ready to seek and want help for an acknowledged problem. Referrals are most efficacious if the officer can best match the services needed by the couple with the most appropriate agency. This requires that officers be familiar with the different types of help available in their community.

5. *Arbitration.* If all of the above actions fail or are inappropriate, an officer might have to directly impose a solution. Arbitration, however, seldom has lasting effects on resolving the problem.

CRIMINAL VICTIMIZATION OF THE ELDERLY

Three commonly held and popular beliefs about crime and older people are: (1) Crime is one of the most serious problems that elderly people face; (2) the elderly are more frequently victimized by crime than other age groups; and (3) fear of crime among the elderly is exceptionally great relative to other age groups. Speaking to an American Senate Subcommittee on Housing for the Elderly in 1972, Senator Edward Kennedy stated: "The threat of crime and violence against our older citizens demands a response from all levels of government. . . . A decent and safe living environment is an inherent right of all elderly citizens" (quoted in Cook and Cook 1976, 633). Over the last twenty years, social gerontologists have documented and generally supported the elderly's concern about criminal victimization. Fear of crime by the elderly has apparently made many older persons prisoners in their own homes, afraid to go outside at certain times, suspicious of strangers, and desirous of extreme security measures (Braungart, Hoyer, and Braungart 1979; Garofalo 1972).

The following vignette illustrates the experiences of an elderly person as a witness to a crime.

She sat quietly on the edge of the long bench; tightly clutching her purse. Her other hand firmly gripped the top of her cane and she looked as if she were about to rise; but she did not. She was attired in her Sunday best including matching hat and gloves. Her silver-gray curls peeked out from underneath the rim of her hat and an educated guess would place her in her middle eighties. She had obviously gone to a great deal of care to ready herself for that day; but for some unknown reason, she looked oddly out of place in her surroundings.

She felt rather nervous inside; she had never been to court before. She was amazed at the number of people running up and down the long hall. Lawyers, in their long, black gowns, talking to different people for varying lengths of time and then rushing off, only to disappear and emerge again a few moments later as if they couldn't decide where they wanted to be. Men and women sat or stood around talking and laughing. Laughing, she thought to herself, can you imagine that; and in these sacred halls of justice. She closed her eyes for a few moments as if she were trying to reconcile the thought. When she opened them, a presence came into her visual field that made her start; there he was, the very reason for her being where she was. She felt anger flare up again. He was standing only a few feet away, talking with some friends it seemed (she was just a bit surprised to see he had any). Yes, that was definitely him, she would never forget what he looked like. Then she thought of Sarah, sweet Sarah who wouldn't even hurt a fly. Gosh, their friendship went back some seventy-five years; and now she lay in that hospital with a broken hip. Such a senseless thing for him to do, and all for five dollars. She shut her eyes again, this time to keep the tears in, she might lose the dearest friend in the whole world—and all for five dollars.

Then something in their conversation drew her sharply from her thoughts. "Yes, that's her, what a crazy looking old dame. She's in the wrong place, somebody ought to tell her the funeral home is down the street." "Come on Jeff," a friend replied. "She might hear you." "Hear me? Are you kidding—why just look at her. She's so old she probably couldn't hear if you yelled in her ear."

She lifted her proud head ever so slightly, her lips were firmly pressed together. In a way he was right. Her hearing had been going for a few years now and was a continual source of frustration for her. There were times when she could catch a whisper, and then there were other times . . . Oh well, what can you do? Right now, however, she wished she were deaf.

"Can you imagine me losing this case? Her word against mine, and who is going to believe someone as old as that? I've got it made and when she leaves court today, she'll feel like the old fool she really is for coming in. She should have stayed home with her cats where she belongs."

She hated him even more, if that were possible. She could feel her blood pressure rising. Boy, he wouldn't be feeling so cocky when this day was over, she told herself. Then she smiled inwardly as she thought of reaching over and giving him a good bash on the head with her solid black, oak cane—one good one for Sarah; and maybe even another one for herself.

Then, everything was quiet. She sat there quietly, alone, waiting to be called as the only witness to that heinous crime. She felt suddenly small sitting there in the court hall with its high ceiling and pillar supports. She wished the whole thing was over. Still, she was there to tell the truth. This was her duty; and she had every confidence that it would turn out all right. She remembered when the police had come over to question her. They seemed so impatient and abrupt, but after all, they are so busy and they work so hard all day . . . yes, she could understand it. But in court it would be different. Yes, it sure would. She would get to tell them everything that happened and just how disgusting that young man was. They would sure know what to do with him . . . why . . . MRS. NELLIE BATES. MRS. NELLIE BATES, PLEASE.

She jumped at the sound of her name echoing in the hall. She slowly rose to her feet, feeling somewhat stiff for having sat so long. Then, with the aid of her cane, she made her way toward the open door. The man holding the door took her arm and proceeded to escort her to the front, much faster than she was comfortably used to. Finally, she arrived at the front and seated herself in the chair provided for her.

Everything seemed to go so fast after that, she felt she was in a whirl. The lawyer was asking her questions, turning his head away, she couldn't hear him. She tried to tell them what happened but she was continually being cut off—"Just answer the question, please." "How old are you, Mrs. Bates?" "How good would you say your eyesight is?" "Please speak up Mrs. Bates, no one can hear you." She felt confused and scared. All her confidence disappeared and she wished her husband were alive to help her now. Maybe that Jeff was right—everything was going all wrong. Her eyes misted and she wished she were safe at home. Then it was over, just like that. She was being dismissed, like a child. She looked around pleadingly, she had so much more to tell—no one was interested. She sighed a deep sigh of resignation, and feeling totally defeated, she pulled herself up. The man came hurrying up the aisle to escort her back, but she ignored him. She was not going to be run out of court, they would just have to wait for her to walk.

She approached the table where the young man was sitting with his lawyer. She reached her arm out onto the table for support, and that was when she lost her balance. She desperately tried to regain her footing and her arm made a wild grab for the table. Somehow, she lost her cane in the process, and not knowing exactly how, it sailed out in front where it caught Jeff on the side of the head before it clattered to the floor. Strong arms grabbed her and steadied her on her feet. Her cane was retrieved, and after a quick apology, she was on her way again. She didn't object this time as the man took her arm and walked her to the door. Nor did she grumble when she had to sit in the large hall waiting for over half an hour for the taxi she called. A janitor passed her by several times as he swept the floor but she didn't seem to notice him. He heard her singing a little song to herself; he recognized the tune "The Old Gray Mare," but he didn't recognize the words. He wasn't sure, but he thought he heard her singing: "My old throwing arm, it's just what it used to be . . . just what it used to be." (Yarmey and Kent 1980, 368–70)

Judgments of the accuracy and credibility of witnesses are central to the justice system. The relationship between the accuracy of human observation and recollection and the credibility of the witness is particularly relevant to the police officer's and the court's examination of the elderly. Stereotypes of the aged can influence the way that elderly victims are treated by the justice system (Yarmey 1984).

Contrary to popular beliefs, elderly Americans and Canadians 65 years of age and over are not especially vulnerable to criminal victimization more than any other age group. Young men and women in the 16 to 24 age group are the most likely targets of criminals. Studies using data with large national samples (see U.S. Federal Bureau of Investigation 1974–1985; Solicitor General of Canada 1985; U.S. Department of Justice 1986) indicate that the elderly are the least likely age group to be victimized for most types of serious crimes (burglary, theft, rape, robbery, and assault) and are not likely to be victimized more than other groups in personal crimes such as pocket-picking and purse-snatching.

The relatively lower victimization rates among the elderly than for other age groups, however, should not suggest that crime is of minimal concern. Although older citizens are not more likely to suffer injuries from crimes than younger victims, the elderly who are injured are twice as likely to need medical and dental assistance (Solicitor General of Canada 1985). Furthermore, as the Canadian study showed, the financial impact of criminal victimization is substantially greater for the elderly than for other age groups. Relative to their annual incomes, elderly persons suffer twice as much economic loss from victimization of crimes than do others.

The *fear-victimization paradox*, in which the elderly appear most fearful about the problem of crime but experience least victimization, has been well documented (Garofalo 1981), but the validity of the "fear of crime" is being questioned (see Yin 1982). It is true that some older people are indeed fearful of crime, but fear of crime should not be confused with fear of victimization (Warr 1984). Recent research evidence suggests that older people are not especially afraid of crime in their everyday lives, but that they are more uncertain and anxious about their neighborhood environment. Young people under 25 have concrete fears about specific types of crimes, such as fear of car or property vandalism, home burglary, rape, and murder. In contrast, elderly people are more concerned about the possibility of street robbery or injury by a burglar and a poorer quality of life in their neighborhoods (Ferraro and LaGrange 1988).

To the extent that the elderly feel vulnerable and threatened by changes in the composition and quality of life in their neighborhoods, concern for the possibility of criminal victimization is heightened (Mawby 1982). The elderly who are relatively powerless and perceive little ability to control their futures show a generalized anxiety about their everyday lives, anxiety that includes a greater concern for the possibility of criminal victimization. Perceived safety is related to neighborhood satisfaction, neighborhood convenience, and overall morale. Elderly women who feel most competent, have a strong sense of personal control, and believe that events that impinge on their lives are predictable show little fear of crime (Normoyle and Lavrakas 1984). It is likely that anxiety about criminal victimization is strongly related to personal resources, such as finances, health, and other concerns connected to aging. When these concerns are salient, the elderly person may feel threatened by feelings of self-doubt, incompetence, and an inability to handle general social demands (Ward, LaGory, and Sherman 1986).

Police and Fear-Reduction Strategies

The majority of the public, especially the elderly, are positively disposed toward the police and feel that the local police are doing a good job (Yarmey and Rashid 1983). Most elderly victims of crime perceive the police as approachable, courteous, prompt in their response to calls, but, like other age groups, they are critical about the lack of information made available about the progress of the investigation in their cases (Solicitor General of Canada 1985). The public in general wants a more personable, service-oriented approach taken by the police toward their victimization. That is, they want the police to offer sympathy and interest in their plight, give instruction on better security, and show symbols of thorough criminal investigation such as dusting for fingerprints and questioning of neighbors. In particular, the public wants follow-up contact even when there is little chance for arrest. The police may not see these sorts of "ritualistic" performances as necessary or efficient, but they do assist victims in coping with their fear of crime and emotional distress (Maguire 1981).

The police can play an active role in victimization prevention and, as a consequence, reduce fear of crime among the elderly. The crime prevention literature urges the elderly and women to take greater control over their social environments. However, this exhortation will not succeed unless the police reinforce this advice through practical demonstrations and skills and selected social and environmental supports are developed and maintained (Jones 1987). Several police strategies and programs to reduce citizens' fear of crime have been implemented in the last few years. While police patroling in cars have had little effect on reducing crime or citizens' fears (Kelling et al. 1974), foot patrol does reduce fear of crime among local residents, even though it may not reduce crime itself. The value of foot patrol is attributed to its promotion of "symbolic reassurance" (Bahn 1974) and greater attention to regulation of disorderly behavior and to disreputable, obstreperous, or unpredictable people such as panhandlers, drunks, addicts, rowdy teenagers, prostitutes, loiterers, and the mentally disturbed (Wilson and Kelling

1985). Police involvement in door-to-door surveying to determine specific issues of concern, distribution of valid information about the amount of local crime and risk of criminal victimization, instruction about security measures and the value of neighborhood watch programs may allay citizens' fears (Cordner 1986).

Police intervention tactics must be rational and targeted for specific problems of selected neighborhoods rather than following general strategies to increase citizen contact (Goldstein 1979). In some neighborhoods, but in not others, fear of crime may be a serious but very localized problem. The police should put their energy into solving problems with strategies that fit the issue at hand and are based upon valid, identified needs instead of responding in traditional and more superficial "service call" ways (Cordner 1986). Problem-oriented policing means that police involvement in such activities as Neighborhood Watch should involve more than merely initiating the program or attending a meeting as special guests. Police should be more active in selecting appropriate neighborhoods to implement the program, assisting in setting the agenda, and coordinating regular meetings. A Neighborhood Watch program is not a suitable strategy for all neighborhoods or blocks and may even increase fear of personal crime and heighten prejudices, especially in multiethnic communities (Rosenbaum 1987b).

The elderly are rarely aware of and seldom participate in community crime prevention programs (Solicitor General of Canada 1985). Problem-oriented police departments have the opportunity to confront real concerns and reduce anxieties about crime among older citizens by actively supplying them with crime prevention information and soliciting their assistance in police-directed programs.

SUMMARY

Criminal victimization often has a persistent impact on a persons' emotional and cognitive well-being. Shock, anxiety, depression, and memory loss are common responses and are referred to collectively as posttraumatic stress. Victims of sexual assault share most of these symptoms and must also deal with self-blame and shame because of conflicts and taboos about sexuality and the mythologies surrounding the responsibility of women as victims of rape. How the police deal with sexual assault victims has both immediate and long-term consequences for victims' personal adjustment.

Spouse abuse is any physical or psychological act carried out with the intention of or perceived as having the intention of injuring another person. Wife-batterers are either generally violent men or are relationship-specific violent men. Many abused women leave these types of relationships, but other stay for a number of personal, social, and/or economic reasons. Police have been criticized for their underenforcement of the law in responses to domestic violence and for their crude applications of crisis intervention skills.

Contrary to popular beliefs, the elderly are not especially vulnerable to criminal victimization, but fear of crime is reportedly great among older people. Recent research suggests that the elderly are not especially afraid of crime in their everyday lives, but that they are more uncertain and anxious about the overall quality of life, including the possibility of criminal victimization in their neighborhoods.

10

Decision-Making

Unlike police in many countries, frontline law enforcement officers in the United States and Canada have responsibility for tactical decision-making involving almost all interactions with the public. Patrol officers constantly make choices. Given the responsibility to use discretion, an officer may choose to use force, to arrest, to mediate, to threaten, to warn, to laugh, or even to do nothing. Sometimes these decisions, such as the decision to use deadly force, have to made in a split second.

Selective law enforcement is essential for the criminal justice to function (Goldstein 1960), but what prepares the officer to make such judgments? Police themselves say that experience is the best teacher. Supposedly, decision-making in policing cannot be taught since every situation an officer confronts is unique, and it is impossible to generalize across circumstances. It is also claimed that human behavior is too complex to predict in spite of scientific research efforts to prove otherwise (Bayley and Bittner 1984). The contradiction in these statements, however, should be obvious since police officers do learn to discriminate patterns of behavior through their experiences, and they do share their knowledge with fellow officers. Police officers' main resource, or data base, for making decisions are their collective experiences. This means that decision-making is being taught, but not necessarily in the safest and most effective ways, and not in a way that maximizes scientific knowledge and modern information processing strategies (Sherman 1984). Those situations that are most problematic and give the greatest latitude in decision-making—that is, domestic disputes, proactive traffic stops, and maintenance of order among groups of young people congregating in public places—are also among the most dangerous that an officer faces.

The preparation of authoritative guidelines to assist officers' decision-making is impractical since it is impossible to anticipate the many different circumstances that these rules would have to cover. Still, officers are expected to exercise expert judgment. How police officers estimate the risk factor when entering dangerous situations or how criminals judge their chances for detection and arrest are examples of problems investigated in an area of psychology called *decision-making*. Decision-making is usually subjective, often irrational, and seldom perfect. In spite of the uncertainty that often accompanies choice, decision-making can be improved through knowledge of the fallacies underlying reasoning and judgment and an appreciation of the cognitive processes involved in making inferences and drawing conclusions. This chapter is designed to describe the psychology of decision-making and to show how these principles may be generalized to police and civilian behavior.

REASONING

Rational thought involves deductive and inductive reasoning, judgment, and decision-making. *Deductive reasoning* concerns certainties; if certain premises are true, then certain conclusions will follow. If the premises are wrong, then the conclusions will be wrong, of course. *Induction*, on the other hand, involves finding a common rule or conclusion when given a number of examples or individual instances. Although inferences may appear straightforward, they lead only to probable knowledge rather than to certain conclusions. *Judgment* is the process by which we form opinions, make evaluations, and draw conclusions based upon the information that is available. *Decision-making* is the process of choosing between alternatives and selecting and rejecting courses of action under conditions of uncertainty.

As an example of the reasoning process, suppose that a police officer is called to the scene of a domestic dispute and finds that Mrs. Brown has a nose bleed and two black eyes. The officer learns that Mr. Brown constantly abuses his wife. The officer may conclude through deductive reasoning that Mr. Brown has just beaten his wife, although this may be a faulty deduction if the premises are wrong. The officer might draw the further deduction that Mrs. Brown is similar to other women who live with this type of man. The officer may infer a number of motives for the assault. He may judge that Mrs. Brown is attractive but provocative and may even have deserved the battering. Finally, the officer might make the decision to warn the husband or request that he move to a motel for the night, or he may decide to arrest the man after considering the utility and possible consequences of these different choices for this particular situation.

MEMORY AND JUDGMENT OF FACTS

The traditional view of how people think assumes that we are rational and reasonable creatures, that we weigh the costs and benefits of alternative actions, and that we choose the alternative that has the most value or greatest expected gain. We also assume that we know why we have done something and can trust our explanations for our own behavior. The rational view of judgment and reasoning works in most ordinary and routine situations. However, rational thinking is limited because of perceptual and memory deficits, erroneous reasoning processes, and emotional forces. Furthermore, people are often unaware of their own mental processes. Their explanations, given in all honesty, about why they acted as they did or why they made a certain choice, are often false (Nisbett and Wilson 1977).

Perception and *memory* are biological and social processes by which we gather and interpret information about our environment. Information that is attended to is grouped and organized into concepts on the basis of our needs and interests. Thus, a glimpse of an object in a man's hand may be a dangerous gun, or it may be a harmless toy, or it may not exist except as a figment of imagination. As Schutz (1971), a social philosopher, noted:

All our knowledge of the world, in common-sense as well as in scientific thinking, involves constructs, i.e., a set of abstractions, generalizations, formalizations, and idealizations specific to the respective level of thought organization. Strictly speaking, there are no such things as facts, pure and simple. All facts are from the outset facts selected from a universal context by the activities of our mind. They are, therefore, always interpreted facts. (P. 5)

SCHEMATA AND HEURISTICS

In order to fully appreciate the dynamics involved in understanding the decision-making of police officers and offenders, certain basic psychological concepts must first be understood. Our ability to attend to information, store it in memory, and later retrieve it from storage is limited. To compensate for these shortcomings, we use a number of shortcuts, or cognitive strategies. Mental shortcuts serve to reduce information overload and allow us to make judgments efficiently and effectively as possible. These cognitive strategies involve the use of schemata and heuristics. A *schema* is an organized collection of thoughts, beliefs, and feelings about objects, persons, roles, or events. *Heuristics*, on the other hand, are decision-making principles that act as mental shortcuts for making inferences and drawing conclusions. Errors and distortions occur in thinking because heuristics often involve the use of biases and fallacies when people deal with social information.

The Value of Schemata

Schemata are valuable because they allow us to process information efficiently at each of the three main stages of memory processes: *attention, encoding,* and *retrieval.* What we notice, store in memory, and retrieve from memory depends upon the selective process of the mind. Selection of social information is guided by schemata, which assist in the interpretation of social information, fill in gaps where there are deficiencies in input, draw meaningful inferences from information, assist in problem-solving, and provide normative expectations for what should happen. Our behavior in many respects is efficient on routine tasks because schematic processing is so automatic.

Not everything about schematic processing is constructive, however. Schemata may lead a person to misperceive or fail to recognize a new situation; or to reject legitimate evidence about something because it doesn't fit the schema, as when stereotypes guide thoughts and behaviors; or they may be incorrectly imposed on a situation on the basis of minimal and preliminary information and cause one to "jump the gun." If schematic processing gets too mechanical or too routine, people begin to act mindlessly—that is, they fail to consciously attend to details, and may fail to make necessary adjustments in performance (Langer and Imber 1979).

Police officers, for example, have a schema for juvenile delinquents. Police know that certain kinds of hair styles, demeanour, clothing, and walking habits distinguish offenders from other youths (Pepinsky 1975). The schema might include a number of general group characteristics such as the likelihood of prior records and the probability of dangerousness or threat to others. In short, police have a clear, well-developed picture in their minds about what constitutes a "juvenile delinquent."

Police officers are "primed" to read potential danger in encounters from their career experiences and, in particular, from calls from dispatchers. Even slight differences in wording from dispatchers, such as, "check a burglary" as opposed to " check a break-in" result in different schemata and reactions from patrol officers (Pepinsky 1976). Pepinsky (1977) theorizes that police officers have such high information overload in handling their everyday duties that they make decisions about specific cases based upon institutionalized official schemata.

There are many types of schemata. *Person schemata* organize our impressions and feelings about a person we know well such that we are surprised if this individual behaves out of character. *Self-schemata* help us to process information about our selves and our social world. Events that impinge on our beliefs about our selves are given great attention, are thought about frequently, and are more easily remembered than other events. *Role schemata* represent the organized, abstract images we hold about people in a particular role, such as police officers, delinquents, pickpockets, and the like. These schemata direct our expectations about how these people are supposed to act. Problems sometimes arise when one individual each has a schema for another's role whose behavior does not match expectations, or the schema. Finally, *event schemata* refer to organized beliefs about how events are supposed to proceed. People often expect that an event will follow a script in which there is a standard sequence of behavior over a period of time. For example, in the situation of a police officer moving a gang of kids off a shopping center the script might involve the officer making an order, several kids yelling and protesting, voices getting loud, the officer's staying cool, the kids' getting angry, one or two kids appointing themselves as leaders and speaking for the group, and so on. Event schemata have a causal flow that can be specific and elaborate and allow us to know in advance what to expect in a particular type of situation.

Irrationality of Human Inference and Heuristics

Like everything else, the world of policing is becoming increasingly technical; intuitive knowledge based on practical experience is proving to be insufficient as a guideline for police decision-making (Bayley and Bittner 1984). Police officers are called upon to make decisions that require an ability to make inferences from statistical data. Patrol officers must think in probabilistic terms whenever they take actions involving the possibility of personal injury to self and others. In this section, I will look at the use of different heuristics people use to make inferences or draw conclusions rapidly and effortlessly.

Availability Heuristic

Consider the following research findings: When people were asked to estimate the frequency of deaths from accidents, homicides, and tornadoes as compared to deaths from disease such as diabetes, strokes, tuberculosis, asthma, and emphysema, they overestimated the former, which are more rare, vivid, and sensational, and underestimated the latter, which are more frequent, regular, and mundane. Suicides occur 30 percent more frequently than homicides, but homicides were estimated to be about five times as frequent as suicides (Slovic, Fischhoff, and Lichtenstein 1980). It appears that events that are easily recalled or easy to imagine are likely to be judged as more frequent than those that are less readily recalled or less imaginable. This is the *availability heuristic*. Dramatic or sensational incidents are highly salient and, consequently, are given high attention. The high availability of such events may create a false impression of greater frequency and more erroneous judgments (Tversky and Kahneman 1982).

The availability heuristic raises important concerns for police officers who have to make split-second decisions with life and death consequences. Those factors and events that are most emotion-arousing, vivid, concrete, and salient, such as racial characteristics and related beliefs about risk, will be more accessible in memory and therefore believed to be more probable. Thus, officers may make life and death decisions based upon evidence that is most available but not necessarily most relevant.

Several kinds of reasoning errors or fallacies based on the availability principle have been identified:

Illusory Correlation. Police officers often have to decide whether a citizen is drunk or is mentally disturbed, is dangerous or not, should be taken to the police station or hospital, and so on. Judgments of people and the amount of trust and credibility we give to them often depends on the cooccurrences of other events. Inaccurate judgments often occur because of erroneous beliefs about the covariation between events. Because of stereotyped expectations, people often see relationships between events that really are not there (Chapman and Chapman 1982). These are *illusory correlations.* For instance, someone may look suspicious or dangerous because he or she has especially large eyes. The greater the assumed association between large eyes and dangerousness, the more likely it will be decided that they cooccur. However, just because they seem to be related does not mean that they have any predictive value—that is, large eyes do not cause violent behavior and may be totally unrelated to dangerousness.

People are susceptible to making illusionary correlations because of the tendency to look for, consider, and recall things that confirm beliefs rather than disconfirm them. In other words, people have a confirmation bias. We often continue to persevere with our beliefs and practices, even when it is shown that they are wrong, because they worked in the past and we are comfortable with our existing theories. We will even try to ignore, reinterpret, or explain away new information that is incongruent with our beliefs. Theories tend to persevere even when supporting evidence is discredited because efforts have been made to rationalize the existing theory and these rationalizations are very available in memory.

Theories also dominate thinking such that other general hypotheses are often not considered. For example, several years ago, the manner in which the British police handled the five-year investigation of the "Yorkshire Ripper" murders was criticized for "grooved" thinking (Steinbruner 1975). Police were convinced that tapes and letters sent to them were authentic and had been sent by the murderer of Joan Harrison, since information in these materials contained unpublicized facts. Their strong commitment to the authenticity of these materials, which later proved to be false, blinded them to other hypotheses (Pennington 1981). In addition, any information that confirmed the police hypothesis that the Yorkshire Ripper had a Sunderland accent was accepted, while information to the contrary was disregarded or devalued. Peter Sutcliffe, the man who was eventually arrested and convicted for the murders, was known to the police early in the investigation, but, in spite of incriminating evidence in one police report, he was not considered a prime suspect because he lacked the Sunderland accent.

Adjustment and Anchoring.   When people are asked to make judgments of the outcome of certain events, initial estimations often serve as *anchors* for subsequent decisions, and these final decisions are often *adjusted* up or down as a function of initial values. Different initial values lead to different final estimates; if the starting point is high, estimates will be higher than if the starting point is low. Consider, for example, the following problem given to high school students (Tversky and Kahneman 1973a). One group was asked to estimate within five seconds the mathematical product of $1 \times 2 \times 3 \times 4 \times 5 \times 6 \times 7 \times 8$. The second group given the same amount of time had to estimate $8 \times 7 \times 6 \times 5 \times 4 \times 3 \times 2 \times 1$. The correct answer in both cases is 40,320, but group one gave a median estimate of 512 whereas group two gave a median estimate of 2,250. In order to make these estimations, each group probably started to calculate the first two or three numbers and then to extrapolate to a final guess. The anchoring principle caused the first group, which started with smaller ascending numbers, to judge the final calculation to be lower than the second group, which started with larger descending numbers.

The principle of an *anchoring bias* raises interesting questions for police decision-making and policy issues. For example, do police administrators' knowledge of patrol officers' traffic ticket quotas for one year anchor the next year's quotas? Does current frequency of use of deadly force in crisis situations anchor beliefs about what is appropriate in future crisis situations?

Conjunctive Bias.   Another availability heuristic that can produce errors in judgment occurs when decisions must be made about compound events and is called *conjunctive bias*. In judging the likelihood of the joint occurrence (conjunction) of two independent events, the proper statistical procedure is to calculate the product of their separate probabilities. Thus, the probability of a coin turning up "tails" two times in a row is .5 (heads versus tails) $\times$ .5 (heads versus tails) or .25. This simple example illustrates that conjunction is less likely than each probability taken alone. However, when research subjects were asked to estimate the probability of the events in following statements "A complete suspension of diplomatic relations between the U.S.A. and the Soviet Union, sometime in 1983" and "A Russian invasion of Poland, and a complete suspension of diplomatic relations between the U.S.A. and the Soviet Union, sometime in 1983," subjects judged the second statement more probable than the first. The conjunction fallacy was probably committed because the added item "a Russian invasion of Poland" provided a vivid image that linked the two independent events into a cause-and-effect relationship. The joint occurrence of these two events is plausible, but they are less likely to occur than a suspension of diplomatic relations alone. People tend to overestimate the likelihood of the occurrence of conjunctive events (Tversky and Kahneman 1983).

False Consensus Effect.   Research indicates that people tend to overestimate the number of individuals like themselves who hold similar attitudes toward specific persons or actions. They also overestimate the number of people who would make the same judgments and choices as themselves in specified situations (Nisbett and Kunda 1985). The *false consensus effect* may occur because people tend to selectively perceive and remember others who agree with them more than people who disagree with them. Also, those persons who are not in agreement are unlikely to spend much time together. Consequently, the greater availability of like-minded persons may give the false impression of higher consensus than is warranted.

Representativeness Heuristic

The difficulty in making social judgments under conditions of uncertainty is simplified by the *representativeness heuristic*, which is used whenever we make an inference or judgment that a person or an event is similar to or resembles or is typical of some general population or category of events. However, by assuming a connection between a specific instance and a general category based merely on resemblance, we are liable to make errors in judgment because of misconceptions of or insensitivity to statistical information.

Gambler's Fallacy.   Misunderstandings regarding the laws of chance can lead someone to adopt a judgment strategy known as the *gambler's fallacy*. Take the following example: If you flipped a fair coin and heads turned up three times in a row, and you decided that tails were most likely to turn up on the next toss, and then heads won again, you might feel more sure than ever that tails would win on the next toss. If the coin did turn up tails, your strategy and the gambler's fallacy would be reinforced. This shifting about in feelings and predictions may be understandable in common sense terms, but it is irrational in probabilistic terms and produces a heuristic bias. The odds for flipping a fair coin remains constant at 50:50 on each toss. Each coin toss in a sequence of tosses is an independent event, and what happens in prior events does not effect the probability of later events. The error in inference occurs because people know that in the long run there will be a 50–50 probability of heads and tails, and they believe that in the short run a small sequence of tosses will be representative of the infinite sequence.

Regression Errors.   If police officers (and other legal officials) are to make rational decisions, they must know and play the odds with an appreciation of statistical reasoning, rather than rely on intuition (Saks and Kidd 1980–1981.) Most people, for example, have little awareness of the notion of regression errors. For example, if you played a round of golf and played much better than normally, would you expect to repeat that good score on the next game? The likelihood is that you wouldn't play as well in your next game. Similarly, if you played a poor game, the likelihood is that you would improve on your next round. This illustrates the statistical principle of *regression to the mean*—that is, on the average, events that are extreme will be less extreme when they recur. The *regression fallacy* occurs when people ignore, discount, or are unaware of this explanation for changes in performance. People tend to think of other reasons for the event, attributing performance changes to praise, criticisms, rewards, punishments, and so on, rather than to the less striking and more probable reason of regression errors.

Base Rate Information. Imagine that a police officer has just stopped a motorist for a traffic violation. In the course of her questioning she notices that the person is polite, shy, neat in appearance, and careful in his grammar and pronunciation. Is this person likely to be a pilot, a business executive, a plumber, a professor, or a professional athlete? One way to make this judgment is to compare his traits with the typical pilot, business executive, plumber, professor, and professional athlete. If this strategy is followed, the representativeness heuristic is being used, and, as we already know, it is prone to error (Tversky and Kahneman 1973b). A better strategy would be to rely on *base rate information*—that is, how common is each alternative in the general population. If there are more business executives in the general population than there are pilots, plumbers, professors, and professional athletes, the probability is greatest that the driver in this example is a business executive.

If predictions are to have value, base rate information drawn from a large number of samples of the population must be available and utilized. Laypersons have been shown to freely use and benefit from statistical information when its situational applicability is made apparent (Kruglanski, Friedland, and Farkash 1984). Although research has yet to be conducted, it is to be expected that police would also benefit from and be able to freely use statistical information when its situational applicability was made apparent. Unfortunately, modern police managers fail to provide frontline officers with feedback information telling them about the consequences of their interventions or whether their arrests resulted in convictions or prison sentences. Without adequate feedback, base rate information is not available and, of course, cannot be used as comparable knowledge in discretionary judgments. This problem promises to be resolved with the introduction of computer terminals in police cars, providing the terminals are properly programed to provide such information (Sherman 1984). However, training police officers to use these sorts of decision-making aids in their job performance will not be feasible for all individuals. Police, like everyone else, differ in their ability and willingness to transfer course learnings to their job tasks (Kleiman and Gordon 1986).

BIASES AND COMMON BELIEFS

Wise decisions depend upon one's knowing the facts and properly interpreting these facts. However, we often rely on experts or other authorities for advice and they may contradict one another as well as differ from common sense. How are we to know which interpretation is most likely to be valid? One solution is to reduce the number of possible explanations about a problem by identifying biases of thinking (Lauer 1978).

Bias of Dramatic Examples

The *bias of dramatic examples* refers to the tendency to generalize from a small number of sensational examples or even a single dramatic instance to a universal proposition. For instance, in discussing the problem of mental illness, people often make judgments about the mentally disturbed on the basis of personally knowing one or two people who have been "sick." This small sample may possess some of the more striking characteristics of the mental ill, but it is unlikely that it represents this population in more than a few exceptional ways. One study has shown, for example, that a juror's belief whether a defendant was legally insane or not depended to a great extent upon the resemblance between the defendant and someone the juror knew who had been mentally ill (Simon 1967).

Generalizations from small samples are always risky. A fundamental concept of reasoning from statistics is that of large samples must be used. If you want to describe a population of people—for example, "men who batter their wives"—larger samples are more likely to accurately represent the characteristics of this population than smaller samples. Although this idea seems self-evident, research shows that it is not intuitively obvious to everyone (Tversky and Kahneman 1973a).

Bias of Retrospective Determinism

The *bias of retrospective determinism* refers to the belief that what happened in the past had to happen that way; history could not have been otherwise (Fischoff 1975). Acceptance of this myth means that all historical events were determined to turn out just the way they did. According to this view, then, all of our present social problems are inevitable and unavoidable. Acceptance of this fallacy permits the perpetuation of unjust conditions on the grounds that if this is the way things are and always have been, then we might as well accept the inescapable and not worry. Alternative reasons for conditions are ignored, and the accepted historical explanation is thought of as a predetermined outcome.

Historical analyses are important in allowing us to appreciate past events. However, the danger of understanding based on hindsight is that it produces an inappropriate "knew-it-all-along" attitude and over-confidence about our present knowledge. That is, we feel that we have the same control in the present that we have in hindsight about explanations for past events. Furthermore, hindsight knowledge, with its associated beliefs of predetermined outcomes, may produce exaggerated expectations and feelings of control when making predictions about future events.

The biasing effects of hindsight wisdom is apparent in the critical treatment the press and television media in Britain made of the police following the arrest and conviction of Peter Sutcliffe for the Yorkshire Ripper murders (Pennington 1981). One paper, for example, asked, "How was it that connections appear not to have been made during the course of the police inquiry, when so many facts, incidents and coincidences—not individually but when taken together—seem with hindsight to have pointed towards Peter Sutcliffe?" *(Guardian,* May 23, 1981). This message suggests that media personnel would have been much more astute than the police if they had been in charge of the investigation. However, knowledge learned in hindsight gave the media advantages not available to the police: They knew how the murders took place, and they could separate relevant facts (signals) from trivia (noise).

Fallacy of Misplaced Concreteness

When people state that "society is to blame" or "law enforcement is unresponsive," a fallacy is created by making something that is abstract into something that is concrete. This process, called *reification*, or the *fallacy of misplaced concreteness*, only gives the appearance of explanation but is misleading because it cannot be tested. What is "society" or "law enforcement"? Where do we begin if we want to complain, and to whom do we complain? Law enforcement and society are abstract concepts that in themselves do not make or do or cause anything. Individual and institutional factors operate separately and in interaction with each other within society and within law enforcement agencies, and they must be isolated if attributions of responsibility are to be made correctly.

Ad Hominem Arguments

If someone states that the crime rate is high in a particular socio-economic community because "the people are lazy," "they lack ambition," "they are ignorant," and so on, the *ad hominem argument* is being used. Rather than looking at the various logical, empirical, and theoretical reasons for the crime rate, people hold the victims responsible for their fate and dismiss the problem. By focusing and attacking character and intelligence traits, the speaker diverts attention away from his or her lack of facts and reasonable argument. This is a favorite tactic among politicians or between couples, who argue by attacking their opponent personally. A strategy related to the ad hominem approach is to arouse people's prejudice when logic fails by appealing to their emotions with popular myths or slogans (the ad populum technique). Thus, the poor and the unemployed can be dismissed as freeloaders who only want handouts from the government by such slogans as I Fight Poverty; I Work (Lauer 1978). Whenever people feel that they are losing power or traditional values are under attack, slogans such as Better Dead than Red, Creeping Socialism, There's No Future in Nuclear Power, and so on, are popularized. When emotional arguments are used in combination with popular myths to support judgments, individuals who challenge these biases may find themselves the victims of attack.

Circular Reasoning

Circular reasoning occurs whenever conclusions are used to support the assumptions that were necessary to make the conclusions. Thus, a speaker may conclude that Native Americans are inferior, and, for proof of their inferiority, cites their lack of education, unemployment, and high frequency of drunkenness. In reply, if it is pointed out that Native Americans lack academic qualifications, fail to find jobs, and drink as a coping defense because of institutionalized discrimination, the speaker might then reply that they could not pass school and could not be hired by employers anyway because they are inferior. Circular reasoning undermines rational judgments and decision-making because conclusions always lead back to assumptions without recourse to independent facts.

Fallacy of Authority

The reasoning, judgments, and decisions of authorities are usually valued because of their recognized knowledge and experience in their field. Most educated people defer to authority since, from a normative point of view, it is usually the wisest thing to do. However, legitimate appeal to authority to assist decision-making has definite boundaries. First, the nature of the authority must be free of contradictory interpretations. For example, some fundamentalists will cite the Bible as the authority for their argument without acknowledging that the Bible is open to different interpretations and inconsistent positions. The scriptures are taken as a literal guide to human conduct by conservatives, whereas liberals view the Bible as only one source of guidance, along with reason, tradition, and experience. Second, the authority must have credibility in the area of the problem. The fact that a man or a woman is a respected scholar in forensic psychology, for example, does not mean that he or she is an authority on nonpsychological aspects of law enforcement. Similarly, the fact that a police chief is a respected authority on crime and violence does not mean that he or she can speak with legitimate authority on the psychology of crime and violence. Furthermore, an authority has no prerogative to make decisions in areas distinct from his or her expertise. Authorities often assume, however, that their expertise in one or more fields of accomplishment means that they have general approval to speak, and should be respected, in areas of nonexpertise. Finally, authorities are not always above personal bias and subjectivity. Citing authorities beyond these limits is the *fallacy of authority*.

The next section will focus on some real-world examples of the application of decision-making principles in police work: the decision to use deadly force; risky decisions resulting in traffic accidents; and shop-lifting as a risky decision.

DECISION-MAKING SITUATIONS

Decision to Use Deadly Force

In August of 1981, rookie police officer Joyce Faye Allen of Nashville, Tennessee, saw a robbery in progress at a local market. Harry Walden ran from the store and Officer Allen shot him dead. Two other men ran from the building and were wounded by the officer. Tragically for all concerned, Walden was the market's night manager and the other two men were innocent bystanders. All three men were running from Billy Guy Anderson, an escaped convict, who was robbing the store armed with a shot gun. Anderson had already shot and killed a fourth man near the market. The investigating officer concluded that police officer Allen had to make a "split-second decision"; however, one week after the incident Allen was dismissed from her job. The chief of police and his colleagues decided that the shooting of the store manager was consistent with the department's policy and regulations involving deadly force. It was considered reasonable to expect that Harry Walden was a robber because he ran out the door first. The administration concluded, however, that it was not reasonably certain that the two customers were involved in the robbery; consequently, Officer Allen was judged as having used poor judgment and deemed unsuitable as a police officer.

Deadly force is defined as force likely to kill or capable of taking life and is probably the most serious single act in which a police officer can be engaged. The decision to employ deadly force often has irreversible consequences. It is imperative that police "use that degree of force necessary to protect human life; however, deadly force is not justified merely to protect property interest. A reverence for the value of human life should always guide officers in considering the use of deadly force" (Broome 1979).

Contrary to media sensationalism, police-civilian shootings are relatively rare events. However, police use of firearms is more frequent in certain neighborhoods than in others within the same city. In the United States, approximately four hundred civilians die yearly at the hands of law enforcement officers, and one hundred police officers are killed in the line of duty. This four-to-one ratio has been constant for a number of years (Geller 1982).

Veteran officers are much less likely to draw a firearm in confrontations with suspects that are inexperienced police (Fyfe 1978). Officers are much more likely to draw their guns as a function of the information given to them by dispatchers' descriptions of the crime and background knowledge about the suspect than as a result of personal observation of behavioral characteristics (such as attitude, actions, alcohol, suspicious bulges in clothing) or physical attributes (such as race, sex, age, size, appearance) (Holzworth and Pipping 1985).

According to Scharf and Binder (1983), when an officer enters a situation that may involve shooting, information is typically assessed in five decision stages. The first phase *(anticipation)* is the time period from the initial notification of the need for assistance to the officer's arrival at the scene. During this period, the officer may receive information about the suspect or the crime. In the second phase *(entry and initial contact)*, the officer personally assesses the nature of the incident and suspect. In the third phase *(information exchange)*, the officer and the suspect exchange verbal and/or nonverbal communication. The fourth phase *(final decision)* involves the decision to shoot or not shoot. The final phase *(aftermath)* involves coping with the consequences of the final decision. Not all confrontations, of course, have these distinctly identifiable phases. Furthermore, the time involved in making the deadly final decision may not be more than a split second.

Because the research literature on police use of deadly force shows considerable methodological differences and is still fragmentary and limited mainly to large urban centers, it is difficult to give a profile of the most common type of incident involving shootings between police and civilians or to generalize across settings (Horvath 1987) or across countries (Chappell and Graham 1985). Keeping these limitations in mind, Horvath (1987) suggests that certain factors are related to an officer's use of a firearm. Black civilians are more likely to be involved in deadly force incidents than other racial groups. This finding is consistently reported, but its interpretation is controversial. Some observers regard this evidence as proof of racial discrimination on the part of the police (Takagi 1974), whereas others claim that the disproportionality of black representation in deadly force incidents is open to alternative interpretations, such as demographic characteristics of a region and general racial involvement in arrest incidents (Binder and Scharf 1980; Horvath 1987; Goldkamp 1976). The vast majority of police using firearms against civilians are on duty, in uniform, and doing routine patrol (Fyfe 1978; Geller 1982). Horvath (1987) concludes that "the outcome of a deadly force incident is probably more strongly related to circumstantial elements, such as the distance between an officer and civilian, than to more readily available but less salient items leading an officer to use a firearm. In other words, to know or understand what factors lead an officer to shoot at a civilian does not necessarily lead to an understanding of why a civilian is shot in a particular circumstance" (p. 237).

The principal reasons or motivations of civilians to shoot police officers have been investigated by Margarita (1980). Police are not generally killed by deranged lunatics or "psychos." Instead, officers are shot at, injured, or killed most frequently by robbers attempting to escape from the scene of a crime. Murder or injury to the officer is not the primary intention of the felon; decisions to shoot are most frequently associated with attempts to escape or to avoid self-injury.

Police officers who survive shootings are victims of deadly force and are typically not prepared to deal with its consequences. In fact, some observers believe that the victimized officer may suffer more general over-all trauma than does the citizen victim (Stratton 1986). Police officers are trained to see themselves as experienced decision-makers and agents who are physically and emotionally stronger than most civilians. They are supposed to have control over their emotions and be able to function under extreme stress. When victimized by deadly force, the officer's prior illusions of invulnerability, autonomy, omnipotence, and control of the environment are often shattered (Reiser and Geiger 1984).

Risky Decisions

Given the fact that most police officers are rational persons, why do some officers, in spite of their training, take foolish risks such as running into a building alone in pursuit of an armed and dangerous suspect? What causes drivers, who in most instances are reasonable persons, to take extreme risks such as tailgating at high speeds? Drug pushers are willing to risk arrest, conviction, and confiscation of property. Even the decision to shoplift is a risky decision since there is a likelihood of begin caught and arrested.

The *rational decision-maker model*, if it is true, assumes that people operate in ways that maximize their gains, minimize their losses, and allocate their resources most efficiently. This theory of behavior also assumes that people make reasoned judgments based upon enough reliable information about the choices in question and that they understand the laws of probability sufficiently to combine information about these events to make sound judgments.

According to *risky decision theory*, when individuals make decisions, each alternative choice has associated with it a subjective expected utility (SEU) (Slovic, Fischoff, and Lichtenstein 1977), which is the product of an event's or outcome's subjective probability of occurrence and its subjective value or attractiveness. In a risky decision, rational persons are expected to evaluate the expected utility of alternative events or outcomes and then choose the course of action with the highest utility, or greatest SEUs. In theory, potential thieves choose to commit criminal acts by comparing the SEUs of stealing and not stealing at various points in time and then decide whether or not to steal.

The assumption that criminal behavior is rational and that potential criminal acts are decided upon after considerations of expected utility —that is, in terms of the likelihood of profit versus the severity and the likelihood of punishment if caught—is central to the concept of deterrence. Cognitive psychologists, however, have shown that the rational view of decision-making is often wrong (Tversky and Kahneman 1982). The rational decision-maker model does not take into account the fact that people are subject to cognitive biases and do not understand or use statistical probability theory as experts do. The model also neglects individual and situational factors that influence decision-making. Potential criminals do make rational judgments, but there is little evidence to show that they acquire and use information about risks and payoffs in probabilistic ways as proposed by the rational view of criminal behavior (Carroll 1982). In the next section, descriptions of traffic accident risks are given to show how personal and situational characteristics interact to influence rational judgments of drivers.

Traffic Accident Risk.   If we assume that drivers are rational, a risk-taking model of driving assumes that drivers decide to drive safely or not by subjectively evaluating the costs and payoffs associated with alternative actions (Brown 1981). Risk-taking, however, does not necessarily imply conscious choice since risks can be taken without awareness (Jonah 1986). One driver, for example, may tailgate another vehicle and not realize the danger involved if the forward driver has to brake suddenly, whereas another driver may drive too closely behind another vehicle and be fully aware of the threat but be willing to take the risk for some reason. These differences in driving behavior illustrate the distinction between risk perception and risk acceptance or utility.

The payoffs for a potential offender for risk-taking include such factors as shortened journey time, being ahead of the line of traffic, increased excitement, satisfaction, pleasure, and so on. Potential offenders also have costs associated with their actions such as receiving abuse, assault or retribution from offended road users; being the cause of an accident or a near-miss for themselves or other road users; and detection, conviction and punishment by the legal system.

Several mediators of risk-taking in young drivers have been identified in terms of both accident risk perceptions and risk utility. Compared to older drivers (51 or older), young drivers (16–25 years) rate the appearance or style of a car more important than the car's safety features when deciding to purchase a vehicle. Also, younger drivers are less knowledgeable about traffic accidents being the major cause of death among adults under the age of 35 (Jonah and Dawson 1982). Young drivers perceive substantially fewer hazards while driving than older drivers, and those they do notice tend to be stationary (parked cars, for example) as opposed to moving (Soliday 1974). Young male drivers (18–24) perceive specific hazards, such as speeding and tailgating, as less risky than older drivers (38–50) (Bragg and Finn 1982). Young male drivers also perceive their skills and ability levels to be equal to that of older drivers and judge their risk of accidents to be similar (Matthews and Moran 1986).

These perceptions, however, are totally inaccurate. Young male drivers are inferior to older male drivers as indicated by their significant overrepresentation among all drivers involved in accidents and fatalities (Finn and Bragg 1986). Young male drivers have a tendency to see their peers as being more at risk than themselves; they believe potential driving hazards to be relevant to their peers, but not to themselves; and they perceive their own driving abilities to be superior to their peers' (Matthews and Moran 1986). Older male drivers see their risk to be similar to that of their peers (Finn and Bragg 1986). All of the above findings suggest that young male drivers "are overrepresented in traffic accidents at least in part because they fail to perceive specific driving situations as being as risky as older drivers perceive them" (p. 289) (Finn and Bragg 1986).

One hypothesis offered to explain the lower perception of risk in young drivers is their great confidence in their abilities and the belief that they can overcome hazardous situations (Bragg and Finn 1982). Each time that drivers speed and arrive at their destination without mishap, the experience "proves" to them their great capabilities as drivers. Increased confidence leads to a belief in personal immunity or invincibility to injury or death, and a belief in other drivers' susceptibility to hazards. High confidence and the perception that hazards are under control and are preventable by personal action are associated with excessive optimism that good events, rather than misfortune, happen (Weinstein 1984). These experiences result in dangerous driving situations being misperceived and faulty conclusions being inferred— for example, "I'm a safe driver, I don't need to wear a safety belt." Death is not a salient and highly available concept to most young people.

In his review of the literature, Jonah (1986) states that risk-taking among young drivers has the following utilities:

> outlet for stress, aggression, expression of independence, means of increasing arousal, impressing others, means to another end (i.e. speeding

to avoid being late) . . . to express opposition to adult authority and conventional society, to cope with anxiety, frustration, fear of failure at school, to gain acceptance into a peer group or to maintain one's position within a peer group, to show that one is "cool", or to demonstrate to others that one has matured and can engage in adult behaviours (e.g. driving after drinking.) . . . A youth who drives at a high speed to show off his driving skill to his friends may perceive being ticketed by the police as useful because it provides him an opportunity to reject authority and show that he is unconcerned about traffic laws. (P. 266)

Finally, researchers believe there is enough evidence to support the classification of a *risk behavior syndrome.* That is, the same drivers who perform one risky manoeuver also perform other risky behaviors and this risk propensity is related to accident involvement (Jonah 1986). For example, drivers not wearing seatbelts are more likely to tailgate (Evans, Wasielewski, and Von Buseck 1981), and drivers who run through yellow lights at intersections are less likely to buckle up (Deutsch, Sameth, and Akinyemi 1981); these behaviors are related to significantly more accidents and traffic violations.

Gadd (1986) vividly describes an incident early in a police officer's career when risky driving and quick decisions led to disastrous results.

Unfortunately, no one can be taught how to handle every situation that comes along in police work, since even similar calls won't be exactly the same. And while this diversity keeps the job exciting, it also creates problems for the officers, who don't know quite what to expect. . . .

I was new on the job, and I was involved in a chase. This kid on a motorcycle zipped around a car illegally, so being the non-ticket writer I was, I was gonna stop him and warn him about the violation. "I was a kid once." That's the way I used to think.

We got up to the next light, and I pulled around the one car that was in between us, then turned on the forward reds. At that point, he looked back, and the chase was on. It went approximately three blocks, and he was driving in the wrong side of traffic, doing better than seventy miles an hour. Then a car he was passing made a left-hand turn in front of him.

Something that I will never forget is the flash of light when that bike hit the car, and seeing the two objects go over the car. The rider went up over a good twenty foot tree and into the corner of a concrete building. It splits his head completely open, and then he came down onto the sidewalk. That's something I'll never forget.

Then standing over this kid in this massive, massive pool of blood. In fact, I broke down and cried. Having been in the business a short time, and then having this happen to me, this needless waste of human life. I felt like I was the cause of it, which I was, but the kid had a choice; he coulda stopped.

That incident was very devastating to me for awhile. I still think about it every once in awhile. As a sidelight, he was known in the area as a guy that would run excessively when you'd try to stop him. That night, I didn't know it. Afterwards, they told me who he was, and I realized that he was gonna run no matter what I did. (P. 26)

Shoplifting as a Risky Decision.   Many of the perceptual and utility risk factors known to operate in driving can be generalized to other situations, such as stealing (Farrington and Knight 1980) and shoplifting (Weaver and Carroll 1985). Shoplifting is said to have some of the following utilities for risk-taking among juveniles: excitement and thrill-seeking, a form of play, and impressing others (Walsh 1978). Shoplifters, like other individuals, are guided by heuristics and are just as susceptible to biased thinking. For example, shoplifters perceive substantial social support for their actions. This false consensus effect is a consequence of knowing personally of other shoplifters and believing that these persons and other intimate associates approve of their behavior (Kraut 1976). In this section, I will compare the differences in risk perceptions of shoplifters defined as "experts" in their field and those who are novices.

An expert, in this case, is an experienced criminal. Such individuals perceive risks as controllable aspects of their work environment (Inciardi 1975). In the past, since their activities have been successful relative to the very few times that they have failed in criminal acts, experienced felons perceive themselves as more immune from the law than do nonfelons, and those that are most experienced perceive a lesser certainty of punishment (Kraut 1976).

Scientific understanding of how experts and novices differ was initially studied by comparing the cognitive strategies of chess masters and novices (Chase and Simon 1973). These strategies, however, are common to all experts, not just chess masters. Experts have a great amount of knowledge about a small set of issues. They have an efficient system of rules, schemata and scripts, and heuristic shortcuts to facilitate their searches through a large amount of stored facts and procedural information. This elaborate knowledge structure is combined with a wide perspective and the ability to use general knowledge to make decisions on technical matters.

Investigations of criminals as experts in their field reveal that, relative to noncriminal novices, experienced criminals differ in their metacognitive knowledge — that is, their knowledge of what they know about committing crimes. Weaver and Carroll (1985), in a field study of seventeen expert shoplifters and seventeen novices, examined their thought processes during consideration of actual crime opportunities. Both experts and noncriminal novices were found to assess crime opportunities in terms of a simple risk-taking model of decision-making. They considered such factors as store security, layout and people, and size of item to be stolen; the attractiveness of the item, and a quick assessment of the risks involved before deciding to steal the item. In contrast to noncriminal novices, few experts considered the long-term consequences of their actions — arrest, trial fines, jail. Experts were found to analyze the opportunities for shoplifting faster and more systematically. Experienced shoplifters were more active in searching out, developing, and evaluating shoplifting opportunities. Experts were observed to be more confident, to follow rules, cognitive schemata or scripts, and plans of action that made them more efficient than the novices. Shoplifting is a skill with component parts. Experts' skills were automatic, rapid, effortless, and efficient such that they could focus their attention on understanding and assessing the constantly changing current situation. In short, expert criminals, in contrast to novices, were more knowledgeable and more efficient in their cognitive skills in "their field."

The next chapter will look at the decisions officers face when they must apprehend mentally disordered individuals. Officers have been called "psychiatrists in blue" since they must consider whether psychiatric diversion is needed rather than legal sanctions (Menzies 1987). This decision presupposes that officers have the skill or can learn to assess situationally the mental health of citizens and deal sensitively with confused and possibly dangerous persons (Yuille 1986). The traditional roles of police officers as law enforcers and maintainers of public order have changed over the last two decades, with police thrust into the role of social service agents. In spite of their reluctance to participate in the "psychiatrization" of accused persons (Menzies 1987) and their relative lack of ability to assume quasipsychiatric functions (Schiffer 1978), contemporary social conditions demand that police be able to manage the mentally disordered and work with psychiatrists and other mental health professionals.

SUMMARY

Rational thought involves deductive and inductive reasoning, judgment, and decision-making. Deductive reasoning entails drawing a particular consequence from certain rules or premises. Inductive reasoning entails drawing a general rule from a number of particular instances. Judgment is the process of forming opinions, making evaluations, and reaching conclusions. Decision-making is the process of choosing among alternatives. Cognitive strategies, mental representations, and schemata help us to organize information and make judgments as efficiently and effectively as possible.

People are prone to make errors in thinking because of the use of cognitive biases such as the availability heuristic and the representative heuristic. People can be biased in their decision-making by the way that a question is framed, by the perception of risk, and by wishful thinking, oversimplification, and misinterpretation of statistical probabilities of information. Discussion in this chapter has focused on some real-world examples of biased decision-making principles in police work; the decision to use deadly force; risky decisions resulting in traffic accidents; and shoplifting as a risky decision.

11

Mental Disorder

The trouble with being a cop is you get all the dirty jobs no one else will touch with a ten-foot pole. Take psychos and alkies. The hospitals won't take them, the doctors don't even want to talk to them, the relatives have given up trying. We're all that's left. We try to humor a guy, talk to them nice, but sometimes they're better off in jail with three squares and a roof over their heads. Next thing you know we've got lawyers and doctors around here screaming about civil rights and us cops keeping sick people in jail. (Matthews 1970)

Police are caught in a dilemma of accepting the responsibility of mentally ill persons as an integral part of their work (Bittner 1967), but not being able to provide them with what they perceive as the best police service. Most jurisdictions allow police to apprehend without warrant a person who is apparently mentally disordered and admit him or her to a mental health facility for treatment. This approach, however, is seldom successful because of contemporary practices resulting from the community treatment movement and the process of deinstitutionalization of psychiatric patients.

A typical scenario involving a police officer and a suspected mentally disordered person consists of a complaint from the community regarding bizarre behavior, police detention and transport of the individual to a general hospital emergency room, an examination by a medical doctor, and an immediate discharge if the patient does not meet the legal criteria for involuntary commitment. At this point, the doctor typically refuses to assume responsibility for any further involvement with the individual. Regardless of the police officer's opinion about the potential dangerousness of this individual, whom he or she may see as a "psycho," if this perception is not shared by the emergency room psychiatrist, the individual will not be committed. However, the officer may not want to book the individual over a minor incident. Furthermore, the officer may feel that this person does not belong in jail because he or she will be disruptive or victimized (Steadman et al. 1986). The officer may release the individual but later receive further complaints from the community about this person. These complaints may or may not include serious criminal actions, but this time the officer usually decides to bring criminal charges.

Police officers are not trained psychiatrists, and psychiatrists are not police officers, but police may have to criminalize the mentally disordered in order to take control of a situation (Teplin 1984). In this chapter, I will look at the interactions of the police and the mentally ill and discuss the meanings of maladaptive behavior and their possible relationship to legal insanity, or what is also called "criminal responsibility."

IDENTIFYING THE MENTALLY ILL

Mental health experts typically identify maladaptive behavior in terms of four functional clinical criteria (Davidoff 1987). First, an assessment is made of the severity of impairment of intellectual abilities such as attention, memory, judgment, and communication. Second, an evaluation is made of the individual's reasonable conformity to generally accepted social standards of conduct in daily functioning and personal relationships. Any behavior that seriously interferes with the well-being of others is typically perceived as abnormal. Third, a judgment is made of the individual's ability to exercise reasonable self-control. Overcontrol or an absence of control are seen as "maladaptive." Finally, the patient's ability to manage his or her distress from anxiety, anger, or sadness is considered. Does the patient show signs of overly frequent suffering or persistent or intense suffering? Obvious public signs of panic, overwhelming happiness, or uncontrollable sadness when situations do not seem to warrant it are often seen as abnormal (Page 1975). Although these four criteria suggest that "abnormality" and "normality" differ in their degree of deviation, they also have qualitative differences. An individual who sees things or hears voices that do not exist, for instance, is hallucinating, not merely using a vivid imagination.

The validity of clinical diagnoses depends upon an awareness of cultural practices. What is socially appropriate behavior in one culture may deviate widely from accepted social customs in another. Maladaptive behaviors are never precisely defined. They are often judged differently across cultural groups and can differ within cultures over time as a function of changing social values, political pressures, and scientific evidence.

ATTITUDES TOWARD
THE MENTALLY DISORDERED

Most people tend to dislike, distrust, fear, avoid, and undervalue the mentally ill (Jones et al. 1984; Rabkin 1974). Once labeled "mentally ill," individuals often see themselves as helpless and not responsible for their actions. Mental patients are expected to be odd, simple, and incompetent and are perceived in these ways even when they are behaving normally (Rosenhan 1973). They often experience a loss of status in the community and substantial avoidance, if not outright rejection. When released from the hospital, the psychiatric patient carries the burden of being labeled a "schizophrenic," or "depressive," and so forth. These labels are damaging since they tend to persist and promote misinterpretations of behavior. Laypersons often assume that labels are equal to clinical explanations, rather than being simply categorizations or descriptions of behavior, and they react to the labels rather than to the everyday behaviors of the individual.

In general, laypersons have two major concerns regarding the mentally ill: their unpredictability and their dangerousness. The belief that mental disorders predispose people to impulsive, violent, and assaultive behavior is an ancient stereotype that can be traced to the early writings of the Greeks and Romans (Rosen 1968). Negative attitudes toward the mentally ill may be lessening over time (Rabkin 1974), but television helps to maintain misleading stereotypes with its images of the mentally disordered as unpredictably dangerous, if not homicidal. Seventeen percent of television drama programs portray mentally disordered characters, and 73 percent of these characters are shown as violent and 23 percent as homicidal lunatics (Gerbner et al. 1981).

Mental illness or bizarre behavior is highly visible in most urban communities. Many "bag" men and women who twenty years ago would have been given custodial care in psychiatric institutions have been released in large numbers because of deinstitutionalization (Teplin 1984). Taking patients out of psychiatric hospitals and treating them in the community were supposed to promote health and independence and facilitate the learning and use of social skills. The civil rights of the mentally disordered to remain and live in the community without treatment has been confirmed by the courts. All of these factors act to upset the public's sense of order and stability and put pressure on the criminal justice system to intervene with the mentally ill.

According to Bittner (1967), the general public's perceptions, knowledge, and fears about people with mental disorders are shared by the police. More recently, Sales (1986) concluded that some police officers, along with attorneys and judges, "create handicaps or barriers for persons in need of rehabilitation services because they all too often rely on myths, stereotypes, and inadequate knowledge in reaching decisions and in executing their responsibilities. . . . Research has demonstrated that police often fail to recognize mental disability symptomatologies for what they are and are 20% more likely to arrest suspects evidencing these symptoms than comparable suspects who are 'normal' " (p. 8).

Police, in general, receive very little formal or informal training about mental retardation (Schilit 1979). Moreover, they feel that their involvement with psychotic or emotionally disturbed people is inappropriate (Teplin et al. 1980). However, when officers receive formal training in mental health and abnormal psychology, research evidence indicates that their interactions with family members of a mentally ill person are more supportive, they are less likely to arrest a suspected disordered person on the basis of his or her disability symptoms, and they are more negative regarding involuntary commitment (Blankenship and Cramer 1976). Police officers' attitudes, knowledge, compassion, and ability to accurately identify and describe mentally disordered persons improve significantly with education (Janus et al. 1980). Recognition of individuals who are mentally ill but not acting in a socially disruptive manner usually results in the police leaving them alone. However, if there is the suggestion of mental illness and a likelihood that the disorder is the cause of socially disturbing behaviors that could be dangerous to self or others, the individual will be apprehended or arrested.

Positive attitudes are related to behavior under specific conditions (Cialdini, Petty, and Cacioppo 1981). Contemporary police policies are to seek recruits with greater formal education, and police forces are encouraging their officers to seek further education. Since attitudes toward persons with disorders are related to education, it is likely that over time police officers will have more positive attitudes toward the mentally disordered and will be more supportive in their everyday interactions (Yuker 1986).

CRIME AND MENTAL DISORDER

The fact that there is a correlation between crime and mental disorder is accepted by authorities (Monahan and Monahan 1986), but there is no evidence that crime rates are higher among mentally disordered individuals than among "normal" people of the same age, gender, race, social class, and prior history of criminality (Monahan and Steadman 1983). Arguments suggesting that former psychiatric patients have higher rates of violent crime than that of the general population and are more dangerous than the average citizen are not supported by the research evidence. The supposedly higher rate of violent crime committed by released mental patients can be entirely accounted for by those patients having a criminal record for activities that predated their hospitalization (Monahan 1981).

Dangerousness, or the propensity to cause serious injury or harm to others, is not a personality trait but a consequence of a multiple chain of interacting events that vary as a function of an individual's actions in certain social or interpersonal situations (Diamond 1974; Monahan 1981). It is now recognized that clinical judgments based on current diagnostic techniques regarding the future dangerousness of mentally disordered persons have very low validity. Mentally disordered persons as a class are no more or no less dangerous than "normal" individuals (Monahan and Cummings 1975). Mental health professionals are more likely to be wrong than accurate when predicting that an individual will be violent over an extended period. Predicting a particular person's probability to be violent is especially difficult since all behavior including "dangerousness" is the product of a complex interaction of both situational and individual variables. Laypersons, psychiatrists, forensic social workers, forensic psychiatric nurses, and lawyers have been shown to be similar in making judgments of dangerousness after viewing videotapes of actual psychiatric interviews of accused individuals. The only significant difference among these groups was the higher levels of confidence shown by psychiatrists and lawyers in making their decisions (Jackson 1988). It is my guess that police officers are just as competent as the above groups in making decisions about dangerousness, perhaps more so, since police make their judgments in situ, rather than from psychiatric interviews.

POLICE DECISION-MAKING INVOLVING MENTALLY DISORDERED PERSONS

Over twenty years ago, just prior to the beginnings of the community treatment movement, Bittner (1967) found that the police make an emergency commitment rather than an arrest or nothing, in five types of cases: (1) when there is evidence that the person has attempted suicide; (2) when the signs of a serious mental disorder are accompanied by distortion of normal physical appearance such as nudity, extreme dirtiness, or bizarre movements; (3) when there is evidence of extreme agitation and threats of incipient or actual acts of violence; (4) when there are instances of severe disorientation and public nuisance; and (5) when the request for committal comes from people in an instrumental relationship to the person (physician, lawyer, teacher, employer, landlord, and so on). These observations suggest that the average police officer's decision to make an emergency psychiatric intervention rather than a criminal intervention is primarily dependant on observations of overt behavior and antisocial actions, rather on attributions of the behavior to internal distress. Few people would disagree that these types of problems warrant police action. Police are competent to make judgments concerning mental disorders when normality is defined in terms of overt social behaviors and moral and legal categories, rather than in scientific and medical categories (Bartol 1983). Furthermore, the argument has been made that the police and the legal system should not get wrapped up in the psychiatric jargon surrounding abnormal behavior, but, instead, should communicate in more accurate and meaningful terms for legal purposes, using terms such as *crazy behavior* for an individual's antisocial actions (Morse 1978).

Few studies conducted since the mid-1960s, however, support the findings of Bittner (1967) that police officers have a propensity to make emergency commitments in certain circumstances. Several investigations indicate that serious signs of mental illness increase the probability of the officer's decision to arrest rather than to refer the individual for psychiatric treatment (see Matthews 1970; Rock, Jacobson, and Janepaul 1968). In the most rigorous study to date involving nearly 1,400 police-citizen encounters, Teplin (1984) concluded "that the mentally ill are being criminalized, in that mentally disordered persons had a significantly higher arrest rate than those who were not mentally disordered" (p. 800). Officers choose to arrest rather than to commit persons for several reasons: (1) to maintain legal authority and to let the courts decide if the individual is insane or not; (2) mental disorders often produce annoying symptoms (verbal abuse, disrespect, and so on), which may provoke the officer to arrest rather than to show sensitivity to mental problems; (3) lack of knowledge about mental disorders; and (4) stringent psychiatric requirements for admission to a hospital—that is, the person must be suicidal or clearly delusional rather than mentally retarded, alcoholic, or defined as "dangerous" (Teplin 1984). Finally, police decision-making regarding people with mental disorders is not independent of moral judgments. In a study conducted in Toronto, Menzies (1987) found that police equated "abnormal" with moral judgments of "bad": They pointed to the mentally disordered individuals' "reprehensible and unconscionable conduct," and "marginal and intransigent moral careers," and, as a consequence, recommended that "they *merited* the full force of their forensic dispositions" (p. 443).

MALADAPTIVE BEHAVIOR

When people show "disturbed" behavior in public places or there is a report of loud and violent behavior in a domestic setting, police officers typically become involved in the situation. The police have been the primary source of psychiatric referral for the general public and, in particular, the needy and the underprivileged for decades. This section discusses some of the factors that can assist the police officer in assessing situationally the mental condition of citizens in disturbed states.

For a number of years, mental illness was classified in terms of two major categories, *neurosis* and *psychosis*, with a third classification, *personality disorders*, also thrown in between the two. In 1980, the American Psychiatric Association removed neurosis as a category from its diagnostic manual (the *Diagnostic and Statistical Manual of Mental Disorders*, third edition, also called *DSM-III*). Although the terms *neurotic* and *psychotic* are familiar to the general public and are part of our everyday language, these labels have been replaced with classifications such as anxiety disorder and psychotic disorder in an attempt to make the diagnosis more descriptive of specific behaviors and symptoms than those used earlier. My discussion will conform to the new system, but I will look at only a few of these categories.

Anxiety Disorders

Anxiety, which is both an emotional and a physical experience, is defined as an intense, diffuse, vague, unpleasant feeling of fear and apprehension (Sarason and Sarason 1987). Common symptoms of anxiety are loss of breath, rapid heart rate, diarrhea, loss of appetite, tremors, dizziness, fainting, and sleeplessness. Phobia, panic, generalized anxiety, and obsessive-compulsive disorders are the major syndromes of maladaptive anxiety.

A *phobic disorder* involves a persistent and irrational fear of a specific object, person, or situation. Phobias may include almost anything from *claustrophobia* (fear of closed spaces) to *agoraphobia* (fear of being alone, particularly in public places). Most people have some irrational fears, but when an individual is disabled by fear that is out of proportion to situational demands and he or she desperately attempts to avoid the feared situation, the fear is categorized as a phobic disorder.

Persons with *panic disorder* suffer recurrent *panic attacks* after periods of normal functioning. The attacks appear suddenly and unpredictably without any known stimulus to trigger the symptoms. Severe feelings of overwhelming terror associated with tremors, nausea, heavy perspiration, rapid heart beat, shortness of breath, and feelings of dizziness mark the attack. Victims fear losing control, going crazy, or dying. Panic attacks can last for a few seconds to several hours. Panic disorders are disabling because sufferers live in a general state of tension, are afraid of a reoccurrence, and deliberately try to avoid situations in which panic previously developed.

Generalized anxiety disorder is a general state of anxiety or constant tension that is not linked to a specific situation or object. Because of their general apprehensiveness and "free-floating anxiety," individuals feel that they are not in control of events and that disaster is imminent. They are apprehensive about their future and for the people close to them. Individuals with this disorder tend to overreact to minor irritations and have difficulty concentrating and making decisions.

Obsessive-compulsive disorders are shown by people who feel bound to repeat unwanted thoughts over and over or feel compelled to carry out actions or rituals again and again. An *obsession* is a preoccupation with an idea to the exclusion of almost everything else; the individual may, for example, have thoughts only of killing relatives or thoughts of dying and so on. A *compulsion* is an irresistible need to repeat an act or ritual against one's will, such as the need to wash one's hands fifty times a day or the compulsive need to set fires. Victims may experience extreme anxiety attacks if they attempt to resist their obsessions and compulsions. The compulsive rituals become a form of protection against anxiety, and, although the individual recognizes the absurdity and irrationality of the obsession or compulsion, he or she cannot ignore repeating these ideas or urges even when others are present and distressed by these symptoms.

Many sufferers of anxiety disorders seek psychiatric help and do not have contact with police, but others may need police assistance. The immediate task of the police officer giving emergency assistance is to provide a "safe place." Fears and phobias should be taken seriously since something about the situation has great importance for the person who is not in control of his or her symptoms. An individual experiencing an anxiety reaction is usually highly suggestible. If this individual is forced to face the source of the phobia, he or she is likely to panic, struggle, or fight in an attempt to escape the anxiety-arousing situation. The consequences of forcing the individual to confront this situation can lead to fainting or even a heart attack. The officer should help the person to relax and to master his or her immediate panic by showing a calm manner and a willingness to listen, even though the individual may be uncomfortable, uncooperative, or unreasonable (Bassuk and Birk 1984).

Psychotic Disorders

Psychotic disorders, unlike anxiety disorders, are much more likely to bring an individual into contact with the police (Bull et al. 1983). These individuals are often so impaired that the term *madness* is most descriptive. Impairment usually involves cognitive disorders. The individual shows an inability to distinguish what is real from what is not. A difficulty in focusing attention, a lack of concentration, and severe memory failures are common symptoms, along with profound deficits in reasoning and communication (Sarason and Sarason 1987).

Emotional disturbances are also common symptoms of psychotic disorders. Patients may display an extremely flat emotional response, or apathy, extreme despair, or depressed affect, extreme agitation consisting of screaming, giggling, laughing, jumping about, and so forth. Anxiety and ambivalence are not unusual. Emotions are often inappropriate and exaggerated such that a patient may laugh at sad news, become depressed when one might expect joy, or start to cry for no known reason.

Schizophrenia is the best known and most frequently cited psychotic disorder. The term *schizophrenia* originates from early Greek writings and means "split mind," suggesting the break-up of the mind's unity. A common misconception is that schizophrenics have a "split personality." More accurately, their thought processes are highly disorganized or organized in a bizarre fashion that distorts reality and confuses fantasy with fact. Their tendency to withdraw from those around them into their own private world may give the impression of "a splitting away." Psychotic disordered individuals are typically not aware of or do not have insight into their problems. The disorder generally starts in late adolescence or young adulthood and lasts a lifetime. The person may show symptoms of delusions and hallucinations. Unusual postures, strange facial expressions, exaggerated walking style, silliness, a lack of cleanliness, and a disinterest in maintaining dignity or social manners with family members and friends may be signals of schizophrenia.

There are several subtypes of schizophrenia, but I will describe only one of them. *Paranoid schizophrenia* is distinguished by multiple delusions and hallucinations about persecution or grandeur. Paranoid schizophrenics may have the delusions that "they" (the Soviets, the FBI, and so on) are plotting against them. Paranoid schizophrenics will take innocent events, such as a lost letter or an airplane flying over their houses, as proof of their suspicions. Some patients have delusions of grandeur, believing that they are Jesus, the king of England, or the president of the United States. Hallucinations may take the form of voices or tactile feelings or visual signs from the television or other objects that confirm these delusions. Paranoid schizophrenics can react to delusions of persecution with anger and aggression, but the probability of unprovoked violence is small.

The following example illustrates the psychotic thought patterns and speech disturbance of a schizophrenic patient:

> Everybody needs sex. . . . I haven't had sex for five years. The clock is in this room because they want patients to learn how to tell time. I know Mary Poppins, and she lives in Massachusetts. I didn't like the movie "Mary Poppins." They messed up the book, so they could try to win the Oscar. Movies come from real life. This morning, when I was at Hillside, I was making a movie. I was surrounded by movie stars. The x-ray technician was Peter Lawford. The security guard was Don Knotts. . . . Is this room painted blue to get me upset? My grandmother died four weeks after my eighteenth birthday. (Quoted in Sheehan 1981, 69)

Theories of the causes of psychosis are complex and controversial, and a thorough discussion of these causes is beyond the focus of this book. In brief, it is believed that schizophrenia is probably associated with hereditary and environmental factors as well as having biochemical determinants (brain chemicals, hormones, perhaps even viruses). Psychotic symptoms may be seen as a result of brain injury, tumors, diseases affecting the central nervous system, and drug and alcohol abuse. Regardless of its source, the individual who is hallucinating and acting in an uncontrolled fashion, screaming, threatening, and so on, needs emergency attention in order to prevent harm to him- or herself or to others. Police officers in contact with psychotic disordered persons are advised to be compassionate, supportive, and protective (Bull et al. 1983). However, temporary physical restraints or other protective techniques may be necessary in some cases to protect the disordered person or insure the safety of others (Cumming 1983). Reasoning with a schizophrenic about his or her delusions is fruitless since the delusions are usually meaningless to others, although they do form a logical pattern to the schizophrenic. Rather than try to argue the delusion away, officers should listen and be empathic. When hallucinations or bizarre motor behaviors occur during a crisis intervention, the individual may be frightened and trying to tell the officer something of importance, but anxious because of the situation or wanting to tune the officer out. Schizophrenics can be assisted, providing one is willing to tolerate their bizarreness.

SUICIDE AND PARASUICIDE

Police officers have traditionally played and will continue to play a large role in crisis intervention in dealing with suicide attempts. About ten out of every one hundred thousand deaths in the United States are due to suicide. This proportion ranks about average on an international scale of rates of successful suicides. An additional twenty persons out of one hundred thousand in the general population attempt suicide. Mental disorders account for the highest incidence of completed suicides, with alcoholics and the mentally depressed having higher rates than others (Lester 1983). Groups that are considered at high suicide risk are drug abusers, schizophrenic and depressed persons, people who have a family history of suicides, people who have made earlier suicide attempts, single people, especially among the divorced, separated, and widowed, young people between the ages of 20 and 24, and the elderly over 70. The motivation for suicide for high-risk groups appears to be related to "escapist" causes. There may be a desire to leave an "intolerable" situation. The individual may have lost a partner through death or divorce, for example, and feel depressed, guilty, anxious, or worthless. The future may be seen as hopeless. Suicide appears to be on the increase among adolescents and a number of warning signs of teenage suicide are now known (Sarason and Sarason 1987).

> *Verbal comments*   Statements such as "I wish I'd never been born" and "You'll be sorry when I'm gone" should be taken just as seriously as the direct threat, "I'm going to kill myself."
>
> *Behavior changes*   These cover a wide range and include giving away treasured possessions, taking life-threatening risks, and having frequent accidents. Other signs may be complaints of intense loneliness or boredom, a marked increase in agitation or irritability, or getting into trouble with school or the police. There may also be the more customary signs of depression: changes in appetite and sleep habits, suddenly dropping grades, complaints of inability to concentrate, and withdrawal from friends and from favorite activities.
>
> *Situational factors*   Inability to communicate with parents, recent problems at school, end of a love relationship, recent involvement with drugs or alcohol all increase the situational risk.
>
> *What to do*   Parents and friends should take action by asking questions such as "Are you very unhappy?" "Do you have a plan about taking your life?" "Do you think you really don't want to live anymore?" Asking direct questions about suicide doesn't put ideas into someone's head. Instead it may be a life-saving measure if the answers are taken seriously. Both parents and friends often don't believe that such statements might be carried out or they may be too frightened to take such action. Although friends are sometimes sworn to secrecy about suicidal thoughts, they should contact a parent or responsible adult immediately if they suspect thoughts of suicide, and professional help should be obtained at once. If the suicidal threat seems immediate, the nearest suicide prevention center (usually listed under "suicide" or "crisis" in the phone book) should be contacted. (Sarason and Sarason 1987, 289)

Twice as many males kill themselves, but twice as many females attempt suicide. Suicide and parasuicide (suicide attempts that are not completed) differ. People who succeed in killing themselves typically plan the event carefully and anticipate possible failures. In contrast, suicide attempters may act impulsively, plan to be rescued, and use a method that is slow to take effect. The suicide attempter's main goal is

to manipulate others (Sarason and Sarason 1987). Suicide risk is difficult to predict in alcoholics and many "accidental" deaths on the
highway involving drinking and driving may involve suicides.

Several common myths about suicide are listed below (Davidoff 1987,
493).

1. *Myth:* People who discuss suicide rarely follow through. *Fact:*
   Approximately 75 percent of those who take their lives are thought
   to communicate intent beforehand. They may talk about suicide,
   ask for help, threaten, or taunt. In some cases, the signal is an
   indirect one, such as tidying up loose ends (paying bills, giving
   away possessions, making apologies).
2. *Myth:* Suicide occurs mainly among the poor. *Fact:* Financially
   advantaged individuals often take their own lives. Suicide rates
   are very high among physicians, lawyers, and psychologists, for
   example.
3. *Myth:* People of specific religious affiliations do not commit suicide. *Fact:* Although some religions (Catholicism, for instance)
   prohibit suicide, identification with these faiths is no guarantee
   against suicide. Catholics do have somewhat lower rates of self-
   destruction (Templer and Veleber 1980). People who attend church
   regularly are also at lower risk for suicide (Martin 1984).
4. *Myth:* People with terminal illnesses do not kill themselves. *Fact:*
   The fatally ill sometimes take their own lives, especially when
   they are suffering greatly or disrupting the lives of loved ones.
5. *Myth:* Primarily, insane people kill themselves. *Fact:* Suicide is
   relatively common among hospitalized mental patients and among
   people with psychotic symptoms (Robins 1985). Still, most people
   who kill themselves do not appear to be irrational or out of touch
   with reality. The social relationships of presuicides, however, are
   often troubled, and their thinking is often rigid and extreme.
6. *Myth:* Suicide is influenced by latitude, weather fronts, barometric
   pressure, humidity, precipitation, cloudiness, wind speed, temperature, sunspots, and phases of the moon. *Fact:* there are no
   clear-cut relationships between suicide rates and any of these
   phenomena. Suicide rates do peak gently in May and dip to a low
   in December. Weather may influence the timing of a suicide
   attempt (Breuer et al. 1984).
7. *Myth:* Suicides are particularly prevalent during festive holidays,
   when people feel keenly aware of misery and loneliness. *Fact:*
   Although clinicians and lay public continue to endorse this reason-

able idea, controlled studies find either no relationship between holidays and suicide rates or a reduction in suicides around major public holidays (Lester and Lester 1971; Philips and Liu 1980; Zung and Green 1974).

8. *Myth:* An improved emotional state removes the risk of suicide. *Fact:* Depressed people sometimes commit suicide after their spirits rise at a time when they feel less paralyzed or passive.

9. *Myth:* Suicidal people want to die. *Fact:* Many suicidal individuals, perhaps most, appear ambivalent about death, so professionals view suicidal acts as "cries for help." In a British study of people who attempted suicide in Bristol, fully half of the interviewees claimed to be seeking relief from an intolerable situation without having consciously evaluated the consequences (Morgan 1979). They reported feeling convinced at the time that they would not die.

LEGAL INSANITY

On March 30, 1981, John W. Hinckley, Jr., tracked former President Ronald Reagan to a Washington hotel. As the president walked to his car, Hinckley, firing from a shooter's crouch and using specially purchased Teflon-coated bullets, attempted to assassinate him. At his trial, Hinckley's defense lawyers did not deny that he committed the crime, but, they argued, his actions were the product of a diseased mind. The defense claimed that "a mind that is [so] influenced by the outside world is a mind out of control and beyond responsibility" (Quoted in Winslade and Ross 1983, 188). The argument was put forth that since Hinckley could not control himself, he could not have a "guilty mind" *(mens rea)*. Consequently, the defense argued, Hinckley should be considered legally insane and not held criminally responsible for his actions. In June 1982, a Washington, D.C., jury found Hinckley not guilty by reason of insanity (NGRI) on all charges related to his attempt to assassinate the president.

The defense presented the jury the following picture of their client. As a teenager, John Hinckley, Jr., was a withdrawn, socially isolated boy. He spent much of his time alone listening to music in his bedroom. He had an above average IQ (113) and received good grades in college. His alienation from others and the fantasy world in which he lived became integrated with his reenactment of scenes seen from repeated viewings of the movie *Taxi Driver*. Hinckley became obsessed with Jodie Foster, an actress who played a 12-year-old prostitute. He identified with a character in the film who stalks the president and is involved in a wild shooting as part of a heroic rescue attempt. The defense argued that the movie script became the master plan that drove Hinckley to attempt the assassination. Hinckley decided that he had to meet and win the girl of his dreams by going to New Haven where Foster was attending Yale University. He repeatedly called and wrote letters to her, but she refused to meet him. Since his plans were not succeeding and he felt emotionally exhausted and disillusioned, he decided that he had to impress her and prove with one heroic act the depth of his love. He wrote a final love letter. Soon after sending the letter, Hinckley shot and wounded the president and three other men.

The insanity defence is one of the most controversial issues in Anglo-American law, yet it is a defence that is used in fewer than 2 percent of all criminal trials (Simon 1983). Legal observers feel that the insanity plea touches at the core of legal and philosophical foundations of democracy. As Stone (1975) stated:

> The insanity defense touches on ultimate social values and beliefs. It purports to draw a line between those who are morally responsible and those who are not, those who have free will and those who do not, those who should be punished and those who should not and those who can be deterred and those who cannot. (P. 218)

In spite of these lofty ideals and the public's general support for the principle that justice is a human product and that all mitigating circumstances must be appreciated and applied where necessary, many people are dissatisfied with the insanity plea. Some feel that the insanity defense is a legal loophole that allows "guilty" people to escape conviction and punishment (Hans and Slater 1983). An ABC News poll conducted one day following the conclusion of the Hinckley verdict revealed that 75 percent of those surveyed felt "justice had not been done" (ABC News 1982). Similarly, a sample of 434 men and women residents of Delaware "thought the verdict was unfair, believed Hinckley was not insane, had little faith in the psychiatric testimony presented at the trial, and asserted they would have reached a guilty verdict had they been jurors in the trial" (Hans and Slater 1983, 209). These types of reactions put pressure on legislators either to do away with the insanity defense completely or to change the criterion of legal insanity. In the next section, I will look at the two legal steps used by the courts to resolve the issue of insanity, competence to stand trial and criminal responsibility. These classifications refer to the defendant's mental status at two different points in time (Schwitzgebel and Schwitzgebel 1980).

Competence to Stand Trial

Questions of intellectual and emotional fitness, or *competence*, refer to the state of mind of the defendant at the time of preparation for trial and at trial. The focus of concern centers on whether or not the accused understands the charges, trial procedures, and consequences, and whether he or she can communicate with counsel to assist in the defense. Most statutes dealing with fitness to stand trial allow psychological or psychiatric examination of the defendant on request of the prosecution, the defense, or the trial judge. If the accused is assessed to be intellectually or psychologically deficient, the court usually judges him or her "incompetent to stand trial." Such a decision could result in a defendant's being confined in a mental institution or psychiatric security institution for an indefinite period of time, sometimes for the remainder of his or her life. Confinement can also be undertaken on an outpatient basis. Competence to stand trial evaluations are far more common than conclusions of criminal responsibility (Bartol 1983).

Criminal Responsibility

In general, according to the law, individuals are held to be responsible for their behavior and are considered to be capable of exercising control over their actions. The issue of legal insanity pertains to the defendant's mental status at the time the crime was committed. Was there a "disease of the mind" or mental illness? If there was a mental disorder, did the mental condition "cause" the loss of control and lead to the criminal act? If the person lacked sufficient awareness or control as a result of the mental disorder, the person is said to be legally insane (Slovenko 1984).

In early biblical times, little attention was given to mitigating circumstances; societies were more concerned with the need to preserve law and order, and punishments for criminal acts were imposed regardless of the mental state of the person concerned. The first evidence of diminishment of responsibility was introduced in Roman times, and by the fourteenth century, during the reign of Edward III (1326–1377), complete madness was recognized by the English courts as a defense to criminal charges (Simon 1983). Toward the end of the sixteenth century, English courts recognized that the lack of a guilty mind or criminal intent of a mad person meant a lack of legal responsibility. In 1723, an English judge in the trial of Edward Arnold introduced the concept of the *wild beast test:* "In order to avail himself of the defense of insanity a man must be totally deprived of his understanding and memory so as not to know what he is doing, no more than an infant, a brute, or a wild beast" (Quoted in Simon 1983, 184–185). The idea that an individual must be able to distinguish good from evil in order to be judged responsible remained as the court's standards of insanity until 1800 and the trial of James Hadfield. Hadfield believed that he was the savior of all humanity and, in order to get widespread recognition, he attempted (unsuccessfully) to assassinate King George III. Through risking his own life in a shoot-out or by sacrificing himself on the gallows, he believed that he would become a martyr and thereby prove, like Jesus, his love for mankind. Hadfield's reasoning nearly two hundred years ago was not too dissimilar from that of John Hinckley. Likewise, the jury acquitted Hadfield on the grounds of insanity. What is notable in this trial was the court's decision that the defendant need not be totally mentally incapacitated before he or she could be acquitted. Furthermore, the court declared that mere knowledge of right from wrong and an awareness of the nature and consequences of the criminal act did not make the individual criminal responsible. If at the time of the crime the person suffered a mental disorder that caused the criminal act, he or she was to be regarded as insane. These opinions, formulated in 1800, are similar to present practices.

The classic test of legal insanity, which continues to be followed in Canada, Britain, and about twenty state courts in the United States is the *McNaughten rule.* In 1843, Daniel McNaughten shot and killed Edward Drummond, secretary to the prime minister, Sir Robert Peel, in the mistaken belief that Drummond was the prime minister. McNaughten was described in court as a paranoid with the persecutory delusions that

Sir Robert Peel conspired financially and personally against him. After two days of medical testimony and hearing about new psychiatric insights into mental illness, the jury found the defendant not guilty on the grounds of insanity. McNaughten was sent to a mental institution where he remained for the rest of his life. The public, the press, the House of Lords, and Queen Victoria were outraged by the verdict. The queen demanded the acquittal be reexamined. The House of Lords demanded that the chief justice and his fifteen judges of the common law courts resolve the "error." The response of the judges was to establish a criterion of criminal responsibility of the insane, the McNaughten rule. It states that a defendant is not responsible if he or she committed a criminal act "while labouring under such a defect of reason, from disease of the mind, as not to know the nature and quality of the act he was doing; or, if he did know it, that he did not know he was doing what was wrong" (Bartol 1983, 117). Simply put, the jury must decide whether or not the defendant was aware and knew what he or she was doing at the time of the offense or knew or realized that what he or she was doing was wrong.

In some jurisdictions, an *irresistible impulse test* has been added to the responsibility criterion. Individuals may be aware of the moral and legal consequences of their acts and know that they are wrong, but lack the will power to resist the impulse to commit the illegal act (Slovenko 1984). Some states and the federal courts in the United States now follow the American Law Institute (ALI) Model Penal Code that combines the cognitive elements of the McNaughten rule and the irresistible control test: "A person is not responsible for criminal conduct if at the time of such conduct as a result of mental disease or defect he lacks substantial capacity either to appreciate the criminality [wrongfulness] of his conduct or to conform his conduct to the requirements of law" (Slovenko 1984). The Model Penal Code definition of insanity was used in the Hinckley trial.

It should be clear that *insanity* is a legal term, constructed by jurists for judicial decisions. It is not a medical or psychological classification and is not found in the diagnostic criteria of DSM-III. The public mistakenly considers insanity identical to mental illness or craziness and generally fails to appreciate that it is a legal term for an excusing condition dependant upon both the existence of mental disorder and an incapacity of mind due to that disorder (Hans and Slater 1983). Most laypersons hold misconceptions about the criminally insane (Steadman and Cocozza 1977) and lack knowledge about the legal test of insanity —which could explain why negative attitudes toward the insanity plea exist. A person can be considered legally sane by the court, but mentally disordered by psychiatrists and clinical psychologists. Although the courts make liberal use of clinical psychologists and psychiatrists in trials involving insanity pleas, it has been argued that clinicians are being asked "to do things they are not able to do or trained to do—for example, to express certainty rather than ambiguity, to predict dangerousness" (Wrightsman 1987, 273). Often, psychiatrists and clinical psychologists are ridiculed for their expert testimony, perhaps justifiably so in some cases. But at the same time, the courts and the public should not expect clinicians to resolve legal decisions when their expertise is psychiatry or psychology.

SUMMARY

Police officers must accept the responsibility of managing mentally ill persons as an integral part of their work, and they may have to criminalize the mentally disordered in order to take control of a situation. Maladaptive behavior is generally identified in terms of defective cognitive or social functioning, severe distress, and an inability to exercise self-control. There is no evidence that crime rates are higher among the mentally disordered than among "normal" people of the same age, social class, and race.

Anxiety disorders involve both emotional disturbances of fear and apprehensions, and physical experiences of tremors, dizziness, and so forth. Psychotic disorders are much more debilitating than anxiety disorders and entail distortions of reality, severe mood swings, and cognitive deficits. Police commonly play a large role in crisis intervention dealing with individuals suffering from psychotic disorders and suicide attempts.

Individuals who fail to possess the mental capacity to be responsible for a criminal act may be declared not guilty by reason of insanity.

12

Eyewitness Testimony

> When giving testimony as an expert on eyewitness identification, I focus
> my analysis on the police procedures that were employed following the
> crime. In particular, I focus on police procedures involving photographic
> spreads, the elicitation of descriptions, and show-up or line-up proce-
> dures. (Hastie 1986, 81)

Police officers are generally the first professional interviewers of victims
and witnesses of crime or accidents. The assessment of eyewitness
identification evidence includes judgments of the competency and credibility of eyewitnesses. Ultimately, it is the judge and/or jury who must
make credibility judgments of eyewitnesses and decisions of the guilt or
innocence of the defendant. If the police affect the reliability of eyewitness evidence, their work will be attacked at trial by defense attorneys.
In the opinion of one deputy district attorney, the police officer and not
just the defendant is on trial: "Your credibility, your judgment, your
conduct in the field, your use of force, your adherence to official
policies, your observance of the defendant's rights—they're all on trial"
(Rutledge 1979, 12).

Extensive research evidence on eyewitness testimony suggests that
police practices can influence the validity and reliability of witness
statements (see, for example, Clifford and Bull 1978; Loftus 1979;

Lloyd-Bostock and Clifford 1983; Shepherd, Ellis, and Davies 1982; Wells and Loftus 1984; Yarmey 1979). A person's normal ability to observe an incident or person(s), retain that information in memory, and retrieve the information later when called to identify the suspect(s) or reconstruct the events are subject to defects that may affect the reliability of evidence. In addition, suggestive interview techniques or suggestive mugshots, photo-spreads, and line-up procedures can contribute to misidentification and affect witness credibility. Few police investigators in the United States (Sanders 1986) or in Canada (Yuille 1984) are trained in these issues, and few legal professionals, including defense attorneys, prosecutors, and trial judges, are knowledgeable about the psychological research on eyewitness testimony (Brigham and WolfsKeil 1983; Winterdyk 1988; Yarmey and Jones 1982, 1983; Yarmey and Popiel 1988).

Despite the United States Supreme Court's recognition of the "dangers inherent in eyewitness testimony" *(United States v. Wade* 1967), some legal scholars argue that "existing safeguards against wrongful conviction through misidentification are limited and inadequate" (Sanders 1984, 203). In addition to the major factors of perjury and police and prosecutorial overzealousness, which contribute to wrongful convictions (Sanders 1984), eyewitness misidentification is the principle factor in over half of all wrongful felony convictions (Rattner 1988). Police officers, prosecutors, defense attorneys, the courts, and the public have mutual interests in protecting against the dangers of misidentification: "If the police and public erroneously conclude, on the basis of an unnecessarily suggestive confrontation, that the right man has been caught and convicted, the real outlaw must still remain at large. Law enforcement has failed in its primary function and has left society unprotected from the depredations of an active criminal" *(Manson v. Brathwaite* 1977, 127). Take, for example, the following situation:

> In 1979 and 1980 (Bob) Dillen, a freelance photographer, was arrested 13 times for armed robberies of Fotomat and Foto Hut booths in Pittsburgh, Pennsylvania. He had to stand trial for 5 of those cases; each time, fortunately, the jury did not convict him. Nevertheless, stress and the loss of time and money were immense. Finally, in the 13th case, a cashier who had been kidnapped and held hostage overnight led police to the cabin where they arrested the real criminal. Dillen's only "crime" was that he looked too much like the real criminal *(Tallahassee Demo-*

crat, December 23, 1980, p. 1). . . . Two rape victims picked William Jackson out of a police lineup in 1977; he was convicted of rape and sentenced to 14 to 50 years in prison. Five years later a prominent local internist, Dr. Edward Jackson (no relation), was arrested while burglarizing a house and police identified him as the "Grandville rapist," suspected of nearly 100 assaults in an affluent Ohio neighborhood. They also deduced that he had committed the rapes for which William Jackson had been in prison for five years. The two men looked remarkably alike: tall slender blacks with short Afros, sparse beards, mustaches, and similar facial features. William Jackson was released from prison seven and one half hours after Dr. Edward Jackson was indicted in September, 1982. (Brigham 1986, 465)

This chapter shows how the scientific study and understanding of eyewitness testimony can facilitate the police. More specifically, I will look at the principal factors that promote or hinder the accuracy and credibility of eyewitnesses.

PERCEPTION AND MEMORY

It has been suggested that trial judges, lawyers, and the police hold a traditional but outdated view of human perception and memory (Ellison and Buckhout 1981). In this traditional nineteenth-century model, men and women are seen as passive observers of the environment similar in many respects to a video recorder; everything that is seen and heard is presumably accurately recorded. It is assumed that the perception and memory of eyewitnesses involve a copying process that produces a permanent record of all that was observed and that skillful questioning or mere refreshment of one's memory allow for the recovery of exact details.

In contrast to this common belief, contemporary cognitive psychologists conceptualize the memory process as divided into three information processing stages: *the acquisition stage,* in which information is perceived; the *retention,* or *storage, stage,* involving the period between acquisition and recollection; and the *retrieval stage,* when the individual recalls or recognizes the stored information. Observation and recollection are seen to be active, selective, decision-making processes that are "affected by the totality of a person's abilities, background, attitudes, motives, and beliefs, by the environment and by the way his recollection is eventually tested" (Buckhout 1974, 24). Furthermore, memory theorists understand perception and memory to involve social processes — that is, perception and memory are affected by the actions and reactions of other people and by their real or imagined evaluations.

When witnesses are asked to describe an incident, certain events are readily recalled, but not others. The mechanisms by which we remember information are beyond our personal inspection. Some of the contents of memory can be accessed, but the processes of memory and decision-making that retrieve this information are not conscious acts. Memory involves a complex system of reconstructive and constructive processes that affect the contents of both short-term and a long-term store.

Short-term memory is a theoretical concept describing an active memory of general awareness. It holds the contents of conscious attention for fairly short durations of time — approximately twenty to thirty seconds. The storage capacity of short-term memory is limited to about seven items of information. For example, if we look up a telephone number in our city directory, we normally can hold that number long enough to dial it without forgetting it. Information can be held indefinitely in short-term memory if we choose to actively rehearse it, providing we are not distracted during that time. Use of coding strategies such as elaboration, imagery, and repetition increases the likelihood that information will be transferred from short-term memory into long-term memory.

Long-term memory is understood to be a relatively permanent store with an apparently infinite capacity to retain information. It is an active reconstructive and constructive process that constantly manipulates its contents and transforms information into more organized and meaningful units. Not all information that is potentially available in long-term memory is accessible, however. Forgetting may occur due to decay of the memory trace, to interference from internal sources or external information that alters, adds to, or replaces the stored material, or to use of inadequate retrieval cues to guide the memory search.

Witnesses typically make errors in memory through omission or commission. A failure to pay attention or the decision to select some material over others may mean that *errors of omission* occur. *Errors of commission* refer to distortions and intrusions from associated thoughts and experiences being confused with the sought-after information. Retrieval is also influenced by expectations and inferences of what should have happened, as opposed to what did happen, so the witness "fills in the gaps." Errors of omission and commission can also be caused by alcohol and drug abuse, physical and emotional trauma, and such bodily changes as those associated with advanced aged and senility. Accordingly, eyewitness identifications that appear obvious and based on common sense may in fact be much more complex.

In the next sections, I will look at the chief factors that have been found to affect memory during the acquisition, retention, and retrieval stages of eyewitness memory.

Acquisition Stage

At its most basic level, the perception of an incident involves the encoding of information hitting sensory receptors and being transformed into memory codes. Perception entails more than a mere passive recording of an event: What witnesses observe depends on what they selectively pay attention to. Factors determining attention include sudden changes in stimulation, the novelty and complexity of information, and the repetition and intensity of stimuli. Attention is also influenced by motivation, interest, and expectations.

Perception involves making sense of the stimulus information activating the receptors. It is a constructive process involving subprocesses of figure-ground discrimination, feature detection and analysis, pattern recognition, and identification (Neisser 1976). An individual in an ambiguous situation may have to test his or her hypothesis of what is being perceived, and interpretations may be based more on beliefs and wishes than on facts (is that a man in the doorway, or is it a mere shadow?). Perception can be influenced by an observer's attitudes and prejudices, and, of course, defects of vision or hearing contribute to faulty perception. Because more information strikes the receptors than can be encoded, decisions must be made regarding which stimuli to encode and which to ignore. As a consequence, some important information may be excluded.

One study describes the optimal conditions for memory retention and eyewitness accuracy:

Accuracy is likely to be enhanced when eyewitnesses have had repeated opportunities to make observations and/or have had an opportunity to observe events or persons over an extended period of time; when events are meaningful and the target events or persons are a central aspect of the events; when the events are arousing or stressful, but not so arousing or stressful that they impair eyewitness performance; and when the events are of sufficient severity that they attract attention without also motivating eyewitnesses to make excessive numbers of false identifications. . . . Reliability is likely to be enhanced when eyewitnesses have advance information that allows them to anticipate events or stimulus persons. . . . If the stimulus information has been processed in some "deep" or meaningful way that is appropriate to the events . . . an immediate rehearsal of events (perhaps a prompt reporting of events to the police) will improve subsequent witness performance. (Penrod, Loftus, and Winkler 1982, 133–134)

A number of the situational and witness factors relevant to the acquisition stage of eyewitness memory are outlined next. These factors may also influence the storage and retrieval stages, but for descriptive purposes, I categorize them as follows:

Exposure Time.　　As expected, the longer the exposure time the better the performance in accuracy of verbal recall (Hintzman 1976), facial recognition (Ellis, Davies, and Shepherd 1977; Shapiro and Penrod 1986) and voice recognition (Goldstein and Chance 1985). Conversely, the shorter the amount of time for observation, the poorer the memory performance. However, long periods of observation time involving several hours with a perpetrator can still lead to witness misidentifications (see Watson 1924).

The amount of time that a witness has available for observation is less important than the type of attention given to persons or events in that time period. Memory for faces is superior, for example, if the faces are "deeply processed," involving consideration of the personality attributes that fit each face, for example, than if attention is given only to specific facial features (Patterson and Baddeley 1977). Incidents that seem to be more important or more serious will be selectively attended to, and memory for those events will be superior to events that are perceived to be less serious (Leippe, Wells, and Ostrom 1978). Furthermore, even in relatively short time spans, a person is better able to encode incidents and people in those events he or she expects to occur than unexpected ones.

How much time passed in a criminal incident or in a traffic accident often is a crucial factor to the courts. Judgments of time durations are usually highly inaccurate and depend upon the complexity and type of events that filled the period (Fraisse 1984). Experimental research on simulated crimes indicates that witnesses overestimate time durations on the order of 2.5 to 1 (Buckhout 1977). Females overestimate substantially more than males, and overestimations are significantly longer in highly stressful conditions than in low stress situations (Loftus et al. 1987). The study of Loftus et al. also showed that the accuracy of time estimation was not related to the amount of material that a witness could recall about the event or to the accuracy of memory. Because time judgments are typically overestimated, police are advised to judge witnesses' time estimations against corroborating evidence whenever possible.

Observation Conditions. Professional criminals typically attempt to minimize the opportunity for witnesses to make studied observations; crimes often occur where the lighting is poor and events are complex, fast-changing, or chaotic. Descriptions of suspects by victims of crime are less complete for crimes committed at twilight than for those committed at night or by day (Kuehn 1974). People have a limited capacity to process information. Research on staged crimes shows that memory for a thief is negatively correlated with memory for peripheral details because attention given to one stimulus reduces the amount of processing capacity available for other stimuli (Kahneman 1973). Memory is not "holistic," even though jurors may believe it is (Wells and Leippe 1981). If a perpetrator is observed during the crime from a profile view, witnesses should be tested at the line-up with profile rather than frontal views of suspects. Witnesses, however, are significantly more accurate in identification when they have had a full-face view than a profile view of the perpetrator during the crime (Memon et al. 1988).

Attention given to visual details of a criminal incident may produce good memory for visual events, but then less attention is available for other sensory channels. For example, I found (1986a) that subject-witnesses persist in trying to pick up visual information while observing a simulated crime even when there is little light available. Although the witnesses knew they would have to identify the perpetrator at some later time, they did not spontaneously switch to the auditory channel and attend specifically to his voice, even in conditions of near darkness.

Stress and Violence.   Contrary to beliefs held by some police officers and the general public (Brigham and WolfsKeil 1983; Yarmey and Jones 1982), extreme stress and anxiety interfere with, rather than promote, a person's ability to acquire and process information. Perception of stimuli under high stress is fragmented, unstructured, reckless, short-circuited, narrow in focus, and often nonsensically interpreted (Postman and Bruner 1948). There is a need for victims to escape the situation; energy is focused on survival and immediate needs rather than on cognitive strategies to facilitate transfer of information from short-term memory to long-term memory. A mentally shocking event can produce loss of memory (retrograde amnesia) for stimuli that occurred up to nearly two minutes before the shocking episode (Loftus and Burns 1982). The notion that an extremely violent incident produces a "flashbulb memory" or burns an indelible print in memory, capturing all perceptions of the moment in a permanent, vivid, and accurate memory, simply is false (Brown and Kulik 1977; Neisser 1982). There is no physiological or behavioral evidence for a special flashbulb-memory mechanism that creates a detailed and permanent record of all that was observed (McCloskey, Wible, and Cohen 1988). Memory for some of the stimuli that occur during a highly stressful event can be very accurate, resistant to suggestion, and persistent over time (Yuille and Cutshall 1986), but not all stimuli that were present will be attended to, and even those that may have been central or salient at the time may not be recalled if they were not selectively processed.

Extreme stress produces a narrowing of attention, and the more that attention is divided the poorer the performance, particularly for peripheral stimuli (Baddeley 1972). Attention to salient or central cues increases at optimal levels of stress, but then decreases as stress increases (Easterbrook 1959). On the average, poorer recall is found in witnesses to a violent crime than witnesses to a nonviolent incident, with women's ability to recall inferior to that of men (Clifford and Scott 1978). Accuracy of recall decreases with an increase in the number of perpetrators, from one up to five in total, especially in a violent situation (Clifford and Hollin 1981).

Attention and memory are highly affected by the presence of a weapon, since a hand-held weapon serves as a distracting cue that interferes with the witness' encoding of the perpetrator's face (Yarmey 1988). Experimental research indicates that weapon focus causes poor line-up recognition and poor recall for situational details (Loftus, Loftus, and Messo 1987; Maass and Kohnken 1986; Tooley et al. 1987).

In an ideal world, witnesses would reach a suitable level of arousal that would result in the best possible performance in remembering the perpetrator. However, if a witness is either overaroused or underaroused, acquisition and storage of information will not be optimum. Witnesses typically do not have practice in observing threatening, violent criminal incidents, and we do not know exactly what level of arousal is ideal for any specific person. According to the *inverted-U hypothesis* (Yerkes and Dodson 1908), performance is lowest when stress and anxiety is very high or low, and highest when arousal is moderate or optimum. Police officers should have less confidence in the accuracy of witness descriptions if the witness reports being extremely fearful and attempting to escape, as opposed to being moderately anxious and intentionally set to remember the suspect.

Witness Expectations.   In discussing of schemata and heuristics (Chapter 10), I noted that people use rules of thumb to reduce the burden of gathering and evaluating large amounts of information. The preference for economy in information processing produces faster judgments at the risk of greater inaccuracy. In order to predict and understand behavior, we tend to categorize people in stereotyped fashion. Criminals, for example, are supposed to look generally tough, vicious, and unsavory (Yarmey 1982), and the general public even shares stereotypic beliefs about which face best fits certain types of crimes (Bull and Green 1980). People may hold stereotypes of racial and ethnic group differences that promote images of violence and crime. For example, most white people hold a stereotype that blacks are more violent than whites (Boon and Davies 1987). Stereotyped beliefs about criminals could influence whom a witness selectively attends to and remembers from an incident (Shoemaker, South, and Lowe 1973). Stereotypes may also increase a person's confidence or certainty of identification in a line-up (Mueller, Thompson, and Vogel 1988).

Social expectations and stereotypes appear to influence the perception and memory for criminal suspects mainly when situational conditions are complex and the event is short in duration, factors that lead to fragmentary or incomplete encodings of information (Boon and Davies 1987; Yarmey 1982). Because of such conditions, witnesses may misidentify the suspect or fail to recognize the suspect when he or she is present in a set of photographs. In either case, an innocent person may be accused of a crime or a guilty person set free.

Effects of Alcohol and Marijuana on Memory.   Researchers have confirmed the common belief that persons under the influence of alcohol or marijuana are less able subsequently to remember events and experiences that were acquired during the impaired state (see the review by Loftus 1980). Moderate, or social, drinking does not impair short-term memory or the ability of the individual to retrieve old memories from long-term memory. However, the ability to store long-lasting memories in long-term memory while even moderately impaired (the equivalent of five ounces of 80-proof alcohol for a 160-pound person) is affected. Similarly, marijuana interferes with the ability to transfer information from the short-term memory store to long-term memory. Yuille (1987) found that both alcohol and marijuana influence eyewitness recall. Along with a control group, subjects under the influence of alcohol (experiment 1) and subjects under the influence of marijuana (experiment 2) were presented with staged crimes. Alcohol was found to interfere with the completeness of recall after a one-week delay. Alcohol did not influence the rate of accuracy of photo line-up identification of the suspect one week later, but alcohol did increase the number of false identifications. Similar results were found for the affects of marijuana. Both the completeness and the accuracy of free recall of subjects given the drug and questioned immediately after the event were influenced by the drug. Recall after one week was also inferior in the marijuana group of subjects. Marijuana had no effect on the rate of accuracy of identification of the suspect, but the rate of false identifications was significantly increased.

Retention Stage

Since memory is an active, continuing process, rather than a fixed or static one, several factors that occur during storage of information in short-term memory and long-term memory can influence the reliability of recall and recognition. Witnesses asked to tell the police what they observed cannot provide an exact replication or reproduction of the event. Instead, they remember certain general and specific features of their experience. Reconstruction of experiences usually appear organized and logical because internal factors work on stored materials to make them more meaningful and reasonable, even though the original experience may have been ambiguous. Stored information tends to be shortened or leveled out, with seemingly redundant materials dropped out; certain characteristics of the experience become dominant or salient; and omissions or gaps in memory tend to be filled in, or confabulated, with inferred details in order to have a more coherent picture (Bartlett 1932). Information is also organized in meaningful or associated clusters. Unless asked to recall experiences in the sequence in which events occurred, individuals are likely to impose their own subjective organization onto the stored information, emphasizing some events and overlooking others.

External factors also can influence stored information. External factors that have great importance for eyewitness accuracy include the following:

Length of Retention Interval.   Memory for stimuli tends to become increasingly less accurate with the passage of time unless it is renewed through periodic use. Most forgetting takes place soon after acquisition; as time passes, forgetting is more gradual (Ebbinghaus 1964).

For the majority of crimes or accidents, descriptions of the incident and the perpetrator are given within hours or within a day, but it is not unusual for police to contact some eyewitnesses until a week or longer after the incident (Ellis, Shepherd, and Davies 1980). Verbal descriptions of faces made after a week's delay are less detailed and are less likely to lead to accurate identifications than those given within a day of the incident. Upper facial features are more likely to be attended to and better recalled than lower facial features at both short and long intervals. However, memory for all facial features degrades at the same rate over time (Ellis, Shepherd, and Davies 1980). Ruback, Westcott, and Greenberg (1981) found that the accuracy of verbal descriptions of a perpetrator given by victims of a theft declined from questioning given immediately after the crime to two months later. Accuracy of descriptions decreased from 86 percent to 70 percent for hair color, from 40 percent to 30 percent for eye color, from 58 percent to 36 percent for weight, and from 31 percent to 14 percent for age. Memory for physical attributes of strangers' age, hair color, and height are usually inaccurate. Judgments of height and weight are often anchored by a person's own weight, with tall and short people and heavy and thin people overestimating or underestimating as a function of their own size (for example, tall people tend to overestimate the heights of others) (Wells 1988). Estimations of weight and age are also highly susceptible to postevent suggestions. Referring to a previously observed person, for example, as either a "man" or "young man" produces significantly different estimations of that person's age (Christiaansen, Sweeney, and Ochalek 1983). If officers have doubt about witnesses' general ability to estimate age, height, and weight, they can ask them to judge an officer's age, height, and weight, keeping in mind, however, that this is a perceptual task that is less difficult than a memory task.

There is evidence that recognition memory for strangers' faces seen only once for thirty to forty-five seconds remains relatively stable over delays from one week to four months (Shepherd 1983; Shepherd, Ellis, and Davies 1982). However, the greater weight of evidence suggests that most forgetting of faces occurs within the first hours after observation (see Deffenbacher 1983; Krouse 1981). Long-term recognition memory for faces tested after delays of a week or more are more likely to lead to an increase in false identifications of distractors, rather than to a definite decrement in correct identifications (Chance and Goldstein 1987). Also, compared to immediate testing (ten-minute delay), recognition memory for faces tested after a one-week retention interval is significantly inferior when witnesses have only a brief period of time, such as three seconds or less, to observe the individuals (McKelvie 1988).

Some cases involve considerable delay between the perception and subsequent eyewitness testimony. For example, the 1987 trial in Jerusalem of John Demjanjuk, the man accused and found guilty of being "Ivan the Terrible," the infamous Treblinka camp guard in World War II, raised the question of whether the police and the courts can trust the accuracy of person identifications from witnesses who see an individual in the present following a retention interval of forty or more years, when the first observation occurred. Upon seeing Demjanjuk, one witness stated, "I say it unhesitatingly, without the slightest doubt . . . I saw

Figure 12.1 (A) Photograph from a 1942 SS Pass, Claimed by the Prosecution at John Demjanjuk's Trial to Be Ivan the Terrible; and (B) Photograph of John Demjanjuk in 1987. From *Applied Cognitive Psychology*, vol. 2, by Hadyn D. Ellis, copyright © 1988 by John Wiley and Sons, Ltd. Reprinted by permission of John Wiley and Sons, Ltd.

his eyes, I saw those murderous eyes." Another eyewitness was equally certain, claiming "He is indelibly embedded in my memory" (quoted in Ellis 1988). Cognitive psychology presently has no empirical studies that examine identifications of persons after such very long intervals. Any advice from cognitive psychologists as expert witnesses on this issue can only be based upon educated guesses and inference.

Figure 12.1 shows a recent photograph of John Demjanjuk and a photograph claimed to be that of Ivan the Terrible.

Postevent Interference.   One theoretical explanation for forgetting is that related events occurring during the storage period interfere with the information to be remembered (Bower 1978). If a photo line-up is considered by the police to be a critical test of witnesses' memory, all activities related to the crime that occur between the time of the crime and the presentation of the photo line-up are liable to interfere with facial memory. Police practices such as using suggestive statements or leading questions with witnesses, failure to prevent witnesses from communicating with each other, failure to interview witnesses at the first reasonable opportunity, presenting large numbers of mugshots, and construction of artist's facial sketches or commercial composites (Identi-Kit or Photofit) can introduce misleading information prior to a witness' viewing a line-up (Hall, Loftus, and Tousignant 1984; Wells 1988).

Researchers have found that "innocent" suggestions given to witnesses, such as showing a photograph of an individual and describing him or her in some way ("She is a multiple murderer," or "He is a lifeboat captain recently decorated for bravery") distorts subjects' subsequent verbal descriptions of that person as well as Photofit composites constructed from witnesses' memory of the target person (Shepherd et al. 1978). Similarly, Loftus and Greene (1980) found that over a third of their subjects shown a "suspect" and subsequently exposed to inaccurate facial information about this person from another witness (told, for example, that he had straight hair or had a mustache when the man they had earlier seen had curly hair or was clean-shaven) incorporated these false details into their verbal descriptions of this person. In contrast, 5 percent of the control subjects included those descriptions in their verbal recall. Seventy percent of another group of subjects exposed to these false details later misidentified an individual in a line-up with these characteristics. In contrast, only 13 percent of the control subjects "recognized" an individual with those features. When subjects were asked leading questions containing the erroneous information, over 30 percent of the subjects stated that they had seen such a facial feature. Only 4 percent of the controls did so. These studies indicate that verbal descriptions given during the storage period can contaminate memory for faces.

Loftus and her associates (Loftus 1975, 1977; Loftus and Palmer 1974; Loftus, Miller, and Burns 1978; Loftus and Zanni 1975) have demonstrated several variations of postevent interference activities on eyewitness memory. In addition to the influence of misleading information on facial identification, Loftus has shown that new evidence can be created from the use of misleading questions and that people will compromise responses, or "blend memories," to conform to the interrogator's expectations. For example, if a witness initially observes a blue car involved in an accident and later is misled to believe that it was green, he or she is likely to report that the color of the car was bluish-green. Misleading postevent information has its greatest impact on witnesses' reports if it is administered after a relatively long delay after the original event was observed, rather than being introduced immediately after the incident, and if witnesses are questioned just after the misinformation is given, rather than at a later time (Loftus, Miller, and Burns, 1978). Misinformation is also more likely to be incorporated into witnesses' testimony for memories of peripheral details of witnessed events than for memories of more central or salient features of the incident (Dristas and Hamilton 1977).

The issue of whether or not the misleading information effect results in the new information replacing or altering the original memory, as Hall, Loftus, and Tousignant (1984) argue, or whether witnesses' reports are altered while the original memories remain intact coexisting in memory with the misleading information, as McCloskey and Zaragoza (1985) and Read and Bruce (1984) believe, is theoretically important to psychologists. Regardless of the outcome of this scientific debate, it is clear that for some witnesses, misleading postevent information can distort the reliability of their testimony. The police are advised to avoid suggesting to witnesses that they already have knowledge about crimes since an inadvertent suggestive question in these circumstances is likely to influence the accuracy of witnesses' reports. Misleading information from police is less likely to bias witnesses' reports if police are able to convince witnesses that they are ignorant of what took place (Smith and Ellsworth 1987).

Facial Sketches.   Facial sketches can be useful in the apprehension of suspects, as the following incident illustrates:

CALGARY (CP)—A thief who tried to rifle the cash registers of several Calgary stores was nabbed thanks to the sketches of a freelance artist who witnessed the daylight robberies.

Rande Michael Livingstone, 23, pleaded guilty to theft under $1,000 in provincial court Tuesday and was sentenced to six months in jail.

The woman, who asked that her name not be published, is a freelance artist who sketches courtroom scenes for Calgary television stations.

The artist said she watched Livingstone use a master key to try to unlock several unattended cash registers at Calgary's Sunridge Mall Oct. 14, then followed him and an accomplice in hopes they would stop. "I looked him right in the face and it startled him so much he dropped his keys," she said in an interview. "Then I waggled my finger at him in the best fundamentalist manner and I said, 'God is watching you. He knows where that money is.' "

"He was so surprised at that he fell right over a chair in Grandma Lee's (restaurant)."

Livingstone entered a guilty plea halfway through his trial, after the woman's sketch was entered as evidence against him. His accomplice has not yet been apprehended. (*Guelph Mercury*, January 5, 1989, 2)

Although the use of a facial sketch was central to this case, this technique has some difficulties. Even when police operate in the most professional, objective manner there are errors built into identification procedures themselves that can bias witness memory. When witnesses, for example, are asked to provide a description of the suspect's appearance to a police artist, the procedures used in this process can interfere with the subsequent identification of the suspect in a photo-spread or live line-up.

Police artists in the United States and Canada generally follow a five-step procedure in drawing a facial sketch (Homa 1983). The sketch typically requires two or three hours of cooperative interaction between the artist and the witness. The first task of the artist is to establish rapport with the witness. He or she is asked to give a simple account of the incident leading up to the observation of the suspect. This description informs the artist about such things as the lighting, time of day, event duration, viewing distance between the witness and the perpetrator, and the approximate level of detail to expect in facial recall. Second, the witness is asked to give a detailed description of the suspect, including body build and clothing. Third, the artist may make use of reference materials such as showing the witness several different representative photographs of facial features that might resemble features of the suspect. Fourth, the artist begins to sketch a facial portrait and repeatedly questions, clarifies, and modifies the drawing following witness comments. Fifth, the artist adds shading and specific details, such as glasses, facial hair, and so on, to provide a lifelike and realistic drawing. When completed, the witness is asked to give an overall assessment of its likeness to the suspect.

Police artists generally attempt to construct a three-dimensional, lifelike representation of the suspect; they do not try to produce a photographically precise representation. Although the goal of producing realism without specificity may appear contradictory, the artist's goal is to produce a sketch that may remind others in the general community of someone they recognize. Some artists can do this through drawing a facial caricature, emphasizing or accenting reportedly unusual features of the suspect's face. Some artists also attempt to sketch the suspect's predominant facial expression—a practice, however, that is error-prone and unlikely to facilitate recognition (Bruce and Young 1986).

Several factors influence the quality of the final drawing, and these can account for different representations of a suspect being produced when more than one artist or more than one eyewitness is involved in the same case (see, for example, the different New York newspaper sketches of David Berkowitz, the infamous "Son of Sam," published in 1977). Each artist has his or her own interview skills, facial concepts, and techniques, which can create subtle changes in a drawing. Witnesses themselves differ in their ability to verbalize and accurately describe a facial image from memory. Artists' requests for small, obscure, physical details, which the witness initially may not be sure about, force witnesses to describe details that may not be anything more than guesses or logical inferences. The overall predictive validity of this approach is low in spite of the fact that police officers on occasion report some spectacular resemblances that do lead to arrests.

The use of artist sketches is especially problematic if the only witness available to identify the suspect in a line-up is the witness who assisted in the construction of the artist's sketch. It is probable that a witness who had only a short time in which to observe the perpetrator will have a weak memory trace for that person. The original facial memory trace is likely to be altered or perhaps even replaced by the more familiar and well-studied artist drawing. It is possible that the memory trace for the sketch, rather than the original memory representation, will be more available for subsequent photo-spread and line-up decisions. Hall (1977) found that subjects who participated with artists in drawing a sketch of a mock suspect's face were unable later to identify that person in a videotape line-up with greater than chance accuracy. In contrast, performance of subjects not asked to assist in a drawing of the suspect was significantly better than chance.

Describing a suspect's face to a technician constructing an Identi-Kit composite also can interfere with the ability of that witness to recognize the suspect in a line-up (Comish 1987). The Identi-Kit is a set of transparencies of line drawings of facial features (different types of eyes, chins, and so forth). Selected transparencies of each facial feature are superimposed to construct a composite face (see Davies 1983; Laughery and Fowler 1980). Furthermore, witnesses' ability both to describe the suspect and to recognize the suspect in a photo-spread are negatively affected by previously viewing other witnesses' composite constructions (Jenkins and Davies 1985). These findings suggest that publication of police artist sketches or commercial composites in newspapers or on television could interfere with subsequent line-up identification.

Although the police want to gather as much information as possible, overzealous interview techniques requiring witnesses to produce increasingly greater amounts of facial details can unwittingly lead to false descriptions and subsequent misidentifications. Facial composites should be published only as a last resort since composites are usually only general representations of wanted persons rather than specific photographic copies. As Jenkins and Davies (1985) stated: "If the composites should be seriously misleading in one or more features, and these misleading features are shared by a second and innocent person, there is a danger of double jeopardy. Not only will suspicion fall upon the innocent victim, but other witnesses may also have their memories of the suspect's appearance altered through their observation of the composite. Thus when they attend the line-up, they may select the same innocent suspect, and compound the original error!" (p. 175).

Retrieval Stage

Two of the most common ways of testing memory are those of recall and recognition. Free recall tends to be highly accurate but important details may be omitted (Lipton 1977). Witnesses questioned in a free narrative manner are usually conservative in their reports — that is, they do not mention a detail unless they are quite sure of it, but, as a consequence, there are gaps in their responses. Free narration often produces a serial position effect, whereby level of recall is highest for information at the beginning and end of the event to be remembered and poorest in the middle (Wessels 1982). Memory may be facilitated by the use of cued recall in which witnesses are asked such questions as "Can you state the suspect's age? Was he 25, 23, 21, or 19?" Interrogation of this sort increases the completeness of witness reports, but accuracy is not as high as that in free recall since witnesses are forced to respond with answers they are not always certain of. Witnesses asked to identify a suspect from photographs or a live line-up employ recognition memory. The individual compares the photograph or visual appearance or voice of persons on display with stored information and makes a decision based upon a familiar or nonfamiliar match.

The quality of police work in questioning eyewitnesses, taking notes, showing mugshots, photo-spreads, and live line-ups is crucial to the justice process. Witness factors such as age, sex, race, and so on, are not controlled by the police, and their influence on eyewitness accuracy can only be estimated. For most crimes, police are not involved until after a crime has been committed, and the police cannot affect the witnesses' accuracy of perception of the incident. Once the police intervene, however, their questions and other activities with witnesses and victims are part of the eyewitness identification process. These factors, referred to as *system variables*, can influence the validity of witness reports (Wells 1978, 1988). I will look at some of the major system factors and present some of the recommendations offered by Wells (1988) and others in the next sections.

Questioning Witnesses.   Failure to recall at a given moment in time is often a function of the way that information is retrieved, rather than a function of acquisition or storage (Tulving 1974). Recollections may be available but unaccessible for recall because inappropriate retrieval cues are used. The first questions put to witnesses should be general, open-ended ones asking for a description of viewing conditions and what happened and a description of the perpetrator. Following witnesses' free reports, specific questions can be asked about matters not mentioned earlier, such as those concerning the perpetrator's clothing, age, height, and so on.

Use of leading questions should be minimized if possible, and witnesses should be cautioned not to guess (Wells 1988). Leading questions are particularly damaging to memory if they deal with peripheral aspects of the event rather than central or salient ones (Dodd and Bradshaw 1980). However, police should not suppose that central and peripheral aspects of the event are intuitively obvious; witnesses and police may differ on what they feel was salient in any situation. Poorly worded questions often create false memories rather than elicit true accounts. For example, if a witness is asked the question, "Did you see the gun?" this question presupposes that a gun existed. In contrast, a question that includes an indefinite article such as "Did you see a gun?" does not presuppose that the perpetrator had a weapon (Loftus 1979). Subtle differences in the construction of questions can produce different descriptions from witnesses. Experimental subjects, for example, in answer to questions about a film of an automobile collision they had just seen, gave different estimations of the speeds at which the cars were traveling when questioned with sentences containing verbs with different emotional characteristics (*smashed, collided, bumped, hit,* and *contacted*) (Loftus and Palmer 1974). Similarly, questions using adverbs implying no upper limit (such as How *fast* was Car 1 going? How *much* damage was done to Car 1? How *long* were the skid marks made by Car 1? How *many* bruises did the driver of Car 1 suffer?), as opposed to questions using adverbs having no such implication, produce significantly higher estimates of property damage, personal injury, noise, and skidding (Lipscomb, McAllister, and Bregman 1985).

Questions about the actions of the suspect and person descriptions such as those including height and weight should be simple, direct, and free of assumptions. The question "What is his height?" is preferred over the question "How tall is he?" since the former question does not suggest to the witness to think of tallness (Wells 1988). Officers should expect to find suspect descriptions more poorly recalled than action descriptions (Marshall 1966; Clifford and Scott 1978). Complex questions involving two or more questions embedded within one another are to be avoided since they are likely to include suggestive statements that will produce distorted reports and confuse the witness. It is not recommended that police provide witnesses with a complete checklist of all facial characteristics typically used to describe individuals, since this may encourage uncertain witnesses to guess in answering every question on the checklist (Deffenbacher and Horney 1981). If witnesses have to resort to guesses in order to satisfy their questioner or to meet their own expectations of being a "good" witnesses (Trankell 1972; Yarmey 1979), they will tend to forget over time that parts of their initial report were guesses and will accept with increasing confidence their later incorrect recollections of the incident (Hastie, Landsman, and Loftus 1978). Finally, accuracy of recall is greater when specific questions follow the likely time sequence of the incident or begin with the central character, as opposed to being randomly ordered or focused on the main event of the incident (Morris and Morris 1985).

In contrast to the information gathered by standard police interview procedures, research evidence shows that police can improve the percentage of correct recalls from witnesses by up to 35 percent and not increase the number of incorrect recalls or confabulations (partial recalls and inferences) by using interview techniques based upon scientific principles of memory and cognition. This interrogation approach, referred to as the *cognitive interview*, can be used in both interviews and in line-up identification procedures (Fisher, Geiselman, and Raymond 1987; Geiselman et al. 1984; Geiselman et al. 1985; see also, Malpass and Devine 1981a).

The cognitive interview consists of four empirically validated memory retrieval techniques. This procedure is less time consuming than standard police questioning techniques but yields more accurate information. Geiselman and his associates suggest that the following instructions be given to witnesses:

1. *Reinstate the context.* Try to reinstate in your mind the context surrounding the incident. Think about what the surrounding environment looked like at the scene, such as rooms, the weather, any nearby people or objects. Also think about how you were feeling at the time and think about your reactions to the incident.
2. *Report everything.* Some people hold back information because they are not quite sure that the information is important. Please do not edit anything out of your report, even things you think may not be important.
3. *Recall the events in different order.* It is natural to go through the incident from beginning to end. However, you also should try to go through the events in reversed order. Or, try starting with the things that impressed you the most in the incident and then go from there, going both forward in time and backward.
4. *Change perspectives.* Try to recall the incident from the different perspectives that you may have had or adopt the perspectives of others that were present during the incident. For, example, try to place yourself in the role of a prominent character in the incident and think about what he or she must have seen. (Geiselman et al. 1986, 390–91)

The cognitive interview is able to generate the same amount of correctly recalled information at that elicited by hypnosis interviews but has the advantage that it can be learned and applied with little training and does not have the inherent limitations of hypnosis (Geiselman et al. 1985). Hypnotic memory enhancement in eyewitness retrieval has been criticized by experimental psychologists and legal experts.

Most laboratory studies have failed to find hypnotically assisted retrieval superior to standard memory retrieval procedures (Smith 1983; Yuille and McEwan 1985). Furthermore, hypnosis can distort eyewitness memory reports (Orne et al. 1984). Hypnotized witnesses are more susceptible to leading questions (Putnam 1979; Sanders and Simmons 1983) and are more likely to believe that their hypnotically assisted recalls are accurate and, therefore, must be the truth (Sheehan and Tilden 1983). If investigative hypnosis is to be used in identification cases, it should be administered only by fully qualified persons trained in psychology or medicine with specialization in hypnosis (Orne et al. 1984). Many states now have policies against the admission of hypnotically assisted identification testimony. Wells (1988) recommends that "police should consider hypnosis only as a last resort with the expectation that testimony obtained through hypnosis is likely to be of investigative value only and not of probative value to the courts" (p. 101).

It is relatively easy to second guess the police and their interview techniques from the luxury of one's psychology laboratory (Fisher, Geiselman, and Raymond 1987). The intent of criticism, however, is to show how eyewitness recall can be improved and to indicate how interviews can be conducted more effectively. Fisher and his colleagues (Fisher, Geiselman, Raymond, Jurkevich, and Warhaftig 1987) suggest that police will be more successful in eliciting accurate eyewitness recall if the following conditions are met: (1) They reduce or eliminate persistent interruptions of witnesses' narrative descriptions, since constant interruptions interfere with witnesses' concentration on the memory retrieval process, and frequent interruptions set an expectation that interruptions are part of the interview format and that only short answers with few details are expected before the next interruption. (2) Interviewers should emphasize open-ended questions that allow the witness the freedom to develop and elaborate upon answers. Direct, short-answer questions used only after the witness has completed his or her narrative response and failed to mention some pertinent details. (3) Police should structure interviews to fit the sequence of witness thoughts and mental representations of the crime. Any follow-up questions have to be appropriate to the mental representation being described by the witness rather than following some predetermined order or standardized police checklist. Finally, Fisher, Geiselman, Raymond, Jurkevich, and Warhaftig (1987) found that some police interviewers have a bias in asking questions in a negative rather than a positive form. Instead of "You don't remember whether . . . ?" questions should be worded, for example, "Do you remember whether . . . ?" Questions should be neutral in wording, such as "Can you describe his complexion?"; free of police jargon and highly stylistic speech patterns; free of surrounding distractions; adequately spaced apart in order to allow witness elaborations; and nonjudgmental of the witness and the crime situation. Officers should strive to have witnesses translate their subjective descriptions or interpretations, such as "He reminded me of a sailor," into objective statements about what it was in that situation that led to that interpretation.

Eyewitness recall, of course, depends upon the physical condition and psychological state of the witness. Eyewitness statements should be taken at the first reasonable opportunity since accuracy of memory declines with the passage of time. However, those witnesses who are functionally uncommunicative because of trauma, fear, and anxiety have to be given pyschological support and reassurance before descriptions are taken. Once personal rapport is established, it is the interviewer's responsibility to control the situation as much as possible so that witness anxiety and situational anxiety do not interfere with retrieval. Eyewitness descriptions should also be taken before showing a witness a photographic or live line-up; otherwise, the line-up will bias the description, making it merely a confirmation of the characteristics of the suspect seen in the line-up.

Questioning the Mentally Handicapped.   The courts are unlikely to accept the confession statements of a suspect if it is shown at trial that the suspect is mentally handicapped. Trial judges, of course, have the advantage over police officers of receiving professional advice regarding the intellectual capabilities of an accused. Police officers, in contrast, must judge the cognitive abilities of a suspect or witness from his or her public behaviors and ability to communicate.

The intellectually handicapped are generally distinguished by three levels of retardation. The largest group of retarded individuals, classified as mild or educably mentally retarded, have IQs that range between 50 to 69. This group is most likely to have contact with police since they usually live outside institutions and, depending upon their social skills, are able to hold employment in selected occupations, such as welders, miners, house painters, and so on. The moderately or trainably retarded have IQs that range from 25 to 49. They are usually institutionalized and rarely hold jobs except for minimal employment in sheltered workshops. The most severe and profoundly retarded, with IQs below 25, are almost always institutionalized since they are unable to provide even the most basic kinds of self-care (Liebert, Poulos, and Marmor 1977).

A systematic analysis of police awareness and interview methods used in gathering recollections from mildly mentally handicapped adult eyewitnesses has been conducted by Tully and Cahill (1984). One week after observing a twelve-minute, staged incident, mentally handicapped and control (normal) subjects were questioned by fifteen highly experienced police officers regarding what occurred during the incident. As expected, control subjects on the average were superior in recall to the handicapped. The retarded recalled about 80 percent of material remembered by the controls and made approximately 50 percent more errors in recall. However, since a few of the retarded subjects performed as well as the controls, there is support for the argument that some mildly mentally handicapped persons should not be disregarded as witnesses. The greater error production by the handicapped was related to their greater suggestibility or readiness to read contextual cues from officers as encouragement to "find" more and more details. The police were found to have a good appreciation of the problems involved in interviewing the mentally retarded and accurately judged their general level of intelligence, with one exception. The police consistently underestimated the memory impairment of the handicapped: They judged the quality of their recollections to be better than they actually were. The police also showed a strong tendency to prompt or use leading questions with the handicapped. No relationship was found between reported levels of confidence in memory and accuracy of recollection, although the police interpreted confidence as a predictor of good memory (see Tully 1986).

Tully and Cahill (1984) offer the following suggestions for interviewing mentally handicapped persons:

1. Establish a personal rapport with the individual. This will allow the interviewer to judge styles of communication, idiosyncrasies, nervousness, openness or guardedness, certainty, and so forth. The officer can tell the person at this point that it is acceptable to be unsure.

2. If possible, two officers should independently share the task of interviewing the witness in order to minimize any preconceived biases or hypotheses about the witness and about the incident. Similarly, two or more officers should interview each witness in multiple-eyewitness cases. The handicapped witness should be constantly reminded of the importance of accuracy since this is likely to maintain the individual's concentration and carefulness.

3. Several short interviews are recommended. This will serve to minimize the mentally retarded witness' need to "find" details because of a perceived expectation that interview time, regardless of its length, must be filled with statements.

4. Mentally handicapped persons should be allowed to start their narrative where they choose, rather than have a starting point arbitrarily imposed.

5. In order to minimize deference to police authority and seeking of social approval, officers have to guard against giving the mentally handicapped person undue social consideration while interviewing. In addition, the police must not press for additional details, use suggestive prompts, or use leading questions with the mentally retarded.

Note-Taking. Recording witness statements is a fundamental procedure for police officers, and officers can expect to be thoroughly cross-examined about the contents of their notes in court by defense attorneys. Communications between witnesses and police can be distorted at several points in interviews, but I will restrict my attention to only a small portion of this process (McCroskey and Wheeless 1976). The police officer can be an effective note-taker only if he or she is a good listener. Without listening, there is no communication, no gain of information, and no understanding. Most people are poor listeners because they believe that listening is a passive function rather than an active process requiring energy and thought. Listening is more than simply hearing, since listening involves speech recognition, memory retrieval, association of ideas, evaluation, and decision-making. People usually listen to what they want to hear. To truly listen, the officer must understand the witness' cultural background, be able to interpret his or her words in terms of the trauma or violation just experienced, and consider what has been implied or left unsaid. The police officer who holds prejudices toward the witness and the situation and lacks professional objectivity and a caring attitude may misinterpret and misrepresent what was said. Assuming that the officer is listening, witness statements should be copied down as given, not paraphrased (Wells 1988). Verbal statements of witnesses can easily be misinterpreted later by the police and by the courts if statements are only slightly paraphrased. Furthermore, in order for the courts to have full understanding, police should record both the questions that were asked and the witness' responses as well as any questions asked by the witness and the police responses.

Visual Identification. Witnesses may be asked to search through police mugshots, construct a facial composite or artist's sketch, look at a photo-spread, attend a live line-up, or confirm whether or not a person is the suspect from a one-on-one confrontation (a show-up). Each of these activities may yield important information, but each can also distort memory through suggestive practices.

1. *Mugshots.* Research evidence suggests that having an eyewitness search through a large set of photographs in the hope of finding the perpetrator may cause interference with later recollections of the suspect. The major problem with a search of mugshots is that a suspect is likely to be missed, especially if his or her photograph happens to be positioned later in the file than earlier (Laughery, Alexander, and Lane 1971). Experimental research indicated that subjects who searched through a set of one hundred mugshots without finding three perpetrators were inferior on a subsequent recognition test to a control group of subjects who had not done the mugshot search (Davies, Shepherd, and Ellis 1979). Police mugshots vary in their age and photographic quality and may not reflect the current physical appearance of the perpetrator.

If there is only one witness and he or she fails to identify the perpetrator in a search of mugshots but is later given a photo line-up or a live line-up, there is the possibility that an identification made from either line-up is a result of having seen the suspect earlier in the mugshots (Brown, Deffenbacher, and Sturgill 1977). The testimony of that sole witness may be invalidated by this potential bias of unconscious transference (see Loftus 1979). Police are advised that in the case of multiple witnesses, only one witness be presented with mugshots. Also, police should not use the same photograph of the perpetrator shown in the mugshots subsequently in a photospread, since a witness may be recognizing characteristics of the photograph rather than identifying a familiar face from the scene of the crime. Mugshots should only be used in the investigation if all other reasonable attempts to find the suspect have failed, since the search itself may interfere with memory (Devlin 1976; Wells 1988). Witnesses should also be warned that the set of mugshots may or may not contain the suspect.

2. *Photo-spreads and live line-ups.* The two major goals of eyewitness identification procedures are to facilitate the confirmation of guilty suspects and to avoid the identification of innocent suspects. When witnesses are asked to participate in an identification, with either a photo-spread or a live line-up, the police usually have a suspect in mind, although at this stage, he or she is not known to be guilty or innocent. Supposedly, witnesses base their decision to select a suspect on a match in familiarity between their memory of the perpetrator and the appearance of the suspect and distractors in the display. The act of choosing depends upon the magnitude of memory strength and the willingness of the witness to make a decision between the selected person and police-selected distractors. A witness will be accurate if he or she selects the perpetrator if the perpetrator is present or rejects the display if the guilty suspect is absent. A witness is inaccurate if an innocent suspect is chosen when the perpetrator is not present or overlooks the guilty suspect when the perpetrator is present (see Malpass and Devine 1984).

Although there is no empirical evidence demonstrating that identifications obtained from live line-ups in contrast to photo-spreads are more accurate (see Shepherd, Ellis, and Davies 1982), live line-ups are recommended because a photographic identification may be seen as artificial or less realistic than a live line-up and body cues such as posture, movement, and idiosyncratic mannerisms are impossible to perceive in photographs (Wells 1988). On the other hand, photo-spreads are easier to conduct, and suitable distractors are more readily found. Also, photo-spreads are less time-consuming and are not dependant upon the cooperation of the accused to behave in an orderly manner. However, use of photo-spreads may lead to a lax decision criteria, resulting in more guessing or less sensitivity in discrimination (Hilgendorf and Irving 1978). Investigators found a higher false alarm rate (rate at which innocent persons are misidentified) with facial photographs (80 percent) than on a live line-up (25 percent), when the guilty suspect was not present in the display (a blank line-up) (Hilgendorf and Irving 1978). Blank photo-spreads and blank line-ups are used in order to identify subjects who are merely choosing the individual who most looks like the suspect or who are prone to guessing. If there is any indication that witnesses are "too eager" to make an identification and are likely to make a false one, a blank photo-spread composed entirely of distractors known to be innocent can be an effective screening procedure. Eyewitnesses who reject this line-up can then be trusted to be more objective when viewing a line-up known to contain the suspect. Research indicates that good eyewitnesses tend to reject the blank photo-spread and select the correct photo when it is present, whereas poor eyewitnesses often choose an innocent distractor from the blank photo-spread (Wells 1984). The next sections review a number of factors related to photo-spread and line-up identifications.

EYEWITNESS CERTAINTY

Unlike accuracy of eyewitness memory, which is determined by learning and memory factors (such as acquisition, storage, and retrieval), confidence in decision-making is influenced primarily by social and individual factors such as feedback and support from others and self-esteem (Leippe 1980). Accuracy of memory and subjective confidence in identification performance are separate, independent psychological factors, and most eyewitness identification studies have found little or no predictive relationship between the two (Deffenbacher 1980). A witness' statement of high certainty in his or her identification of an unfamiliar suspect is not always a good predictor of an accurate identification (Malpass and Devine 1981a; Wells and Murray 1984). Eyewitnesses have been found to be equally as confident in their choices when the guilty suspect is in the line-up and is identified as when he or she is absent and an innocent look-alike suspect is selected (Lindsay 1986; Lindsay and Wells 1980). The lack of correspondence between eyewitness certainty and eyewitness accuracy is apparent from studies showing that eyewitnesses' level of confidence remains constant regardless of the accuracy or inaccuracy of eyewitness identification (see Lindsay, Wells, and Rumpel 1981). Similarly, confidence levels of witnesses may change over time as a function, for example, of being prepared for cross-examination, but accuracy of identification is unaffected (Wells, Ferguson, and Lindsay 1981). Since factors that may affect accuracy do not influence certainty and since certainty can be influenced by factors that do not affect accuracy, eyewitness certainty should not be used in most criminal cases as an indicator of eyewitness accuracy, except under the most ideal conditions for memory and cognition.

Several researchers emphasize, however, that confidence and accuracy are not totally unrelated in all situations. Confidence is a reliable predictor of accuracy of identification when the perpetrator is viewed under optimal conditions (such as good opportunity to view the target, long exposure duration, short retention interval) (Deffenbacher 1980). A conservative estimate of the relationship between eyewitness confidence and accuracy of recognizing an unfamiliar face is at least .25 and may even be as high as .42 when the target is viewed under optimal conditions (Bothwell, Deffenbacher, and Brigham 1987). The longer that a witness has to view a person, the greater the predictability of accuracy from confidence statements. However, researchers caution that the greater the stress and emotional arousal of an incident the less likely that recognition accuracy will be related to subjective confidence (Bothwell, Deffenbacher, and Brigham 1987). Finally, it is recommended that police query eyewitnesses about their confidence after they attempt an identification rather than before an identification is tested. Questions about certainty of identification before an attempt is made decreases the probability of an accurate decision (Fleet, Brigham, and Bothwell 1987).

Suggestion in Eyewitness Identification

According to the Supreme Court of the United States:

> The influence of improper suggestion upon identifying witnesses probably accounts for more miscarriages of justice than any other single factor — probably it is responsible for more such errors than all other factors combined. (*United States v. Wade* 1967, 26)

Most witnesses probably assume that the police will show a photo-spread or a line-up only if the incriminating evidence points to a good suspect. Thus, any line-up has an inherent quality of suggestion since witnesses suspect that the police feel that the offender is present. This suspicion will be confirmed if there is any direct or indirect suggestion from the police that the perpetrator is present. Police can communicate their belief about the suspect's identity through their verbal and nonverbal behaviors and through the manner in which the line-up is structured. If witnesses feel for any reason that they must choose a member of the line-up as the offender, regardless of their memory for that person, a miscarriage of justice is possible.

The wording of the police instructions to witnesses can influence whether or not a selection is made (Malpass and Devine 1981b). Witnesses must be instructed that the perpetrator "may or may not be present" and given the options of rejecting the whole line-up or indicating that they do not know. If these conditions are not given, witnesses may feel pressured to treat the situation as a problem-solving puzzle in which their task is to determine which person in the display most closely resembles the perpetrator. Witnesses also have been found to show a committment effect to someone (a distractor) they previously selected from a photo-spread. If this person and the guilty suspect are both present in a subsequent viewing of the photo lineup, witnesses will disregard the real suspect and select the person they previously chose (Gorenstein and Ellsworth 1980). It must be emphasized to witnesses that a line-up or a photo-spread is an identification test and that they are to select someone only if they recognize that person as the individual who committed the crime. Witnesses should also be encouraged to indicate in writing at the time of their identification their reasons for their choice.

The tendency of witnesses to identify a member of a line-up who most resembles the suspect relative to other line-up members can be counteracted by the use of a sequential line-up. Line-up members are presented one at a time and the witness must respond positively or negatively to each individual (Lindsay and Wells 1986). The sequential procedure forces witnesses to make more of an absolute choice (is this the suspect or not?), in contrast to the traditional line-up approach, in which witnesses can adopt a best-choice strategy (that is, who best resembles the perpetrator?). Lindsay and Wells (1986) found that the sequential procedure resulted in fewer false identifications than the traditional line-up with no significant difference in accuracy. The positive affects of sequential presentation in reducing the number of false identifications with no equivalent loss in correct identifications has been replicated in a study by Cutler and Penrod (1988).

Line-Up Fairness. Line-ups and photo-spreads should be constructed from the descriptions a witness first gives to police about the suspect when memory is strongest and least likely to be influenced by postevent interferences. One of the goals in line-up construction is to ensure that the suspect does not appear distinctive or salient in the display. Persons used as *distractors (foils)* should be selected in terms of their physical similarity to the perpetrator (height, weight, age, race, hair, and so forth), as described earlier by the witness. However, one or more suspect characteristics that make him or her salient compared to all other line-up members, such as a moustache or facial scar, may not have been mentioned in the original witness descriptions. In this situation, the distractors must also have these distinctive characteristics. This may be done through careful selection of foils or by make-up artists' altering distractors (Wells 1988). Control over suspect and distractor characteristics also includes the clothing of all line-up participants. Lindsay, Wallbridge, and Drennan (1987) found that unless all line-up members were similarly dressed at the time of the line-up, clothing could be a suggestive factor in identification. In their study, similarity in clothing did not influence the ability to identify the suspect, but fewer false identifications were found when all members of the line-up were dressed alike. It also made no difference whether members of a similarly dressed line-up wore clothing identical, similar, or dissimilar to that worn during the crime. In addition, subjects who correctly selected the clothing worn by the criminal during the crime from a six-picture photo-array were significantly more accurate in selecting the perpetrator from an independent photographic line-up than were eyewitnesses who failed to select the suspect clothing. Thus, obtaining clothing identifications separately from person identifications can provide the police with a second, independent source of direct evidence.

Selection of foils may be especially problematic in the case of "other race" identifications. Brigham and Ready (1985) found that the fairness of a line-up depends upon the race of the line-up constructor being the same as the race of the members of the line-up. Both white subjects and black subjects displayed an own-race bias: They were more selective in choosing suitable own-race photo distractors than other-race photo distractors. These findings indicate that the greater difficulty in recognizing other-race individuals also includes police officers who experience difficulties in making fine discriminations in similarity in preparing line-ups and photo-arrays (see also Brigham and Malpass 1985; Johnson 1984).

Photo-spreads or line-ups typically range in size between five and eleven distractor members plus the suspect. The question of line-up fairness, however, involves not merely its *nominal size* (the number of line-up members present) but its *functional size* (the number of line-up members who match the description of the suspect) (Wells, Leippe, and Ostrom 1979). To take an extreme example, a line-up might nominally have six or twelve members, but functionally have only one if all the distractors were short and fat and the suspect were tall and thin. Such a line-up constructed from the witnesses's descriptions of a tall man would obviously be biased toward the selection of the police suspect. A biased line-up that appears fair on the surface because of its nominal size but in reality has only one or two suspects is no different than a line-up with no distractors (a show-up).

Instructions to witnesses regarding line-up procedures should be given by an officer who does not know the identity of the police suspect, and witnesses should be told that the officer does not know whether or not the perpetrator is present. Line-up procedures should be recorded, and the photo-spread or line-up should be photographed or videotaped. Police can check the fairness of a photo-array or line-up by determining whether a sample of mock witnesses (people who had never seen the suspect) could pick out the police suspect at a better than chance ratio after being given only a general description of the perpetrator (Bytheway and Clarke 1976).

Voice Identification

In criminal cases involving masked perpetrators, crimes committed in darkness, obscene phone calls, ransom demands, and the like, memory for an unfamiliar voice may be the only evidence the police have that can lead to an arrest and court conviction. Voice identification evidence has been routinely accepted by both law enforcement agencies (Mayor 1985) and the courts for several decades (Tosi 1979).

The best known example of a witness identifying a defendant by his voice is the kidnapping case of *United States v. Hauptmann* (1935) in which Colonel Charles Lindbergh claimed to make a positive identification of the defendant's voice almost three years after hearing it (see McGehee 1937). In the Supreme Court decision in the Wade-Gilbert-Stovall trilogy (1967), voice identification played a major role in convictions in two of the cases. In the Wade case, Billy Joe Wade and the distractors in the line-up were required to wear strips of tape over their faces and to say "Put the money in the bag." A witness to the bank robbery identified Wade. In the *Stovall v. Denno* case (1967), Stovall was asked to say a few words for voice identification purposes at the hospital bedside of one of the injured victims. Stovall was identified, found guilty, and sentenced to death.

Voice identification evidence has been accepted by the justice system from three different perspectives: from operators conducting spectrographic analysis of voice recognition by machine; from the analysis of similarities and differences in speech samples of voices conducted by expert phoneticians; and from experimental psychologists involved in the study of voice identification by humans. My discussion is limited to the third type of evidence.

Voice recognition by listeners is susceptible to all of the interfering factors that influence memory for eyewitness identification (see reviews by Bull and Clifford 1984; Clifford 1983) and is clearly inferior to facial identification performance (Goldstein and Chance 1985). Some voices are very distinctive and readily recognized (Thompson 1985), but even under the best conditions, most unfamiliar voices are difficult to identify and are easily confused with other voices. The confidence-accuracy relationship in most voice identification studies is positive, but very modest, and subjective confidence is not a good predictor of earwitness performance.

Several factors, such as disguise and delay of testing, can significantly impair accuracy of voice recognition. A change in tone of voice, for example, from an angry voice when the crime was committed to a normal tone at the voice line-up, substantially affects accuracy (Saslove and Yarmey 1980). Delay in presentation of the recognition test is also a critical factor in voice identification. Clifford, Rathborn, and Bull

(1981) found that accuracy of recognition for voices declined from 55 percent correct ten minutes after presentation to 32 percent, 30 percent, and 37 percent correct after delays of one day, seven days, and fourteen days, respectively. Saslove and I (1980), however, found no significant difference in accuracy of speaker identification on an immediate test (60 percent correct) compared to a test given twenty-four hours later (70 percent correct). At longer delays, of a week or more, recognition accuracy has been shown to fall much more dramatically. Clifford and Denot (1982) found that subjects asked to identify the voice of a suspect were 50 percent accurate after one week, 43 percent correct after two weeks, and at chance level of 9 percent accuracy after three weeks. Long-term voice identification beyond twenty-four hours should be treated by the criminal justice system with the utmost caution. In the opinion of one researcher,

> Voice identification should not be accepted as courtroom evidence without precautions to minimize the obviously large potential for false identification. Specifically, I would recommend that positive voice identifications of a suspect be acceptable as evidence in a courtroom only if a controlled study shows the suspect to have a highly identifiable voice. Obviously, the lure voices used in the police line-up should have been picked to have the same general characteristics (e.g. regional accent) as the suspect's voice. (Thompson 1985, 26–27)

Most of the recommendations for the conduction of a "fair" police voice line-up are similar to those made for the presentation of "fair" visual line-ups and will not be repeated. In addition, however, it is recommended that a high fidelity tape-recorded voice line-up rather than a live voice line-up be used (Wells 1988). Tape recordings, in contrast to live performances, allow greater control over variables such as disguise, slurs, and other qualitative factors, without any loss in accuracy of witness identification. At least five distractor voices should be selected to match the general characteristics of the suspect's voice as described previously by the witness. There should be no extreme differences among members of the line-up in terms of factors affecting voice distinctiveness, such as rate of speech, pitch, expressive style, enunciation, inflection, pauses, tremor, nasality, age, and cultural backgrounds. At the same time, the distractor voices cannot be selected to sound too similar to each other or to the target voice (Handkins and Cross 1985).

All voices should be naturalistic, and all should say the same twenty or more words in the same order (Hammersley and Read 1983).

Children's Eyewitness Testimony

Until recently, trial judges were cautious about permitting children to testify as witnesses in court. Expert advice from the early part of the century supported the belief that children's memory was unreliable because of an inability to distinguish reality from fantasy (Piaget 1972), a tendency to fantasize sexual events (Freud 1940), an inherent suggestibility (Binet 1900; Varendonck 1911), and a susceptibility to errors produced through uncritical fabrications (see Saywitz 1987). Today, mainly because of the justice system's greater appreciation of individual differences in children's cognitive and moral development and widespread recognition of the frequency of physical and sexual abuse of children by adults, children are testifying in court about their victimization (Berliner and Barbieri 1984) and as eyewitnesses to such matters as homicide (Pynoos and Eth 1984), traffic accidents (Sheehy and Chapman 1982), and other criminal and civil issues.

Contemporary studies testing children in situations that simulate real eyewitness tasks indicate that children are not always inferior to adults. Children as young as 6 years of age are generally as accurate in their free recall descriptions as adults, although they usually recall less (see Goodman, Aman, and Hirschman 1987; Yarmey 1987). However, very young children of 3 years of age are less accurate and less complete than 6-year-olds (Goodman, Aman, and Hirschman 1987).

Compared to older children and adults, children under 11 years of age are more likely to be unreliable eyewitnesses in recognition memory for faces (Brigham, Van Verst, and Bothwell 1986) and recognition memory for voices (Peters 1987). Children aged 3 to 6, in particular, make fewer correct identifications of target persons and significantly more misidentifications of innocent distractors compared to older children (Goodman, Aman, and Hirschman 1987; King and Yuille 1987; Peters 1987; Yarmey 1987). Identification "performance of children up to 11 years is particularly dismal" (Cole and Loftus 1987, 206).

The relationship between age and suggestibility is far from definite. Children testifying about an event or experience that is familiar and understandable are no more likely to be vulnerable to suggestion and leading questions than adults (Duncan, Whitney, and Kunen 1982). Children's susceptibility to suggestions *depends* upon their memory of the original event (Loftus and Davies 1984) and the dynamics of the interview situation. Children are likely to conform to expectations of authority figures (Ceci, Ross, and Toglia 1987) and are highly sensitive to contextual cues presented by interviewers (King and Yuille 1987; Zaragoza 1987).

Research into children's ability to distinguish between fantasies and the reality of their memories for an event and between memories of their thoughts about the event and memories of what other people may have said about it has not been extensive. Preliminary investigations (see Lindsay and Johnson 1987) reveal that 6-year-olds are as accurate as older children and young adults in remembering whether they had said something or whether another person had said it, whether they imagined themselves saying a test word or hearing another person saying it, and judging which of two persons had said a test word. Young children are also as accurate as adults in remembering whether they performed some actions or imagined themselves performing these actions. Younger children, however, were inferior to older children in discriminating between having said and having imagined saying a test word.

Police should be aware that interviewing child witnesses, especially victims of sexual abuse, has special problems. Children as a group are not inherently untrustworthy (Melton 1981), although some may lie to protect themselves from rejection, punishment, shame, guilt, fear, or manipulation, among other reasons (Faller 1984). The police practice of using anatomically detailed dolls during interviews of alleged sexually abused children may be highly suggestive, and the play that children exhibit with these dolls may be misinterpreted as evidence for abuse (King and Yuille 1987; Yuille 1988). Interviews of children should be conducted so that the child's cognitive skills are enhanced without violating due process. Since children tend to represent knowledge in terms of scripts rather than as categories (Nelson and Gruendel 1981), they should be interviewed in a narrative manner rather than through the use of standard, set questions. For example, children should be asked to describe their experiences in questions such as "What happens when Daddy dresses you?" "What happens when Uncle Bob tucks you into your bed?" They should not be asked about specific details in questions such as "When did Daddy or Uncle Bob do . . . ?"

Asking children to relate their memory as a script in a sequential form may facilitate memory retrieval by eliciting information about patterns of experiences.

Police as Eyewitnesses

Jurors and the general public have great confidence and trust in the testimony of police officers (*State v. Wheeler* 1982). Whether or not police are more capable than nonpolice as eyewitnesses and are more believable to the general public and to officers of the court are empirical issues that can be tested (Yarmey 1986b). The evidence reviewed below indicates that police are not superior to civilians as eyewitnesses.

It is generally agreed that short-term memory has a limited capacity of about seven chunks of information. Police officers, like nonpolice, share this processing capacity. Bull and Reid (1975) found that police were able to recall seven items of information following both face-to-face briefing sessions and television briefing sessions, but that recall declined substantially when they were given eight items of information. The influence of amount of observation time on recall is similar for police and nonpolice at short durations, but police are superior at longer durations. Clifford and Richards (1977) tested police and civilians in a field situation for their ability to recall details of a target person to whom they had spoken thirty seconds earlier. The target person interacted with the police and the civilians for either fifteen seconds (to get the time) or for thirty seconds (to seek directions). No reliable recall differences were found at the short exposure interval, but police were significantly more accurate at the longer exposure interval.

In a study designed to investigate whether police are more observant than civilians, Ainsworth (1981) compared the perceptions of a group of experienced police officers (average length of experience nine years, three months) with those of a group of inexperienced police (average length of experience 11.9 months) and with a group of civilians. Subjects were shown a videotape of an urban street corner where a number of incidents were staged—criminal offenses, suspicious circumstances, and traffic offenses. They were asked to record any offenses or suspicious circumstances. No reliable differences were found among these groups in the total number of incidents identified. However, in contrast to the other two groups, inexperienced police saw proportionately more traffic and fewer criminal incidents. The claim that police officers are especially vigilant in their perception of offenses or suspicious circumstances was not supported. Similarly, Tickner and Poulton (1975) found no reliable differences between police and civilians in accuracy of detections of wanted persons and criminal activities while viewing filmed street scenes of one, two, or four hours' duration. Police officers, however, reported reliably more alleged thefts than did civilian observers.

There is no evidence to support the hypothesis that police are superior to civilians in facial identification. Billig and Milner (cited in Clifford and Bull 1978) found no significant differences between police and civilians in recognition memory for whites and blacks. Yuille (1984) discovered that police trainees were prone to making false identifications on a photo-spread and concluded that "police may suffer from a bias to select from line-ups, even if it consists entirely of foils." Some cognitive skills, such as police judgments of intoxication levels, can be improved with extensive training (Langenbucher and Nathan 1983), but eyewitness identification has not been found to improve with practice (Malpass 1981; Woodhead, Baddeley, and Simmonds 1979). Eyewitness memory is probabilistic and fallible in some circumstances in all observers, including the police. Training of police officers in skills of person and incident observations may not necessarily improve accuracy, but it may minimize the tendency to make guesses and false alarms and may assist the officer in handling any cognitive overload of information.

SUMMARY

This chapter has examined the major psychological factors affecting eyewitness identifications and recall. Errors result from those factors that influence the normal processes of perception, retention, and retrieval of information. In addition, suggestive interview techniques and identification procedures can contribute to misidentification.

Police can improve the accuracy of eyewitness memory by focusing their attention on system variables and using interview techniques based upon scientific principles of memory and cognition. Police interviews of the mentally handicapped and children present special problems; their solution can be facilitated by greater knowledge of cognitive and applied social psychology.

References

ABC News *Nightline*. 1982. "Insanity plea on trial." June 22.

Abel, G., J. Becker, and L. Skinner. 1980. Aggressive behavior and sex. *Psychiatric Clinics of North America* 3:133–51.

Adlam, K. R. C. 1982. The police personality: Psychological consequences of being a police officer. *Journal of Police Science and Administration* 10:344–49.

Adorno, T. W., E. Frenkel-Brunswik, D. J. Levinson, and R. N. Sanford. 1950. *The authoritarian personality*. New York: Harper and Row.

Ageton, S. S. 1983. *Sexual assault among adolescents*. Lexington, Mass.: D. C. Heath.

Aichhorn, A. 1935. *Wayward youth*. New York: Viking Press.

Ainsworth, P. G. 1981. Incident perception by British police officers. *Law and Human Behavior* 5:231–36.

Albrecht, S. L., and M. Green. 1977. Attitudes toward the police and the larger attitude complex: Implications for police-community relationships. *Criminology* 15:67–86.

Alcock, J. E. 1978. Social psychology and the importation of values. Paper presented at the Canadian Psychological Association annual conference. Ottawa.

Alder, C. M. 1982. An explanation of self-reported sexual aggression. Ph.D. dissertation, University of Oregon, Eugene.

Alexander, C. S. 1980. Blaming the victim: A comparison of police and nurses' perceptions of victims of rape. *Women and Health* 5:65–79.

Alkus, S., and C. Padesky. 1980. Special problems of officers: Stress-related issues and interventions. *Counseling Psychologist* 11:55–64.

Allen, B. L., and J. M. Levine. 1971. Consensus and conformity. *Journal of Personality and Social Psychology* 7:48–58.

Alldridge, P. 1984. Brainwashing as a criminal law defence. *Criminal Law Review* 726–37.

Allport, G. W. 1955. *Becoming.* New Haven: Yale University Press.

American Psychiatric Association. 1980. *Diagnostic and statistical manual of mental disorders,* 3rd ed. Washington, D.C.

American Psychological Association. 1979. *Ethical standards of psychologists.* Washington, D.C.: American Psychological Association.

————. 1984. *Final Report of the Task Force on the Victims of Crime and Violence.* Washington, D.C.: American Psychological Association.

Amir, M. 1971. *Patterns in forcible rape.* Chicago: University of Chicago Press.

Amoroso, D. M., and E. Ware. 1981. Adolescents' perception and evaluation of police. *Canadian Journal of Behavioural Science* 13:326–35.

Andenaes, J. 1983. Deterrence. In S. H. Kadish, ed., *Encyclopedia of crime and justice,* vol. 2. New York: Free Press.

Anderson, M. A. 1973. *Women in law enforcement: A primer for policewomen.* Portland, Oreg.: Metropolitan Press.

Anderson, W., and B. Bauer. 1987. Law enforcement officers: The consequences of exposure to violence. *Journal of Counseling and Development* 65:381–84.

Anderten, P., V. Staulcup, and T. Grisso. 1980. On being ethical in legal places. *Professional Psychology* 11:764–73.

Apple, N., and D. J. O'Brien. 1983. Neighborhood racial composition and residents' evaluation of police performance. *Journal of Police Science and Administration* 11:76–84.

Arbuthnot, J., and D. A. Gordon. 1988. Crime and cognition: Community applications of sociomoral reasoning development. *Criminal Justice and Behavior* 15:379–93.

Arbuthnot, J., D. A. Gordon, and G. Jurkovic. 1987. Personality and delinquency. In H. C. Quay, ed., *Handbook of juvenile delinquency.* New York: Wiley.

Asch, S. E. 1956. Studies of independence and conformity: A minority of one against a unanimous majority. *Psychological Monographs* 70 (416).

Ashworth, C. D., and S. Feldman-Summers. 1978. Perceptions of the effectiveness of the criminal justice system. *Criminal Justice and Behavior* 4:227–40.

Astrand, P. O. 1956. Human physical fitness with special reference to sex and age. *Physiological Review* 36:307–35.

Atwater, E., B. Bernhart, and S. Thompson. 1980. The authoritarian cop: An outdated stereotype? *Police Chief* (January):58–59.

Ayllon, T., and N. Azrin. 1968. *The token economy: A motivational system for therapy and rehabilitation.* New York: Viking.

Back, K. W. 1977. *Social psychology.* New York: Wiley.

Badalamente, R. V., C. E. George, P. J. Halterlein, T. T. Jackson, S. A. Moore, and R. Rio. 1973. Training police for their social role. *Journal of Police Science and Administration* 1:440–53.

Baddeley, A. D. 1972. Selective attention and performance in dangerous environments. *British Journal of Psychology* 63:537–46.

Bae, R. P. 1981. Ineffective crisis intervention techniques: The case of the police. *Journal of Crime and Justice* 4:61–82.

Bahn, C. 1974. The reassurance factor in police patrol. *Criminology* 12:338–45.

Bailey, W. C. 1982. Capital punishment and lethal assaults against police. *Criminology* 19:608–25.

Balch, R. W. 1972. The police personality: Fact or fiction? *Journal of Criminal Law, Criminology and Police Science* 63:106–19.

Baldwin, J. 1963. *The fire next time.* New York: Dial.

Balkin, J. 1988. Why policemen don't like policewomen. *Journal of Police Science and Administration* 16:29–38.

Ball-Rokeach, S. J. 1973. Values and violence: A test of the subculture of violence thesis. *American Sociological Review* 38:736–49.

Bandura, A. 1973. *Aggression: A social learning analysis.* Englewood Cliffs, N.J.: Prentice-Hall.

———. 1977. *Social learning theory.* Englewood Cliffs, N.J.: Prentice-Hall.

Banks, C., E. Maloney, H. D. Willcock. 1975. Public attitudes to crime and the penal system. *British Journal of Criminology* 15:228–40.

Banton, M. 1964. *The policeman in the community.* London: Tavistock.

Barber, T. X., and M. W. Ham. 1974. *Hypnotic phenomena.* Morristown, N.J.: General Learning.

Bard, M., and D. Sangrey. 1979. *The crime victim's book.* New York: Scribner's.

Bard, M., and J. Zacker. 1974. Assaultiveness and alcohol use in family disputes: Police perceptions. *Criminology* 12:281–92.

Baron, R. A. 1977. *Human aggression.* New York: Plenum.

Bart, P. B., and P. H. O'Brien. 1985. *Stopping rape: Effective avoidance strategies.* New York: Pergamon.

Bartlett, F. C. 1932. *Remembering.* London: Cambridge University Press.

Bartol, C. R. 1982. Psychological characteristics of small-town police officers. *Journal of Police Science and Administration* 10:58–63.

————. 1983. *Psychology and American law.* Belmont, Calif.: Wadsworth.

Bascelli, J. R. 1985. A cry for help: An analysis of wife abuse. *The Journal of Psychiatry and Law* (Spring–Summer):165–95.

Bassuk, E. L., and A. W. Birk, eds. 1984. *Emergency psychiatry: Concepts, methods, and practices.* New York: Plenum.

Bayley, D. H., and E. Bittner. 1984. Learning the skills of policing. *Law and Contemporary Problems* 47:35–59.

Bayley, D. H. and H. Mendelsohn. 1969. *Minorities and the police: Confrontation in America.* New York: Free Press.

Bazelon, D. L. 1973. Psychologists in corrections—Are they doing good for the offender or well for themselves? In S. L. Brodsky, ed., *Psychologists in the criminal justice system.* Urbana: University of Illinois Press.

Beccaria, C. 1953. *On crimes and punishments.* Indianapolis: Bobbs-Merrill. (Originally published 1776.)

Bell, D. J. 1982. Policewomen: Myths and reality. *Journal of Police Science and Administration* 10:112–20.

Bem, D. J. 1966. Inducing belief in false confessions. *Journal of Personality and Social Psychology* 3:707–10.

————. 1970. *Beliefs, attitudes and human affairs.* Belmont, Calif.: Brooks/Cole.

————. 1972. Self-perception theory. In L. Berkowitz, ed., *Advances in experimental social psychology,* vol. 6. New York: Academic Press.

Bem, S. L. 1981. Gender schema theory: A cognitive account of sex typing. *Psychological Review* 88:354–64.

Bennis, W., and C. Cleveland. 1980. Ripping off the cops. *Chronicle of Higher Education,* April 7, vol. 20, no. 6, p. 64.

Bent, A. E., and R. A. Rossum. 1976. *Police, criminal justice and the community.* New York: Harper and Row.

Bentham, J. 1962. The works of Jeremy Bentham, J. Bowing, ed. vol. 1. New York: Russell and Russell.

Berg, B. L., and K. J. Budnick. 1986. Defeminization of women in law enforcement: A new twist in the traditional police personality. *Journal of Police Science and Administration* 14:314–19.

Berg, B. L., E. J. True, and M. G. Gertz. 1984. Police, riots, and alienation. *Journal of Police Science and Administration* 12:186–90.

Berk, R. A., D. R. Loseke, S. F. Berk, and D. Rauma. 1980. Bringing the cops back in: A study of efforts to make the criminal justice system more responsive to incidents of family violence. *Social Science Research* 9:193–215.

Berkowitz, L. 1969. Simple views of aggression, an essay review. *American Scientist* 57:372–83.

————. 1970. Experimental investigations of hostility catharsis. *Journal of Consulting and Clinical Psychology* 35:1–7.

————. 1974. Some determinants of impulsive aggression: The role of mediated associations with reinforcements for aggression. *Psychological Review* 81:165–176.

————. 1978. Is criminal violence normative behavior? Hostile and instrumental aggression in violent incidents. *Journal of Research in Crime and Delinquency* (July):148–61.

————. 1980. *A survey of social psychology*, 2nd ed. New York: Holt, Rinehart, and Winston.

————. 1981. On the difference between internal and external reactions to legitimate and illegitimate frustrations: A demonstration. *Aggressive Behavior* 7:83–96.

Berliner, L., and M. K. Barbieri. 1984. The testimony of the child victim of sexual assault. *Journal of Social Issues* 40:125–37.

Bickman, L. 1974. The social power of a uniform. *Journal of Applied Social Psychology* 4:47–61.

Biderman, A. D. 1960. Social psychological needs and "involuntary" behavior as illustrated by compliance in interrogation. *Sociometry* 23: 120–47.

Binder, A., and P. Scharf. 1980. The violent police/citizen encounter. *Annals of the American Academy of Political and Social Science* 452:82–97.

Binet, A. 1900. *La Suggestibilité*. Paris: Schleicher Frères.

Bittner, E. 1967. Police discretion in emergency apprehension of mentally ill persons. *Social Problems* 14:278–92.

Black, D. 1979. Common sense in the sociology of law. *American Sociological Review* 44:18–27.

Blackmore, J. 1978. Are police allowed to have problems of their own? *Police Magazine* 1:47–55.

Blair, I. 1985. *Investigating rape: A new approach for police*. Dover, NH: Croom Helm.

Blake, R., and J. Mouton, 1964. *The managerial grid: Key orientations for achieving production through people*. Houston: Gulf.

Blanchard, F. A., L. Adelman, and S. W. Cook. 1975. Effect of group success and failure upon interpersonal attraction in cooperating interracial groups. *Journal of Personality and Social Psychology* 31:1020–30.

Blanchard, F. A., and S. W. Cook, 1976. Effects of helping a less competent member of a cooperating interracial group on the development of interpersonal attractions *Journal of Personality and Social Psychology* 34:1245–55.

Blanchard, F. A., R. H. Weigel, and S. W. Cook. 1975. The effect of relative competence of group members upon interpersonal attraction in cooperating interracial groups. *Journal of Personality and Social Psychology* 32:519–30.

Blankenship, R. L. and J. A. Cramer. 1976. The effects of education and training on police perceptions of mentally disordered juvenile behaviors. *Journal of Police Science and Administration* 4:426–35.

Blasi, A. 1980. Bridging moral cognition and moral action: A critical review of the literature. *Psychological Bulletin* 88:1–45.

Blau, T. H. 1984. *The psychologist as expert witness*. New York: Wiley.

Bloch, P., and C. Ulberg. 1972. The beat commander concept. *Police Chief* 39:55–63.

Blum, R. H. 1981. The problems of being a police officer. In G. Henderson, ed., *Police human relations*. Springfield, Ill.: Thomas.

Blumer, H. 1961. Race prejudice as a sense of group position. In J. Masuoka and P. Valien, eds., *Race relations*. Chapel Hill: University of North Carolina Press.

Blumstein, P. W. 1975. Identity bargaining and self-conception. *Social Forces* 53:476–85.

Bogomolny, R. 1976. Street Patrol: The decision to stop a citizen. *Criminal Law Bulletin* 12:544–82.

Boneau, C. A., and J. M. Cuca. 1974. An overview of psychology's human resources. *American Psychologist* 29:821–40.

Boon, J. C. W., and G. M. Davies. 1987. Rumours greatly exaggerated: Allport and Postman's apocryphal study. *Canadian Journal of Behavioural Science* 19:430–40.

Bopp, W. J. 1974. *Police personnel administration: The management of human resources*. Boston: Holbrook.

Bordens, K. S. 1984. The effects of likelihood of conviction, threatened punishment, and assumed role on mock plea bargaining decisions. *Basic and Applied Social Psychology* 5:59–74.

Bordua, D. J., and A. J. Reiss, Jr. 1966. Command, control and charisma: Reflections on police bureaucracy. *American Journal of Sociology* 72: 68–76.

Bothwell, R. K., K. A. Deffenbacher. and J. C. Brigham. 1987. Correlation of eyewitness accuracy and confidence: Optimality hypothesis revisited. *Journal of Applied Psychology* 72:691–95.

Bower, G. H. 1978. Interference paradigms for meaningful propositional memory. *American Journal of Psychology* 91:575–85.

Bowers, K. S. 1973. Situationalism in psychology: An analysis and a critique. *Psychological Review* 80:307–36.

Bowker, L. E. 1983. *Beating wife-beating*. Lexington, Mass.: Lexington Books.

Bragg, W. E., and P. Finn. 1982. *Young driver risk-taking research: Technical report of experimental study.* Contract no. DTNH 20-80-R-07360. Washington, D.C.: National Highway Traffic Safety Administration.

Bram v. United States, 168 U.S 532 (1897).

Brannigan, A. 1984. *Crimes, courts and, corrections.* Toronto: Holt, Rinehart, and Winston.

Braungart, M. M., W. J. Hoyer, and R. G. Braungart. 1979. Fear of crime and the elderly. In A. P. Goldstein and W. J. Hoyer eds., *Police and the elderly.* New York: Pergamon.

Brent, E. E. Jr., and R. E. Sykes. 1980. The interactive bases of police-suspect confrontation. *Simulation and Games* 11:347–63.

Breslin, W. 1978. Police intervention in domestic confrontations. *Journal of Police Science and Administration* 6:293–301.

Breuer, H. W., B. R. Fischbach-Breuer, J. Breuer, G. Goeckenjan, and J. M. Curtius. 1984. Suicide and weather. *Deutsche Medzinische Wochenschrift* 9:1716–20.

Brigham, J. C. 1986. *Social psychology.* Toronto: Little, Brown.

Brigham, J. C., and R. S. Malpass. 1985. The role of experience and contact in the recognition of faces of own- and other-race persons. *Journal of Social Issues* 41:139–55.

Brigham, J. C., and D. J. Ready. 1985. Own-race bias in lineup construction. *Law and Human Behavior* 9:415–24.

Brigham, J. C., M. Van Verst, and R. K. Bothwell. 1986. Accuracy of children's eyewitness identifications in a field setting. *Basic and Applied Social Psychology* 7:295–306.

Brigham, J. C., and M. P. WolfsKeil. 1983. Opinions of attorneys and law enforcement personnel on the accuracy of eyewitness identifications. *Law and Human Behavior* 7:337–49.

Brisson, N. J. 1981. Battering husbands: A survey of abusive men. *Victimology: An International Journal* 6:338–44.

Broder, P. K., N. Dunivant, E. C. Smith, and L. P. Sutton. 1980. *Further observations on the link between learning disabilities and juvenile delinquency.* Williamsburg, Va.: National Center for State Courts.

Brodsky, S. L. 1976. Psychology and criminal justice. In P. J. Woods, ed., *Career opportunities for psychologists: Expanding and emerging areas.* Washington, D.C.: American Psychological Association.

Brodsky, S. L., and G. D. Williamson. 1985. Attitudes of police toward violence. *Psychological Reports* 57:1179–80.

Broome, H. F. 1979. *A community concern: Police use of deadly force.* Washington, D.C.: U.S. Department of Justice, Law Enforcement Assistance Administration.

Brosseau, J., and G. Lock. 1979. *Report of the task force on children and others with learning disabilities.* Edmonton: The Senate, University of Alberta.

Brown, E., K. A. Deffenbacher, and W. Sturgill. 1977. Memory for faces and the circumstances of the encounter. *Journal of Applied Psychology* 62:311–18.

Brown, I. D. 1981. The traffic offence as a rational decision: Exposure of a problem and suggested countermeasures. In S. M. A. Lloyd-Bostock, ed., *Psychology in legal contexts.* London: Macmillan.

Brown, L. and A. Willis. 1985. Authoritarianism in British police recruits: Importation, socialization or myth? *Journal of Occupational Psychology* 58:97–108.

Brown, R., and J. Kulik. 1977. Flashbulb memories. *Cognition* 5:73–99.

Brown, S. E. 1984. Police responses to wife beating: Neglect of a crime of violence. *Journal of Criminal Justice* 12:277–88.

Browne, A. 1983. Battered women, the self-defense plea, and the role of the district attorney. Paper given at a presentation-workshop to district attorneys of Kansas, Nebraska, and Missouri.

———. 1987. *When battered women kill.* New York: Free Press

Brownmiller, S. 1975. *Against our will: Men, women, and rape.* New York: Simon and Schuster.

Bruce, V., and A. Young. 1986. Understanding face recognition. *British Journal of Psychology* 77:305–27.

Buckout, R. 1974. Eyewitness testimony. *Scientific American* 231:23–31.

———. 1977. Eyewitness identification and psychology in the courtroom. *Criminal Defense* 4:5–10.

Bull, R., B. Bustin, P. Evans, and D. Gahagan. 1983. *Psychology for police officers.* Toronto: Wiley.

Bull, R., and B. R. Clifford. 1984. Earwitness voice recognition accuracy. In G. L. Wells and E. F. Loftus, eds., *Eyewitness testimony: Psychological perspectives.* New York: Cambridge University Press.

Bull, R., and J. Green. 1980. The relationship between physical appearance and criminality. *Medicine, Science and the Law* 20:79–83.

Bull, R., and R. L. Reid. 1975. Recall after briefing: Television versus face-to-face presentation. *Journal of Occupational Psychology* 48:73–78.

Burbeck, E., and A. Furnham. 1985. Police officer selection: A critical review of the literature. *Journal of Police Science and Administration* 13:58–69.

Burgess, A. W., and L. L. Holmstrom. 1974. Rape trauma syndrome. *American Journal of Psychiatry* 131:981–86.

———. 1979. *Rape crisis and recovery.* Bowie, Md.: Robert J. Brady.

Burris, C. A., and P. Jaffe. 1983. Wife abuse as a crime: The impact of police laying charges. *Canadian Journal of Criminology* (July):309–18.

Burt, M. R. 1980. Cultural myths and supports for rape. *Journal of Personality and Social Psychology* 38:217–30.

Buss, A. H. 1971. Aggression pays. In J. L. Singer, ed., *The control of aggression and violence.* New York: Academic Press.

Butler, A. J. P., and R. Cochrane. 1977. An examination of some elements of the personality of police officers and their implications. *Journal of Police Science and Administration* 5:441–50.

Butterfield, E. C. 1979. From data to testimony: By whose rules should we play? Paper presented at the meeting of the American Psychological Association, New York.

Bytheway, W. R., and M. Clarke. 1976. The conduct and uses of identification parades. *Journal of Criminal Law* 40:198–205.

Cadoret, R. J., L. Cunningham, R. Loftus, and J. Edwards. 1975. Studies of adoptees from psychiatrically disturbed biological parents. 2. Temperament hyperactive, antisocial and developmental variables. *Journal of Pediatrics* 86:301–6.

Caiden, G. C. 1977. *Police revitalization.* Lexington, Mass.: Lexington Books.

Cain, M. 1973. *Society and the policeman's role.* London: Routledge and Kegan Paul.

Calhoun, L. G., J. W. Selby, G. T. Long, and S. Laney. 1980. Reactions to the rape victim as a function of victim age. *Journal of Community Psychology* 8:172–75.

Campagna, A. F., and S. Harter. 1975. Moral judgment in sociopathic and normal children. *Journal of Personality and Social Psychology* 31:199–205.

Campbell, J. P., M. D. Dunnette, E. E. Lawler, and K. E. Weick. 1970. *Managerial behavior, performance, and effectiveness.* New York: McGraw-Hill.

Cannavale, F. J., H. A. Scarr, and A. Pepitone. 1970. Deindividuation in the small group: Further evidence. *Journal of Personality and Social Psychology* 16:141–147.

Caplan, G. 1981. Mastery of stress: Psychosocial aspects. *American Journal of Psychiatry* 138:413–20.

Carlson, H. M., and M. S. Sutton. 1979. Some factors in community evaluation of police street performance. *American Journal of Community Psychology* 7:583–91.

Carroll, J. S. 1982. Committing a crime: The offender's decision. In V. J. Konecni and E. B. Ebbesen, eds., *The criminal justice system: A social-psychological analysis.* San Francisco: Freeman.

Carson, S. 1982. Post-shooting stress reactons. *Police Chief* (October):66–68.

Carter, D. L. 1983. Hispanic interaction with the criminal justice in Texas: Experiences, attitudes, and perceptions. *Journal of Criminal Justice* 11:213–27.

Cattell, R. B. 1946. *Description and measurement of personality*. Yonkers on Hudson, N.Y.: World Book.

Ceci, S. J., D. F. Ross, and M. P. Toglia. 1987. Age differences in suggestibility: Narrowing the uncertainties. In S. J. Ceci, M. P. Toglia, and D. F. Ross, eds., *Children's eyewitness memory*. New York: Springer-Verlag.

Cellini, H. R., and J. Snowman. 1982. Learning disabilities and juvenile delinquents. *Federal Probation* (September):26–32.

Chambliss, W., ed. 1969. *Crime and the legal process*. New York: McGraw-Hill.

———. 1974. The state, the law, and the definition of behavior as criminal or delinquent. In D. Glaser, ed., *Handbook of criminology*. Indianapolis: Bobbs-Merrill.

Chance, J. E., and A. G. Goldstein. 1987. Retention interval and false recognition: Response latency measures. *Bulletin of the Psychonomic Society* 25:415–18.

Chandler, M. J. 1973. Egocentrism and antisocial behavior: The assessment and training of social perspective-taking skills. *Developmental Psychology* 9:326–32.

Chapman, A. W. 1953. Attitudes toward legal agencies of authority for juveniles in Dayton, Ohio. Ph.D. dissertation, Ohio State University.

Chapman, L. J., and J. Chapman. 1982. Test results are what you think they are. In D. Kahneman, P. Slovic, and A. Tversky, eds., *Judgment under uncertainty: Heuristics and biases*. New York: Cambridge University Press.

Chapman, S. G. 1976. *Police murders and effective countermeasures*. Santa Cruz, Calif.: Davis.

Chappell, D., and L. P. Graham. 1985. *Police use of deadly force: Canadian perspectives*. Toronto: University of Toronto Press.

Charles, M. T. 1982. Women in policing: The physical aspect. *Journal of Police Science and Administration* 10:194–205.

Chase, W. G., and H. A. Simon. 1973. Perception in chess. In W. G. Chase, ed. *Visual information processing*. New York: Academic Press.

Chavis, D. M., P. E. Stucky, and A. Wandersman. 1983. Returning basic research to the community: A relationship between scientist and citizen. *American Psychologist* 38:424–34.

Check, J. V. P., and J. F. Klein. 1977. The personality of the American police: A review of the literature. *Crime and/et Justice* (May):33–46.

Chevigny, P. 1969. *Police power*. New York: Pantheon.

Christiaansen, R. E., J. D. Sweeney, and K. Ochalek. 1983. Influencing eyewitness descriptions. *Law and Human Behavior* 7:59–65.

Christiansen, K. O. 1970. Crime in a Danish twin population. *Acta Geneticae Medicae et Gemellologiae* 19:232–36.

Christie, R., and F. Geis, eds. 1970. *Studies in machiavellianism.* New York: Academic Press.

Chwast, J. 1965. Value conflicts in law enforcement. *Crime and Delinquency* 11:152–61.

Cialdini, R. B., R. E. Petty, and J. T. Cacioppo. 1981. Attitude and attitude change. *Annual Review of Psychology* 32:357–404.

Clark, L. M., and D. J. Lewis. 1977. *Rape: The price of coercive sexuality.* Toronto: Women's Press.

Clifford, B. R. 1983. Memory for voices: The feasibility and quality of earwitness evidence. In S. M. A. Lloyd-Bostock and B. R. Clifford, eds., *Evaluating witness evidence.* New York: Wiley.

Clifford, B. R., and R. Bull. 1978. *The psychology of person identification.* London: Routledge and Kegan Paul.

Clifford, B. R., and H. Denot. 1982. Visual and verbal testimony and identification under conditions of stress. Unpublished manuscript, North East London Polytechnic.

Clifford, B. R., and C. R. Hollin. 1981. Effects of the type of incident and the number of perpetrators on eyewitness memory. *Journal of Applied Psychology* 66:364–70.

Clifford, B. R., H. Rathborn, and R. Bull. 1981. The effects of delay on voice recognition accuracy. *Law and Human Behavior* 5: 201–5.

Clifford, B. R., and V. J. Richards. 1977. Comparison of recall by policemen and civilians under conditions of long and short durations of exposure. *Perceptual and Motor Skills* 45:503–12.

Clifford, B. R., and J. Scott. 1978. Individual and situational factors in eyewitness testimony. *Journal of Applied Psychology* 63:352–59.

Clinard, M. B. 1974. *Sociology of deviant behavior,* 4th ed. New York: Holt, Rinehart, and Winston.

Cloninger, C. R., K. O. Christiansen, T. Reich, and I. I. Gottesman. 1978. Implications of sex differences in the prevalences of personality, alcoholism, and criminality for familial transmission. *Archives of General Psychiatry* 35:941–51.

Cloninger, C. R., S. Sigvardsson, M. Bohman, and A. Von Knorring. 1982. Predisposition to petty criminality: 2. Cross-fostering analysis of gene environment interaction. *Archives of General Psychiatry* 39:1242–47.

Coates, T. J., A. C. Peterson, and C. Perry, eds. 1982. *Promoting adolescent health: A dialogue on research and practice.* New York: Academic Press.

Cochrane, R., and A. J. P. Butler. 1980. The values of police officers, recruits, and civilians in England. *Journal of Police Science and Administration* 8:205–11.

Cockerham, W. C., and L. E. Cohen. 1980. Obedience to orders: Issues of morality and legality in combat among U.S. Army paratroopers. *Social Forces* 58:1272–88.

Cohen, S. 1975. A comparison of crime coverage in Detroit and Atlanta newspapers. *Journalism Quarterly* 52:726–30.

Colbert, J. A. 1980. Effect of evaluation apprehension on attitude change in the presence of a police uniform. Ph.D. dissertation, University of Denver.

Cole, C. B., and E. F. Loftus. 1987. The memory of children. In S. J. Ceci, M. P. Toglia, and D. F. Ross, eds., *Children's eyewitness memory*. New York: Springer-Verlag.

Colman, A. M., and L. P. Gorman. 1982. Conservatism, dogmatism, and authoritarianism in British police officers. *Sociology* 16:1–11.

Comish, S. E. 1987. Recognition of facial stimuli following an intervening task involving the Identi-Kit. *Journal of Applied Psychology* 72:488–91.

Cook, F. L., and T. D. Cook. 1976. Evaluating the rhetoric of crisis: A case study of criminal victimization of the elderly. *Social Science Review* 50: 632–46.

Coons, W. H. 1982. Learning disabilities and criminality. *Canadian Journal of Criminology* (July):1–16.

Cordner, G. W. 1986. Fear of crime and the police: An evaluation of a fear-reduction strategy. *Journal of Police Science and Administration* 14:223–33.

Cooper, W. H. 1982. Police officers over career stages. *Canadian Police College Journal* 6:93–112.

Coser, L. 1956. *The functions of social conflict*. New York: Free Press.

Covey, H. C., and S. Menard. 1987. Trends in arrests among the elderly. *Gerontologist* 27:666–72.

Cox, T. 1978. *Stress*. Baltimore: University Park.

Crawford, P. J., and T. J. Crawford. 1983. Police attitudes toward the judicial system. *Journal of Police Science and Administration* 11:290–95.

Creamer, J., and G. Robin. 1970. Assaults on police. In S. Chapman, ed., *Police patrol readings*, 2nd ed. Springfield, IL: Charles C. Thomas.

Crosby, A. 1979. The psychological examination in police selection. *Journal of Police Science and Administration* 7:215–30.

Crosby, F., S. Bromley, and L. Saxe. 1980. Recent unobtrusive studies of black and white discrimination and prejudice: A literature review. *Psychological Bulletin* 87:546–63.

Cruse, D. 1972. *Determinants of police behavior.* Springfield, Va.: National Technical Information Service.

Crutchfield, R. S. 1955. Conformity and character. *American Psychologist* 10:191–98.

Culver, J. H. 1978. Television and the police. *Policy Studies Journal* 7:500–5.

Cumming, E., I. Cumming, and L. Edell. 1965. Policeman as philosopher, guide, and friend. *Social Problems* 12:276–86.

Cumming, R. G. 1983. *Casebook of psychiatric emergencies: The "on call" dilemma.* Baltimore: University Park Press.

Curtis, L. 1976. Rape, race and culture: Some speculations in search of a theory. In M. Walker and S. Brodsky, eds., *Sexual assault: The victim and the rapist.* Lexington, Mass.: Lexington Books.

Cutler, B. L., and S. D. Penrod. 1988. Improving the reliability of eyewitness identification: Lineup construction and presentation. *Journal of Applied Psychology* 73:281–90.

Danish, S. J., and N. Ferguson. 1973. Training police to intervene in human conflicts. In J. R. Snibbe and H. M. Snibbe, eds., *The urban policeman in transition.* Springfield, Ill.: Thomas.

Davidoff, L. L. 1987. *Introduction to psychology,* 3rd ed. New York: McGraw-Hill.

Davies, G. M. 1983. Forensic face recall: The role of visual and verbal information. In S. M. A. Lloyd-Bostock and B. R. Clifford, eds., *Evaluating witness evidence.* New York: Wiley.

Davies, G. M., J. W. Shepherd, H. D. Ellis. 1979. Effects of interpolated mugshot exposure on accuracy of eyewitness identification. *Journal of Applied Psychology* 64:232–37.

Davis, E. 1973. Neighborhood team policing: Implementing the territorial imperative. *Crime Prevention Review* 1:11–19.

Deci, E. L. 1980. *The psychology of self-determination.* Lexington, Mass.: Lexington Books.

Decker, S. H. 1981. Citizen attitudes toward the police: A review of past findings and suggestions for future policy. *Journal of Police Science and Administration* 9:80–87.

Deffenbacher, K. A. 1980. Eyewitness accuracy and confidence: Can we infer anything about their relationship? *Law and Human Behavior* 4:243–60.

———. 1983. Book review of *Identification evidence: A psychological evaluation* by J. W. Shepherd, H. D. Ellis, and G. M. Davies. *American Journal of Psychology* 96:591–95.

Deffenbacher, K. A., and J. Horney. 1981. Psycho-legal aspects of face identification. In G. Davies, H. Ellis, and J. Shepherd, eds., *Perceiving and remembering faces*. New York: Academic Press.

Deitz, S. R., M. Littman, and B. J. Bentley. 1984. Attribution of responsibility for rape: The influence of observer empathy, victim resistance, and victim attractiveness. *Sex Roles* 10:261–80.

DeJong, W. 1979. An examination of self-perception meditation of the foot-in-the-door effect. *Journal of Personality and Social Psychology* 37:2221–39.

Derbyshire, R. 1968. Childrens' perceptions of the police: A comparative study of attitudes and attitude change. *Journal of Criminal Law, Criminology, and Police Science* 59:183–90.

Deutsch, D., S. Sameth, and J. Akinyemi. 1981. Seat belt usage and risk-taking behavior at two major intersections. *American Association Automotive Medicine Quarterly Journal* 3:23–25.

Deutsch, M., and H. Gerard. 1955. A study of normative and informational influence upon individual judgment. *Journal of Abnormal and Social Psychology* 51:629–36.

Devlin, Lord Patrick. 1976. *Report to the Secretary of State for the Home Department of the Departmental Committee on Evidence of Identification in Criminal Cases*. London: Majesty's SO.

Diamond, B. L. 1974. The psychiatric prediction of dangerousness. *University of Pennsylvania Law Review* 123:439–52.

Dittes, J., and H. Kelley. 1956. Effects of different conditions of acceptance upon conformity to group norms. *Journal of Abnormal and Social Psychology* 53:100–7.

Dobash, R. E., and R. Dobash. 1979. *Violence against wives: A case against the patriarchy*. New York: Free Press.

Dodd, D. J. 1967. Police mentality and behaviour. *Issues in Criminology* 3:47–67.

Dodd, D. H., and J. M. Bradshaw. 1980. Leading questions and memory: Pragmatic constraints. *Journal of Verbal Learning and Verbal Behavior* 19:695–704.

Dolan, R., J. Hendricks, and M. S. Meagher. 1986. Police practices and attitudes toward domestic violence. *Journal of Police Science and Administration* 14:187–92.

Dollard, J., N. Miller, L. Doob, O. H. Mowrer, and R. R. Sears. 1939. *Frustration and aggression*. New Haven: Yale University Press.

Doob, A. N. 1970. Catharsis and aggression: The effect of hurting one's enemy. *Journal of Experimental Research in Personality* 4:291–96.

Doob, A. W., and G. E. MacDonald. 1979. Television viewing and fear of victimization: Is the relationship causal? *Journal of Personality and Social Psychology* 37:170–79.

Dristas, W. J., and V. L. Hamilton. 1977. Evidence about evidence: Effect of pressupositions, items salience, stress, and perceiver set on accident recall. Unpublished manuscript, University of Michigan.

Driver, E. 1970. Confessions and the social psychology of coercion. In M. R. Summers and T. E. Barth, eds., *Law and order in a democratic society.* Columbus, Ohio: Charles E. Merrill.

Duncan, E. M., P. Whitney, and S. Kunen. 1982. Integration of visual and verbal information in children's memories. *Child Development* 53:1215–23.

Dutton, D., and S. L. Painter. 1981. Traumantic bonding: The development of emotional attachments in battered women and other relationships of intermittent abuse. *Victimology: An International Journal* 6:139–55.

Easterbrook, J. A. 1959. The effects of emotion on the utilization and organization of behavior. *Psychological Review* 66:183–201.

Ebbinghaus, H. 1964. *Memory: A contribution to experimental psychology.* New York: Dover. (Originally published 1885.)

Edleson, J. L. 1984. Working with men who batter. *Social Work* (May–June):237–42.

Edleson, J. L., Z. Eisikovits, and E. Guttmann. 1985. Men who batter women. *Journal of Family Issues* 6:229–47.

Ehrlich, I. 1975. The deterrent effect of capital punishment: A question of life and death. *American Economic Review* (June):397–417.

Eisenberg, T. 1975. Labor-management relations and psychological stress. *Police Chief* 42:54–58.

Elifson, K. W., D. M. Petersen, and C. K. Hadaway. 1983. Religiosity and delinquency. *Criminology* 21:505–27.

Elliott, J. F., and M. H. States. 1980. The concept of power and the police. *Journal of Police Science and Administration* 8:87–93.

Ellis, H. D. 1988. The Tichborne claimant: Person identification following very long intervals. *Applied Cognitive Psychology* 2:257–64.

Ellis, H. D., G. M. Davies, and J. W. Shepherd. 1977. Experimental studies of face identification. *National Journal of Criminal Defense* 3:219–34.

Ellis, H. D., J. W. Shepherd, and G. M. Davies. 1980. The deterioration of verbal descriptions of faces over different delay intervals. *Journal of Police Science and Administration* 8:101–6.

Ellison, K. W., and R. Buckhout, 1981. *Psychology and criminal justice.* New York: Harper and Row.

Elms, A., ed. 1969. *Role playing, reward, and attitude change.* Princeton: Van Nostrand.

Elwork, A., B. D. Sales, and D. Suggs. 1981. The trial: A research review. In B. D. Sales, ed., *The trial process.* New York: Plenum.

Enter, J. E. 1986. The rise to the top: An analysis of police chief career patterns. *Journal of Police Science and Administration* 14:334–46.

Erez, E. 1984. Self-defined "desert" and citizens' assessment of the police. *Journal of Criminal Law and Criminology* 75:1276–99.

Erickson, M. H. 1938. Criminality in a group of male psychiatric patients. *Mental Hygiene* 22:459–76.

Erikson, E. H. 1959. Identity and the life cycle: Selected papers. *Psychological Issues* 1:1–171.

————. 1963. *Childhood and society*, 2nd ed. New York: Norton.

Erikson, K. T. 1966. *Wayward puritans: A study in the sociology of deviance.* New York: Wiley.

Erlanger, H. S. 1974. The empirical status of the subculture of violence thesis. *Social Problems* 22:280–92.

Ettinger, R., R. C. Marino, N. Endler, S. Geller, and T. Natziuk. 1971. Effects of agreement and correctness of relative competence and conformity. *Journal of Personality and Social Psychology* 19:204–12.

Evans, L., P. Wasielewski, and C. R. Von Buseck, 1981. Compulsory seat belt usage and driver risk-taking behavior. Warren, Mich.: General Motors Research Laboratories, GMR-3413.

Fagan, M. M., and K., Ayers, Jr. 1982. The life of a police officer: A developmental perspective. *Criminal Justice and Behavior* 9:273–85.

Fagan, R. W. 1986. Police attitudes toward capital punishment. *Journal of Police Science and Administration* 14:193–201.

Faller, K. C. 1984. Is the child victim of sexual abuse telling the truth? *Child Abuse and Neglect* 8:473–81.

Farley, F. H. 1973. A theory of delinquency. Paper presented at the annual meeting of the American Psychological Association, Montreal.

Farley, F. H., and S. V. Farley. 1972. Stimulus-seeking motivation and delinquent behavior among institutionalized delinquent girls. *Journal of Consulting and Clinical Psychology* 39:94–97.

Farmer, R. E., and L. H. Monahan, 1980. The prevention model for stress reduction: A concept paper. *Journal of Police Science and Administration* 8:54–60.

Farnham-Diggory, S. 1978. *Learning disability: A psychological perspective.* Cambridge: Harvard University Press.

Farrington, D. P. 1983. Randomized experiments on crime and justice. In M. Tonry and N. Morris, eds., *Crime and justice: An annual review of research,* vol. 4. Chicago: University of Chicago Press.

Farrington, D. P., and B. J. Knight. 1980. Four studies of stealing as a risky decision. In P. D. Lipsitt and B. D. Sales, eds., *New directions in psychological research.* New York: Van Nostrand.

Feild, H. S. 1978. Attitudes toward rape: A comparative analysis of police, rapists, crisis counselors, and citizens. *Journal of Personality and Social Psychology* 36:156–79.

Felkenes, G. T. 1984. Attitudes of police officers towards their professional ethics. *Journal of Criminal Justice* 12:211–20.

Fell, R. D., W. C. Richard and W. L. Wallace. 1980. Psychological job stress and the police officer. *Journal of Police Science and Administration* 8:139–44.

Fennel, J. T. 1981. Psychological stress and the peace officer or stress—A cop killer. In G. Henderson, ed., *Police human relations*, Springfield, Ill.: Charles C. Thomas.

Fenster, C. A., G. Faltico, J. Goldstein, F. Kaslow, B. Locke, M. Musikoff, H. Schlossberg, and R. Wolk. 1976. Careers in forensic psychology. In P. J. Woods, ed., *Career opportunities for psychologists: Expanding and emerging areas*. Washington, D.C.: American Psychological Association.

Fenster, C. A., C. F. Wiedemann, and B. Locke. 1977. Police personality: Social science folklore and psychological measurement. In B. D. Sales, ed., *Psychology in the legal process*. New York: Spectrum.

Ferraro, K. F., and R. L. LaGrange. 1988. Are older people afraid of crime? *Journal of Aging Studies* 2:277–87.

Feshbach, S. 1986. Reconceptualizations of anger: Some research perspectives. *Journal of Social and Clinical Psychology* 4:123–32.

Festinger, L. 1957. *A theory of cognitive dissonance.* New York: Row, Peterson.

Fiedler, F. E. 1967. *A theory of leadership effectiveness.* New York: McGraw-Hill.

———. 1981. Leadership effectiveness. *American Behavioral Scientist* 24:619–32.

Fielding, N. G. 1986. Evaluating the role of training in police socialization: A British example. *Journal of Community Psychology* 14:319–29.

Figley, C., and H. McCubbin, eds. 1983. *Stress and the family.* New York: Bruner-Mazel.

Filley, A. C., R. J. House, and S. Kerr. 1976. *Managerial process and organizational behavior.* Glenview, Ill.: Scott, Foresman.

Finn, P., and B. W. E. Bragg. 1986. Perception of the risk of an accident by young and older drivers. *Accident Analysis and Prevention* 8:289–98.

Fiora-Gormally, N. 1978. Battered wives who kill. *Law and Human Behavior* 2:133–65.

Fischer, C. T. 1984. A phenomenological study of being criminally victimized: Contributions and constraints of qualitative research. *Journal of Social Issues* 40:161–78.

Fischoff, B. 1975. Hindsight and foresight: The effect of outcome knowledge on judgment under uncertainty. *Journal of Experimental Psychology: Human Perception and Performance* 1:288–99.

Fishbein, M. and I. Ajzen. 1974. Attitudes toward objects as predictive of single and multiple behavioral criteria. *Psychological Review* 81:59–74.

Fisher, R. P., E. Geiselman, and D. S. Raymond. 1987. Critical analysis of police interview techniques. *Journal of Police Science and Administration* 15:177–85.

Fisher, R. P., R. E. Geiselman, D. S. Raymond, L. M. Jurkevich, and M. L. Warhaftig. 1987. Enhancing enhanced eyewitness memory: Refining the cognitive interview. *Journal of Police Science and Administration* 15:291–97.

Fishman, M. 1978. Crime waves as ideology. *Social Problems* 25:531–43.

———. 1981. Police news: Constructing an image of crime. *Urban Life* 9:371–94.

Fleet, M. L., J. C. Brigham, and R. K. Bothwell. 1987. The confidence-accuracy relationship: The effects of confidence assessment and choosing. *Journal of Applied Social Psychology* 17:171–87.

Fodor, E. M. 1973. Moral development and parent behavior antecedents in adolescent psychopaths. *Journal of Genetic Psychology* 122:37–43.

Fogelson, R. M. 1977. *Big-city police.* Cambridge: Harvard University Press.

Forssman, H., and T. S. Frey. 1953. Electroencephalograms of boys with behavior disorders. *Acta Psychiatrica et Neurologica Scandinavica* 28:61–73.

Fraisse, P. 1984. Perception and estimation of time. In *Annual Review of Psychology* 35:1–36.

French, J. R. P., Jr., and B. H. Raven. 1959. The bases of social power. In D. Cartwright, ed., *Studies in social power.* Ann Arbor: University of Michigan Press.

Freud, S. 1932. The acquisition of power over fire. *International Journal of Psychoanalysis* 13:405–10.

———. 1940. An outline of psycho-analysis. In J. Strachey, ed., *Standard edition of the complete psychological work of Sigmund Freud,* vol. 23. London: Hogarth.

———. 1950. Why war? In J. Strachey, ed., *Collected papers 5.* London: Hogarth.

Friedlander, K. 1947. *The psychoanalytic approach to juvenile delinquency.* New York: International Universities Press.

Friedman, M. D., and R. H. Rosenman, 1974. *Type A behavior and your heart.* New York: Knopf.

Friedrich, R. J. 1977. The impact of organizational, individual, and situational factors on police behavior. Ph.D. dissertation, University of Michigan.

Frieze, I. H., S. Hymer, and M. S. Greenberg. 1987. Describing the crime victim: Psychological reactions to victimization. *Professional Psychology: Research and Practice* 18:299–315.

Fry, L. W., and L. J. Berkes. 1983. The paramilitary police model: An organizational misfit. *Human Organization* 42:225–34.

Fuller, J. L., and W. R. Thompson. 1978. *Behavior genetics*, St. Louis: Mosby.

Furman v. Georgia. 408 U. S. 238 269 (1972).

Furnham, A. 1983. Social psychology as common sense. *Bulletin of the British Psychological Society* 36:105–9.

Furnham, A., and M. Henderson. 1983. Lay theories of delinquency. *European Journal of Social Psychology* 13:107–20.

Fyfe, J. J. 1978. Shots fired: A typological examination of New York City Police firearms discharges, 1971–1975. Ph.D. dissertation, State University of New York at Albany.

Gabrielli, W. F., and S. A. Mednick. 1983. Genetic correlates of criminal behavior. *American Behavioral Scientist* 27:59–74.

Gadd, I. 1986. *Our cops: Their stories*. Alliston, Ont.: Bulldog Press.

Garofalo, J. 1981. The fear of crime: Causes and consequences. *Journal of Criminal Law and Criminology* 82:839–57.

———. 1982. Fear of crime as a problem for the elderly. *Social Problems* 30:240–45.

Gebotys, R. J., J. V. Roberts, and B. DasGupta. 1988. News media use and public perceptions of crime seriousness. *Canadian Journal of Criminology* 30:3–16.

Geen, R. G., D. Stonner, and G. L. Shope. 1975. The facilitation of aggression by aggression: Evidence against the catharsis hypothesis. *Journal of Personality and Social Psychology* 31:721–26.

Geiselman, R. E., R. P. Fisher, I. Firstenberg, L. A. Hutton, S. Sullivan, I. Avetissian, and A. Prosk. 1984. Enhancement of eyewitness memory: An empirical evaluation of the cognitive interview. *Journal of Police Science and Administration* 12:74–80.

Geiselman, R. E., R. P. Fisher, D. P. MacKinnon, and H. L. Holland. 1985. Eyewitness memory enhancement in the police interview: Cognitive retrieval mnemonics versus hypnosis. *Journal of Applied Psychology* 70:401–12.

———. 1986. Enhancement of eyewitness memory with the cognitive interview. *American Journal of Psychology* 99:385–401.

Geller, W. A. 1982. Deadly force: What we know. *Journal of Police Science and Administration* 10:151–77.

Gelles, R. J., and M. A. Straus. 1979. Violence in the American family. *Journal of Social Issues* 35:15–39.

Gerbner, G., L. Gross, M. Morgan, and N. Signorielli. 1981. Health and medicine on television. *New England Journal of Medicine* 305:901–4.

Gergen, K. J. 1971. *The concept of self.* New York: Holt, Rinehart, and Winston.

Gibbons, D. C. 1973. *Society, crime and criminal careers,* 2nd ed. Englewood Cliffs, N.J.: Prentice-Hall.

Gibbs, J. P. 1975. Assessing the deterrence doctrine. *American Behavioral Scientist* 22:653–77.

Gibbs, J. P., and M. L. Erickson 1979. Conceptions of criminal and delinquent acts. *Deviant Behavior* 1:71–100.

Gibson, L., R. Linden, and S. Johnson. 1980. A situational theory of rape. *Canadian Journal of Criminology* 22:51–65.

Giordano, P. C. 1976. The sense of injustice? An analysis of juveniles' reactions to the justice system. *Criminology* 14:93–112.

Girodo, M. 1983. Undercover operations and law enforcement stress: Getting the pendulum to return. *Royal Canadian Mounted Police Gazette* 45:26–28.

Glaser, D. 1978. The counterproductivity of conservative thinking about crime. *Criminology* 16:209–24.

Glass, D. C. 1977. *Behavior patterns, stress, and coronary disease.* Hillsdale, N.J.: Lawrence Erlbaum.

Glass, D. C., and J. Singer. 1972. *Urban stress.* New York: Academic Press.

Glueck, S. 1925. *Mental disorders and the criminal law.* New York: Little, Brown.

Goldkamp, J. 1976. Minorities as victims of police shootings: Interpretations of racial disproportionality and police use of deadly force. *Justice System Journal* 2:169–83.

Goldsmith, J., and S. S. Goldsmith. 1976. *Crime and the elderly.* Lexington, Mass.: Lexington Books.

Goldstein, A. G., and J. E. Chance. 1985. Voice recognition: The effects of faces, temporal distribution of "practice," and social distance. Paper presented at the meetings of the Midwestern Psychological Association, Chicago.

Goldstein, A. P., P. J. Monti, T. J. Sardino, and D. J. Green. 1977. *Police crisis intervention.* Elmsford, N.Y.: Pergamon Press.

Goldstein, H. 1979. Improving policing: A problem-oriented approach. *Crime and Delinquency* (April):236–58.

Goldstein, J. 1960. Police discretion not to invoke the criminal process: Low-visibility decisions in the administration of justice. *Yale Law Journal* 69: 543–88.

Goldstein, J. H. 1986. *Aggression and crimes of violence,* 2nd ed. New York: Oxford University Press.

Goleman, D. J., and G. E. Schwartz 1976. Meditation as an intervention in stress reactivity. *Journal of Consulting and Clinical Psychology* 44:456–66.

Gondolf, E. W. 1988. Who are those guys? Toward a behavioral typology of batterers. *Violence and Victims* 3:187–203.

Goodman, G. S., C. Aman, and J. Hirschman. 1987. Child sexual and physical abuse: Children's testimony. In S. J. Ceci, M. P. Toglia, and D. F. Ross, eds., *Children's eyewitness memory*. New York: Springer-Verlag.

Gordon, C. 1968. Self-conceptions: Configurations of content. In C. Gordon and K. J. Gergen, eds., *The self in social interaction*, vol. 1. New York: Wiley.

Gorenstein, G. W., and P. C. Ellsworth, 1980. Effects of choosing an incorrect photograph on a later identification by an eyewitness. *Journal of Applied Psychology* 65:616–22.

Gottlieb, B. H. 1981. *Social networks and social support*. Beverly Hills: Sage.

Graber, D. A. 1978. The media and the police. *Policy Studies Journal* 7:493–500.

Gray, T. C. 1975. Selecting for a police subculture. In J. H. Skolnick and T. C. Gray, eds., *Police in America*. Boston: Little, Brown.

Grayson, B., and M. I. Stein, 1981. Attracting assault: Victims' nonverbal cues. *Journal of Communication* 31:68–75.

Greeley, A. M., and P. B. Sheatsley, 1971. Attitudes toward racial integration. *Scientific American* 223:13–19.

Greenberg, D. F. 1981. *Crime and capitalism: Readings in Marxist Criminology*. Palo Alto, Calif.: Mayfield.

Greenberg, M. S., and R. B. Ruback. 1984. Criminal victimization: Introduction and overview. *Journal of Social Issues* 40:1–8.

Greer, G. 1975. Seduction is a four-letter word. In L. G. Schultz, ed., *Rape victimology*. Springfield, Ill.: Charles C. Thomas.

Griffeth, R. W., and T. P. Cafferty. 1977. Police and citizen value systems: Some cross-sectional comparisons. *Journal of Applied Social Psychology* 7:191–204.

Griffin, B. S., and C. T. Griffin. 1981. Victims in rape confrontation. *Victimology: An International Journal* 6:59–75.

Gross, S. 1984. Women becoming cops: Developmental issues and solutions. *Police Chief* (January):33–35.

Groth, A. N. 1979. *Men who rape: The psychology of the offender*. New York: Plenum.

Groth, A. N., and A. W. Burgess. 1977. Motivational intent in the sexual assault of children. *Criminal Justice and Behavior* 4:253–64.

Groth, A. N., A. W. Burgess, and L. Holstrom. 1977. Rape, power, anger, and sexuality. *American Journal of Psychiatry* 134:1239–43.

Gudjonsson, G. H. 1984. Fear of "fear of failure" and "tissue damage" in police recruits, constables, sergeants and senior officers. *Personality and Individual Differences* 5:233–36.

Gudjonsson, G. H., and K. R. C. Adlam. 1983. Personality patterns of British police officers. *Personality and Individual Differences* 4:507–12.

Gudjonsson, G. H., and J. A. C. MacKeith. 1982. False confessions. Psychological effects of interrogation: A discussion paper. In A. Trankell, ed., *Reconstructing the past: The role of the psychologist in criminal trials.* Stockholm: P. A. Norstedt and Soners Forlag.

———. 1988. Retracted confessions: Legal, psychological and psychiatric aspects. *Medicine, Science, and Law* 28:187–94.

Gundersen, D. F. 1987. Credibility and the police uniform. *Journal of Police Science and Administration* 15:192–95.

Hageman, M. J. C. 1978. Occupational stress of law enforcement officers and marital and familial relationships. *Journal of Police Science and Administration* 6:402–12.

Hahn, H. 1971. Ghetto assessments of police protection and authority. *Law and Society Review* 6:183–94.

Hall, D. F. 1977. Obtaining eyewitness identifications in criminal investigations: Two experiments and some comments on the Zeitgeist in forensic psychology. Paper presented at the American Psychology-Law Conference, Snowmass, Colo.

Hall, D. F., E. F. Loftus, and J. P. Tousignant. 1984. Postevent information and changes in recollection for a natural event. In G. L. Wells and E. F. Loftus, eds., *Eyewitness testimony.* New York: Cambridge University Press.

Hall, E. R., J. A. Howard, and S. L. Boezio. 1986. Tolerance of rape: A sexist or antisocial attitude? *Psychology of Women Quarterly* 10:101–18.

Hall, M. N. 1982. Law enforcement officers and death notification: A plea for relevant education. *Journal of Police Science and Administration* 10:189–93.

Hamblin, R. L. 1958. Leadership and crisis. *Sociometry* 21:322–55.

Hamilton, D. L., and G. D. Bishop. 1976. Attitudinal and behavioral effects of initial integration of white surburban neighborhoods. *Journal of Social Issues* 32:47–67.

Hammersley, R., and J. D. Read. 1983. Testing witnesses' voice recognition: some practical recommendations. *Journal of the Forensic Science Society* 23:203–8.

Handkins, R. E., and J. F. Cross. 1985. Can a voice line-up be too fair?

Paper presented at the meetings of the Midwestern Psychological Association, Chicago.

Haney, C., C. Banks, and P. G. Zimbardo. 1973. Interpersonal dynamics in a simulated prison. *International Journal of Crime and Penology* 1:69–97.

Haney, C., and J. Manzolati. 1981. Television criminology: Network illusions of criminal justice realities. In E. Aronson, ed., *Readings about the social animal*, 3rd ed. San Francisco: Freeman.

Hans, V. P., and D. Slater. 1983. John Hinckley, Jr., and the insanity defense: The public's verdict. *Public Opinion Quarterly* 47:202–12.

Hare, R. D. 1965. Temporal gradients of fear arousal in psychopaths. *Journal of Abnormal Psychology* 70:442–45.

———. 1986. Criminal psychopaths. In J. C. Yuille, ed., *Police selection and training*. Boston: Martinus Nijhoff.

Harris, G. T., and M. E. Rice. 1984. Mentally disordered firesetters: Psychodynamic versus empirical approaches. *International Journal of Law and Psychiatry* 7:19–34.

Harris, R. N. 1973. *The police academy: An inside view*. New York: Wiley.

Hart, P. J. 1978. Crime and punishment in the Army. *Journal of Personality and Social Psychology* 36:1456–71.

Hastie, R. 1986. Notes on the psychologist expert witness. *Law and Human Behavior* 10:79–82.

Hastie, R., R. Landsman, and E. F. Loftus. 1978. Eyewitness testimony: The dangers of guessing. *Jurimetrics Journal* 19:1–8.

Haward, L. R. C. 1981. *Forensic psychology*. London: Batsford.

Haynes, S. G., M. Feinleib, and E. D. Eaker. 1983. Type-A behavior and the ten-year incidence of coronary heart disease in the Framingham heart study. In R. H. Rosenman, ed., *Psychosomatic risk factors and coronary heart disease*. Bern: Huber.

Hays, J. R., T. K. Roberts and K. S. Soloway, eds. 1981. *Violence and the violent individual*. New York: S. P. Medical and Scientific Books.

Henderson, G. 1981a. Police leadership. In G. Henderson, ed., *Police human relations*. Springfield, Ill.: Charles C. Thomas.

———. 1981b. On becoming a police officer. In G. Henderson, ed. *Police Human Relations*. Springfield, Ill.: Charles C. Thomas.

Henke, E. 1838. *Handbuch des criminalrechts und der criminal politik*. Vierter Theil. Berlin: Nicolai

Higgins, L. 1951. Historical background of policewomen's service. *Journal of Criminal Law, Criminology, and Police Science* 41:822–33.

Higgins, E. T., and W. S. Rholes. 1978. Saying is believing: Effects of message modification on memory and liking for the person described. *Journal of Experimental Social Psychology* 14: 363–78.

Hilgard, E. R. 1971. Toward a responsible social science. *Journal of Applied Social Psychology* 1:1–6.

Hilgendorf, E. L., and B. L. Irving. 1978. False positive identification. *Medicine, Science and the Law* 18:255–62.

———. 1981. A decision-making model of confessions. In S. M. A. Lloyd-Bostock, ed., *Psychology in legal contexts: Applications and limitations.* London: Macmillan.

Hindelang, M. J. 1974. Public opinion regarding crime, criminal justice, and related topics. *Journal of Research in Crime and Delinquency* 11: 101–16.

Hinkle, L. E., Jr., L. H. Whitney, E. W. Lehman, J. Dunn, B. Benjamin, R. King, A. Plakun, and B. Flehinger. 1968. Occupation, education, and coronary heart disease. *Science* 161:238–46.

Hintzman, D. L. 1976. Repetition and memory. In G. H. Bower, ed., *The psychology of learning and motivation,* vol. 10. New York: Academic Press.

Hirschi, T. 1969. *Causes of delinquency.* Berkeley: University of California Press.

Hirschi, T. and R. Stark. 1969. Hellfire and delinquency. *Social Problems* 17:202–13.

Hoffman, V. J. 1984. The relationship of psychology to delinquency: A comprehensive approach. *Adolescence* 19:55–61.

Holdaway, S. 1986. Police and social work relations—Problems and possibilities. *British Journal of Social Work* 16:137–60.

Hogan, R., C. B. Desoto, and C. Solano. 1977. Traits, tests, and personality research. *American Psychologist* 32:255–64.

Hollin, C. R., and K. Howells. 1987. Lay explanations of delinquency: Global or offence-specific? *British Journal of Social Psychology* 26:203–10.

Holman, B. 1977. Community relations units in police departments. In H. J. Bryce, ed., *Black crime: A police view.* Washington, D.C.: National Institute of Law Enforcement and Criminal Justice, U.S. Department of Justice.

Holmes, S. A. 1982 A Detroit model for police-social work cooperation. *Social Casework: The Journal of Contemporary Social Work* (April):220–26.

Holmes, T. H., and R. H. Rahe. 1967. The social readjustment rating scale. *Journal of Psychosomatic Research* 11:213–18.

Holmstrom, L., and A. W. Burgess, 1978. *The victims of rape: Institutional reactions.* New York: Wiley.

———. 1979. Rapists' talk: Linguistic strategies to control the victim. *Deviant Behavior* 1:101–25.

Holzworth, R. J., and C. B. Pipping. 1985. Drawing a weapon: An analysis of police judgments. *Journal of Police Science and Administration* 13:185–93.

Homa, G. 1983. *The law enforcement composite sketch artist.* Training manual, New Jersey State Police.

Homant, R. J., and D. B. Kennedy. 1982. Battered women and the police: A comparison of perceptions. Paper presented to the Academy of Criminal Justice Sciences, Louisville, Ky.

Horvath, F. 1987. The police use of deadly force: A description of selected characteristics of intrastate incidents. *Journal of Police Science and Administration* 15:226–38.

House, J. S. 1974. Occupational stress and coronary heart disease: A review and theoretical integration. *Journal of Health and Social Behavior* 15: 12–25.

Hunt, I. C., Jr. 1971. *Minority recruiting in the New York City Police Department:* Part 1. New York: Rand Institute.

Hurrell, J. J., and W. H. Kroes. 1975. Stress awareness. In W. H. Kroes and J. J. Hurrell, eds., *Job stress and the police officer: Identifying stress reduction techniques*. Washington, D.C.: GPO.

Hylton, J. H. 1980. The assessment of police job satisfaction. *Canadian Police College Journal 4:* 189–207.

———. 1981a. Some attitudes toward natives in a prairie city. *Canadian Journal of Criminology* 4:189–207.

———. 1981b. Innate criminality revisited. *Canada's Mental Health* 29 (3): 12–15.

———. 1982. The native offender in Saskatchewan: Some implications for crime prevention programming. *Canadian Journal of Criminology* 24: 121–31.

Inbau, F. E., and J. E. Reid. 1962. *Criminal interrogation and confessions*. Baltimore: Williams and Wilkins.

Inciardi, J. A. 1975. *Careers in crime*. Chicago: Rand McNally.

Inman, M. 1981. Police interrogation and confessions. In S. Lloyd-Bostock, ed., *Psychology in legal contexts: Applications and limitations*. London: Macmillan.

In re Gault, 387 U.S. 1 (1967).

Inwald, R. 1984. Psychological testing: Guidelines help managers avoid liability issues. *Training Aids Digest* 9:1–7.

———. 1985. Administrative, legal, and ethical practices in the psychological testing of law enforcement officers. *Journal of Criminal Justice* 13: 367–72.

Jackson, M. W. 1988. Lay and professional perceptions of dangerousness and other forensic issues. *Canadian Journal of Criminology* (July):215–29.

Jackson, S. E. 1983. Managing stress and burnout in law enforcement agencies. *Royal Canadian Mounted Police Gazette* 45:20–25.

Jacob, H. 1971. Black and white perceptions of justice in the city. *Law and Society Review* 5:69–89.

Jacobi, J. 1975. Reducing police stress—A psychiatrist's point of view. In W. Kroes and J. Herrell, Jr., eds., *Job stress and the police officer— Identifying stress reduction techniques.* Washington, D.C.: GPO.

Jacobs, P. A., M. Brunton, H. M. Melville, R. P. Brittain, and W. F. McClemont. 1965. Aggressive behavior, mental subnormality, and the XYY male. *Nature* 208:1351–52.

Jacquith, S. M. 1981. Adolescent marijuana and alcohol use: An empirical test of differential association theory. *Criminology* 19:271–80.

Jaffe, P., and C. A Burris. 1981. No place to turn. *Canadian Lawyer* (October):13–15.

James, W. 1950. *The principles of psychology.* New York: Dover. (Originally published 1890.)

James, J. T. L. 1979. Toward a cultural understanding of the native offender. *Canadian Journal of Criminology* 21:453–62.

Janoff-Bulman, R., and I. Frieze. 1983. A theoretical perspective for understanding reactions to victimology. *Journal of Social Issues* 39:1–17.

Janus, S. S., B. E. Bess, J. J. Cadden, and H. Greenwald. 1980. Training police officers to distinguish mental illness. *American Journal of Psychiatry* 137:228–29.

Jenkins, C. D. 1971a. Psychologic and social precursors of coronary disease: I. *New England Journal of Medicine* 284:244–55.

———. 1971b. Psychologic and social precursors of coronary disease: II. *New England Journal of Medicine* 284:307:17.

Jenkins, F., and G. Davies. 1985. Contamination of facial memory through exposure to misleading composite pictures. *Journal of Applied Psychology* 70:164–76.

Jensen, G. 1981. *Sociology of delinquency: Current issues.* London: Sage.

Johnson, E. 1970. Police: An analysis of role conflict. *Police* 14:47–52.

Johnson, R. E. 1979. *Juvenile delinquency and its origins: An integrated theoretical approach.* Cambridge: Cambridge University Press.

Johnson, R. N. 1972. *Aggression in man and animals.* Philadelphia: Saunders.

Johnson, S. L. 1984. Cross-racial identification errors in criminal cases. *Cornell Law Review* 69:934–87.

———. 1985. Black innocence and the white jury. *Michigan Law Review* 83:1611–1708.

Jonah, B. A. 1986. Accident risk and risk-taking behaviour among young drivers. *Accident Analysis and Prevention* 18:255–71.

Jonah, B. A., and N. E. Dawson. 1982. The national vehicle occupant restraint survey: Attitudes toward the use of restraints by Canadians, TP3593E. Road Safety Directorate, Transport Canada.

Jones, E. E., A. Farina, A. H. Hastorf, H. Markus, D. T. Miller, and R. A. Scott. 1984. *Social stigma.* San Francisco: Freeman.

Jones, G. M. 1987. Elderly people and domestic crime. *British Journal of Criminology* 27:191–201.

Jones, S. 1986. Police and public perceptions of the police role: Moving towards a reappraisal of police professional. In J. C. Yuille, ed., *Police selection and training.* Dordrecht: Martinus Nijhoff.

Joseph, N., and N. Alex. 1972. The uniform: A sociological perspective. *American Journal of Sociology* 77:719–30.

Jurkovic, G. J. 1980. The juvenile delinquent as a moral philosopher: A structural-developmental perspective. *Psychological Bulletin* 88:709–22.

Kaci, J. H. 1982. Confessions: A comparison of exclusion under Miranda in the United States and under the Judges' Rule in England. *American Journal of Criminal Law* 10:87–112.

Kahneman, D. 1973. *Attention and effort.* Englewood Cliffs, N.J.: Erlbaum.

Kalin, R., and R. C. Gardner. 1981. The cultural context of social psychology. In R. C. Gardner and R. Kalin, eds., *A Canadian social psychology of ethnic relations.* Toronto: Methuen.

Kantor, G. K.., and M. A. Straus. 1987. The "drunken bum" theory of wife beating. *Social Problems* 34:214–31.

Kaplan, S. G., and E. G. Wheeler. 1983. Survival skills for working with potentially violent clients. *Social casework: The Journal of Contemporary Social Work* (June):339–46.

Kassin, S. M., and L. S. Wrightsman. 1985. Confession evidence. In S. M. Kassin and L. S. Wrightsman, eds., *The psychology of evidence and trial procedure.* Beverly Hills: Sage.

Kaufmann, H. 1970. *Aggression and altruism.* New York: Holt, Rinehart, and Winston.

Keilitz, I., B. Zaremba, and P. K. Broder. 1979. *The link between learning disabilities and juvenile delinquency: Some issues and answers.* Williamsburg, Va.: National Center for State Courts.

Keller, O. J., and C. B. Vedder. 1965. The police and middle-class conflicts. *Police* 9:6–8.

Kelley, H. H., and J. Thibault. 1978. *Interpersonal relations: A theory of interdependence.* New York: Wiley.

Kelling, G. L., T. Pate, D. Dieckman, and C. E. Brown. 1974. *The Kansas City preventive patrol experiment: A summary report.* Washington, D.C.: Police Foundation.

Kelly, R. M., and G. West. 1973. The racial transition of a police force: A profile of white and black policemen in Washington, D.C. In J. R. Snibbe and H. M. Snibbe, eds., *The urban policeman in transition.* Springfield, Ill.: Charles C. Thomas.

Kennedy, D. B., and R. J. Homant. 1981. Nontraditional role assumption and the personality of the policewoman. *Journal of Police Science and Administration* 9:346–55.

————. 1983. Attitudes of abused women toward male and female police officers. *Criminal Justice and Behavior* 10:391–405.

Kidd, R. F., and E. F. Chayet. 1984. Why do victims fail to report? The psychology òf criminal victimization. *Journal of Social Issues* 40:39–50.

Kidder, L. H., J. L. Boell, and M. M. Moyer. 1983. Rights consciousness and victimization prevention through personal defense and assertiveness training. *Journal of Social Issues.* 39:1–17.

Kiernan, M. 1979. Police vs. the press: "There's always tension." *Police Magazine* 2:38–43.

Kilpatrick, D. G., P. A. Resick, and L. J. Veronen. 1981. Effects of a rape experience: A longitudinal study. *Journal of Social Issues* 37:105–22.

Kilpatrick, D. G., B. E. Saunders, L. J. Veronen, C. L. Best, and J. M. Von. 1987. Criminal victimization: Lifetime prevalence, reporting to police, and psychological impact. *Crime and Delinquency* 33:479–89.

King, S. 1971. Coping mechanisms in adolescents. *Psychiatric Annuals* 1:4–29.

King, M. A. and J. C. Yuille. 1987. Suggestibility and the child witness. In S. J. Ceci, M. P. Toglia, and D. F. Ross, eds., *Children's eyewitness memory.* New York: Springer-Verlag.

Kipnis, D. 1976. *The powerholders.* Chicago: University of Chicago Press.

Klaas, E. T. 1978. Psychological effects of immoral actions: The experimental evidence. *Psychological Bulletin* 85:756–71.

Kleiman, L. S., and M. E. Gordon. 1986. An examination of the relationship between police training academy performance and job performance. *Journal of Police Science and Administration* 14:293–299.

Klein, J. F., J. R. Webb, and J. E. DiSanto. 1978. Experience with the police and attitudes towards the police. *Canadian Journal of Sociology* 3:441–56.

Kleinman, P., and D. S. David. 1973. Victimization and perception of crime in a ghetto community. *Criminology* 11:307–43.

Klockars, C. B. 1984. Blue lies and police placebos: The moralities of police lying. *American Behavioral Scientist* 27:529–44.

Knapp Commission report on police corruption. 1973. New York: George Braziller.

Koenig, D. 1975. Police perceptions of public respect and extra-legal use of force: A reconsideration of folk wisdom and pluralistic ignorance. *Canadian Journal of Sociology* 1:313–24.

Kohlberg, L. 1963. The development of children's orientation toward a moral order. 1: Sequence in the development of human thought. *Vita Humana* 6:11–33.

―――. 1969. Stage and sequence: The cognitive developmental approach to socialization. In D. A. Goslin, ed., *Handbook of socialization theory of research*. Chicago: Rand McNally.

Kohlberg, L., and D. Freundlich. 1973. Moral judgment in youthful offenders. In L. Kohlberg, and E. Turiel, eds., *Moralization, the cognitive developmental approach*, New York: Holt, Rinehart, and Winston.

Kolko, D. J. 1985. Juvenile firesetting: A review and methodological critique. *Clinical Psychology Review* 5:345–76.

Kolko, D. J., and A. E. Kazdin. 1986. A conceptualization of firesetting in children and adolescents. *Journal of Abnormal Child Psychology* 14:49–61.

Konecni, V. J. 1975. Annoyance, type and duration of postannoyance activity, and aggression: The "cathartic" effect. *Journal of Experimental Psychology: General* 104:76–102.

Koss, M. P. 1985. The hidden rape victim: Personality, attitudinal, and situational characteristics. *Psychology of Women Quarterly:* 9:193–212.

Kraut, R. E. 1976. Deterrent and definitional influences on shoplifting. *Social Problems* 23:358–68.

Kroes, W. H. 1976. *Society's victim—The policeman*. Springfield, Ill.: Charles C. Thomas.

―――. 1983. Stress: The other side of policing. *Royal Canadian Mounted Police Gazette* 45:4–7.

Kroes, W. H., and J. J. Hurrell. eds. 1975. *Job stress and the police officer: Identifying stress reduction techniques*. Washington, D.C.: GPO.

Kroes, W. H., B. L. Margolis, and J. J. Hurrell. 1974. Job stress in policemen. *Journal of Police Science and Administration* 2:145–55.

Krouse, F. L. 1981. Effects of pose, pose change, and delay on face recognition performance. *Journal of Applied Psychology* 66:651–54.

Kruglanski, A. W., N. Friedland, and E. Farkash. 1984. Lay person's sensitivity to statistical information: The case of high perceived applicability. *Journal of Personality and Social Psychology* 46:503–18.

Krulewitz, J. E. 1981. Sex differences in evaluations of female and male victims' responses to assault. *Journal of Applied Social Psychology* 11: 460–74.

Kruelwitz, J. E., and J. E. Nash. 1979. Effects of rape victim resistance, assault outcome, and sex of observer on attributions about rape. *Journal of Personality* 47:557–74.

Krulewitz, J. E., and E. J. Payne. 1978. Attributions about rape: Effects of rapist force, observer, and sex role attitudes. *Journal of Applied Social Psychology* 8:291–305.

Kübler-Ross, E. 1969. *On death and dying*. New York: Macmillan.

Kubzansky, P. E. 1961. The effects of reduced environmental stimulation on human behavior: A review. In A. D. Biderman and H. Zimmer, eds., *The manipulation of human behavior*. New York: Wiley.

Kuehn, L. L. 1974. Looking down a gun barrel: Person perception and violent crime. *Perceptual and Motor Skills* 39:1159–64.

Kurtines, W., and E. B. Greif. 1974. The development of moral thought: Review and evaluation. *Psychological Bulletin* 81:453–70.

Kuykendall, J., and R. R. Roberg. 1982. Mapping police organizational change: From a mechanistic toward an organic model. *Criminology* 20: 241–56.

LaFave, W. R. 1965. *Arrest: The decision to take a suspect into custody*. Boston: Little, Brown.

Lamborn, L. 1981. The vulnerability of the victim. In B. Galaway and J. Hudson, eds., *Perspectives on crime victims*. St Louis: Mosby.

Langenbucher, J. W., and P. E. Nathan. 1983. Psychology, public policy, and the evidence for alcohol intoxication. *American Psychologist* (October): 1070–77.

Langer, E. J., and L. G. Imber. 1979. When practice makes imperfect: Debilitating effects of overlearning. *Journal of Personality and Social Psychology* 32:311–28.

Langone, J. 1981. When cops crack up. *FBI/DOJ Discover* 84 (May):86–87.

La Prairie, C. P. 1984. Selected criminal justice and socio-demographic data on native women. *Canadian Journal of Criminology* (April):161–69.

Larson, K. S. 1968. Authoritarianism and attitudes toward police. *Psychological Reports* 23:349–50.

Lassiter, G. D., and A. A. Irvine. 1986. Videotaped confessions: The impact of camera point on view of judgments of coercion. *Journal of Applied Social Psychology* 16:268–76.

Lauer, R. H. 1978. *Social problems and the quality of life*. Dubuque, Iowa: Brown.

Laughery, K. R., J. F. Alexander, and A. B. Lane. 1971. Recognition of human faces: Effects of target exposure time, target positions, pose position, and type of photograph. *Journal of Applied Psychology* 51:477–83.

Laughery, K. R., and R. H. Fowler. 1980. Sketch artist and Identi-Kit procedures for recalling faces. *Journal of Applied Psychology* 65:307–16.

Lautman, B. 1984. Handgun laws work. *Washington Report* 10(1):2. Washington, D.C.: Handgun Control.

Law Enforcement Assistance Administration (LEAA). 1977. *The police and public opinion*. Washington, D.C.: National Criminal Justice Information and Statistics Service.

Lawrence, R. A. 1984. Police stress and personality factors: A conceptual model. *Journal of Criminal Justice* 12:247–63.

Lazarus, R. S. 1968. Emotions and adaptations: Conceptual and empirical relations. In W. J. Arnold, ed., *Nebraska symposium on motivation.* Lincoln: University of Nebraska Press.

―――. 1976. *Patterns of adjustment.* New York: McGraw-Hill.

Lazin, F. A. 1980. How the police view the press. *Journal of Police Science and Administration* 8:148–59.

LeDoux, J. C., and R. R. Hazelwood. 1985. Police attitudes and beliefs toward rape. *Journal of Police Science and Administration* 13:211–20.

Lefkowitz, J. 1973. Attitudes of police toward their job. In J. R. Snibbe and H. M. Snibbe, eds., *The urban policeman in transition*, Springfield, Ill.: Charles C. Thomas.

―――. 1974. Job attitudes of police: Overall description and demographic correlates. *Journal of Vocational Behavior* 5:221–30.

―――. 1975. Psychological attributes of policemen: A review of research and opinion. *Journal of Social Issues* 31:3–26.

―――. 1977. Industrial-organizational psychology and the police. *American Psychologist* 32:346–64.

Lefkowitz, M. M., L. D. Eron, L. O. Walder, and L. R. Huesmann. 1977. *Growing up to be violent.* New York: Pergamon.

Leippe, M. R. 1980. Effects of integrative memorial and cognitive processes on the correspondence of eyewitness accuracy and confidence. *Law and Human Behavior* 4:261–74.

Leippe, M. R., G. L. Wells, and T. M. Ostrom. 1978. Crime seriousness as a determinant of accuracy in eyewitness identification. *Journal of Applied Psychology* 63:345–51.

Lempert, R. 1983. The effect of executions on homicides: A new look in an old light. *Crime and Delinquency* (January):88–115.

Lerner, M. J. 1980. *The belief in a just world: A fundamental delusion.* New York: Plenum.

Lester, D. 1979. The policeman's lot. *Law and order* 27, 58, and 71.

―――. 1983. *Why people kill themselves.* Springfield, Ill.: Charles C Thomas.

Lester, D., and W. T. Brink. 1985. Police solidarity and tolerance for police misbehavior. *Psychological Reports* 57:326.

Lester, D., and J. L. Genz. 1978. Internal-external locus of control, experience as a police officer, and job satisfaction in municipal police officers. *Journal of Police Science and Administration* 6:479–81.

Lester, D., L. A. Leitner, and I. Posner. 1985. A note on locus of control and stress in police officers. *Journal of Community Psychology* 13:77–79.

Lester, G., and D. Lester. 1971. *Suicide.* Englewood Cliffs, N.J.: Prentice-Hall.

Lester, K. D., F. Gronau, and K. Wondrack. 1982. The personality and attitudes of female police officers: Needs, androgyny and attitudes toward rape. *Journal of Police Science and Administration* 10:357–60.

Levens, B. R., and D. G. Dutton. 1980. *The social service role of police: Domestic crisis intervention.* Ottawa: Communication Division, Ministry of the Solicitor General of Canada.

Levine-MacCombie, J., and M. P. Koss. 1986. Acquaintance rape: Effective avoidance strategies. *Psychology of Women Quarterly* 10:311–20.

Levinson, D. J. 1978. *The seasons of a man's life.* New York: Ballantine.

Levy, B. 1968. Cops in the ghetto: A problem of the police system. *American Behavioral Scientist* (March–April):31–34.

Lewin, K. 1951. Problems of research in social psychology. In D. C. Cartwright, ed., *Field theory in social science: Selected theoretical papers by Kurt Lewin,* (155–69). New York: Harper and Brothers.

Lewin, K., R. Lippitt, and R. White. 1939. Patterns of aggressive behavior in experimentally created "social climates." *Journal of Social Psychology* 10: 271–99.

Liaison 1983a. The other side of the coin. 9(2):12–16. Ottawa: Communication Division of the Secretariat, Ministry of the Solicitor General Canada.

———. 1983b. Spies, victims and other business. 9(9). Ottawa: Communication Division of the Secretariat, Ministry of the Solicitor General Canada.

Liebert, R. M., R. W. Poulos, and G. S. Marmor. 1977. *Developmental Psychology,* 2nd ed. Englewood Cliffs, N.J.: Prentice-Hall.

Linden, R. 1983. Women in policing: A study of lower mainland R. C. M. P. detachments. *Canadian Police College Journal* 7:217–29.

Lindsay, D. S., and M. K. Johnson. 1987. Reality monitoring and suggestibility: Children's ability to discriminate among memories from different sources. In S. J. Ceci, M. P. Toglia, and D. F. Ross, eds., *Children's eyewitness memory.* New York: Springer-Verlag.

Lindsay, R. C. L. 1986. Confidence and accuracy of eyewitness identification from lineups. *Law and Human Behavior* 10:229–39.

Lindsay, R. C. L., H. Wallbridge, and D. Drennan. 1987. Do the clothes make the man? An exploration of the effect of lineup attire on eyewitness identification accuracy. *Canadian Journal of Behavioural Science* 19:463–78.

Lindsay, R. C. L., and G. L. Wells. 1980. What price justice? Exploring the relationship of lineup fairness to identification accuracy. *Law and Human Behavior* 4:303–14.

———. 1986. Improving eyewitness identifications from lineups: Simultaneous versus sequential lineup procedures. *Journal of Applied Psychology* 80:556–64.

Lindsay, R. C. L., G. L. Wells, and C. Rumpel. 1981. Can people detect eyewitness identification accuracy within and across situations? *Journal of Applied Psychology* 66:79–89.

Lipscomb, T. J., H. A. McAllister, and N. J. Bregman. 1985. Bias in eyewitness accounts: The effects of question format, delay interval, and stimulus presentation. *Journal of Psychology* 119:207–12.

Lipset, S. M. 1972. National values: Canada and the United States. In J. W. Berry and G. J. S. Wilde, eds., *Social psychology: The Canadian context.* Toronto: McClelland and Stewart.

Lipton, D. N., E. C., McDonel, and R. M. McFall. 1987. Heterosocial perception in rapists. *Journal of Consulting and Clinical Psychology* 55: 17–21.

Lipton, J. P. 1977. On the psychology of eyewitness testimony. *Journal of Applied Psychology* 62:90–95.

Lloyd-Bostock, S., and B. R. Clifford, eds. 1983. *Evaluating witness evidence.* Chichester: Wiley.

Loftus, E. F. 1975. Leading questions and the eyewitness report. *Cognitive Psychology* 7:560–72.

———. 1977. Shifting human color memory. *Memory and Cognition* 5: 696–99.

———. 1979. *Eyewitness testimony.* Cambridge: Harvard University Press.

———. 1980. "Did I really say that last night?" Alcohol, marijuana, and memory. *Psychology Today* (March):42–56, 92.

Loftus, E. F., and T. Burns. 1982. Mental shock can produce retrograde amnesia. *Memory and Cognition* 10:318–23.

Loftus, E. F., and G. M. Davies. 1984. Distortions in the memory of children. *Journal of Social Issues* 40:51–67.

Loftus, E. F., and E. Greene. 1980. Warning: Even memory for faces may be contagious. *Law and Human Behavior* 4:323–34.

Loftus, E. F., G. R. Loftus, and J. Messo. 1987. Some facts about "weapon focus." *Law and Human Behavior.* 11:55–62.

Loftus, E. F., D. G. Miller, and H. J. Burns. 1978. Semantic integration of verbal information into a visual memory. *Journal of Experimental Psychology: Human Learning and Memory* 4:19–31.

Loftus, E. F., and J. P. Palmer. 1974. Reconstruction of automobile destruction: An example of the interaction between language and memory. *Journal of Verbal Learning and Verbal Behavior* 13:85–589.

Loftus, E. F., J. W. Schooler, S. M. Boone, and D. Kline. 1987. Time went by so slowly: Overestimation of event duration by males and females. *Applied Cognitive Psychology* 1:3–13.

Loftus, E. F., and G. Zanni. 1975. Eyewitness testimony: The influence of the wording of a question. *Bulletin of the Psychonomic Society* 5:86–88.

Loh, W. D. 1981. Psychological research: Past and present. *Michigan Law Review* 79:659–707.

Loo, R. 1986. Post-shooting stress reactions among police officers. *Journal of Human Stress* (Spring):27–31.

———. 1987. Policies and programs for mental health in law enforcement organizations. *Canada's Mental Health* 35:18–22.

Lopez-Rey, M. 1968. Defining police-community relations. In A. F. Brandstatter and L. A. Radelet, eds., *Police and community relations: A source book.* Beverly Hills: Glencoe.

Lord, L. K. 1986. A comparison of male and female peace officers' stereotypic perceptions of women and women peace officers. *Journal of Police Science and Administration* 14:83–97.

Lorenz, K. 1966. *On aggression.* New York: Harcourt, Brace, and World.

Loseke, D. R., and S. E. Cahill. 1984. The social construction of deviance: Experts on battered women. *Social Problems* 31:296–310.

Loving, N. 1980. *Responding to spouse abuse and wife beating: A guide for police.* Washington, D.C.: Police Executive Research Forum.

Maass, A., and G. Kohnken. 1986. Weapon focus and arousal in eyewitness recognition. Paper presented at the twenty-first International Congress of Applied Psychology, Jerusalem.

Maccoby, E. E., and C. N. Jacklin. 1974. *The psychology of sex differences.* Stanford: Stanford University Press.

Macdonald, J. M. 1971. *Rape: Offenders and their victims.* Springfield, Ill.: Charles C. Thomas.

———. 1977. *Bombers and firesetters.* Springfield, Ill.: Charles C. Thomas.

MacInnes, C. 1962. *Mr. Love and Justice.* London: New English Library.

Maguire, M. 1981. Victims of residential burglary. In S. Lloyd-Bostock, ed., *Law and psychology.* Wolfson College, Oxford: Centre for Socio-Legal Studies.

Malamuth, N. M. and J. V. P. Check. 1980a. Penile tumescence and perceptual responses to rape as a function of victim's perceived reactions. *Journal of Applied Social Psychology* 10:528–47.

———. 1980b. Sexual arousal to rape and consenting depictions: The importance of the woman's arousal. *Journal of Abnormal Psychology* 89:763–66.

Malloy, T. E., and G. L. Mays. 1984. The police stress hypothesis: A critical evaluation. *Criminal Justice and Behavior* 11:197–224.

Malpass, R. S. 1981. Training in face recognition. In G. Davies, H. Ellis, and

R. Shepherd, eds., *Perceiving and remembering faces*. New York: Academic Press.

Malpass, R. S., and P. G. Devine. 1981a. Guided memory in eyewitness identification. *Journal of Applied Psychology* 66:343–50.

———. 1981b. Eyewitness identification: Lineup instructions and the absence of the offender. *Journal of Applied Psychology* 66:482–89.

———. 1984. Research on suggestion in lineups and photospreads. In G. L. Wells and E. F. Loftus, eds., *Eyewitness testimony: Psychological perspectives*. New York: Cambridge University Press.

Manning, P. K. 1977. *Police work: The sociological organizations of policing*. Cambridge: MIT Press.

———. 1978. Real police work. In P. K. Manning and J. Van Maanen eds., *Policing: A view from the street*. Santa Monica: Goodyear.

Manson v. Brathwaite, 432 U.S. 98, 127 (1977) (J. Marshall dissenting).

Margarita, M. 1980. Killing the police. *Annals* 452:63–71.

Marin, R. J. 1978. Professionalization of the Canadian policeman through education and training: Myth or reality? *Crime and/et Justice* 6:188–93.

Marshall, J. 1966. *Law and psychology in conflict*. New York: Bobbs-Merrill.

Marshall, P. 1973. Policewomen on patrol. *Manpower* 5:14–20.

Marshall, W. L. and H. E. Barbaree. 1984. A behavioral view of rape. *International Journal of Law and Psychiatry* 7:51–77.

Martin, W T. 1984. Religiosity and United States suicide rates, 1972–1978. *Journal of Clinical Psychology* 40:1166–69.

Marx, K. 1963. *Early writings*, T. B. Bottomore, trans. New York: McGraw-Hill.

Maslach, C., and S. E. Jackson. 1979. Burned-out cops and their families. *Psychology Today* 12:59–62.

Matarazzo, J. D., B. V. Allen, G. Saslow, and A. N. Wiens. 1964. Characteristics of successful policemen and firemen applicants. *Journal of Applied Psychology* 48:123–33.

Matthews, A. R., Jr. 1970. Observations on police policy and procedures for emergency detention of the mentally ill. *Journal of Criminal Law, Criminology and Police Science* 61:283–95.

Matthews, M. L., and A. R. Moran. 1986. Age differences in male drivers' perception of accident risk: The role of perceived driving ability. *Accident Analysis and Prevention* 18:299–313.

Mauro, R. 1984 The constable's new clothes: Effects of uniforms on perceptions and problems of police officers. *Journal of Applied Social Psychology* 14:42–56.

Mawby, R. I. 1982. Crime and the elderly: A review of British and American research. *Current Psychological Reviews* 2:301–10.

Maxfield, M. G. 1988. The London metropolitan police and their clients: Victim and suspect attitudes. *Journal of Research in Crime and Delinquency* 25:188–206.

Maykovich, M. K. 1975. Correlates of racial prejudice. *Journal of Personality and Social Psychology* 32:1014–20.

May, R. 1972. *Power and innocence.* New York: Norton.

Mayor, D. 1985. Subjective voice identification. *Royal Canadian Mounted Police Gazette* 47:6–10.

McCloskey, M., C. G. Wible, and N. J. Cohen. 1988. Is there a special flashbulb-memory mechanism? *Journal of Experimental Psychology: General* 117:171–81.

McCloskey, M., and M. Zaragoza. 1985. Misleading postevent information and memory for events: Arguments and evidence against memory impairment hypotheses. *Journal of Experimental Psychology: General* 114:1–16.

McConahay, J. B., and J. C. Hough, Jr. 1976. Symbolic racism. *Journal of Social Issues* 32:23–45.

McConville, M., and J. Baldwin. 1982. The role of interrogation in crime discovery and conviction. *British Journal of Criminology* 22:165–75.

McCroskey, J. C., and L. R. Wheeless. 1976. *Introduction to human communication.* Boston: Allyn and Bacon.

McEvoy, D. W. 1974. Training for the centurions. In J. L. Steinberg and D. W. McEvoy eds., *The police and the behavioral sciences.* Springfield, Ill.: Charles C. Thomas.

McGee v. State, 2 Tenn. Crim. App. 100, 451 S.W.2d 709 (1969).

McGehee, F. 1937. The reliability of the identification of the human voice. *Journal of General Psychology* 17:249–71.

McKelvie, S. J. 1988. The role of spectacles in facial memory: A replication and extension. *Perceptual and Motor Skills* 66:651–58.

McNamara, J. A. 1967. Uncertainties in policework: The relevance of police recruits' backgrounds and training. In D. J. Bordua, ed., *The police: Six sociological essays.* New York: Wiley.

Mednick, S. A. 1986. The inheritance of human deviance: Anti-genetic bias and the facts. In J. C. Yuille, ed., *Police selection and training.* Boston: Martin Nijhoff.

Mednick, S. A., W. F. Gabrielli, and B. Hutchings. 1984. Genetic influences in criminal convictions: Evidence from an adoption cohort. *Science* 224:891–94.

Mednick, S. A., and J. Volavka. 1980. Biology and crime. In N. Morris and M. Tonry, eds., *Crime and justice: An annual review,* vol. 2. Chicago: University of Chicago Press.

Mednick, S. A., J. Volavka, W. F. Gabrielli, and T. Itel. 1981. EEG as a predictor of antisocial behavior. *Criminology* 19:219–31.

Meehl, P. E. 1971. Law and the fireside inductions: Some reflections of a clinical psychologist. *Journal of Social Issues* 27:65–100.

Megargee, E. I. 1982a. Reflections on psychology in the criminal justice system. In J. Gunn and D. P. Farrington, eds., *Abnormal offenders, delinquency, and the criminal justice system*. New York: Wiley.

———. 1982b. Psychological determinants and correlates of criminal violence. In M. E. Wolfgang and N. A. Weiner, eds., *Criminal violence*. Beverly Hills: Sage.

Melton, G. B. 1981. Children's competency to testify. *Law and Human Behavior* 5:73–85.

Memon, A., R. Dionne, L. Short, S. Maralani, D. MacKinnon, and R. E. Geiselman. 1988. Psychological factors in the use of photospreads. *Journal of Police Science and Administration* 16:62–69.

Menzies, R. J. 1987. Psychiatrists in blue: Police apprehension of mental disorder and dangerousness. *Criminology* 25:429–53.

Meyer, C. K., T. C. Magedanz, S. G. Chapman, D. C. Dahlin, and C. Swanson. 1982. An analysis of factors related to robbery-associated assaults on police officers, part 1. *Journal of Police Science and Administration* 10:1–27.

Meyer, C. K., T. C. Magedanz, D. C. Dahlin, and S. G. Chapman. 1981. A comparative assessment of assault incidents: Robbery-related, ambush, and general police assaults. *Journal of Police Science and Administration* 9:1–18.

Middleton, R. 1976. Regional differences in prejudice. *American Sociological Review* 41:94–117.

Mieszala, P. 1981. Juvenile fire setters. *Rekindle*, August 11–13.

Milburn, T. W. 1977. The nature of threat. *Journal of Social Issues* 33:126–39.

Milgram, S. 1963. Behavioral study of obedience. *Journal of Abnormal and Social Psychology* 67:371–78.

———. 1974. *Obedience to authority: An experimental view*. New York: Harper and Row.

Miller, J. 1974. Professional dilemmas in corrections. *Seminars in Psychiatry* 3:357–62.

Milton, C. 1972. *Women in policing*. Washington, D.C.: Police Foundation.

Miranda v. Arizona, 384 U.S. 436 (1966).

Mischel, W. 1968. *Personality and assessment*. New York: Wiley.

Mitchell, C. N. 1988. The intoxicated offender—Refuting the legal and medical myths. *International Journal of Law and Psychiatry* 11:77–103.

Monahan, J. 1980. *Who is the client?* Washington, D.C.: American Psychological Association.

————. 1981. *The clinical prediction of violent behavior.* Washington, D.C.: Department of Health and Human Service.

Monahan, J., and L. Cummings. 1975. Social policy implications of the inability to predict violence. *Journal of Social Issues* 31:153–64.

Monahan, J., and D. Klassen. 1982. Situational approaches to understanding and predicting individual violent behavior. In M. E. Wolfgang and N. A. Weiner, eds., *Criminal violence.* Beverly Hills: Sage.

Monahan, J., and B. Monahan. 1986. Police and the mentally disordered. In J. C. Yuille, ed., *Police selection and training.* Boston: Martinus Nijhoff.

Monahan, J., R. W. Novaco, and G. Geis. 1979. Corporate violence: Research strategies for community psychology. In T. R. Sarbin, ed., *Challenges to the criminal justice system: The perspectives of community psychology.* New York: Human Sciences Press.

Monahan, J., and H. Steadman 1983. Crime and mental disorder: An epidemiological approach. In N. Morris and M. Tonry, eds., *Crime and justice: An annual review,* vol. 3. Chicago: University of Chicago Press.

Moore, R. J. 1983. The relationship of perceived quality of life, socio-political-economic attitudes and contact with the legal system to perceptions and evaluations of the legal system. Paper presented at the Annual meeting of the Canadian Psychological Association, Winnipeg, Canada.

Moretz, W. J., Jr. 1980. Kids to cops: "We think you're important but we're not sure we understand you." *Journal of Police Science and Administration* 8:220–24.

Morgan, H. G. 1979. *Death wishes.* New York: Wiley.

Morris, V., and P. E. Morris. 1985. The influence of question order on eyewitness accuracy. *British Journal of Psychology* 76:365:71.

Morse, S. J. 1978. Crazy behavior, morals, and science: An analysis of mental health law. *Southern California Law Review* 51:527–654.

Mueller, J. H., W. B. Thompson, and J. M. Vogel. 1988. Perceived honesty and face memory. *Personality and Social Psychology Bulletin* 14:114–24.

Muchmore, J. M. 1975. Uniform—Its effect. *Police Chief* 42:70–71.

Mummendey, A. 1984. *The social psychology of aggression.* Heidelberg: Springer-Verlag.

Murphy, J. J. 1965. Improving the law enforcement image. *Journal of Criminal Law, Criminology and Police Science* 56:107.

Myers, T. 1982. Alcohol and violent crime re-examined: Self-reports from two sub-groups of Scottish male prisoners. *British Journal of Addictions* 77: 399–400.

National Institute of Law Enforcement and Criminal Justice. 1975–1978. *Forcible rape.* Washington, D.C.

Neisser, U. 1976. *Cognition and reality.* San Francisco: Freeman.

———. 1982. Snapshots or benchmarks? In U. Neisser, ed., *Memory observed.* San Francisco: Freeman.

Nelson, K., and J. Gruendel. 1981. Generalized event representations: Basic building blocks of cognitive development. In A. Brown and M. Lamb, eds., *Advances in developmental psychology,* vol. 1. Hillsdale, N.J.: Erlbaum.

Nelson, Z. P., and W. Smith. 1970. The law enforcement profession: An incident of high suicide. *Omega* 1:293–99.

Niederhoffer, A. 1967. *Behind the shield: The police in urban society.* Garden City, N.Y.: Doubleday.

Nielsen, E. 1982. Post shooting stress reactions. *Utah Peace Officers Association* (12–16).

———., and D. L. Eskridge. 1982. Post shooting procedures: The forgotten officer. *Police Product News* (July):41–43.

Nisbett, R. E., and Z. Kunda. 1985. Perception of social distributions. *Journal of Personality and Social Psychology* 27:154–64.

Nisbett, R. E., and T. D. Wilson, 1977. Telling more than we can know: Verbal reports on mental processes. *Psychological Review* 84:231–59.

Normoyle, J., and P. J. Lavrakas. 1984. Fear of crime in elderly women: Perceptions of control, predictability, and territoriality. *Personality and Social Psychology Bulletin* 10:191–202.

Norton, W. A. 1981. Ethics and the work of psychologists in the field of criminal justice. *Social Science Medicine* 15:39–49.

O'Hara, C. E. 1970. *Fundamantals of criminal investigation.* Springfield, Ill.: Charles C. Thomas.

O'Malley, H. 1973. *Evaluation report on the Holyoke team police experiment of the Holyoke Police Department.* Holyoke, Mass.: Holyoke Police Department.

Oppenlander, N. 1982. Coping or copping out: Police service delivery in domestic disputes. *Criminology* 20:449–65.

Orne, M. T., D. A. Soskis, D. F. Dinges, and E. C. Orne. 1984. Hypnotically induced testimony. In G. L. Wells and E. F. Loftus, eds., *Eyewitness testimony: Psychological perspectives.* New York: Cambridge University Press.

Oros, C. J., K. Leonard, and M. P. Koss. 1980. Factors related to a self-attribution of rape by victims. *Personality and Social Psychology Bulletin* 6:193.

Osterburg, J. W. 1981. The scientific method and criminal investigation. *Journal of Police Science and Administration* 9:135–42.

Page, J. D. 1975. *Psychopathology*, 2nd ed. Chicago: Aldine.

Parke-Davis & Co. v. H. K. Mulford Co., 189 F. 95, (1911).

Parkes, C. 1975. Unexpected and untimely bereavement: A statistical study of young Boston widows and widowers. In B. Schenberg, et al., eds. *Bereavement: Its psychological aspects*. New York: Columbia University Press.

Parkinson, G. C. 1980. Cooperation between police and social workers: Hidden issues. *Social Work Journal* 25:12–18.

Patterson, K. E., and A. D. Baddeley. 1977. When face recognition fails. *Journal of Experimental Psychology: Human Learning and Memory* 3:406–17.

Payne, D. E., and K. P. Payne. 1970. Newspapers and crime in Detroit. *Journalism Quarterly* 47:233–38.

Pennington, D. C. 1981. The 'Yorkshire Ripper' police inquiry: Hindsight and social cognition. *British Journal of Social Psychology* 20:225–27.

Penrod, S., E. Loftus, and J. Winkler. 1982. The reliability of eyewitness testimony: A psychological perspective. In N. L. Kerr and R. M. Bray, eds., *The psychology of the courtroom*. New York: Academic Press.

Pepinsky, H. E. 1975. Police decision-making. In D. M. Gottfredson, ed. *Decision-making in the criminal justice system: Reviews and essays*. Rockville, Md.: National Institute of Mental Health.

———. 1976. Police patrolmen's offense-reporting behavior. *Journal of Research in Crime and Delinquency* 13:33–47.

———. 1977. Stereotyping as a force for increasing crime rates. *Law and Human Behavior* 1:299–308.

Perloff, L. S. 1983. Perceptions of vulnerability to victimization. *Journal of Social Issues* 39:41–61.

Perlstein, G. R. 1972. Policewomen and policemen: A comparative look. *Police Chief* 39:72–74, 83.

Peters, D. P. 1987. The impact of naturally occurring stress on children's memory. In S. J. Ceci, M. P. Toglia, and D. F. Ross, eds., *Children's eyewitness memory*. New York: Springer-Verlag.

Phares, E. J. 1971. Internal-external control and the reduction of reinforcement value after failing. *Journal of Consulting and Clinical Psychology* 37:386–90.

Phares, E. J., D. E. Ritchie, and W. L. Davis. 1968. Internal-external control and reaction to threat. *Journal of Personality and Social Psychology* 10:402–5.

Phares, E. J., R. G. Wilson and N. W. Klymer. 1971. Internal-external control and the attribution of blame under neutral and distractive conditions. *Journal of Personality and Social Psychology* 18:285–88.

Philips, D. P., and J. Liu. 1980. The frequency of suicides around major public holidays. *Suicide and Life-Threatening Behavior* 10:41–50.

Piaget, J. 1965. *The moral judgment of the child.* New York: Free Press. (Originally published in 1932).

———. 1972. *Judgment and reasoning in the child,* M. Warden, trans. Totawa, N.J.: Littlefield, Adams. (Originally published in 1924).

Piliavin, I., and S. Briar. 1964. Police encounters with juveniles. *American Journal of Sociology* 70:206–14.

Poister, T. H., and J. C. McDavid. 1978. Victim's evaluation of police performance. *Journal of Criminal Justice* 6:133–49.

Poole, E. D., and M. R. Pogrebin 1988. Factors affecting the decision to remain policing: A study of women officers. *Journal of Police Science and Administration* 16:49–55.

Pope, C. E., and W. Feyerherm. 1976. A review of recent trends: The effects of crime on the elderly. *Police Chief* (February):48–51.

Posluns, D. 1981. An introduction to psychological expert testimony. *Advocates' Quarterly* 3:1–17.

Postman, L., and J. S. Bruner. 1948. Perception under stress. *Psychological Review* 55:314–23.

Preiss, J. R., and H. J. Ehrlich. 1966. *An examination of role theory: The case of the state police.* Lincoln: University of Nebraska Press.

President's Commission on Law Enforcement and Administration of Justice. 1967. *The challenge of crime in a free society.* Washington, D.C.

President's Task Force on Victims of Crime. 1983. *Report of the President's Task Force on Victims of Crime.* Washington, D.C.

Price, B. R. 1974. A study of leadership strength of female police executives. *Journal of Police Science and Administration* 2:219–26.

Pugh, G. C. 1985. Situation tests and police selection. *Journal of Police Science and Administration* 13:30–35.

Putnam, W. H. 1979. Hypnosis and distortions in eyewitness memory. *International Journal of Clinical and Experimental Hypnosis* 27:437–48.

Pynoos, R. S., and S. Eth. 1984. The child as a witness to homicide. *Journal of Social Issues* 40:87–108.

Quinsey, V. L., and D. Upfold. 1985. Rape completion and victim injury as a function of female resistance strategy. *Canadian Journal of Behavioural Science* 17:40–50.

Rabkin, J. 1974. Attitudes towards mental illness. *Schizophrenia Bulletin* 10:7–33.

Radelet, L. A. 1980, *The police and the community,* 3rd ed. Encino, Calif.: Glencoe.

Rafky, D. M. 1973. Police race attitudes and labelling. *Journal of Police Science and Administration* 1:65–86.

————. 1977. The cognitive gap between the police and the policed: An exploratory study in attitude organization. *Law and Human Behavior* 1:63–79.

Rand, M. 1970. Unit beat policing—Time for a fresh approach? *The Criminologist* 5:52–61.

Rankin, J. H. 1979. Changing attitudes toward capital punishment. *Social Forces* 58:194–211.

Rattner, A. 1988. Convicted but innocent: Wrongful conviction and the criminal justice system system. *Law and Human Behavior* 12:283–93.

Ray, J. J. and F. H. Lovejoy. 1983. The behavioural validity of some recent measures of authoritianism. *Journal of Social Psychology* 120:91–99.

Read, J. D. and D. Bruce. 1984. On the external validity of questioning effects in eyewitness testimony. *International Review of Applied Psychology* 33: 33–49.

Reese, W. L. 1983. What chiefs are saying about media relations. *Police Chief* 11:38.

Regoli, R. M., and E. D. Poole. 1980. Police professionalism and role conflict: A comparison of rural and urban departments. *Human Relations* 33: 241–52.

Reiser, M., and S. P. Geiger. 1984. Police officer as victim. *Professional psychology: Research and practice* 15:315–23.

Reiss, A. J. 1967. Career orientations, job satisfaction and the assessment of law enforcement problems by officers. *Studies in crime and law enforcement in major metropolitan areas*, vol. 2. Washington, D.C.: GPO.

————. 1971. *The police and the public.* New Haven: Yale University Press.

Renner, K. E., and D. A. Gierach. 1975. An approach to the problem of excessive force by police. *Journal of Police Science and Administration* 3:377–83.

Report of the Task Force on the Role of Psychology in the Criminal Justice System. 1978. *American Psychologist* 33:1099–1113.

Reuterman, N. A. 1978. The public's view of delinquency causation: A consideration in comprehensive juvenile justice planning. *Juvenile and Family Court Journal* 29:39–45.

Rhodes, A. L., and A. J. Reiss, Jr. 1970. The "religious factor" and delinquent behavior. *Journal of Research in Crime and Delinquency* 7: 83–98.

Richardson, J. F. 1974. *Urban police in the U.S.* Port Washington. New York: Kennikat Press.

Risin, L. I., and M. P. Koss. 1988. The sexual abuse of boys. In A. W. Burgess, ed., *Rape and sexual assault II*. New York: Garland.

Ritchie, E., and E. J. Phares. 1969. Attitude change as a function of internal-external control and communicator staters. *Journal of Personality* 37: 429–33.

Robins, E. 1985. Psychosis and suicide. Paper presented at the annual meeting of the American Psychiatric Association, Dallas.

Rochin v. California, 342 U.S. 165 (1952).

Rock, R., M. Jacobson, and R. Janepaul. 1968. *Hospitalization and discharge of the mentally ill.* Chicago: University of Chicago Press.

Rokeach, M., M. G. Miller, and J. A. Snyder. 1971. The value gap between police and policed. *Journal of Social Issues* 27:155–77.

Rosen, G. 1968. *Madness in society.* Chicago: University of Chicago Press.

Rosenbaum, A., and K. D. O'Leary. 1981. Marital violence: Characteristics of abusive couples. *Journal of Consulting and Clinical Psychology* 49:63–71.

Rosenbaum, D. P. 1987a. Coping with victimization: The effects of police intervention on victims' psychological readjustment. *Crime and Delinquency* 33:502–19.

———. 1987b. The theory and research behind neighborhood watch: Is it a sound fear and crime reduction strategy? *Crime and Delinquency* 33: 103–34.

Rosenhan, D. L. 1973. On being sane in insane places. *Science* 179:250–58.

Ross, H. L. 1983. *Deterring the drinking driver.* Lexington, Mass.: Lexington Books.

Ross, L. 1977. The intuitive psychologist and his short comings: Distortions in the attribution process. In L. Berkowitz, ed., *Advances in Experimental Social Psychology*, vol. 10. New York: Academic Press.

Rotter, J. B. 1966. Generalized expectancies for internal versus external control of reinforcement. *Psychological Monographs* 80:1–28.

Roy, M. (1982). *The abusive partner.* New York: Van Nostrand Reinhold.

Ruback, R. B., D. R. Westcott, and M. S. Greenberg. 1981. Eyewitness identification by theft victims. Paper presented at the meeting of the American Psychology-Law Society, Cambridge, Mass.

Rubenstein, J. 1972. *City police.* New York: Farrar, Straus, and Giroux.

Rubin, J. G. 1974. Police identity and the police role. In J. Goldsmith and S. S. Goldsmith, eds., *The police community.* Pacific Palisades, Calif.: Palisades Publishers.

Russell, K. 1978. *Complaints against the police: A sociological view.* Leicester: Milltak.

Rutledge, D. (1979). *Courtroom survival: The officer's guide to better testimony.* Flagstaff, Ariz.: Flag Books.

Ryan, C. 1981. On becoming a police officer. In G. Henderson, ed., *Police human relations*, Springfield, Ill.: C. Charles Thomas.

Safer, M. A. 1980. Attributing evil to the subject, not the situation: Student reaction to Milgram's film on obedience. *Personality and Social Psychology Bulletin* 6:205–9.

Saks, M. J., and R. F. Kidd. 1980–1981. Human information processing and adjudication: Trial by heuristics. *Law and Society Review* 15:123–60.

Sales, B. 1986. Rehabilitation psychology and law. *Rehabilitation Psychology* 31:5–11.

Sallmann, P. A. 1981. The police and the criminal justice system. *Australian and New Zealand Journal of Criminology* 14:23–39.

Samenow, S. E. 1984. *Inside the criminal mind.* New York: Times Books.

Samuelson, W. 1969. Why was capital punishment restored in Delaware? *Journal of Criminal Law, Criminology and Police Science* 60:148.

Sanders, G. S. 1986. On increasing the usefulness of eyewitness research. *Law and Human Behavior* 10:333–35.

Sanders, G. S., and W. L. Simmons. 1983. Use of hypnosis to enhance eyewitness accuracy: Does it work? *Journal of Applied Psychology* 68: 70–77.

Sanders, R. 1984. Helping the jury evaluate eyewitness testimony: The need for additional safeguards. *American Journal of Criminal Law* 12:189–224.

Sanford, N. 1973a. Authoritarian personality in contemporary perspective. In J. Knutson, ed., *Handbook of political psychology.* San Francisco: Jossey-Bass.

———. 1973b. The roots of prejudice: Emotional dynamics. In P. Watson, ed., *Psychology and race.* Chicago: Aldine.

Sarason, I. G. 1975. Anxiety and self-preoccupation. In I. G. Sarason and C. D. Spielberger, eds., *Stress and anxiety*, vol. 2. New York: Halsted Press.

Sarason, I. G., J. H. Johnson, J. P. Berberich, and J. M. Siegel. 1979. Helping police officers to cope with stress: A cognitive behavioral approach. *American Journal of Community Psychology* 7:593–603.

Sarason, I. G., and B. R. Sarason. 1987. *Abnormal psychology: The problem of maladaptive behavior*, 5th ed. Englewood Cliffs, N.J.: Prentice-Hall.

Sarat, A., and N. Vidmar. 1976. Public opinion, the death penalty, and the eighth amendment: Testing the Marshall hypothesis. *Wisconsin Law Review* 1976:171–206.

Sarbin, T. R. 1979. The myth of the criminal type. In T. R. Sarbin, ed., *Challenges to the criminal justice system: The perspectives of community psychology.* New York: Human Sciences Press.

Saslove, H., and A. D. Yarmey, 1980. Long-term auditory memory: Speaker identification. *Journal of Applied Psychology* 65:111–16.

Sasaki, D. W. 1988. Guarding the guardians: Police trickery and confessions. *Stanford Law Review* 40:1593–1616.

Saywitz, K. J. 1987. Children's testimony: Age-related patterns of memory errors. In S. J. Ceci, M. P. Toglia, and D. F. Ross, eds., *Children's eyewitness memory*. New York: Springer-Verlag.

Scharf, P., and A. Binder. 1983. *The badge and the bullet*. New York: Praeger.

Schein, E. H. 1956. The Chinese indoctrination program for prisoners of war: A study of attempted brainwashing. *Psychiatry* 19:149–72.

Scheppele, K. L., and P. B. Bart. 1983. Through women's eyes: Defining danger in the wake of sexual assault. *Journal of Social Issues* 39:63–81.

Schiffer, M. E. 1978. *Mental disorder and the criminal trial process*. Toronto: Butterworths.

Schilit, J. 1979. The mentally retarded offender and criminal justice personnel. *Exceptional Children* 46:16–22.

Schoenfeld, L. S., J. L. Kobos, and I. R. Phinney. 1980. Screening police applicants: A study of reliability with the MMPI. *Psychological Reports* 47:419–25.

Schrink, J., E. Poole, and R. Regoli. 1982. Sexual myths and ridicule: A content analysis of rape jokes. *Psychology* 19:1–6.

Schuessler, K. 1952. The deterrent influence of the death penalty. *Annals of the American Academy of Political and Social Science* 284:54–63.

Schuman, H., and B. Gruenberg. 1972. Dissatisfaction with city services: Is race an important factor? In H. Hahn, ed., *People and politics in urban society*. Beverly Hills: Sage.

Schutz, A. 1971. *Collected papers*. The Hague: Martinus Nijhoff.

Schwitzgebel, R. L., and R. K. Schwitzgebel. 1980. *Law and psychological practice*. New York: Wiley.

Scott, E. M., and K. L. Scott. 1983. Healthy families. *International Journal of Offender Therapy and Comparative Criminology* 27:71–78.

Sears, R., E. E. Maccoby, and H. Levin. 1957. *Patterns of child rearing*. Evanston, Ill.: Row and Peterson.

Seligman, C., J. Brickman, and D. Koulack. 1977. Rape and physical attractiveness: Assigning responsibility to victims. *Journal of Personality* 45: 555–63.

Seligman, M. 1975. *Helplessness: On depression, development and death*. San Francisco: Freeman.

Sellin, T. 1959. *The death penalty*. Philadelphia: American Law Institute.

Selye, H. 1976. *The stress of life*, rev. ed. New York: McGraw-Hill.

Sewell, J. D. 1983. The development of a critical life events scale for law enforcement. *Journal of Police Science and Administration* 11:109–16.

Shapiro, P., and S. D. Penrod. 1986. A meta-analysis of the facial identification literature. *Psychological Bulletin* 100:139–56.

Shaw, L. 1973. Role of clothing in the criminal justice system. *Journal of Police Science and Administration* 1:414–20.

Sheehan, P. W., and J. Tilden. 1983. Effects of suggestibility and hypnosis on accurate and distorted retrieval from memory. *Journal of Experimental Psychology: Learning, Memory, and Cognition* 9:283–93.

Sheehan, S. 1981. A reporter at large (Creedmoor, Part 1). *New Yorker* (May): 25.

Sheehy, N. P., and A. J. Chapman. 1982. Eliciting children's and adults' accounts of road accidents. *Current Psychological Reviews* 2:341–48.

Sheldon, W. H. 1942. *The varieties of temperament.* New York: Harper and Row.

Shepherd, J. W. 1983. Identification after long delays. In S. M. A. Lloyd-Bostock and B. R. Clifford, eds. *Evaluating witness evidence.* New York: Wiley.

Shepherd, J. W., H. D. Ellis, and G. M. Davies. 1982. *Identification evidence: A psychological evaluation.* Aberdeen: Aberdeen University Press.

Shepherd, J. W., H. D. Ellis, M. McMurran, and G. M. Davies. 1978. Effect of character attribution on photofit construction of a face. *European Journal of Social Psychology* 8:263–68.

Sherman, L. J. 1973. A psychological view of women policing. *Journal of Police Science and Administration* 3:434–38.

————. 1975. An evaluation of policewomen on patrol in a surburban police department. *Journal of Police Science and Administration* 3:434–38.

Sherman, L. W. 1984. Experiments in police discretion: Scientific boon or dangerous knowledge? *Law and Contemporary Problems* 47:61–81.

Shoemaker, D. J., D. R. South, and J. Lowe. 1973. Facial stereotypes of deviants and judgments of guilt or innocence. *Social Forces* 51:427–33.

Silverman, D. 1946. The psychotic criminals: A study of 500 cases. *Journal of Clinical Psychopathology* 8:703–30.

Simon, R. J. 1967. *The jury and the defense of insanity.* Boston: Little, Brown.

————. 1983. The defense of insanity. *Journal of Psychiatry & Law* (Summer):183–201.

Sjoberg, L. 1982. Logical versus psychological necessity: A discussion of the role of common sense in psychological theory. *Scandinavian Journal of Psychology* 23:65–78.

Skinner, B. F. 1953. *Science and human behavior.* New York: Macmillan.

————. 1969. *Contingencies of reinforcement.* New York: Appleton-Century-Crofts.

Skogan, W. G., and M. G. Maxfield. 1981. *Coping with crime: Individual and neighborhood reactions.* Beverly Hills: Sage.

Skogan, W. G., and M. A. Wycoff. 1987. Some unexpected effects of a police service for victims. *Crime and Delinquency* 33:490–501.

Skolnick, J. H. 1966. *Justice without trial: Law enforcemant in democratic society.* New York: Wiley.

Slovenko, R. 1984. The meaning of mental illness in criminal responsibility. *Journal of Legal Medicine* 5:1–61.

Slovic, P., B. Fischhoff, and S. Lichtenstein. 1977. Behavioral decision theory. *Annual Review of Psychology* 28:1–39.

———. 1980. Risky assumptions. *Psychology Today* (June):44–48.

Smith, K. A. B., B. Locke, and A. Fenster. 1970. Authoritarianism in policemen who are college graduates and non-college police. *Journal of Criminal Law, Criminology, and Police Science* 61:313–15.

Smith, M. 1983. Hypnotic memory enhancement of witnesses: Does it work *Psychological Bulletin* 94:387–407.

Smith, P. E., and R. O. Hawkins. 1973. Victimization, types of citizen-police contacts, and attitudes toward the police. *Law and Society Review* 8: 135–52.

Smith, V. L., and P. C. Ellsworth. 1987. The social psychology of eyewitness accuracy: Misleading questions and communicator expertise. *Journal of Applied Psychology* 72:294–300.

Smithyman, S. D. 1978. The undetected rapist. Ph.D. dissertation, Claremont Graduate School.

Sobelman, S. A., and J. Glorioso. 1980. Law enforcement and psychology: The action concept. *Police Chief* (August):44, 46.

Solicitor General of Canada. 1975. *Ministry of Native Peoples and Justice.* Ottawa: Information Canada.

———. 1985. Criminal victimization of elderly Canadians. *Canadian Urban Victimization Survey Bulletin.* Ottawa: Communications Group, Program Branch.

Soliday, S. M. 1974. Relationship between age and hazard perception in automobile drivers. *Perceptual and Motor Skills* 39:335–38.

Spielberger, C. D. 1979. *Police selection and evaluation: Issues and techniques.* New York: Praeger.

Spielberger, C. D., R. L. Gorsuch, and R. E. Lushere. 1970. *Manual for the state-trait anxiety inventory.* Palo Alto, Calif.: Consulting Psychologists Press.

Sporer, S. L. 1982. A brief history of the psychology of testimony. *Current Psychological Reviews* 2:323–40.

Stang, D. 1972. Conformity, ability, and self-esteem. *Representative Research in Social Psychology* 3:97–103.

Stang, D. P. 1969. The police and their problems. *Law and order reconsidered.* Washington, D.C.: GPO.

Stang, D. J. 1976. Group size effects on conformity. *Journal of Social Psychology* 98:175–81.

Stark, R., and J. McEvoy, III. 1970. Middle-class violence. *Psychology Today* (November)4:52–54.

State v. Biron, 266 Minn. 272, 123 N.W. 2 d 392 (1963).

State v. Garcia, Cr. No. 4259 (Sup. Ct. Monterrey CA 1977).

State v. Jackson, 308 N.C. 549, 566–68, 304 S.E.2d 134, 143–44 (1983).

State v. Little, 74 Cr. No. 4176 (Sup. Ct. Beaufort N.C. 1975).

State v. Reilly, No, 5285 (Conn. Super. Ct. April 12, 1974). *vacated,* 32 Conn. Supp. 349, 355 A.2d 324 (Sup. Ct. 1976).

State v. Wheeler, 416 So. 2d 78, 79–80 (La. 1982).

Steadman, H. J., J. P. Morrissey, J. Braff, and J. Monahan. 1986. Psychiatric evaluations of police referrals in a general hospital emergency room. *International Journal of Law and Psychiatry* 8:39–47.

Steadman, H. J., and J. Cocozza. 1977. Selective reporting and the public's misconceptions of the criminally insane. *Public Opinion Quarterly* 41: 523–33.

Steinbruner, J. D. 1975. *The cybernetic theory of decision: New dimensions of political analysis.* Princeton: Princeton University Press.

Stekette, G., and E. B. Foa. 1987. Rape victims: Post-traumatic stress responses and their treatment: A review of the literature. *Journal of Anxiety Disorders* 1:69–86.

Stenmark, D. E., L. C. DePiano, J. H. Wackwitz, C. D. Cannon, and S. Walfish. 1982. Wifes of police officers: Issues related to family-job satisfaction and job longevity. *Journal of Police Science and Administration* 10: 229–34.

Stone, A. 1975. *Mental health and law: A system in transition.* DHEW Pub. no. (ADM) 75–176. Rockville, Md.: NIMH.

Stotland, E. 1975. Self-esteem and stress in police work. In W. Kroes and J. Hurrel, Jr., eds., *Job stress and the police officer - Identifying stress reduction techniques.* Washington, D.C.: GPO.

Stovall v. Denno, 388 U.S. 293, 302 (1967).

Strasser, G., N. L. Kerr, and R. M. Bray. 1982. Problems and prospects for research on the psychology of the courtroom. In N. L. Kerr and R. M. Bray, eds., *The psychology of the courtroom.* New York: Academic Press.

Stratton, J. G. 1978. Departmental psychologist—Is there any value? *Police Chief* (May):73–78.

————. 1980. Psychological services for police. *Journal of Police Science and Administration* 8:31–39.

————. 1986. Officer-involved shootings: Effects, suggested procedures and treatment. In J. C. Yuille, ed., *Police selection and training.* Dordrecht: Martinus Nijhoff.

Stratton, J. G., B. Tracy-Stratton, and G. Alldredge. 1982. The effects of a spouses' training program: A longitudinal study. *Journal of Police Science and Administration* 10:297–301.

Sutherland, E. H., and D. R. Cressey. 1970. *Principles of criminology*, 7th ed. New York: Lippincott.

Symonds, M. 1980. The "second injury" to victims. In L. Kivens, ed., *Evaluation and change: Services for survivors.* Minneapolis: Minneapolis Medical Research Foundation.

Takagi, P. 1974. A Garrison State in a "democratic society." *Crime and Social Justice* 5:27–33.

Tapp, J. L. 1982. Reflections on a decade of law and psychology in the United States. In J. Gunn and D. P. Farrington, eds., *Abnormal offenders, delinquency, and the criminal justice system.* New York: Wiley.

Tapp, J. L., and F. J. Levine, eds. 1977. *Law, justice, and the individual in society: Psychological and legal issues.* New York: Holt, Rinehart, and Winston.

Templer, D. I., and D. M. Veleber. 1980. Suicide rate and religion within the United States. *Psychological Reports* 4:898.

Tenny, E. 1953. Women's work in law enforcement. *Journal of Criminal Law, Criminology, and Police Science* 54:239–46.

Teplin, L. A. 1984. Criminalizing mental disorder: The comparative arrest rate of the mentally ill. *American Psychologist* 39:794–803.

Teplin, L. A., W. J. Filstead, G. M. Hefter, and E. P. Sheridan. 1980. Police involvement with the psychiatric-emergency patient. *Psychiatric Annals* 10: 46–54.

Terman, L. M. 1917. A trial of mental pedagogical tests in a civil service examination for policemen and firemen. *Journal of Applied Psychology* 1:17–19.

Territo, L. K., and H. J. Vetter, eds. 1981. *Stress and police personnel.* Boston: Allyn and Bacon.

Terry, W. C. 1981. Police stress: The empirical evidence. *Journal of Police Science and Administration* 9:61–75.

————. 1985. Police stress as a professional self-image. *Journal of Criminal Justice* 13:501–12.

Theilgaard, A. 1983. Aggression and the XYY personality. *International Journal of Law and Psychiatry* 6:413–21.

Thomas, C. W. 1977. Eighth amendment challenges to the death penalty: The relevance of informed public opinion. *Vanderbilt Law Review* 30:1005–30.

Thompson, C. P. 1985. Voice identification: Speaker identifiability and a correction of the record regarding sex effects. *Human Learning* 4:19–27.

Thornton, L. M. 1975. People and the police: An analysis of factors associated with police evaluation and support. *Canadian Journal of Sociology* 1:325–42.

Thurstone, L. L. 1922. The intelligence of policemen. *Journal of Personality Research* 1:64–74.

Tickner, A. H., and E. C. Poulton. 1975. Watching for people and actions. *Ergonomics* 18: 35–51.

Tingle, D., G. W. Barnard, L. Robbins, G. Newman, and D. Hutchinson. 1986. Childhood and adolescent characteristics of pedophiles and rapists. *International Journal of Law and Psychiatry* 9:103–16.

Tittle, C. R., and C. H. Logan. 1973. Sanctions and deviance; evidence and remaining questions. *Law and Society Review* 7:371–92.

Toch, H. 1976. *Peacekeeping: Police, prisons, and violence.* Lexington, Mass.: Lexington Books.

———. 1978. Police morale—Living with discontent. *Journal of Police Science and Administration* 6:249–52.

Tooley, V., J. C. Brigham, A. Maass, and R. K. Bothwell. 1987. Facial recognition: Weapon effect and attentional focus. *Journal of Applied Social Psychology* 17:845–59.

Tosi, O. 1979. *Voice identification: Theory and legal applications.* Baltimore: University Park Press.

Trankell, A. 1972. *Reliability of evidence.* Stockholm: Rotobeckman.

Treger, H. 1972. Breakthough in preventive corrections: A police-social work team model. *Federal Probation* 36:53–58.

Tully, B. 1986. "Special care questioning" of mentally vulnerable victims and witnesses of crime. In J. C. Yuille, ed., *Police selection and training.* Boston: Martinus Nijhoff.

Tully, B., and D. Cahill. 1984. *Police interviewing of the mentally handicapped: An experimental study.* London: The Police Foundation.

Tulving, E. 1974. Cue-dependent forgetting. *American Scientist* 62:74–82.

Tversky, A., and D. Kahneman. 1973a. Availability: A heuristic for judging frequency and probability. *Cognitive Psychology* 5:207–32.

———. 1973b. Judgment under uncertainty: Heuristics and biases. *Science* 185:1124–31.

———. 1982. Judgment under uncertainty: Heuristics and biases. In D. Kahneman, P. Slovic, and A. Tversky, eds., *Judgments under uncertainty.* New York: Cambridge University Press.

————. 1983. Availability: A heuristic for judging frequency and probability. *Cognitive Psychology* 5:207–32.

Tyson, G. A. 1981. Locus of control and stressful life events. *South African Journal of Psychology* 11:116–17.

U.S. Department of Justice. 1986. *Criminal Victimization in the United States, 1984.* Washington, D.C.: Bureau of Justice Statistics.

U.S. Federal Bureau of Investigation. 1974–1985. *Crime in the United States.* Washington, D.C.: GPO.

United States v. Hauptmann. 1935. *Atlantic Report* 180:809–29.

United States v. Wade, 388 U.S. 218 (1967).

Van den Haag, E. 1975. *Punishing criminals.* New York: Basic Books.

Van Maanen, J. 1973. Observations on the making of policemen. *Human Organization* 32:407–18.

Varendonck, J. 1911. Les témoignages d'enfants dans un procès retentissant. *Archives de psychologie* 11:129–71.

Vaughan, G. 1964. The trans-situational aspect of conforming behavior. *Journal of Personality* 32:335–54.

Vennard, J. 1984. Disputes within trials over the admissibility and accuracy of incriminating statements: Some research evidence. *Criminal Law Review* (January):15–24.

Veroff, J., and J. Veroff. 1972. Reconsideration of a measure of power motivation. *Psychological Bulletin* 78:279–91.

Vidmar, N., and T. Dittenhoffer. 1981. Informed public opinion and death penalty attitudes. *Canadian Journal of Criminology* 23:43–56.

Vincent, C. L. 1979. *Policeman.* Toronto: Gage.

Violanti, J. M., J. R. Marshall, and B. Howe. 1985. Stress, coping, and alcohol use: The police connection. *Journal of Police Science and Administration* 13:106–10.

Waaland, P., and S. Keeley. 1985. Police decision making in wife abuse: The impact of legal and extralegal factors. *Law and Human Behavior* 9:355–66.

Wagner, A. E. 1980. Citizen complaints against the police: The complainant. *Journal of Police Science and Administration* 8:247–52.

Waldo, G., and S. Dinitz. 1967. Personality attributes of the criminal: An analysis of research studies 1950–1965. *Journal of Research in Crime and Delinquency* 4:185–202.

Walker, L. E. 1979. *The battered woman.* New York: Harper and Row.

————. 1983. The battered woman syndrome study. In D. Finkelhor, R. J. Gelles, G. T. Hotaling, and M. A. Straus, eds., *The dark side of families.* Beverly Hills: Sage.

Walker, L. E., R. K. Thyfault, and A. Browne. 1982. Beyond the juror's ken: Battered women. *Vermont Law Review* 7:1–14.

Wall, S. M., and M. Furlong. 1985. Comprehension of Miranda rights by urban adolescents with law-related education. *Psychological Reports* 56: 359–72.

Walsh, D. P. 1978. *Shoplifting: Controlling a major crime*. London: Mcmillan.

Walsh, F. 1982. *Normal family processes*. New York: Guildford.

Walster, E., G. W. Walster, and E. Berscheid. 1978. *Equity: Theory and research*. Boston: Allyn and Bacon.

Walter, P. D. 1982. Expert testimony and battered women. *Journal of Legal Medicine* 3:267–94.

Wambaugh, J. 1975. *The choirboys*. New York: Delacourt.

Ward, R. A., M. LaGory, and S. R. Sherman. 1986. Fear of crime among the elderly as person/environment interaction. *Sociological Quarterly* 27: 327–41.

Ward, R. H. 1970. The police role: A case of diversity. *Journal of Criminal Law, Criminology and Police Science* 61:580–86.

Warr, M. 1984. Fear of victimization: Why are women and the elderly more afraid? *Social Science Quarterly* 65:681–702.

Warren, M. Q. and M. J. Hindelang. 1979. Current explanations of offender behavior. In H. Toch, ed., *Psychology of crime and criminal justice*. New York: Holt, Rinehart and Winston.

Watson, E. R. 1924. *Trial of Adolf Beck*. Notable British Trials. London: W. Hodge.

Weaver, F. M., and J. S. Carroll. 1985. Crime perceptions in a natural setting by expert and novice shoplifters. *Social Psychology Quarterly* 48:349–59.

Webster, J. A. 1970. Police task and time study. *Journal of Criminal Law, Criminology and Police Science* 61:94–100.

Weinstein, N. D. 1984. Why it won't happen to me: Perceptions of risk factors and susceptibility. *Health Psychology* 3:431–57.

Weis, K., and S. S. Borges. 1973. Victimology and rape: The case of the legitimate victim. *Issues in Criminology* 8:71–114.

Weiss, J. 1972. Psychological factors in stress and disease. *Scientific American* 226:104–13.

Wells, G. L. 1978. Applied eyewitness testimony research: System variables and estimator variables. *Journal of Personality and Social Psychology* 36:1546–57.

———. 1984. The psychology of lineup identifications. *Journal of Applied Social Psychology* 14:89–103.

———. 1988. *Eyewitness identification: A system handbook*. Toronto: Carswell.

Wells, G. L., T. J. Ferguson, and R. C. L. Lindsay. 1981. The tractibility of eyewitness confidence and its implications for triers of fact. *Journal of Applied Psychology* 66:688–96.

Wells, G. L., and M. R. Leippe. 1981. How do triers of fact infer the accuracy of eyewitness identifications? Using memory for peripheral detail can be misleading. *Journal of Applied Psychology* 66:682–87.

Wells, G. L., M. R. Leippe, and T. M. Ostrum. 1979. Guidelines for empirically assessing the fairness of a lineup. *Law and Human Behavior* 3:285–93.

Wells, G. L., and E. F. Loftus, eds. 1984. *Eyewitness testimony: Psychological perspectives.* New York: Cambridge University Press.

Wells, G. L., and D. M. Murray. 1984. Eyewitness confidence. In G. L. Wells and E. F. Loftus, eds., *Eyewitness testimony: Psychological perspectives.* New York: Cambridge University Press.

Wertlieb, E. C. 1982. Juvenile delinquency and the schools: A review of the literature. *Journal of Juvenile and Family Courts* 33:15–24.

Wessells, M. G. 1982. *Cognitive psychology.* New York: Harper and Row.

Westley, W. A. 1970. *Violence and the police.* Cambridge: MIT Press.

Wexler, J. G., and D. D. Logan. 1983. Sources of stress among women police officers. *Journal of Police Science and Administration* 11:46–53.

White, H. R., E. W. Labouvie, and M. E. Bates. 1985. The relationship between sensation seeking and delinquency: A longitudinal analysis. *Journal of Research in Crime and Delinquency* 22:197–211.

White, M. F., and B. A. Menke. 1982. On assessing the mood of the public toward the police: Some conceptual issues. *Journal of Criminal Justice* 10:211–30.

White, S. O., and M. Straus. 1981. The implication of family violence for rehabilitation strategies. In S. Martin, ed., *New directions in the rehabilitation of criminal offenders.* Washington, D.C.: National Academy of Sciences Press.

White, W. S. 1979. Police trickery in inducing confessions. *University of Pennsylvania Law Review* 127:581–629.

Wicker, A. W. 1969. Attitudes versus actions: The relationship of verbal and overt behavioral responses to attitude objects. *Journal of Social Issues* 25:41–78.

Wicks, R. J. 1974. *Applied psychology for law enforcement and correction officers.* New York: McGraw-Hill.

Wilbanks, W. 1988. Are elderly felons treated more leniently by the criminal justice system? *International Journal of Aging and Human Development* 26:275–88.

Wilbanks, W., and P. K. Kim. 1984. *Elderly criminals.* Washington, D.C.: University Press of America.

Williams, K. M. 1976. The effect of victim characteristics on the disposition of violent crimes. In W. F. McDonald, ed., *Criminal justice and the victim.* Beverly Hills: Sage.

Williams, L. S. 1984. The classic rape: When do victims report? *Social Problems* 31:459–67.

Willoughby, K. R., and W. R. Blount. 1985. The relationship between law enforcement officer height, aggression, and job performance. *Journal of Police Science and Administration* 13:225–28.

Wilmore, J. 1973. Weight training for women. *Fitness for living* 7 (November–December):40–45.

Wilson, J. Q. 1968. *Varieties of police behavior*. Cambridge: Harvard University Press.

Wilson, J. Q., and G. L. Kelling. 1985. Broken windows: The police and neighborhood safety. In A. S. Blumberg and E. Niederhoffer, eds., *The ambivalent force*. New York: Holt, Rinehart, and Winston.

Winfree, L. T., and C. T. Griffiths. 1977. Adolescent attitudes toward the police: A survey of high school students. In T. N. Ferdinand, ed., *Juvenile delinquency: Little brother grows up*. Beverly Hills: Sage.

Winterdyk, J. 1988. Canadian police officers and eyewitness evidence: A time for reform. *Canadian Police College Journal* 12:175–91.

Winslade, W. J., and J. W. Ross. 1983. *The insanity plea*. New York: Scribner's.

Witkin, H. A., S. A. Mednick, F. Schulsinger, E. Bakkestrom, K. O. Christiansen, D. R. Goodenough, K. Hirschorn, C. Lundstean, D. R. Owen, J. Philip, D. B. Rubin, and M. Stocking. 1976. XYY and XXY men: Criminality and aggression. *Science* 193:547–55.

Wolfgang, M. E. 1959. *Patterns in criminal homicide*. Philadelphia: University of Pennsylvania Press.

Wolfgang, M. E., and F. Ferracuti. 1967. *The subculture of violence: Towards an integrated theory in criminology*. London: Tavistock.

Wolfgang, M. E., and M. Riedel. 1976. Rape, racial discrimination and the death penalty. In H. Bedau and C. Pierce, eds., *Capital punishment in the United States*. New York: AMS Press.

Wood, P. L. 1973. The victim in a forcible rape case: A feminist view. *American Criminal Law Review* 11:335–54.

Wood, S. D., R. Kreitner, G. M. Friedman, M. Edwards, and M. A. Sova. 1982. Cost-effective wellness screening: A case study of 4,524 law enforcement officers. *Journal of Police Science and Administration* 10:273–78.

Woodhead, M. M., A. D. Baddeley, and D. C. V. Simmonds. 1979. On training people to recognize faces. *Ergonomics* 22:333–43.

Woods, P. J. 1976. *Career opportunities for psychologists: Expanding and emerging areas*. Washington, D.C.: American Psychological Association.

Wrightsman, L. S. 1987. *Psychology and the legal system*. Monterey, Calif: Brooks/Cole.

Wrightsman, L. S., and K. Deaux. 1981. *Social psychology in the 80's*, 3rd ed. Monterey, Calif.: Brooks/Cole.

Yarmey, A. D. 1979. *The psychology of eyewitness testimony*. New York: Free Press.

Yarmey, A. D. 1982. Eyewitness identification and stereotypes of criminals. In A. Trankell, ed., *Reconstructing the past: The role of psychologists in criminal trials*. Deventer, The Netherlands: Kluwer.

———. 1984. Accuracy and credibility of the elderly witness. *Canadian Journal on Aging* 3:79–90.

———. 1985a. Older and younger adults' attributions of responsibility toward rape victims and rapists. *Canadian Journal of Behavioural Science* 17: 327–38.

———. 1985b. Attitudes and sentencing for sexual assault as a function of age and sex of subjects. *Canadian Journal on Aging* 4:20–28.

———. 1986a. Verbal, visual, and voice identification of a rape suspect under different levels of illumination. *Journal of Applied Psychology* 71: 363–70.

———. 1986b. Perceived expertness and credibility of police officers as eyewitnesses. *Canadian Police College Journal* 10:31–52.

———. 1987. Streetproofing and bystanders' memory for a child abduction. In M. M. Gruneberg, P. E. Morris, and R. N. Sykes, eds., *Practical aspects of memory: Current research and issues. Volume 1*. New York: Wiley.

———. 1988. Victims and witnesses to deadly force. *Canadian Police College Journal* 12:99–109.

Yarmey, A. D., and H. T. Jones. 1982. Police awareness of the fallibility of eyewitness identification. *Canadian Police College Journal* 6:113–24.

———. 1983. Is the psychology of eyewitness identification a matter of common sense? In S. Lloyd Bostock and B. R. Clifford, eds., *Evaluating witness evidence*. New York: Wiley.

Yarmey, A. D., H. P. T. Jones and S. Rashid. 1984. Eyewitness memory of elderly and young adults. In D. J. Muller, D. E. Blackman, and A. J. Chapman, eds. *Psychology and law*. New York: Wiley.

Yarmey, A. D., and J. Kent. 1980. Eyewitness identification by elderly and young adults. *Law and Human Behavior* 4:359–71.

Yarmey, A. D., and P. K. Popiel. 1988. Judged value of medical versus psychological expert testimony. *International Journal of Law and Psychiatry* 11:195–204.

Yarmey, A.D., and S. Rashid. 1983. Perceptions of the public and legal professionals toward police officers. *Canadian Police College Journal* 7: 89–95.

Yerkes, R. M., and J. D. Dodson. 1908. The relationship of strength of stimulus to rapidity of habit formation. *Journal of Comparative Neurology and Psychology* 18:459–82.

Yin, P. 1982. Fear of crime as a problem for the elderly. *Social Problems* 30:240–45.

Yochelson, S., and S. E. Samenow. 1976. *The criminal personality. Volume 1: A profile for change.* New York: Jason Aronson.

Yuille, J. C. 1984. Research and teaching with police: A Canadian example. *International Review of Applied Psychology* 33:5–23.

———. 1987. The effects of alcohol and marijuana on eyewitness recall. Paper presented at the Second International Conference on Practical Aspects of Memory, Swansea, Wales.

———. 1988. The systematic assessment of children's testimony. *Canadian Psychology* 29:247–62.

———, ed. 1986. *Police selection and training: The role of psychology.* The Hague: Martinus Nijhoff.

Yuille, J. C., and J. L. Cutshall. 1986. A case study of eyewitness memory of a crime. *Journal of Applied Psychology* 71:291–301.

Yuille, J. C., and N. H. McEwan. 1985. Use of hypnosis as an aid to eyewitness memory. *Journal of Applied Psychology* 70:389–400.

Yuker, H. E. 1986. Disability and the law: Attitudes of police, lawyers, and mental health professionals. *Rehabilitation Psychology* 31:13–25.

Yukl, G. 1974. Effects of the opponents's initial offer, concession magnitude, and concession frequency on bargaining behavior. *Journal of Personality and Social Psychology* 30:323–35.

———. 1981. *Leadership in organizations.* Englewood Cliffs, N.J.: Prentice-Hall.

Zamble, E., and P. Annesley. 1987. Some determinants of public attitudes toward the police. *Journal of Police Science and Administration* 15:285–90.

Zaragoza, M. S. 1987. Memory, suggestibility, and eyewitness testimony. In S. J. Ceci, M. P. Toglia, and D. F. Ross, eds., *Children's eyewitness memory.* New York: Springer-Verlag.

Zawitz, M. W., ed. 1983. *Report to the nation on crime and justice: The data.* Washington, D.C.: U.S. Department of Justice.

Zelig, M. 1988. Ethical dilemmas in police psychology. *Professional Psychology: Research and Practice* 19:336–38.

Zimbardo, P. G. 1967. The psychology of police confessions. *Psychology Today* (June):17–27.

———. 1970. The human choice: Individuation, reason, and order versus deindividuation, impulse, and chaos. In W. J. Arnold and D. Levine, eds., *Nebraska symposium on motivation.* Lincoln: University of Nebraska Press.

Zimbardo, P. G., E. B. Ebbeson, and C. Maslach. 1977. *Influencing attitudes and changing behavior*, 2nd ed. Reading, Mass.: Addison-Wesley.

Zimbardo, P. C., C. Haney, and W. C. Banks. 1973. A Pirandellian prison. *New York Times Magazine*, April 8.

Zimring, F. 1977. Determinants of the death rate from robbery: A Detroit time study. *Journal of Legal Studies* 6:317–32.

Zimring, F. E., and G. Hawkins. 1971. The legal threat as an instrument of social change. *Journal of Social Issues* 27:33–48.

Zuckerman, M. 1978. Sensation seeking and psychopathy. In R. D. Hare and D. Schalling, eds., *Psychopathic behavior: Approaches to research*. New York: Wiley.

———. 1979. *Sensation seeking beyond the optimal level of arousal*. Hillsdale, N.J.: Lawrence Erlbaum.

Zung, W. W. K., and R. L. Green. 1974. Seasonal variation of suicide and depression. *Archives of General Psychiatry* 30:89–91.

Name Index

Subject Index

Aggression and violence, 196–97; causes and correlates of, 138–42; defined, 197–200; prediction of, 202–4

Alcohol abuse: and family disputes, 226–27; in police, 93; and violence, 201

Anticipatory socialization, 103–4

Antisocial personality disorders, 178–79, 185

Anxiety, 93, 275–77

Arbitration, 235

Arousal. *See* Stress

Artist sketches, 301–5

Attention, 292–97

Attitudes, 42; and age, 123–24; authoritarian, 39, 74, 122; and behavior, 110–13; changes in, 113–15; and cultures, 131–36; defined, 109–10; and likelihood of victimization, 130; and mass media, 136–40; and mental disorder, 270–72; negative, 115–22; and neighborhood and community beliefs, 130; and personal experiences with police, 128–29; and personality,

122; and prejudice, 115–22; and race, 125; and roles, 113–15; and sex differences, 124–25; and socio-economic status, 127–28; toward police, 108, 122–30

Authoritarian attitudes, 39, 74, 122

Authoritarian personality, 37–39

Authoritarian style of leadership, 74

Authority: fallacy of, 257–58; obedience to, 11–12; and power of police, 143–45

Battered woman's syndrome, 227–29

Battered women, 224–31

Batterers, 225–27

Battering, 225

Biases and common beliefs: ad hominem arguments, 256–57; of authority, 257–58; circular reasoning, 185, 210, 257; dramatic examples, 254–55; of misplaced concreteness, 256; of retrospective determinism, 255–56

Bigotry, 39

DATE DUE

MAY 28 '0?			
JE 12 '04			
DE 17 '06			

GAYLORD   PRINTED IN U.S.A